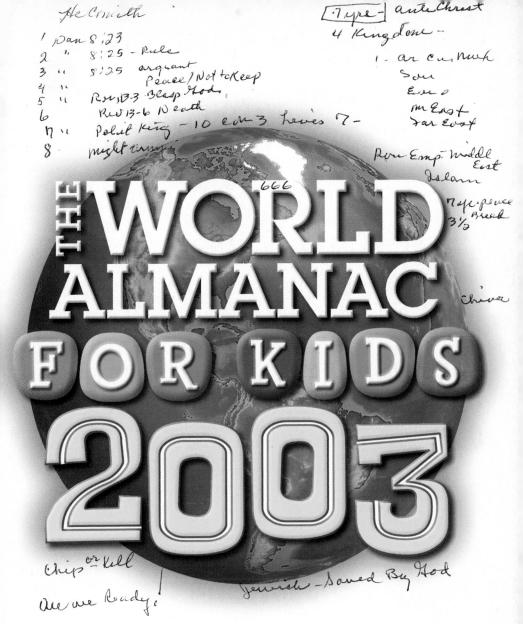

THE WORLD ALMANAC FOR KIDS 2003

666

Handwritten annotations:

He Smith

1 Dan 8:23
2 " 8:25 - Rule
3 " 8:25 arrogant
Peace/Not to Keep
4 " Rev 13-3 Blasp God,
5 " Rev 13-6 Death
6 " Polit King - 10 edm 3 Leves 7 -
7 "
8 might army

Type - ante Christ
4 Kingdom -

1 - or Current
Sour
Euro
Me East
Far East

Rom Emp. Middle
East
Islam

Type peace
3½ Break

Chive

Chip or Kill
are we Ready!
Jewish - Saved By God

D1089293

WORLD ALMANAC BOOKS
A Division of World Almanac Education Group, Inc.
A WRC Media Company

EDITOR: Kevin Seabrooke

CURRICULUM CONSULTANT:
Susan Ohanian, Senior Fellow, Vermont Society for the Study of Education

CONTRIBUTORS: Sean Alfano, Elizabeth Barden, Russell Cobb, Benjamin Dean, Steve de las Heras, Peter Falcier, Matt Friedlander, Joseph Gustaitis, Raymond Hill, Matthew Kiernan, Rachael Mason, Catherine McHugh, Randi Metsch-Ampel, Donna Mulder, Eileen O'Reilly, Ann Pulido-Smith, Donald Young
Consultant: Lee T. Shapiro, Ph.D. (Astronomy)

KID CONTRIBUTORS: Maria Acosta, Andrew Barral, Ashley Bruggeman, Adriana Garcia, Nilufar Khan, Elana Metsch-Ampel, Christin Mulder, Christopher Presley, Kimberly Renner, Alexis Shine, Joseph Van Domelen

Thanks to all the kids who wrote to us with their great ideas!

DESIGN: Bill SMITH STUDIO
Creative Director: Jay Jaffe
Design: Jason Roumas **Photo Research:** Christie Silver **Production:** Karin Campbell

WORLD ALMANAC BOOKS

Vice President– Sales and Marketing	Editorial Director	Managing Editor
James R. Keenley	William McGeveran Jr.	Lori P. Wiesenfeld

Desktop Production Manager: Elizabeth J. Lazzara
Editorial Staff: Mette Bahde, Olivia Smith, Associate Editors; Lloyd Sabin, Desktop Publishing Associate

WORLD ALMANAC EDUCATION GROUP
Chief Executive Officer, WRC Media Inc.: Martin E. Kenney Jr.
President: Robert Jackson
Publisher: Ken Park
Director–Purchasing and Production/Photo Research: Edward A. Thomas
Director of Indexing Services: Marjorie B. Bank; **Index Editor:** Walter Kronenberg
Marketing Coordinator: Sarah De Vos

Rapture of Church – Washington Goose has flown away
American will collapse –
① – money
② Mock America. Burn Flag
③ I.D. crisis
obstruction of Christian Faith

CONTENTS

Any Small Goodness
a novel of the barrio

3

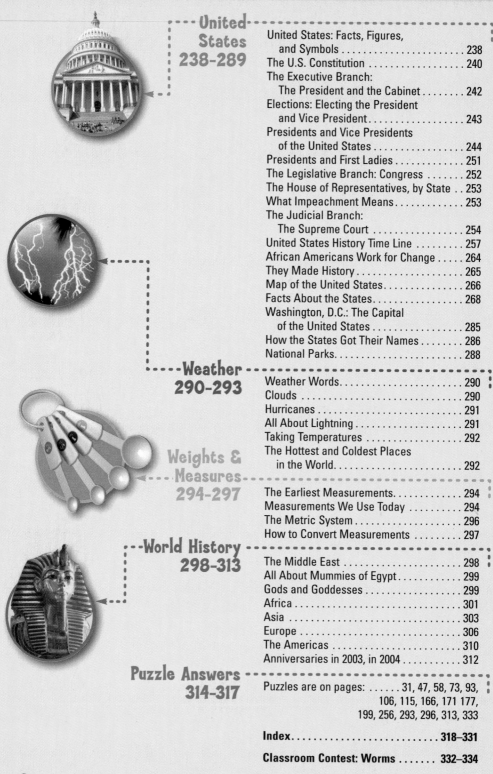

REMEMBERING SEPTEMBER 11:
The Tribute in Light honoring victims of the World Trade Center attack, as viewed from the Empire State Building

REMEMBERING

TRAGEDY AND RESPONSE—A TIME LINE

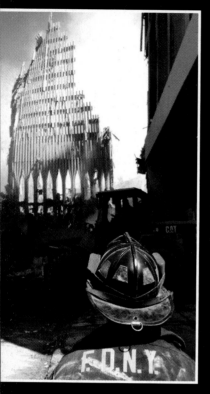

Above: a firefighter surveys the ruins of one of the World Trade Center towers. Below: the wreckage at the Pentagon.

9/11 2001 Around 9 A.M., hijackers fly passenger jets into the twin towers of the World Trade Center in New York City. Soon after, another hijacked plane crashes into the Pentagon near Washington, D.C. A fourth crashes in southwest Pennsylvania after heroic passengers apparently try to overcome the hijackers.

New York Mayor Rudolph Giuliani rushes to the Trade Center and has to scramble from the scene to escape the devastation. Firefighters help evacuate thousands of people from the towers before they collapse.

About 3,000 people from some 90 nations die in all the attacks, including some 400 New York City firefighters and police officers.

9/12 Volunteers from near and far begin arriving at the attack scenes to remove rubble and search for survivors. Memorials spring up, with posters showing missing loved ones.

9/14 On a national day of mourning, President George W. Bush attends a prayer service in Washington, D.C., and visits Ground Zero in New York. He thanks rescue workers and promises to punish those behind the attacks.

9/19 President Bush calls for the Taliban, the Islamic fundamentalist group ruling Afghanistan, to hand over Osama bin Laden and other leaders of the al-Qaeda terrorist network, which the U.S. blames for the attacks.

10/7 U.S. planes bomb targets in Afghanistan, beginning Operation Enduring Freedom, a U.S.-led military campaign to root out terrorist networks.

10/8 President Bush creates an Office of Homeland Security, headed by Tom Ridge.

SEPTEMBER 11

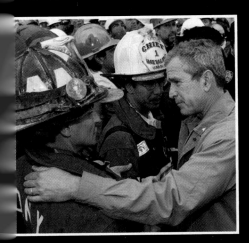

11/13 Afghan guerrillas supported by the U.S. capture the capital city of Kabul from the Taliban.

Oct.– Nov. Five people die and 14 get sick in the U.S. from anthrax in letters mailed to Senate offices and elsewhere; authorities try without success to figure out who sent them.

12/16 Afghan guerrillas report that the battle against al-Qaeda fighters hiding in Tora Bora, a huge cave complex in the mountains along the Afghan border with Pakistan, is ending. But many fighters have apparently escaped.

12/22 A new government, under Hamid Karzai, takes office in Afghanistan.

3/11 2002 Six months after the attacks, progress is reported in restoring the damaged Pentagon. New York City starts a Tribute in Light to the victims—two beams of light shine upward from the site of the former towers into the night sky.

4/14 As dawn lights up the sky, the beams of the Tribute in Light are switched off. By this time, America's Fund for Afghan Children, proposed by President Bush in September, has received over $4 million from American kids.

Above: President Bush greets New York City firefighters; New York Mayor Giuliani at a football game; a memorial at a New York City fire station. Right: U.S. soldiers in Afghanistan.

FACES & PLACES

A STAR IS BORN

One of the many remarkable new images from NASA's Hubble Space Telescope shows part of the CONE NEBULA, a huge column of gas and dust (7 light-years long) in the middle of a star-forming region.

OUT OF THIS WORLD

Astronaut JERRY ROSS (also shown in inset) does repairs to get the International Space Station ready for space walks. Jerry, 54, was on his record seventh trip into space.

KING OF SWING

San Francisco outfielder **BARRY BONDS** set a new single-season home run record in 2001 (breaking Mark McGwire's 1998 mark of 70). Here he blasts number 73, his last homer of the year.

GOLDEN GIRL

In a major upset, teenager **SARAH HUGHES** dazzled the crowd—and judges—to win the gold medal for figure skating at the 2002 Winter Olympics.

BEST BEATS

FALLIN' FOR ALICIA

R & B singer and pianist **ALICIA KEYS** won five Grammys in 2002, including Song of the Year (Fallin'), best R & B Album (Songs In A Minor), and Best New Artist. This tied the record for a female artist set by Lauryn Hill.

MOVIN' LIKE THIS

Named Favorite Band at the 2002 Kids' Choice Awards, the BAHA MEN are known for their upbeat music with Caribbean rhythms.

MORE MANDY

She only recently turned 18, but singer MANDY MOORE already has 3 top albums to her credit and has co-starred in a bunch of films, including Try Seventeen and A Walk to Remember.

15

MOVIE MAGIC

SPIDER-MAN, starring Tobey Maguire, took in a record $114 million in its opening weekend. At right, the wall-crawler gets cozy with Mary Jane Watson (Kirsten Dunst) in a scene from the film.

HARRY & FRIENDS

To the delight of millions of fans, J.K. Rowling's fan-tastic **HARRY POTTER** books have come to life on the screen, with (left to right) Daniel Radcliffe, Rupert Grint, and Emma Watson starring as Harry, Ron Weasley, and Hermione Granger.

OSCAR BREAKTHROUGH

HALLE BERRY and **DENZEL WASHINGTON** both won top acting Oscars in 2002. She was the first African American actress to win the top award. He was the second black actor, following Sidney Poitier back in 1963.

TV TIME

ANIMAL TALES

On Animal Planet's **THE JEFF CORWIN EXPERIENCE,** Jeff, shown here with an armadillo friend, takes you everywhere from Australia to Zanzibar in search of furry and scaly creatures of all kinds.

EVERYBODY LOVES HIM

RAY ROMANO looks like he's in trouble. That's what usually happens to the character he plays on his popular TV series, *Everybody Loves Raymond*. Romano also did the voice for Manny in the 2002 hit film *Ice Age*.

BUSY LIZZIE

HILARY DUFF plays a typical teen in the Disney TV series *Lizzie McGuire*. Though she only turned 15 in April 2002, she's signed to star in two upcoming films. All that and homework, too!

19

MARVELOUS MEDALISTS

ICE GOLD

A former inline skating champ, **DEREK PARRA** switched to ice and struck gold in the 2002 Winter Olympics. He set a world record in the 1,500 meters, and took a silver in the 5,000.

CROATIAN SENSATION

JANICA KOSTELIC was the first Croatian to win a Winter Olympic medal, and the first Alpine skier to win four medals at one Olympics. She took home three golds (slalom, combined, and giant slalom) and a silver (Super-G).

FAST TRACKS

JILL BAKKEN and **VONETTA FLOWERS** hit almost 80 miles an hour to win the first-ever women's Olympic bobsled race. Vonetta also became the first African-American to earn a Winter Olympic medal.

SWEEP, DUDE!

ROSS POWERS gets big air on his way to the gold in the men's halfpipe at the 2002 Winter Olympics. Danny Kass and Jarret Thomas took silver and bronze, for a U.S. sweep.

CHAMPS

PATRIOT POWER

TOM BRADY started the season as a backup for the New England Patriots, but ended up as Super Bowl MVP. At 24, Tom was the youngest quarterback to lead his team to a Super Bowl win.

CYBER-CELEBRATION

Thori Staples Bryan (2), Kelly Lindsay (5), Julie Murray, and goalie LaKeysia Beene (1) of the Bay Area (San Jose) **CYBERRAYS** celebrate their 4-3 win over the Atlanta Beat, to take the 2001 WUSA Founders Cup.

NETTING RESPECT

Traded from Phoenix before the season, star guard **JASON KIDD** turned the New Jersey Nets around. In 2001-2002, they won twice as many games as the season before, and were division champs.

SERIOUS HEAT

RANDY JOHNSON, now a four-time Cy Young winner, won Games 2 and 6 of the 2001 World Series for the Diamondbacks. Then the 6' 10" hurler came in as a relief pitcher and won Game 7, as Arizona took the series from the Yankees.

ANIMALS

What's the biggest venomous snake? ➤ page 30

ANIMAL NEWS & FACTS

HANGING OUT WITH CLOWNS. Only a clown fish can safely swim among the swaying "arms" of the sea anemone. Other fish are stung by those poisonous tentacles, but clown fish are immune. And by staying close to the anemone, they also stay safe from predators. In return, clown fish help the sea anemone by cleaning its tentacles. This kind of close cooperation between two species is called **symbiosis.**

THE GREAT WHITE WAY. It was once thought that real-life great white sharks stayed close to shore, like the shark in the movie *Jaws*. But new electronic tagging technology has shown that there is still a lot to learn about these predators. Scientists found that great whites sometimes swim thousands of miles into the open ocean, and no one knows why.

DEEP-SEA SQUID DISCOVERED. If you ever get down to the bottom of the sea, you may meet the deep-sea squid, an odd creature that has been sighted for the first time, in several places in the Pacific, Atlantic, and Indian oceans. It has ten thin tentacles that stretch out 6 to 8 feet, nearly 10 times its body length and far longer than the arms of any other known squid! It also has two big fins that flap out like elephant ears!

PELICANS IN KANSAS? Miles from any ocean, the marshes of Cheyenne Bottoms in central Kansas are an important stopping place for migrating saltwater birds, including gulls, ducks, swans, and pelicans. Every year tens of thousands of American White pelicans, with 9-foot wingspans, stop there on their way south to Florida, to rest and feed in the 41,000 acres of wetlands.

THAT'S A BIG OLD COCKROACH! About 300 million years ago, much of Ohio was a tropical swamp filled with cockroaches—some of them pretty big. In 2001, scientists identified the fossil of a 3.5-inch cockroach found in a coal mine in eastern Ohio. It's the biggest complete cockroach fossil ever found, and twice as big as the average American roach today, though a bit smaller than those that live in some tropical areas.

Did You KNOW?

CHESSIE IS BACK! *Florida manatees rarely migrate farther up the U.S. Atlantic coast than North Carolina. But "Chessie," who got his nickname for visiting Chesapeake Bay in 1994, is a well-traveled celebrity. He really became famous in 1995, when he went past the Statue of Liberty in New York Harbor and swam on all the way to Rhode Island. In the fall of 2001, Chessie visited Chesapeake Bay again.*

A manatee ▶

ANTS ARE AMAZING

Some 9,500 species of ants have been discovered and named so far. Myrmecologists (scientists who study ants) estimate that there are about 20,000 species in all. Ants have been around for about 100 million years, and are found in just about every type of land environment.

WHERE DO ANTS LIVE? Ants are social insects that live together in large groups, or colonies. Their group home is usually a system of underground tunnels and chambers, with mounds above formed out of the dirt or sand they removed in digging. But some ants are different. **Carpenter ants** carve tunnels in wood (but don't eat it). In the rain forests of South America, the **Aztec ant** lives inside trees. **Tailor ants** from the tropics of Africa use leaves to build their nests. And **Army ants** don't build at all. They travel in big groups looking for food.

DO ANTS HAVE JOBS? Each ant has a specific job. The **queen** lays eggs to populate the colony. **Workers** collect food, feed members of the colony, and enlarge the nest. **Soldiers** are large workers that defend the colony and sometimes attack ants who are strangers. All these hard-working ants are female. **Males** have wings to fly to another colony, where they mate with a queen and die soon afterwards.

A leaf-cutter ant

WHAT DO ANTS EAT? Ants are very fond of eating sweet foods, seeds, and other insects. Sweets provide energy for worker ants, and the protein from other insects helps build up the ant's body. The **Dalmatie ant** actually cooks its food by chewing it into patties and baking them in the sun. **Harvester ants** collect and store seeds. **Leaf-cutter ants** grow fungus for food.

HOW DO ANTS COMMUNICATE? Ants communicate by touching each other with their antennae. They show other ants where food is by making a path with a chemical (called a pheromone) that leaves a scent that the ants follow.

COOL FACTS ABOUT ANTS

▶ The world's biggest ant colony was discovered in 2002. This supercolony has billions of ants living in millions of nests. It stretches 3,600 miles, all the way from Italy to northwest Spain.

▶ An ant can lift 50 times its own weight—which is as much of a feat for them as lifting a car would be for you!

▶ Ants don't have lungs. They breathe through tiny holes in their sides called **spiracles**.

▶ Ants display many behaviors similar to ours. For example, worker ants take care of larvae by feeding and washing them.

▶ No one knows whether ants "sleep" in the way we do. They don't have eyelids, so they can't close their eyes. They do rest, but trying to monitor their brain activity at this time would interfere with it so much that the results wouldn't tell us anything. Ants do look for food only during the day. And in the winter, their breathing and metabolism slows way down.

LARGEST, SMALLEST, FASTEST IN THE WORLD

WORLD'S LARGEST ANIMALS

MARINE MAMMAL: blue whale (110 feet long, 209 tons)

LAND MAMMAL: African bush elephant (13 feet high, 8 tons)

TALLEST MAMMAL: giraffe (19 feet tall)

REPTILE: saltwater crocodile (16 feet long, 1,150 pounds)

SNAKE: Heaviest: anaconda (27 feet, 9 inches long, 500 pounds)
Longest: reticulated python (26–32 feet long)

FISH: whale shark (41½ feet long)

BIRD: ostrich (9 feet tall, 345 pounds)

INSECT: stick insect (15 inches long)

WORLD'S FASTEST ANIMALS

MARINE MAMMAL: blue whale (30 miles per hour)

LAND MAMMAL: cheetah (70 miles per hour)

FISH: sailfish (68 miles per hour)

BIRD: peregrine falcon (100–200 miles per hour)

INSECT: dragonfly (36 miles per hour)

WORLD'S SMALLEST ANIMALS

MAMMAL: bumblebee bat (1.1 to 1.3 inches)

FISH: dwarf goby (length 0.3 inches)

BIRD: male bee hummingbird (2.2 inches)

SNAKES: thread snake and brahminy blind snake (4.25 inches)

LIZARD: Jaragua lizard (0.63 inches)

INSECT: fairy fly (0.01 inches)

FROG: Brazilian frog (0.33 inches)

HOW FAST DO ANIMALS RUN?

Some animals can run as fast as a car. But a snail needs more than 30 hours just to go one mile. If you look at this table, you will see how fast some land animals can go.

MILES PER HOUR	
Cheetah	65
Antelope	60
Lion	50
Coyote	43
Hyena	40
Rabbit	35
Giraffe	32
Grizzly bear	30
Elephant	25
Wild turkey	15
Squirrel	12
Snail	0.03

How Long Do Animals Live?

Most animals do not live as long as human beings do. A monkey that is 14 years old is thought to be old. A person who is 14 is still considered young. The average life span of a human being in the world today is 65 to 70 years. The average life spans of some animals are shown here.

Galapagos tortoise	200+ years
Box turtle	100 years
Blue Whale	80 years
Gray Whale	70 years
Human	67 years
Alligator	50 years
Humpback Whale	50 years
Bald Eagle	40 years
African elephant	35 years
Bottlenose Dolphin	30 years
Grizzly bear	25 years
Horse	20 years
Chimpanzee	20 years
Black bear	18 years
Tiger	16 years
Lion	15 years
Cow	15 years
Rhinoceros (black)	15 years
Moose	12 years
Cat (domestic)	12 years
Dog (domestic)	12 years
Sea lion	12 years
Giraffe	10 years
Pig	10 years
Squirrel	10 years
Goat	8 years
Kangaroo	7 years
Rabbit	5 years
Mouse	3 years

KITS, CUBS, AND OTHER ANIMAL BABIES

ANIMAL	MALE	FEMALE	YOUNG
alligator	bull	cow	hatchling
bear	boar	sow	cub
cheetah	male	female	cub
duck	drake	duck	duckling
ferret	hob	jill	kit
fox	reynard	vixen	kit, cub, pup
giraffe, whale, hippopotamus	bull	cow	calf
gorilla	male	female	infant
hawk	tiercel	hen	eyas
horse	stallion	mare	foal, filly (female), colt (male)
opossum	jack	jill	joey
tiger	tiger	tigress	cub

27

HABITATS: Where Animals Live

The area in nature where an animal lives is called its habitat. The table below lists some large habitats and some of the animals that live in them.

HABITAT	SOME ANIMALS THAT LIVE THERE
DESERTS (hot, dry regions)	camels, bobcats, coyotes, kangaroos, mice, Gila monsters, scorpions, rattlesnakes
TROPICAL FORESTS (warm, humid climate)	orangutans, gibbons, leopards, tamandua anteaters, tapirs, iguanas, parrots, tarantulas
GRASSLANDS (flat, open lands)	African elephants, kangaroos, Indian rhinoceroses, giraffes, zebras, prairie dogs, ostriches, tigers
MOUNTAINS (highlands)	yaks, snow leopards, vicunas, bighorn sheep, chinchillas, pikas, eagles, mountain goats
POLAR REGIONS (cold climate)	polar bears, musk oxen, caribou, ermines, arctic foxes, walruses, penguins, Siberian huskies
OCEANS (sea water)	whales, dolphins, seals, manatees, octopuses, stingrays, coral, starfish, lobsters, many kinds of fish

ANIMAL ARCHITECTS

Many animals build nests or burrows to provide a safe place to raise their young. But few can compare with these animal cities:

CLIFF SWALLOWS are found in the western United States and across Canada. Their colonies average about 300 nests, but can have as many as 3,000. The jug-like nests are made of mud and can be found attached to cliffs, bridges, or buildings. It takes about 1,000 pellets of mud carried one beakful at a time to make each nest!

PRAIRIE DOGS live in underground "towns." Each family has its own den, with "bedrooms," a "nursery," and a "bathroom." A 25,000-square-mile town with about 400 million prairie dogs was discovered in north-central Texas in 1901.

TERMITES in Australia and Africa are the champion builders of the animal world. They use soil and saliva to make cement towers that reach up to 20 feet tall. ▶

WHAT ARE GROUPS OF ANIMALS CALLED?

The next time you describe a group of animals, try using one of the phrases below.

CATS: *chowder* or *clutter* of cats
CHICKS: *clutch* of chicks
CROWS: *murder* of crows
DUCKS: *brace* of ducks
ELKS: *gang* of elks
FOXES: *skulk* of foxes
GEESE: *flock* or *gaggle* of geese
GOLDFINCHES: *charm* of goldfinches
HAWKS: *cast* of hawks
KITTENS: *kindle* or *kendle* of kittens

LEOPARDS: *leap* of leopards
LIONS: *pride* of lions
RHINOCEROSES: *crash* of rhinoceroses
SEALS: *pod* of seals
SWANS: *bevy* of swans
SWINE: *drift* of swine
TOADS: *knot* of toads
TURTLES: *bale* of turtles
WHALES: *pod* of whales
WOLVES: *pack* of wolves

ENDANGERED SPECIES

When an animal species begins to die out, the animal is said to be endangered or threatened. Throughout the world today, 1,070 species of animals are endangered or threatened, according to the National Wildlife Federation.

SOME ENDANGERED ANIMALS

Blue whale—the largest animal ever to live. Whaling almost made them extinct. There are about 5,000 in the world today.

California condor—North America's largest bird. There are about 60 of them now living in the wild.

California red-legged frog—believed to be the species from the Mark Twain story "The Celebrated Jumping Frog of Calaveras County." About 350 remain in the wild.

Giant panda—China's most loveable animal. As few as 1,000 of these creatures remain in the mountains of southwest China.

DID YOU KNOW? *Giant pandas must eat up to 83 pounds of bamboo a day, which takes them up to 14 hours.*

HOW DO ANIMALS AND PLANTS BECOME ENDANGERED?

CHANGES IN CLIMATE. Animals are endangered when the climate of their habitat (where they live) changes in a major way. For example, if an area becomes very hot and dry and a river dries up, the fish and other plant and animal life in the river will die.

HABITAT DESTRUCTION. Sometimes animal habitats are destroyed when people need the land. For example, wetlands, where many types of waterfowl, fish, and insects live, might be drained for new houses or a mall. The animals that lived there would have to find a new home or else die out.

OVER-HUNTING. Bison or buffalo once ranged over the entire Great Plains of the United States, but they were hunted almost to extinction in the 19th century. Since then, they have been protected by laws, and their numbers are increasing.

OPERATION MIGRATION

Whooping cranes are one of America's best known and rarest endangered species. These five-foot-tall birds are white with black wing tips and a red patch on top of their heads. There are only about 400 left, and too many breed in the same place in winter. To avoid disease and other dangers they needed to have another breeding place.

A group called Operation Migration tried an experiment to help cranes breed. They used an ultralight aircraft to guide 11 sandhill cranes from Wisconsin to a wildlife refuge in Florida for the winter. The pilot wore a crane disguise, and the birds learned to follow the aircraft as they would follow their own parents. The plan worked. In October 2001, seven whooping cranes made the same trip. Forty-eight days and 1,218 miles later, they got to Florida. In April 2002, the five birds who survived flew back to Wisconsin. Operation Migration's goal is to have 125 birds in this flock by the year 2020.

DANGER! POISON!

What's the difference between poisonous animals and venomous animals? **Poisonous animals** contain a toxin (poison) in a part of their body, like the skin, organs, or feathers. Touching or eating these animals causes sickness, pain, or death. But, these animals don't do anything to spread their poison. **Venomous animals** do deliver their poison. They use body parts such as fangs, stingers, or tentacles to poison others.

Here are some kinds of poisonous or venomous animals.

▶ **Black widow spiders** are armed with venom that is 15 times more poisonous than the venom of a prairie rattlesnake. They are found in warm and temperate climates around the world and like to live in dark places such as drain pipes and under rocks and logs. Their bite rarely kills humans. Why do we call them the black widow? Because the female sometimes eats the smaller male after mating!

▶ The **blue ring octopus**, the deadliest kind of octopus, uses its arms to capture its prey. Then it bites the victim, sending in a poison through its saliva strong enough to kill a human.

▶ Although its name means "100 legs," the common **centipede** is about 2 inches long with only 15 pairs of legs. Centipedes eat insects, earthworms, spiders, slugs, and some small animals. They move fast and use venom, which comes from glands near the first pair of legs, to kill their prey. Although their bite can be painful to humans, it is not deadly.

▶ The largest venomous snake, the **king cobra**, uses its half-inch-long hollow fangs to inject its prey with toxin (poison) strong enough to kill an elephant. King cobras mainly eat lizards and other snakes.

▶ **Komodo dragons'** mouths are full of disease-causing bacteria. When they bite their prey, the victim gets sick and slowly dies of blood poisoning. Then the lizard returns after this has happened, to eat the body.

▲ *Komodo dragon*

▶ The skin glands of **poison dart frogs** produce a foul-smelling, bitter-tasting substance that warns away predators. A single drop can kill an animal that ignores the warning. People can get sick from touching the frog's skin. In Colombia, people have used the toxin in hunting darts (blowguns).

▶ The skin, liver, and eggs of the **puffer fish** contain deadly toxins. Some chefs in Japan are trained and licensed to prepare a special treat made out of puffers. The chefs are usually able to make this dish safely. But not always. At least a few people die each year from eating it.

▲ *Poison dart frog*

▶ **Scorpions** have eight legs and a hard outer skeleton like spiders and ticks. They live in nearly every type of habitat, including deserts, rain forests, prairies, grasslands, forests, mountains, caves, ponds, and seashore. The stinger at the tip of their tails injects a paralyzing poison into their prey. The sting of most scorpions is only irritating to people, but there about 25 species of scorpions that can kill a person.

▶ Although **sea anemones** look like beautiful flowers attached to coral or rocks on the ocean floor, they are actually predatory animals. The sea anemone's tentacles are studded with microscopic stinging capsules to protect it and catch its food. Sea anemones have few enemies and live for a very long time.

◀ *Sea anemone*

PETS AT THE TOP

TOP TEN DOG BREEDS

Here are the ten most popular U.S. dog breeds with the numbers of dogs registered by the American Kennel Club in 2001:

❶	Labrador retriever	154,897	❻	Poodle	45,852
❷	Golden retriever	62,652	❼	Chihuahua	42,013
❸	German shepherd	57,256	❽	Rottweiler	41,776
❹	Dachshund	50,772	❾	Yorkshire Terrier	40,684
❺	Beagle	49,080	❿	Boxer	34,998

MOST POPULAR PETS

Here are the ten most popular pets in the U.S. today:

❶ Cats
❷ Dogs
❸ Parakeets
❹ Small animals, such as rabbits, cavies, gerbils, and hamsters
❺ Fish
❻ Reptiles
❼ Finches
❽ Cockatiels
❾ Canaries
❿ Parrots

TOP TEN PET NAMES

Here's what veterinarians told the American Society for the Prevention of Cruelty to Animals (ASPCA), when asked to list the ten most popular names for pets:

❶ Max
❷ Maggie
❸ Buddy
❹ Bailey
❺ Jake
❻ Sam
❼ Molly
❽ Nicky
❾ Coco
❿ Sadie

WORM SEARCH

```
S  C  O  C  O  O  N  C  M
C  U  R  R  F  A  R  U  S
S  A  N  A  H  O  L  C  E
E  W  S  A  P  L  Z  P  G
T  K  G  T  E  V  F  J  M
A  Y  U  T  I  L  K  K  E
E  Y  I  P  D  N  C  Y  N
K  L  R  Y  K  D  G  W  T
C  M  U  C  U  S  Q  S  S
```

WORD BOX

Anus	Crop
Castings	Mucus
Clitellum	Segments
Cocoon	Setae

For more about worms, see pages 332-333

ANSWERS ON PAGES 314-317. FOR MORE PUZZLES GO TO WWW.WORLDALMANACFORKIDS.COM

ANIMAL KINGDOM

The world has so many animals that scientists looked for a way to organize them into groups. A Swedish scientist named Carolus Linnaeus (1707–1778) worked out a system for classifying both animals and plants. We still use it today.

The animal kingdom is separated into two large groups—animals with backbones, called **vertebrates**, and animals without backbones, called **invertebrates**.

These large groups are divided into smaller groups called **phyla**. And phyla are divided into even smaller groups called **classes**. The animals in each group are classified together when their bodies are similar in certain ways.

CLASSIFYING ANIMALS

How can you remember the different animal classifications? A good memory aid is to think of the sentence:

King Philip Came Over From Great Spain.

Each capital letter stands for a classification going from most general to most specific.

K = Kingdom; **P** = Phylum; **C** = Class; **O** = Order; **F** = Family; **G** = Genus; **S** = Species.

King Philip Came Over From Great Spain. Now you've got it!

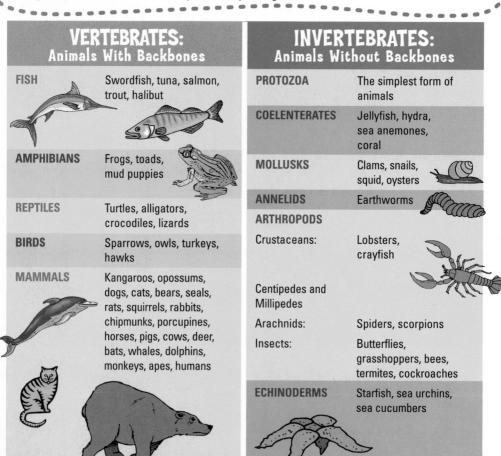

VERTEBRATES:
Animals With Backbones

FISH	Swordfish, tuna, salmon, trout, halibut
AMPHIBIANS	Frogs, toads, mud puppies
REPTILES	Turtles, alligators, crocodiles, lizards
BIRDS	Sparrows, owls, turkeys, hawks
MAMMALS	Kangaroos, opossums, dogs, cats, bears, seals, rats, squirrels, rabbits, chipmunks, porcupines, horses, pigs, cows, deer, bats, whales, dolphins, monkeys, apes, humans

INVERTEBRATES:
Animals Without Backbones

PROTOZOA		The simplest form of animals
COELENTERATES		Jellyfish, hydra, sea anemones, coral
MOLLUSKS		Clams, snails, squid, oysters
ANNELIDS		Earthworms
ARTHROPODS	Crustaceans:	Lobsters, crayfish
	Centipedes and Millipedes	
	Arachnids:	Spiders, scorpions
	Insects:	Butterflies, grasshoppers, bees, termites, cockroaches
ECHINODERMS		Starfish, sea urchins, sea cucumbers

LIFE ON EARTH

This time line shows how life developed on Earth and when land plants developed. The earliest animals are at the top of the chart. The most recent are at the bottom of the chart.

	YEARS AGO		ANIMAL LIFE ON EARTH
PRECAMBRIAN	4.5 BILLION		Formation of the Earth. No signs of life.
	2.5 BILLION		First evidence of life in the form of bacteria and algae. All life is in water.
PALEOZOIC	570–500 MILLION		Animals with shells (called trilobites) and some mollusks. Some fossils begin to form.
	500–430 MILLION		Jawless fish appear, oldest known animals with backbones (vertebrates).
	430–395 MILLION		Many coral reefs, jawed fishes, and scorpion-like animals. First land plants.
	395–345 MILLION		Many fishes. Earliest known insect. Amphibians (animals living in water and on land) appear.
	345–280 MILLION		Large insects appear. Amphibians increase in numbers. First trees appear.
	280–225 MILLION		Reptiles and modern insects appear. Trilobites, many corals, and fishes become extinct.
MESOZOIC	225–195 MILLION		Dinosaurs and turtles appear. Many reptiles and insects develop further. Mammals appear.
	195–135 MILLION		Many giant dinosaurs. Reptiles increase in number. First birds and crab-like animals appear.
	135–65 MILLION		Dinosaurs develop further and then become extinct. Flowering plants begin to appear.
CENOZOIC	65–2.5 MILLION		Modern-day land and sea animals begin to develop, including such mammals as rhinoceroses, whales, cats, dogs, apes, seals.
	2.5 MILLION– 10,000		Earliest humans appear. Mastodon, mammoths, and other huge animals become extinct.
	10,000– PRESENT		Modern human beings and animals.

THE WORLD OF

WHEN DID DINOSAURS LIVE?

Dinosaurs roamed the Earth during the Mesozoic Era, which is divided into three periods:

TRIASSIC PERIOD, from 225 to 195 million years ago

➤ **Pangea**, Earth's one big continent, began to break up in this period.

➤ The earliest known mammals, such as the tiny, rat-like Morganucodon, began to appear.

➤ Evergreen plants were the most common vegetation.

➤ The earliest known dinosaur, **Eoraptor**, or "dawn thief," was a meat-eater only about 40 inches long. Herrersaurus, also a meat-eater, was about 10 feet long.

➤ Large marine reptiles, like long-necked **plesiosaurs** and dolphin-like **ichthyosaurs**, ruled the sea.

JURASSIC PERIOD, from 195 to 135 million years ago

➤ Flowering plants appeared.

➤ Plant-eating **sauropods**, like **Apatosaurus** and **Brachiosaurus**, were the biggest land creatures ever! These dinosaurs were eaten by meat-eaters like **Allosaurus** and **Megalosaurus**.

➤ **Archaeopteryx** was born—the earliest link between dinosaurs and birds.

➤ Flying reptiles called **pterosaurs**, close relatives of the dinosaur, dominated the sky.

CRETACEOUS PERIOD, from 135 to 65 million years ago

➤ The climate was warm, with no polar ice caps.

➤ Meat-eating **theropods** like **Tyrannosaurus Rex** and **Gigantosaurus** walked on two legs.

➤ All dinosaurs and other reptiles such as **ichthyosaurs** and **pterosaurs** became extinct by the end of this period. It may have been because a huge asteroid or comet hit the Earth. This would have filled the atmosphere with dust and debris, blocking most of the sun's light and heat. As a result many plants and animals would die out.

CELEBRITIES OF the DINOSAUR WORLD

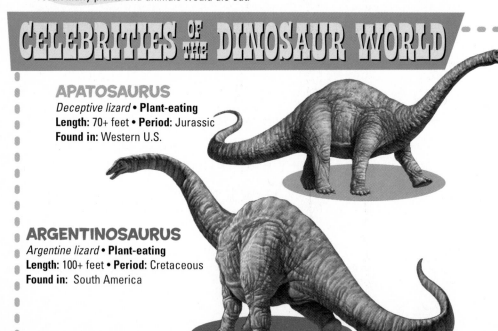

APATOSAURUS
Deceptive lizard • **Plant-eating**
Length: 70+ feet • **Period:** Jurassic
Found in: Western U.S.

ARGENTINOSAURUS
Argentine lizard • **Plant-eating**
Length: 100+ feet • **Period:** Cretaceous
Found in: South America

DINOSAURS

THE FOSSIL RECORD

Paleontologists are scientists who use fossils to study the past. **Fossils** are the remains of animals and plants. Most fossils are found in rocks formed from the mud or sand that collects at the bottom of oceans, rivers, and lakes. They usually come from hard materials, such as bones, teeth, shells, or leaves. Fossils are the main clues we have about ancient plants and animals. The age and type of rocks that fossils are found in can help show how long ago they lived.

DID YOU KNOW? *Discovered in Germany in 1861, the* **Archaeopteryx** *is one of the most famous fossils in history. This creature had bones, teeth, and a skull similar to a dinosaur's. But it also had feathers and could fly.*

EARLY DISCOVERIES

▶ In 1824 British geologist William Buckland recognized some fossils as part of a giant extinct reptile. He named this first dinosaur **Megalosaurus**, from the Greek words *megalos* ("big") and *sauros* ("lizard").

▶ In 1842 Sir Richard Owen used the Greek word *deinos* ("terrible") and *sauros* to coin the term *dinosaur*.

▶ The partial skeleton of a **Hadrosaurus** was found in New Jersey in 1858. This was the first major dinosaur discovery in North America. The remains were made into a full dinosaur skeleton, the first ever to be put on display, at the Philadelphia Academy of Natural Science.

DID YOU KNOW? **JURASSIC VOMIT** *In December 2001, British scientist Peter Doyle said he had found the world's oldest fossilized vomit. About 160 million years ago, an* **ichthyosaur** *ate some shellfish and then spit out the shells. Ichthyosaurs were ocean-going reptiles that looked like modern dolphins.*

VELOCIRAPTOR
Speedy thief
Meat-eating
Length: 6 feet
Period: Cretaceous
Found in: Asia

STEGOSAURUS
Plated lizard • **Plant-eating** • **Length:** 30 feet
Period: Jurassic • **Found in:** North America

TYRANNOSAURUS REX ("T-REX")
King of the tyrant lizards • **Meat-eating**
Length: 40 feet • **Period:** Cretaceous
Found in: Western U.S., Canada, Asia

TRICERATOPS
Three-horned face • **Plant-eating**
Length: 30 feet • **Period:** Cretaceous
Found: North America

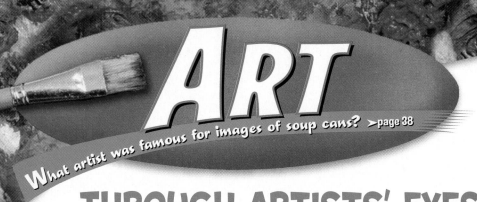

What artist was famous for images of soup cans? ➤page 38

THROUGH ARTISTS' EYES

Artists look at the world in a new way. Their work can be funny or sad, beautiful or disturbing, real-looking or strange.

Throughout history, artists have painted pictures of nature (called landscapes), or pictures of people (called portraits), or pictures of flowers in vases, food, and other objects (known as still lifes).

► Many artists still paint these kinds of pictures. But some artists today create pictures that do not look like anything in the real world. These paintings are examples of **abstract art**, or modern art.

► **Photography**, too, may be a form of art. Photos record both the commonplace and the exotic, and help us look at events in new ways.

► **Sculpture** is a three dimensional form made from clay, stone, metal, or other material. Many sculptures stand freely so that you can walk around them. Some are mobiles that hang from the ceiling. Sculptures can be large, like the Statue of Liberty, or small. Some sculptures are real-looking. Others have no form that can be recognized.

The Thinker, *a sculpture by Auguste Rodin* ►

••-*All About*... ANIMALS ON PARADE

Lizards and horses and pigs—oh my! Visitors to big cities in the U.S. and Canada may have noticed some pretty strange life-sized animals in the past couple of years: Brightly colored cows in Chicago and New York. Pigs in Cincinnati. Fish in New Orleans and Moose in Toronto. Orlando was invaded by lizards. Lexington, Kentucky, had horses, and in Buffalo, New York—what else?—buffalo!

The fiberglass animal statues were decorated by local artists and put on display around each city. These temporary exhibits made a lot of people stop and smile. When the shows were over, the statues were sold at auction, and the money was donated to charity.

The first "cow parade" was in Zurich, Switzerland, in 1998. Chicago had one in 1999. Since then, some 50 U.S. cities have put on animal parades. In 2002, Washington, D.C., had a parade of "party animals"—Republican elephants and Democratic donkeys. Cow parades were also planned for Portland, Oregon; Las Vegas; London; and Sydney, Australia.

All About... IMPRESSIONISM

Impressionism was an art movement that began in the 1860s in France. At the time some painters wanted to rebel against the accepted art styles. They created paintings different from anything that had been seen before. At first, their work was rejected by art critics.

The Impressionists were influenced by the invention of photography. They used rapid brush strokes to try and capture the moment—like a snapshot. This informal style of painting was very concerned with the effect of the light on the scene at a specific time. They especially liked to paint outdoors in natural light. Impressionists used bold contrasts of color, often playing rich warm highlights against blue shadows. The results were usually bright and colorful, without a lot of detail.

The movement's name came from artist Claude Monet's early work, *Impression: Sunrise*. Other famous Impressionist painters include Pierre Auguste Renoir, Alfred Sisley, Camille Pissarro, and Edgar Degas.

▲ The Beach at Sainte-Adresse, *by Claude Monet*

The Starry Night, *by Vincent van Gogh* ▶

SOME FAMOUS WORKS OF ART

PAINTING	ARTIST	WHEN PAINTED	WHERE IT IS
American Gothic	Grant Wood	1930	Art Institute of Chicago
Guernica	Pablo Picasso	1937	Reina Sofía Museum, Madrid, Spain
Lavender Mist	Jackson Pollock	1950	National Gallery of Art, Washington, DC
Mona Lisa	Leonardo da Vinci	1503-1506	Louvre Museum, Paris, France
Paul Revere	John Singleton Copley	around 1768	Museum of Fine Arts, Boston
The Persistence of Memory	Salvador Dalí	1931	Museum of Modern Art, New York City
The Scream	Edvard Munch	1893	National Gallery, Oslo, Norway
The Starry Night	Vincent van Gogh	1889	Museum of Modern Art, New York City
George Washington	Gilbert Stuart	1796	National Portrait Gallery, Washington, DC

WHO AM I?

I was born in Paris in 1848 and became a successful stockbroker. In my late 20s, I began collecting art and soon became a full-time painter. The portrait you see of me is one I made myself. I lived with artist Vincent van Gogh in southern France for a short time in 1888. Three years later, when I was poor and in debt, I sailed to the South Pacific and spent the rest of my life living on tropical islands. I liked to paint the people and scenes I found there, and made just enough money to get by. ⤳ Answer: Paul Gauguin

Art History Highlights

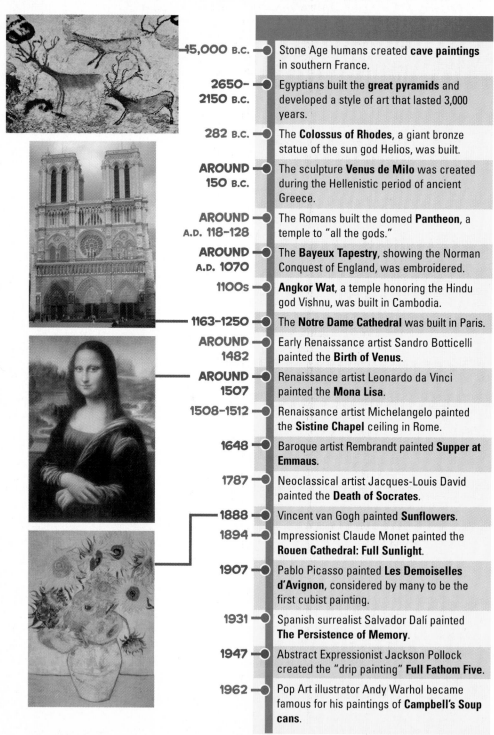

45,000 B.C.	Stone Age humans created **cave paintings** in southern France.
2650–2150 B.C.	Egyptians built the **great pyramids** and developed a style of art that lasted 3,000 years.
282 B.C.	The **Colossus of Rhodes**, a giant bronze statue of the sun god Helios, was built.
AROUND 150 B.C.	The sculpture **Venus de Milo** was created during the Hellenistic period of ancient Greece.
AROUND A.D. 118–128	The Romans built the domed **Pantheon**, a temple to "all the gods."
AROUND A.D. 1070	The **Bayeux Tapestry**, showing the Norman Conquest of England, was embroidered.
1100s	**Angkor Wat**, a temple honoring the Hindu god Vishnu, was built in Cambodia.
1163–1250	The **Notre Dame Cathedral** was built in Paris.
AROUND 1482	Early Renaissance artist Sandro Botticelli painted the **Birth of Venus**.
AROUND 1507	Renaissance artist Leonardo da Vinci painted the **Mona Lisa**.
1508–1512	Renaissance artist Michelangelo painted the **Sistine Chapel** ceiling in Rome.
1648	Baroque artist Rembrandt painted **Supper at Emmaus**.
1787	Neoclassical artist Jacques-Louis David painted the **Death of Socrates**.
1888	Vincent van Gogh painted **Sunflowers**.
1894	Impressionist Claude Monet painted the **Rouen Cathedral: Full Sunlight**.
1907	Pablo Picasso painted **Les Demoiselles d'Avignon**, considered by many to be the first cubist painting.
1931	Spanish surrealist Salvador Dalí painted **The Persistence of Memory**.
1947	Abstract Expressionist Jackson Pollock created the "drip painting" **Full Fathom Five**.
1962	Pop Art illustrator Andy Warhol became famous for his paintings of **Campbell's Soup cans**.

BIRTHDAYS

Who shares your birthday?

JANUARY

1 J.D. Salinger, *writer*, 1919
2 Cuba Gooding Jr., *actor*, 1968
3 J.R.R. Tolkien, *writer*, 1892
4 Louis Braille, *inventor*, 1809
5 Warrick Dunn, *football player*, 1975
6 Joan of Arc, *warrior, saint*, 1412
7 Katie Couric, *TV personality*, 1957
8 Elvis Presley, *singer*, 1935
9 A.J. McLean, *singer*, 1978
10 George Foreman, *boxer*, 1949
11 Mary J. Blige, *singer*, 1971
12 John Hancock, *statesman*, 1737
13 Julia Louis-Dreyfus, *actress*, 1961
14 L.L. Cool J, *rapper*, 1968
15 Rev. Martin Luther King Jr., *civil rights leader*, 1929
16 Aaliyah, *singer*, 1979
17 Jim Carrey, *actor*, 1962
18 Kevin Costner, *actor*, 1955
19 Edgar Allan Poe, *author*, 1809
20 Edwin "Buzz" Aldrin, *astronaut*, 1930
21 Hakeem Olajuwon, *basketball player*, 1963
22 Beverly Mitchell, *actress*, 1981
23 Tiffani-Amber Thiessen, *actress*, 1974
24 Mary Lou Retton, *gymnast*, 1968
25 Virginia Woolf, *writer*, 1882
26 Vince Carter, *basketball player*, 1977
27 Wolfgang Amadeus Mozart, *composer*, 1756
28 Joey Fatone, *singer*, 1977
29 Oprah Winfrey, *TV personality*, 1954
30 Franklin D. Roosevelt, *32nd president*, 1882
31 Justin Timberlake, *singer*, 1981

◀ *January 20*

FEBRUARY

▲ *February 4*

1 Langston Hughes, *poet*, 1901
2 Garth Brooks, *singer*, 1962
3 Norman Rockwell, *artist*, 1894
4 Rosa Parks, *civil rights activist*, 1913
5 Jennifer Jason Leigh, *actress*, 1952
6 Babe Ruth, *baseball player*, 1895
7 Chris Rock, *comedian/actor*, 1966
8 Alonzo Mourning, *basketball player*, 1970
9 Mena Suvari, *actress*, 1979
10 Greg Norman, *golfer*, 1955
11 Jennifer Aniston, *actress*, 1969
12 Abraham Lincoln, *16th president*, 1809
13 Chuck Yeager, *pilot*, 1923
14 Drew Bledsoe, *football player*, 1972
15 Matt Groening, *cartoonist, 1954*
16 Jerome Bettis, *football player*, 1972
17 Michael Jordan, *basketball player*, 1963
18 John Travolta, *actor*, 1955
19 Benicio Del Toro, *actor*, 1967
20 Brian Littrell, *singer*, 1975
21 Kelsey Grammer, *actor*, 1955
22 Drew Barrymore, *actress*, 1975
23 Julio Iglesias, *singer*, 1943
24 George Harrison, *musician*, 1943
25 Tea Leoni, *actress*, 1966
26 Marshall Faulk, *football player*, 1973
27 Chelsea Clinton, *President Clinton's daughter*, 1980
28 Eric Lindros, *hockey player*, 1973
29 Ja Rule, *rapper*, 1976

MARCH

1 Ron Howard, *director*, 1954
2 Jon Bon Jovi, *singer*, 1962
3 Jackie Joyner-Kersee, *Olympic champion*, 1962
4 Patricia Heaton, *actress*, 1959
5 Niki Taylor, *model*, 1975
6 Shaquille O'Neal, *basketball player*, 1972
7 Michael Eisner, *CEO*, 1942
8 Freddie Prinze Jr., *actor*, 1976
9 Bobby Fischer, *chess champion*, 1943
10 Sharon Stone, *actress*, 1958
11 Thora Birch, *actress*, 1982
12 James Taylor, *musician*, 1948
13 William H. Macy, *actor*, 1950
14 Albert Einstein, *scientist*, 1879
15 Mark McGrath, *singer*, 1968
16 James Madison, *4th president*, 1751
17 Mia Hamm, *soccer player*, 1972
18 Queen Latifah, *rapper/actress*, 1970
19 Bruce Willis, *actor*, 1955
20 Spike Lee, *director, actor*, 1957
21 Rosie O'Donnell, *TV personality*, 1962
22 Reese Witherspoon, *actress*, 1976
23 Jason Kidd, *basketball player*, 1973
24 Peyton Manning, *football player*, 1976
25 Sheryl Swoopes, *baksetball player*, 1971
26 Steven Tyler, *singer*, 1948
27 Mariah Carey, *singer*, 1970
28 Julia Stiles, *actress*, 1981
29 Jennifer Capriati, *tennis player*, 1976
30 Celine Dion, *singer*, 1968
31 Ewan McGregor, *actor*, 1971

March 22 ▶

39

APRIL

1 Debbie Reynolds, *actress*, 1932
2 Hans Christian Andersen, *author*, 1805
3 Amanda Bynes, *actress*, 1986
4 Heath Ledger, *actor*, 1979
5 Colin Powell, *secretary of state*, 1937
6 Paul Rudd, *actor*, 1969
7 Russell Crowe, *actor*, 1954
8 Kofi Annan, *UN secretary general*, 1938
9 Dennis Quaid, *actor*, 1954
10 Mandy Moore, *singer*, 1984
11 Jordana Brewster, *actress*, 1980
12 Claire Danes, *actress*, 1979
13 Thomas Jefferson, *president*, 1743
14 Sarah Michelle Gellar, *actress*, 1977
15 Jason Sehorn, *football player*, 1971
16 Kareem Abdul-Jabbar, *basketball player*, 1947
17 Liz Phair, *singer*, 1967
18 Melissa Joan Hart, *actress*, 1976
19 Hayden Christensen, *actor*, 1981
20 Carmen Electra, *actress*, 1973
21 Queen Elizabeth II of Great Britain, 1926
22 Jack Nicholson, *actor*, 1936
23 William Shakespeare, *playwright*, 1564
24 Chipper Jones, *baseball player*, 1972
25 Jacob Underwood, *singer*, 1980
26 Kevin James, *comedian*, 1965
27 Ulysses S. Grant, *18th president*, 1822
28 Jay Leno, *TV personality*, 1950
29 Andre Agassi, *tennis player*, 1970
30 Kirsten Dunst, *actress*, 1982

▲ *April 5*

MAY

▲ *May 29*

1 Tim McGraw, *musician*, 1967
2 The Rock, *wrestler*, 1972
3 James Brown, *singer*, 1933
4 Lance Bass, *singer*, 1979
5 Danielle Fishel, *actress*, 1981
6 George Clooney, *actor*, 1961
7 Johannes Brahms, *composer*, 1833
8 Enrique Iglesias, *singer*, 1975
9 Billy Joel, *songwriter*, 1949
10 Bono, *singer*, 1960
11 Natasha Richardson, *actress*, 1963
12 Jason Biggs, *actor*, 1978
13 Harvey Keitel, *actor*, 1939
14 George Lucas, *filmmaker*, 1944
15 Emmitt Smith, *football player*, 1969
16 Janet Jackson, *singer*, 1966
17 Bob Saget, *actor*, 1955
18 John Paul II, *pope*, 1920
19 Malcolm X, *black nationalist, civil rights activist*, 1925
20 Busta Rhymes, *rapper*, 1972
21 Fairuza Balk, *actress*, 1974
22 Naomi Campbell, *model*, 1970
23 Jewel (Kilcher), *singer*, 1974
24 Billy Gilman, *singer*, 1988
25 Mike Myers, *actor*, 1963
26 Lenny Kravitz, *musician*, 1964
27 Jeff Bagwell, *baseball player*, 1968
28 Rudolph Giuliani, *politician*, 1944
29 John F. Kennedy, *35th president*, 1917
30 Lisa Kudrow, *actress*, 1963
31 Brooke Shields, *actress*, 1965

JUNE

1 Alanis Morissette, *singer*, 1974
2 Dana Carvey, *comedian*, 1955
3 Curtis Mayfield, *songwriter*, 1942
4 Angelina Jolie, *actress*, 1975
5 Mark Wahlberg, *actor*, 1971
6 Dalai Lama, *Tibetan spiritual leader*, 1935
7 Anna Kournikova, *tennis player*, 1981
8 Keenen Ivory Wynans, *actor*, 1958
9 Natalie Portman, *actress*, 1981
10 Leelee Sobieski, *actress*, 1982
11 Joshua Jackson, *actor*, 1978
12 George H. W. Bush, *41st president*, 1924
13 Ashley and Mary-Kate Olsen, *actresses*, 1986
14 Steffi Graf, *tennis player*, 1969
15 Courteney Cox-Arquette, *actress*, 1964
16 Yasmine Bleeth, *actress*, 1968
17 Venus Williams, *tennis player*, 1980
18 Paul McCartney, *musician*, 1942
19 Kathleen Turner, *actress*, 1954
20 Nicole Kidman, *actress*, 1967
21 Prince William of Great Britain, 1982
22 Carson Daly, *TV personality*, 1973
23 Kurt Warner, *football player*, 1971
24 George Pataki, *N.Y. governor*, 1945
25 Chris Isaak, *songwriter*, 1956
26 Derek Jeter, *baseball player*, 1974
27 Tobey Maguire, *actor*, 1975
28 John Cusack, *actor*, 1966
29 Theo Fleury, *hockey player*, 1968
30 Vincent D'Onofrio, *actor*, 1959

▼ *June 9*

JULY

1 Liv Tyler, *actress*, 1977
2 Richard Petty, *auto racer*, 1937
3 Tom Cruise, *actor*, 1962
4 Neil Simon, playwright, 1927
5 P. T. Barnum, *circus founder*, 1810
6 George W. Bush, *43rd president*, 1946
7 Michelle Kwan, figure skater, 1980
8 Beck, *singer*, 1970
9 Tom Hanks, *actor*, 1956
10 Jessica Simpson, *singer*, 1980
11 Lil' Kim, *rapper*, 1975
12 Bill Cosby, *comedian*, 1937
13 Harrison Ford, *actor*, 1942
14 Gerald R. Ford, *38th president*, 1913
15 Jesse Ventura, *governor/wrestler*, 1951
16 Barry Sanders, *football player*, 1968
17 David Hasselhoff, *actor*, 1952
18 Nelson Mandela, *anti-apartheid leader*, 1918
19 Anthony Edwards, *actor*, 1962
20 Carlos Santana, *musician*, 1947
21 Josh Hartnett, *actor*, 1978
22 David Spade, *actor*, 1965
23 Daniel Radcliffe, *actor*, 1989
24 Barry Bonds, *baseball player*, 1964
25 Matt LeBlanc, *actor*, 1967
26 Kelly Clark, *snowboarder*, 1983
27 Alex Rodriguez, *baseball player*, 1975
28 Beatrix Potter, *author*, 1866
29 Peter Jennings, *TV anchor*, 1938
30 Arnold Schwarzenegger, *actor*, 1947
31 J. K. Rowling, *author*, 1966

▲ July 5

AUGUST

▲ *August 14*

1 Edgerrin James, *football player*, 1978
2 Edward Furlong, *actor*, 1977
3 Tom Brady, *football player*, 1977
4 Jeff Gordon, *auto racer*, 1971
5 Patrick Ewing, *basketball player*, 1962
6 David Robinson, *basketball player*, 1965
7 Charlize Theron, *actress*, 1975
8 Joshua "JC" Chasez, *singer*, 1976
9 Whitney Houston, *singer*, 1963
10 Antonio Banderas, *actor*, 1960
11 Hulk Hogan, *wrestler*, 1953
12 Pete Sampras, *tennis player*, 1971
13 Fidel Castro, *president of Cuba*, 1927
14 Halle Berry, *actress*, 1968
15 Ben Affleck, *actor*, 1972
16 Madonna, *singer/actress*, 1958
17 Sean Penn, *actor/director*, 1960
18 Edward Norton, *actor*, 1969
19 Matthew Perry, *actor*, 1969
20 Connie Chung, *journalist*, 1946
21 Fred Durst, *singer*, 1971
22 Howie Dorough, *singer*, 1973
23 Kobe Bryant, *basketball player*, 1978
24 Cal Ripken Jr., *baseball player*, 1960
25 Regis Philbin, *TV personality*, 1934
26 Tom Ridge, *homeland security director*, 1945
27 Sarah Chalke, *actress*, 1976
28 LeAnn Rimes, *singer*, 1982
29 Michael Jackson, *singer*, 1958
30 Cameron Diaz, *actress*, 1972
31 Hideo Nomo, *baseball player*, 1968

SEPTEMBER

1 Tim Duncan, *basketball player*, 1966
2 Salma Hayek, *actress*, 1966
3 Charlie Sheen, *actor*, 1965
4 Mike Piazza, *baseball player*, 1968
5 Jesse James, *outlaw*, 1847
6 Rosie Perez, *actress*, 1964
7 Devon Sawa, *actor*, 1978
8 Pink, *singer*, 1979
9 Adam Sandler, *actor*, 1966
10 Randy Johnson, *baseball player*, 1963
11 Moby, *singer*, 1965
12 Joe Pantoliano, *actor*, 1954
13 Fiona Apple, *singer*, 1977
14 Sam Neill, *actor*, 1947
15 Prince Harry of Great Britain, 1984
16 B. B. King, *blues musician*, 1924
17 David Souter, *Supreme Court justice*, 1939
18 Lance Armstrong, *cyclist*, 1971
19 Trisha Yearwood, *singer*, 1964
20 Guy Lafleur, *hockey player*, 1951
21 Faith Hill, *singer*, 1967
22 Andrea Bocelli, *opera singer*, 1958
23 Erik-Michael Estrada, *singer*, 1979
24 Kevin Sorbo, *actor*, 1958
25 Will Smith, *actor*, 1968
26 Serena Williams, *tennis player*, 1981
27 Meat Loaf, *musician*, 1947
28 Gwyneth Paltrow, *actress*, 1973
29 Bryant Gumbel, *TV personality*, 1948
30 Martina Hingis, *tennis player*, 1980

September 5

September 4 ▶

41

OCTOBER

1 Mark McGwire, *baseball player*, 1963
2 Sting, *musician*, 1951
3 Kevin Richardson, *singer*, 1971
4 Rachel Leigh Cook, *actress*, 1979
5 Kate Winslet, *actress*, 1975
6 Rebecca Lobo, *basketball player*, 1973
7 Vladimir Putin, *Russian president*, 1952
8 Matt Damon, *actor*, 1970
9 John Lennon, *musician*, 1940
10 Brett Favre, *football player*, 1969
11 Orlando Hernandez, *baseball player*, 1969
12 Marion Jones, *Olympic champion*, 1975
13 Paul Simon, *songwriter*, 1941
14 Usher, *singer*, 1979
15 Sarah Ferguson, *British royalty*, 1959
16 Kordell Stewart, *football player*, 1972
17 Eminem, *rapper*, 1972
18 Wynton Marsalis, *jazz musician*, 1961
19 John Lithgow, *actor*, 1945
20 Snoop Dogg, *rapper*, 1972
21 Björk, *singer*, 1966
22 Ichiro Suzuki, *baseball player*, 1973
23 Michael Crichton, *author*, 1942
24 Monica, *singer*, 1980
25 Midori, *violinist*, 1971
26 Hillary Rodham Clinton, *U.S. senator*, 1947
27 Patty Sheehan, *golfer*, 1956
28 Julia Roberts, *actress*, 1967
29 Winona Ryder, *actress*, 1971
30 Nia Long, *actress*, 1971
31 Chris Tucker, *comedian*, 1973

◄ *October 26*

NOVEMBER

▲ *November 2*

1 Jenny McCarthy, *TV personality*, 1972
2 Daniel Boone, *frontiersman*, 1734
3 Phil Simms, *football player/sportscaster*, 1956
4 Laura Bush, *first lady*, 1946
5 Bryan Adams, *singer*, 1959
6 Ethan Hawke, *actor*, 1970
7 Marie Curie, *scientist*, 1867
8 Tara Reid, *actress*, 1975
9 Sean "Puffy" Combs, *rapper/businessman*, 1969
10 Isaac Bruce, *football player*, 1972
11 Leonardo DiCaprio, *actor*, 1974
12 David Schwimmer, *actor*, 1966
13 Whoopi Goldberg, *actress*, 1949
14 Condoleezza Rice, *national security advisor*, 1954
15 Sam Waterston, *actor*, 1940
16 Trevor Penick, *singer*, 1979
17 Danny DeVito, *actor*, 1944
18 Jason Williams, *basketball player*, 1975
19 Meg Ryan, *actress*, 1961
20 Ming-Na Wen, *actress*, 1967
21 Ken Griffey Jr., *baseball player*, 1969
22 Jamie Lee Curtis, *actress*, 1958
23 Billy the Kid, *outlaw*, 1859
24 Scott Joplin, *composer*, 1868
25 Jenna and Barbara Bush, *President Bush's daughters*, 1981
26 Shawn Kemp, *basketball player*, 1969
27 Caroline Kennedy Schlossberg, *President Kennedy's daughter*, 1957
28 Jon Stewart, *TV personality*, 1962
29 Mariano Rivera, *baseball player*, 1969
30 Ben Stiller, *actor*, 1965

DECEMBER

1 Bette Midler, *singer/actress*, 1945
2 Britney Spears, *singer*, 1981
3 Brendan Fraser, *actor*, 1967
4 Marisa Tomei, actress, 1964
5 Frankie Muniz, *actor*, 1985
6 Macy Gray, *singer*, 1969
7 Aaron Carter, *singer*, 1987
8 Teri Hatcher, *actress*, 1964
9 Tom Daschle, *senate majority leader*, 1947
10 Emily Dickinson, *poet*, 1830
11 John Kerry, *U.S. senator*, 1943
12 Jennifer Connelly, *actress*, 1970
13 Jamie Foxx, *comedian*, 1967
14 Craig Biggio, *baseball player*, 1965
15 Mo Vaughn, *baseball player*, 1967
16 Ludwig van Beethoven, *composer*, 1770
17 Bill Pullman, *actor*, 1954
18 Steven Spielberg, *film producer*, 1947
19 Alyssa Milano, *actress*, 1972
20 Kiefer Sutherland, *actor*, 1966
21 Ray Romano, *comedian*, 1957
22 Diane Sawyer, *TV journalist*, 1945
23 Susan Lucci, *actress*, 1948
24 Ricky Martin, *singer*, 1971
25 Dido, *singer*, 1971
26 Susan Butcher, *sled dog racer*, 1954
27 Cokie Roberts, *TV journalist*, 1943
28 Denzel Washington, *actor*, 1954
29 Jude Law, *actor*, 1972
30 Tiger Woods, *golfer*, 1975
31 Val Kilmer, *actor*, 1959

▼ *December 16*

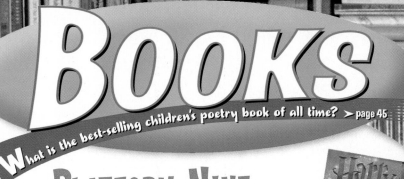

BOOKS

What is the best-selling children's poetry book of all time? ➤ page 45

PLATFORM NINE AND THREE QUARTERS

By now, millions of people around the world (kids and adults!) know about Platform Nine and Three Quarters at London's Kings Cross Station—if they aren't a Muggle, that is. Muggles are non-magical people that can't even see Platform Nine and Three Quarters, or the Hogwarts Express train that takes you from there to the Hogwarts School of Witchcraft and Wizardry.

Harry Potter first appeared in England, in J.K. Rowling's 1997 book, *Harry Potter and the Philosopher's Stone*. It was published in the U.S. in 1999 as *Harry Potter and the Sorcerer's Stone*. Next came *Harry Potter and the Chamber of Secrets* (1999), *Harry Potter and the Prisoner of Azkaban* (1999), and *Harry Potter and the Goblet of Fire* (2000). Each one topped the best-seller lists. *Harry Potter and the Order of the Phoenix* was expected to be out in late 2002 or early 2003, and the first of three movies based on the books came out in December 2001.

If you like fantasy, you might want to check out these series too:

The Chronicles of Narnia, by C.S. Lewis. Secret passages lead four children to Narnia, a land of talking animals, evil witches, wicked dragons, magic spells, and amazing adventures. *The Lion, the Witch, and the Wardrobe* was first in the series.

His Dark Materials Trilogy, by Philip Pullman. Lyra, Will, and their companions learn heart-wrenching lessons about love, friendship, and death as they travel heroically through strange, magical worlds. *The Golden Compass* was the first in the series.

The Dark is Rising, by Susan Cooper. In these books about the timeless conflict between the forces of Light and Darkness, brave children embark on a series of journeys to find magical objects—a grail, six powerful signs, a golden harp, and a crystal sword—that will help goodness triumph over evil. *Over Sea, Under Stone* was the first in the series.

The Redwall Series, by Brian Jacques. Life is very happy for the community of mice, moles, badgers, and other furry creatures that live in Redwall Abbey, until they must defend their home from the evil rats that want to take it over. *Redwall* was the first in the series.

BOOKS TO ENJOY

FICTION
Fiction books are stories that come out of the writer's imagination. Some fiction books are set in a world of fantasy. Others seem very real.

Anna of Byzantium, by Tracy Barrett. Anna looks forward to the day she will succeed her father as ruler of the Byzantine Empire. But her hopes are dashed by the birth of her baby brother. Based on the true story of Anna Comnena, an 11th-century princess.

Any Small Goodness: A Novel of the Barrio, by Tony Johnston. Eleven-year-old Arturo and his family move from Mexico to a rough neighborhood in East Los Angeles, where they find a loving and gentle community of family and friends.

The Black Stallion, by Walter Farley. After a shipwreck, a boy and a magnificent black horse are stranded on a deserted island, where they form a lifelong friendship.

The Cricket in Times Square, by George Selden. An exciting tale of a country cricket who accidentally hitches a ride to New York City in a picnic basket.

Golem, by David Wisniewsky. Striking paper-cut images tell the legend of a clay giant that comes to life to protect the Jews of Prague from persecution in the 16th century.

Hatchet, by Gary Paulsen. Brian is on his way to visit his father in the Canadian oil fields when the small plane he's in crashes in the wilderness. Alone in the woods with only the new hatchet his mother gave him, Brian struggles to survive.

Misty of Chincoteague, by Marguerite Henry. A thrilling story of a boy's and a girl's attempts to capture a wild pony on Assateague island off the coast of Virginia.

My Side of the Mountain, by Jean Craighead George. A young boy runs away from his home in New York City. Living in a big, hollowed-out tree in the Catskill Mountains of upstate New York, he learns to survive on his own.

The Phantom Tollbooth, by Norton Juster. Ten-year-old Milo rides his toy car through a tollbooth that mysteriously appears in his bedroom. It leads him to a magical world of weirdly funny characters.

Tales of a Fourth Grade Nothing, by Judy Blume. Peter Hatcher is the "fourth grade nothing." And it's his little brother's fault. Fudge gets all the attention, while Peter gets all the trouble.

A Wrinkle in Time, by Madeleine L'Engle. Meg Murray travels through space with her brother and friend to find her father, a scientist who disappeared while working on a secret government project.

TONY JOHNSTON
Any Small Goodness
a novel of the barrio

WHO AM I?

I was born in South Africa, in 1892, but grew up in England. I became an orphan at the age of 11. I loved languages and became a professor of Old and Middle English at Oxford University.

One day when I was getting bored marking papers, a sentence came into my head about an imaginary creature. Soon I had thought up a whole imaginary world. I wrote a series of books about this world that became famous.

Answer: J. R. R. Tolkien

POETRY
Poems use language in new and imaginative ways, sometimes in rhyme.

The Gargoyle on the Roof, by Jack Prelutsky; illustrated by Peter Sis. Illustrated poems about werewolves, vampires, trolls, gremlins, and other scary creatures.

One Hundred Years of Poetry, edited by Michael Harrison and Christopher Stuart-Clark. Large book of poems by 150 authors; organized by themes like mystery, animals, childhood, and war.

Remember the Bridge: Poems of a People, by Carole Boston Weatherford. Poems and photos celebrating 400 years of African-American heroes.

Where the Sidewalk Ends, by Shel Silverstein. The best-selling children's poetry book of all time. It is filled with poems and drawings that will make you laugh and cry.

NONFICTION
These books prove facts can be fascinating.

Machu Picchu, by Elizabeth Mann. The incredible story of the Incas and the breathtaking city they built high in the Andes Mountains.

Planet Zoo: One Hundred Animals We Can't Afford to Lose, by Simon Barnes; illustrated by Alan Marks. Watercolor paintings and descriptions of 100 endangered species, with ways we can try to save them.

So, You Want to Be President?, by Judith St. George; illustrated by David Small. This book captures the funny, personal side of the presidents' lives.

Visions of Beauty: The Story of Sarah Breedlove Walker, by Kathryn Lasky. Born to poor sharecroppers, Madame C.J. Walker started a successful beauty care business in the early 1900s. She used her power and wealth to help other African-American women.

What You Never Knew About Fingers, Forks, and Chopsticks, by Patricia Lauber. A fun, fascinating, and sometimes disgusting history of table manners and eating utensils.

REFERENCE
Many reference materials are stored on CD-ROMs and are also available on the Internet.

Almanac: A one-volume book of facts and statistics.

Atlas: A collection of maps.

Dictionary: A book of words in alphabetical order. It gives meanings and spellings and shows how words are pronounced.

Encyclopedia: A place to go for information on almost any subject.

For more on children's books, go to:

WEB SITE *http://www.ala.org/booklist/v96/002.html*

Book Awards, 2001-2002

CALDECOTT MEDAL

This is the highest honor a picture book can receive.

2002 WINNER: *The Three Little Pigs*, by David Wiesner

NEWBERY MEDAL

This is the highest honor for a children's book.

2002 WINNER: *A Single Shard*, by Linda Sue Park

CORETTA SCOTT KING AWARD

These are given to artists and authors whose works encourage expression of the African-American experience.

2002 WINNERS:

Author Award: *The Land*, by Mildred D. Taylor

Illustrator Award: *Goin' Someplace Special*, illustrated by Jerry Pinkney

BEST NEW BOOKS OF THE YEAR

Among those chosen in 2002 by the American Library Association

The Beloved Dearly, by Doug Cooney — A funny story about a group of friends who start a pet funeral business. They soon learn that making money is not the most important thing in the world.

Elusive Glory: African American Heroes of World War II, by John Robert Bruning — Interesting biographies of the Tuskegee Airmen and other African Americans who bravely fought for their country during World War II, even though they faced discrimination at home and in the military.

Harvey Angell, by Diana Hendry — For Henry, an orphan, life in Aunt Agatha's gloomy rooming house is unbearable until magical Harvey Angell moves in. Sometimes compared to books in the Harry Potter series.

The Hungry Year, by Connie Brummel Crook — When Kate's father does not return from hunting, she and her younger brothers are saved from starvation by a group of Mohawk Indians. Set in the Canadian wilderness in 1787.

Seven Wonders of the Ancient World, by Lynn Curlee — Discover the glory of the Hanging Gardens of Babylon, the Colossus of Rhodes, the Temple of Artemis, the Great Pyramid, the Statue of Zeus, the Mausoleum of Halicarnassus, and the Lighthouse of Alexandria with these vivid illustrations and fascinating stories.

Shoeless Joe and Me, by Dan Gutman — Thirteen-year-old Joe Stoshack travels back in time to try to prevent baseball hero Shoeless Joe Jackson from destroying his career in 1919 by getting involved in the Black Sox Scandal.

So, You Wanna Be a Comic Book Artist, by Philip Amara; illustrated by Pop Mhan — Interviews with comic book artists and easy-to-follow instructions may inspire you to create and publish your own comic books.

That's Magic: 40 Fool Proof Tricks to Delight, Amaze, and Entertain, by Richard Jones — Perform dazzling magic tricks with a rope, cup, a deck of cards, a few coins, and the secrets revealed in this book.

All About... COMIC BOOKS

From the time comics started, kids with an extra nickel to spend would use it to buy their favorites. The first comic books were collections of comic strips from newspapers. In the 1930s, original comic books appeared. They always sold well, but by 1938 they really began flying off the shelves. That was the year Superman landed from Krypton.

Every kid (and lots of adults) loved the Man of Steel. He was soon joined by Batman, Green Lantern, and other superheroes.

In the 1940s, during World War II, kids turned to war comics with patriotic heroes like Captain America. During those grim times, funny comics, with characters like Bugs Bunny, Daffy Duck, and Archie, also became popular. By the end of the war in 1945, superheroes were fading away. Kids wanted more realistic, sometimes more violent, stories. But many adults believed comics, especially violent ones, were bad for kids, and most publishers agreed to a code that restricted what comics could show.

Some publishers closed down. It took a real marvel to come to the rescue: Marvel Comics. Marvel introduced new kinds of superheroes, such as Fantastic Four, the Incredible Hulk, Spider-Man, and the X-Men. These characters were cool. They talked and acted more like real people. But they had to battle for kids' attention with TV, and then with computers and video games. To attract new readers, publishers created ever-weirder characters, like Spawn. Drawings and stories became so realistic they began to appeal more to adults than kids.

Although Josie and the Pussycats, Sabrina the Teenage Witch, and the X-Men may have been born in comics, kids today know them mainly through movie and TV spinoffs. Still, comics remain an art form, with their own loyal fans. Don't expect to see The End any time soon.

FIND THAT NAME

Unscramble the letters below to find the authors' names. Then match each author's name to the title of the book or book series he or she wrote.

AUTHORS

CAKJ SLURPETYK   ___ ___ ___ ___   ___ ___ ___ ___ ___ ___ ___ ___

THRANKY SKALY   ___ ___ ___ ___ ___ ___   ___ ___ ___ ___ ___

NONROT RUSTEJ   ___ ___ ___ ___ ___ ___   ___ ___ ___ ___ ___

DRILMED ROYALT   ___ ___ ___ ___ ___ ___   ___ ___ ___ ___ ___

BOOK TITLES

The Gargoyle on the Roof

The Land

The Phantom Tollbooth

Visions of Beauty: The Story of Sarah Breedlove Walker

AUTHORS

ANSWERS ON PAGES 314-317. FOR MORE PUZZLES GO TO WWW.WORLDALMANACFORKIDS.COM

47

BUILDINGS

What unusual building has 17½ miles of hallway? ➤ page 49

Tallest Buildings in the World

Here are the world's tallest buildings, with the year each was completed. Heights listed here don't include antennas or other outside structures. The twin towers of the World Trade Center (1,362 feet and 1,368 feet) were fourth on the list before they were destroyed in September 2001.

PETRONAS TOWERS 1 & 2, Kuala Lumpur, Malaysia (1998) **Height:** each building is 88 stories, 1,483 feet

SEARS TOWER, Chicago, Illinois (1974) **Height:** 110 stories, 1,450 feet ▶

JIN MAO BUILDING, Shanghai, China (1998) **Height:** 88 stories, 1,381 feet

CITIC PLAZA, Guangzhou, China (1997) **Height:** 80 stories, 1,283 feet

SHUN HING SQUARE, Shenzhen, China (1996) **Height:** 69 stories, 1,260 feet

ROOFS THAT MOVE

A lot of new sports stadiums these days use a new technology—**a retractable roof**. These roofs can be opened when the weather's good and closed when it's bad. The first one built was Toronto's SkyDome in 1989. By 2002, ballparks in Houston, Milwaukee, Phoenix, and Seattle all had retractable roofs. Except for the SkyDome, all of these stadiums have natural grass fields.

It takes some fancy engineering to work one of these roofs. The roofs are divided into panels. Each panel is moved into place by wheels driven along tracks by electric motors. It's important that the track stays in alignment so that a panel's weight doesn't fall entirely onto one wheel, which could cause structural damage. Engineers have to allow for wind, too. If the wind blows hard, it could make the roof move too fast, which could cause it to fail. The roof at Astros Field weighs 18 million pounds, covers 6½ acres, and yet can open up completely in as little as 12 minutes.

DID YOU KNOW? **THE LEANING TOWER OF PISA** *is one of Italy's best known attractions. But for years tourists couldn't go inside it. The tilt that made it famous also made it dangerous. By 1990, the tower was closed for repairs. Engineers slowly removed tons of earth from beneath the tower's north side. This straightened it enough to make it safe, but still didn't get rid of its famous tilt. In 2001 the tower opened again, and experts say it's good for another 300 years.*

THE PENTAGON

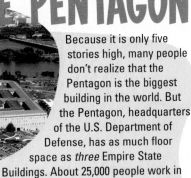

Because it is only five stories high, many people don't realize that the Pentagon is the biggest building in the world. But the Pentagon, headquarters of the U.S. Department of Defense, has as much floor space as *three* Empire State Buildings. About 25,000 people work in the five-sided structure, which is located in Arlington, Virginia, just across the Potomac River from Washington, D.C. The building covers 29 acres, which is about the size of 12 large Home Depot stores. If you were to walk down every hallway, you would cover 17½ miles. There are more than 7,700 windows, 284 restrooms, and enough telephone cable to go around the world four times.

Construction on the Pentagon began in September 1941, in the early days of World War II, and was finished in only 16 months. In 1992 the Pentagon was designated a National Historic Landmark. At that time, the building was showing its age. A huge reconstruction project was begun in 1993. Asbestos and other hazardous materials had to be removed. The building needed new floors and walls, new plumbing and wiring, and new carpets. Fixing it up will cost more than $1 billion, or 10 times the cost of the original building. Adding to the costs will be repairing the damage from September 11, 2001, when terrorists hijacked an airliner and crashed it into a part of the building that was already under reconstruction. The renovation of the whole Pentagon will probably not be finished until 2020.

All About... CASTLES

In Europe in the Middle Ages (roughly 500–1500 A.D.), war was a way of life. For that reason, great lords built the mighty structures known as castles. Castles were both dwelling places and fortifications. They were the homes of the knights, whose job was to defend the territory where their lords lived. The first castles were built of wood and surrounded by moats, which were first dry trenches and were later filled with water. Soon stone replaced wood as a building material. In England alone, some 1,000 castles were constructed between 1135 and 1155.

A typical medieval castle actually consisted of several structures. At the center was the donjon, or keep, which contained the lord's living quarters. It was surrounded by an inner court with towers and walls, a courtyard (also called a "bailey"), and outside walls with towers at different points. People entered the castle complex through a huge gateway that was guarded by a drawbridge and a moveable iron gate called a *portcullis*. From the walls, defenders could shoot arrows, or throw stones and boiling water onto attackers.

Castle-building declined with the development of gunpowder and artillery in the mid-14th century. Since cannons could knock down walls, castles no longer provided reliable protection in wartime. Yet castles continue to fascinate us today. Many castles are popular museums. They attract hordes of visitors hoping for a glimpse into the romance and drama of the past.

Conwy Castle, North Wales ▶

CALENDARS & TIME

Why did George Washington's birthday suddenly change? ➤page 50

Calendars divide time into days, weeks, months, and years. Calendar divisions are based on movements of the Earth, sun, and moon. A year is the time it takes for one revolution of Earth around the sun. Early calendars were lunar—based on the movements of the moon across the sky. The ancient Egyptians were probably the first to develop a solar calendar, based on the movements of Earth around the sun.

THE JULIAN AND GREGORIAN CALENDARS

The ancient Romans had a calendar with a year of 304 days. In 46 B.C., the emperor Julius Caesar decided to use a calendar based on movements of the sun. This calendar, called the Julian calendar, fixed the normal year at 365 days and added one day every fourth year (leap year). It also established the months of the year and the days of the week.

In A.D. 1582, the Julian calendar was revised by Pope Gregory XIII, because the year was 11 minutes and 14 seconds too long. This added up to about three extra days every 400 years. To fix it, he made years ending in 00 leap years only if they can be divided by 400. Thus, 2000 is a leap year, but 2100 will not be. The new calendar, called the Gregorian calendar, is the one used today in most of the world.

THE JEWISH AND ISLAMIC CALENDARS

Other calendars are also used. The Jewish calendar, which began almost 6,000 years ago, is the official calendar of Israel. The year 2002 is the same as 5762–5763 on the Jewish calendar, which starts at Rosh Hashanah. The Islamic calendar starts in A.D. 622. The year 2002 is equivalent to 1422–1423 on the Islamic calendar, which begins with the month of Muharram.

THE CHINESE CALENDAR

The Chinese calendar has years named after animals. There are 12 of them: Rat, Ox, Tiger, Rabbit, Dragon, Snake, Horse, Sheep, Monkey, Rooster, Dog, and Pig. On February 12, 2002, the Year of the Horse (4700) began. On February 5, 2003, the Year of the Sheep begins.

DID YOU KNOW? *The Julian calendar, used in Europe for many centuries, was actually too long by about 11 minutes a year. By 1582, these extra minutes added up to 10 days. So Pope Gregory XIII declared that the day following October 4, 1582, should be known as October 15—wiping out 10 dates. By the time England and the American colonies started using the "Gregorian" calendar in 1752, there were 11 extra days. So the day after September 2 OS (Old Style) became September 14 NS (New Style). George Washington was born on February 11, 1732, but with the calendar change his birthday became February 22.*

BIRTHSTONES

MONTH	BIRTHSTONE
January	Garnet
February	Amethyst
March	Aquamarine
April	Diamond
May	Emerald
June	Pearl
July	Ruby
August	Peridot
September	Sapphire
October	Opal
November	Topaz
December	Turquoise

WHAT ARE TIME ZONES?

A day is 24 hours long—the time it takes Earth to complete one rotation on its axis. Earth is divided into 24 time zones. Each zone is roughly 15 degrees of longitude wide.

The line of longitude passing through Greenwich, England, is the starting point. It is called the prime meridian. In the 12th time zone (and 180th meridian) the International Date Line appears. When you cross the line going west, it's tomorrow. Going east, you travel backward in time and the date is one day earlier.

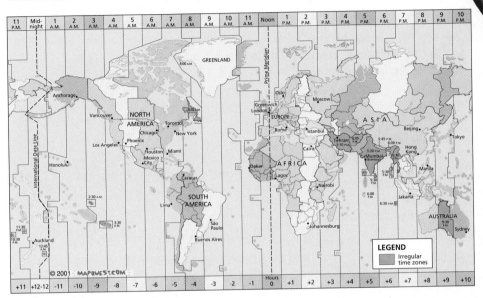

When it is 7 A.M. in New York, New York, it is

7 A.M. in Lima, Peru	Noon in London, England	1 P.M. in Oslo, Norway	2 P.M. in Cairo, Egypt	3 P.M. in Moscow, Russia	7 P.M. in Jakarta, Indonesia	8 P.M. in Hong Kong, China

All About... ATOMIC CLOCKS

There are two key elements to every clock: a "ticker" that moves back and forth (**oscillates**) and something to count the ticks. In a grandfather clock, the pendulum is the "ticker" and the gears that move the hands provide the counter. Steadier ticks make a more reliable clock. Atomic clocks have been around since 1952. They aren't radioactive. They're called that because they use the electrons around cesium **atoms** as the "ticker." Scientists can adjust a microwave beam to the exact **frequency** (oscillation) of the electrons moving in the cesium atoms: 9,192,631,770 cycles in a second. In fact, these 9 billion "back and forth movements" define the unit of time we call a second. Cesium clocks are off by *less than one second per million years*. And scientists are working on clocks that will be even more accurate.

COMPUTERS

What computer is 10 feet tall and weighs 30 tons? ➤ page 58

Computers perform tasks by using programs called software. They tell the computer what to do when the user enters certain information or commands. This is called input.

The computer then processes the information and gives the user the results (output). The computer can also save, or store, the information.

The machines that make up a computer system are kinds of hardware. The largest and most powerful computers are called mainframes. Most people are more familiar with personal computers (PCs). These can be used at a desk (desktops), carried around (laptops), worn on your belt (wearable computers), or even held in your hand (palm computers).

SOFTWARE

KINDS OF SOFTWARE When you write on a computer you use a type of software called a word processing program. This program can be selected by using the **keyboard** or a **mouse**.

Other common types of software include programs for doing math, keeping records, playing games, and creating pictures.

ENTERING DATA In a word processing program, you can input your words by typing on the **keyboard**. The backspace and delete keys are like erasers. You can also press special **function keys** or click on certain symbols (icons) to center or underline words, move words around, check spelling, print out a page, and do other tasks.

HARDWARE

INSIDE THE COMPUTER The instructions from the program you use are carried out inside the computer by the **central processing unit**, or **CPU**. The CPU is the computer's brain.

GETTING THE RESULTS The **monitor** and **printer** are the most commonly used output devices in a computer system. When you type a story, the words show up on a **monitor**, which is like a TV screen. Your story can be printed on paper by using a **printer**.

If you print out a story, you can mail it to a friend. But if you both have **modems**, it can get from your computer to your friend's computer. A **modem** allows information from a computer to travel over telephone lines.

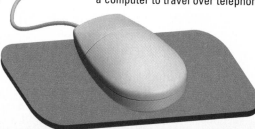

STORAGE KEEPING DATA TO USE IT LATER

A computer also stores information. You can save your work and return to it at your convenience. It is important to save often.

FLOPPY DISK
Information can be saved on a **"floppy" disk** that goes into a slot in the computer called a **disk drive**. If you use a disk to save your story, you can use the disk on another computer and your story will be there to work on. Disks today are usually stiff. Older computers used larger disks that were light and easy to bend, so people began calling them floppy disks.

ZIP DISK
Zip® disks hold much more information than floppy disks. They are used in special Zip drives. A **Jaz® disk** holds a gigabyte of information, 10 times as much as a Zip disk.

CD-ROMs
Many computers have a CD-ROM drive. This allows you to play special disks called **CD-ROMs**, similar to music CDs. A CD-ROM can hold a huge amount of information, including pictures and sound. Almanacs, games, encyclopedias, and many other types of information and entertainment are on CD-ROMs.

DVDs
Digital Versatile Disks look like CD-ROMs, but hold about eight times more information on a single side. DVDs are currently used to store movies, encyclopedias, and other products with lots of data.

HARD DISK
Most computers have a **hard drive**. The hard drive contains a **hard disk** that is not removed. It holds much more information than zip or floppy disks. It stores your software and information you have entered into the computer.

Monitor

CPU

Printer

Keyboard

CD-ROM

Mouse

Floppy Disk

Modem

Zip Drive

COMPUTER TALK

artificial intelligence or AI The ability of computers and robots to imitate human intelligence by learning and making decisions.

bit The smallest unit of data.

browser A program to help get around the Internet.

bug or glitch An error in a program or in the computer.

byte An amount of data equal to 8 bits.

chip A small piece of silicon holding the circuits computers use to store and process information.

database A large collection of information organized so that it can be retrieved and used in different ways.

desktop publishing The use of computers for combining text and pictures to design and produce magazines, newspapers, and books.

download To transfer information from a host computer to a personal computer, often through a modem.

encryption The process of changing data into a secret code.

gig or gigabyte (GB) An amount of information equal to 1,024 megabytes.

hard copy Computer output printed on paper or similar material.

Internet A worldwide system of linked computer networks.

K This stands for *kilo*, or "thousands," in Greek. It is used to represent bytes of data or memory.

megabyte (MB) An amount of information equal to 1,048,516 bytes.

meltdown The collapse of a computer network from heavy traffic.

multimedia Software that includes pictures, video, and sound. In multimedia software, you can see pictures move and hear music and other sounds.

network A group of computers linked together so that they can share information.

password A secret code that keeps people who do not know it from getting into a computer or software.

portal A website that serves as a gateway to the Internet.

program Instructions for a computer to follow.

RAM or random access memory The memory your computer uses to open programs and store your work until you save it to the hard drive or a disk. The information in RAM disappears when the computer is turned off.

ROM or read only memory ROM contains permanent instructions for the computer and cannot be changed. The information in ROM remains after the computer is turned off.

scanner A device that can transfer words and pictures from a printed page into the computer.

spam Electronic junk mail.

thread A series of messages and replies that relate to a specific topic.

upload To send information from a personal computer to a host computer.

virtual reality Three-dimensional images on a screen that are viewed using special equipment (like gloves and goggles). The user feels as if he or she is part of the image and can interact with everything around.

virus A program that damages other programs and data. It gets into a computer through telephone lines or shared disks.

THE BINARY SYSTEM

For a computer to do its work, every piece of information given to it must be translated into **binary code**. You are probably used to using 10 digits, 0 through 9, when you do arithmetic. When the computer uses the binary code, it uses only two digits, 0 and 1. Think of it as sending messages to the computer by switching a light on and off.

Each 0 or 1 digit is called a **bit**, and most computers use a sequence of 8 bits (called a **byte**) for each piece of data. Almost all computers use the same code, called ASCII (pronounced "askey"), to stand for letters of the alphabet, number digits, punctuation, and other special characters that control the computer's operation. Below is a list of ASCII bytes for the alphabet.

A	01000001	H	01001000	N	01001110	T	01010100
B	01000010	I	01001001	O	01001111	U	01010101
C	01000011	J	01001010	P	01010000	V	01010110
D	01000100	K	01001011	Q	01010001	W	01010111
E	01000101	L	01001100	R	01010010	X	01011000
F	01000110	M	01001101	S	01010011	Y	01011001
G	01000111					Z	01011010

COMPUTER GAMES

Backyard Football 2002 *Hasbro Interactive, for Windows and Mac*—Offers over 40 different players (boys, girls, and even NFL players) with unique personalities from which to select the teams. Pick the type of playing field, level of difficulty, and play some football!

Harry Potter and the Sorcerer's Stone *Electronic Arts, for Windows*—Master magic as Harry Potter and interact with more than 20 characters from J.K. Rowling's enchanted world. Explore the 3-D world of the Hogwarts School and play a lightning-fast game of Quidditch.

Rocket Power Extreme Arcade Games *THQ Inc., for Windows*—The main characters from Nickelodeon's hit cartoon, *Rocket Power*—Reggie, Twister, Sam, and Otto—have their own action arcade game. Play hockey with Otto, help Reggie protect her sand castle, use a pogo stick to help Sam collect robot parts, and play roller blade basketball with Twister.

RollerCoaster Tycoon *Hasbro Interactive, for Windows*—Build the perfect theme park (there are 21 to choose from), creating your own roller coasters, log flumes, Ferris wheels, and other rides. But don't forget to include landscaping, garbage cans, benches, bathrooms, and all the other things a park needs. Look for RollerCoaster Tycoon II in the fall of 2002.

Zoo Tycoon *Microsoft Corp., for Windows*—Design a custom zoo from the ground up. Build habitats, adopt animals, hire the zoo staff, and make the visitors happy. There are more than 40 animals to choose from! Sim experts and first-timers will both like this one.

The INTERNET

What is the Internet? The Internet
("Net") connects computers from around the world so people can share information. You can play games on the Net, send e-mail, shop, and find information. By using a program called a **browser**, you can get onto the **World Wide Web** (**www**), which lets you see information using pictures, colors, and sounds. Information on the Web lives on a **Web site**. To get to the Web site you want, you need to use the right **Universal Resource Locator (URL)**, or address. If you know the address, just find the place for it on the screen and type it in carefully.

If you don't know the address, hit **Search**. You may have to pick a **search engine**, which is like a huge index. A few popular search engines are Yahoo, Google, and Lycos. When you have the one you want, type in words that tell what you're searching for. You will get a list of sites. You can choose the site most likely to have the information you want. Some sites have **links**— names of other sites on the same subject.

NET SAFETY

► No one should ask you for personal information, such as your computer password address, school, or telephone number.

► No one should ask for your picture, or ask to meet you in person.

► If you get a "flame," a message that is mean or upsetting, don't respond.

Can you depend on information from the Internet? Watch out when
you use information from the Internet. The source may not be reliable. An official web site produced by a company, organization, or government agency may be more reliable than a site created by a fan. Librarians can often give good advice about sites. And it often may be worth checking more than one source.

SMILEYS

Smileys, or **emoticons**, are letters and symbols that look like faces when turned sideways. They tell things about yourself in messages you send. Here are a few with what they mean.

0:-)	angel	:-)	smile	:-O	shout
}:->	devil	:-(	unhappy	;-)	wink
l(	sleepy	:-D	laugh	:-b..	drool
:-P	sticking out tongue	: x	kiss	>:)	little devil

FAQ: WHAT'S A BL?

Smileys are just one quick way to express an idea or feeling on the Internet. People also use **initials** as a shorthand. For example, FAQ stands for Frequently Asked Question. And BL means Belly Laugh. Here are some other common abbreviations:

BBL: Be back later
FCOL: For crying out loud
GMTA: Great minds think alike

GTG: Got to go
IMHO: In my humble opinion
J/K: Just kidding
OTOH: On the other hand

ROTFL: Rolling on the floor laughing
TTFN: Ta-ta for now

THE WORLD ALMANAC FOR KIDS has its own website at:
WEB SITE http://www.worldalmanacforkids.com

NEW GADGETS

Today's electronic devices not only do many different things; they are often small enough to hold in your hand or carry in your pocket. Here are some of the coolest gadgets around.

① MP3 PLAYER The MP3 is causing a musical revolution. Also known as Jukeboxes, these players let you transfer music from your computer or the Web into a portable device. Though these devices can be as small as a watch or pen, they pack about an hour's worth of music. Some new models can even store thousands of songs. More and more, MP3 players are being packaged with other gadgets such as cell phones and cameras. Some MP3 players even include tiny LCD screens. These let you download photo files, and offer video playback. That means you can watch a music video and play your favorite tunes at the same time!

▲ *MP3 player*

② X BOX This all-in-one gaming system from Microsoft plays DVDs with super sounds and graphics. It also connects to the Internet and to other online players. With the X Box you could race through the streets of your favorite city to the sounds of its own radio stations. Use the four ports to play with three of your friends, or to hook up gamepads, light guns, voice-activated headsets, and more.

③ DIGITAL MOVIE CREATOR This little gadget looks a bit like a water pistol, but it does much more than soak your enemies. You can use it to "film" mini-movies up to four minutes long, and edit them or add special effects and messages on your home computer. It captures audio and video and has a still mode that turns it into a digital camera that can "remember" thousands of images.

④ COMPUTER BRICK The "brick" may some day replace the laptop. It's a pocket-sized container for the guts of a computer. Instead of keeping whole computers at work and at home, for instance, you could carry your brick around like a wallet Whenever you like, you could just slip it into a portal in any one of the many docking stations (screen, keyboard, and mouse) that you find around you in the town of the future.

⑤ WIRELESS E-MAIL Chat is a kid-friendly version of the hand-held wireless e-mail device. Though it isn't a computer, Chat sends or receives e-mails when you plug it into a home or pay phone jack. These e-mails are free. And Chat communicates by radio waves with other Chat machines up to one-half mile away.

WHO AM I?

I was born in England in 1792. In the 1820s I designed a mechanical device I called a difference engine, to do simple math. I could never finish building it because it was so expensive and complicated. But much later, in the 1990s, scientists built it from my drawings, and it worked perfectly! It is the great-grandfather of today's calculators and computers.

➡ Answer: Charles Babbage

·All About... ENIAC·

During World War II a team at the University of Pennsylvania's Computing Lab was helping the Army with calculations for its artillery, but couldn't keep up with the demand. Then two leaders of the team, John Mauchley and Presper Eckert, got an idea. How about building an automatic calculating machine? The result was a huge contraption that stood 10 feet tall, weighed 30 tons, and filled a 50 by 30 ft room. Known as the ENIAC, or Electronic Numerical Integrator and Computer, it used 18,000 vacuum tubes and 6,000 switches to churn out answers. ENIAC was 1,000 times faster than the best calculating machine before it, but no match for today's computers. A computer's speed is often measured in MIPS (millions of instructions per second). ENIAC could execute 0.05 MIPS. A modern computer, with a 1.5 GHz Pentium 4 processor, can perform about 1,700 MIPS.

COMPUTER CROSSWORD

ACROSS

❶ Secret code that keeps software safe
❹ Piece of silicon that holds the computer's circuits
❺ An amount of data equal to 8 bits
❾ An amount of information equal to 1,024 megabytes
❿ The "brain" of the computer
⓫ Certain symbols you click on the computer screen
⓬ Permanent instructions for the computer

DOWN

❷ Letters and symbols that look like a face when turned sideways
❸ A large, organized collection of information
❺ An error in a computer program
❻ Computer code used to stand for letters of the alphabet
❼ A program that damages other programs and data
❽ Device that allows computer information to travel over telephone lines

ANSWERS ON PAGES 314-317. FOR MORE PUZZLES GO TO WWW.WORLDALMANACFORKIDS.COM

ENERGY

What country heats about 85% of its homes with geothermal energy? > page 63

ENERGY KEEPS US MOVING

You can't touch, see, smell, or taste energy, but you can observe what it does. You can feel that sunlight warms objects, and you can see that electricity lights up a light bulb, even if you can't see the heat or the electricity.

What is Energy? Things that you see and touch every day use some form of energy to work: your body, a bike, a basketball, a car. Energy enables things to move. Scientists define energy as the ability to do work.

Why Do We Need Energy to Do Work? Scientists define work as a force moving an object. Scientifically speaking, throwing a ball is work, but studying for a test isn't! When you throw a ball, you use energy from the food you eat to do work on the ball. The engine in a car uses energy from gasoline to make the car move.

Are There Different Kinds of Energy?

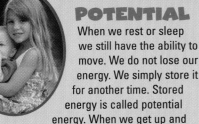

POTENTIAL

When we rest or sleep we still have the ability to move. We do not lose our energy. We simply store it for another time. Stored energy is called potential energy. When we get up and begin to move around, we are using stored energy.

KINETIC

As we move around and walk, our stored (potential) energy changes into kinetic energy, which is the energy of moving things. A parked car has potential energy. A moving car has kinetic energy. A sled stopped at the top of the hill has potential energy. As the sled goes down the hill, its potential energy changes to kinetic energy.

How Is Energy Created? Energy cannot be created or destroyed, but it can be changed or converted into different forms. Heat, light, and electricity are all forms of energy. Other forms of energy are sound, chemical energy, mechanical energy, and nuclear energy.

Where Does Energy Come From? All of the forms of energy we use come from the energy stored in natural resources. Sunlight, water, wind, petroleum, coal, and natural gas are natural resources. From these resources, we get heat and electricity.

The SUN and Its ENERGY

All of our energy comes from the sun. Inside the sun, hydrogen atoms join together and become helium. This process releases energy that radiates into space in the form of waves. These waves give us heat and light. Energy from the sun is stored in our food and provides fuel for our bodies. Some of the energy from the sun is stored in the form of fossil fuels.

Plants absorb energy from the Sun (solar energy) and convert absorbed energy to chemical energy for storage.

Animals eat plants and gain the stored chemical energy.

Food provides the body with energy to work and play.

People eat plants and meat.

Long before humans existed, trees and other plants absorbed the sun's energy. Animals ate plants and smaller animals. After the plants and animals died, they got buried deeper and deeper underground. After millions of years, they turned into coal and petroleum—fossil fuels.

...All About... SOLAR CARS

Solar cars don't have gas tanks. Instead, they have panels of solar cells—small wafer-like units that change light into electrical energy.

Engineers test their latest models by racing them. The 2,300-mile American Solar Challenge, from Chicago to Southern California, is the longest race. The University of Michigan's M-Pulse won in 2001, averaging 40 miles per hour (see below). The 1,800-mile World Solar Challenge in Australia, which began in 1987, is the oldest solar race. In 2001, this race even included solar motorcycles! A Dutch team won, setting a record of 32 hours, 39 minutes—an average of 57 mph.

Engineers admit that solar cars won't replace gas-powered cars any time soon. The big challenge is to design a battery that can store enough energy to keep the car running when the sun isn't shining.

Who Produces and Uses the MOST ENERGY?

The United States produces about 19 percent of the world's energy—more than any other country—but it uses 25 percent of the world's energy. The table at left lists the world's ten top energy-producers and the percent of the world's production that each was responsible for in 1999. The other table lists the world's top energy-users and the percent of the world's energy use that each was responsible for.

Countries That Produce the Most Energy	
United States	19 percent
Russia	11 percent
China	8 percent
Saudi Arabia	5 percent
Canada	5 percent
Great Britain	3 percent
Iran	3 percent
Norway	3 percent
India	2 percent
Mexico	2 percent

Countries That Consume the Most Energy	
United States	25 percent
China	9 percent
Russia	7 percent
Japan	6 percent
Germany	4 percent
Canada	3 percent
India	3 percent
France	3 percent
Great Britain	3 percent
Brazil	2 percent

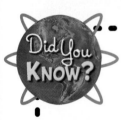

Did You Know?

BOISE, IDAHO, *has the only state capitol building that is kept warm by heat from underground—or geothermal—energy. In fact, Idaho has more than 1,500 hot springs or geothermal wells. These heat thousands of homes, businesses, and public buildings in the state, saving the equivalent of more than 200,000 barrels of oil a year!*

WHERE DOES OUR ENERGY COME FROM?

In 2000, most of the energy used in the United States came from fossil fuels (almost 39% from petroleum, 23% from natural gas, and 22% from coal). The rest came mostly from hydropower (water power), nuclear energy, and renewable resources such as geothermal, solar, and wind energy, and from burning materials such as wood and animal waste.

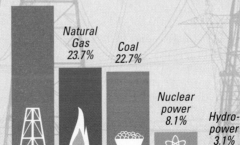

Petroleum 38.6%
Natural Gas 23.7%
Coal 22.7%
Nuclear power 8.1%
Hydro-power 3.1%
Other 3.8%

Sources of Energy

FOSSIL FUELS

Fuels are called "fossil" because they were formed from ancient plants and animals. The three basic fossil fuels are **coal**, **oil**, and **natural gas**. Most of the energy we use today comes from these sources. **Coal** is mined, either at the surface or deep underground.

Oil, or petroleum, is a liquid that is removed by drilling wells. **Natural gas**, which is made up mostly of a gas called methane, also comes from wells. Natural gas is a clean-burning fuel, and it has been used more and more. Oil and coal bring a greater risk of air pollution.

▼ *An oil drill*

All fossil fuels have one problem: they are gradually getting used up. There are special problems about oil, because industrial countries must often import lots of it and can become greatly dependent on other countries for their supply.

WATER POWER

Water power is energy that comes from the force of falling or fast-flowing water. It was put to use early in human history. **Water wheels**, turned by rivers or streams, were common in the Middle Ages. They were used for tasks like grinding grain and sawing lumber.

Today water power comes from waterfalls or from specially built dams. As water flows from a higher to a lower level, it runs a turbine—a device that turns an electric generator. This is called **hydroelectric power** (hydro = water). Today, over half of the world's hydroelectric power is produced in five countries: Brazil, Russia, Canada, China, and the United States.

Hoover Dam, Boulder City, Nevada ▶

NUCLEAR ENERGY

Nuclear power is created by releasing energy stored in the nucleus of an atom. This process is nuclear **fission**, which is also called "splitting" an atom. Fission takes place in a **reactor**, which allows the nuclear reaction to be controlled. Nuclear power plants release almost no air pollution. Many countries today use nuclear energy.

Nuclear power does cause some safety concerns. In 1979 there was a nuclear accident at Three Mile Island in Pennsylvania that led to the release of some radiation. A much more serious accident occurred at Chernobyl in Ukraine in 1986. An explosion there killed about 8,000 people, and a wide area was exposed to dangerous radiation.

A nuclear power plant

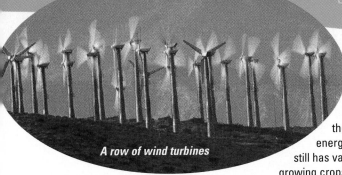

A row of wind turbines

WIND ENERGY

People have used wind as energy for a long time. **Windmills** were popular in Europe during the Middle Ages. Later, windmills became common on U.S. farms. Today, huge high-tech windmills with propeller-like blades are grouped together in **"wind farms."** Dozens of wind turbines are spaced well apart (so they don't block each other's wind). Even on big wind farms, the windmills usually take up less than 1% of the ground space. The rest of the land can still be used for farming or for grazing animals.

Wind power is a rapidly growing technology that doesn't pollute or get used up like fossil fuels. In 2001, there was four times as much electricity generated by wind as there had been in 1996. Unfortunately, the generators only work if the wind blows.

GEOTHERMAL ENERGY

Geothermal energy is heat from the Earth. About 30 miles below the surface is a layer called the **mantle**. This is the source of the gas and lava that erupts from volcanoes. Hot springs and geysers, with temperatures as high as 700 degrees, are also heated by the mantle. Because it's so hot, the mantle holds great promise as an energy source, especially in areas where the hot water is close to the surface. Iceland, which has many active volcanoes and hot springs, uses lots of geothermal energy. About 85% of homes there are heated this way.

BIOMASS ENERGY

Burning wood and straw (materials known as **biomass**) is probably the oldest way of producing energy. It's an old idea, but it still has value. Researchers are growing crops to use as fuel. Biomass fuels can be burned, like coal, in a power plant. They can also be used to make **ethanol**, which is similar to gasoline. Most ethanol comes from corn, which can make it expensive. But researchers are experimenting with other crops, like "switchgrass" and alfalfa.

Recently, a biomass power plant was opened in Burlington, Vermont. It turns wood chips, solid waste, and switchgrass into a substance similar to natural gas.

SOLAR POWER

Energy directly from sunlight is a promising new technology. Vast amounts of this energy falls upon the Earth every day—and it is not running out. Energy from the sun is expected to run for some 5 billion years. Solar energy is also friendly to the environment. One drawback is space. To get enought light, the surfaces that gather solar energy need to be spread out a lot. Also, the energy can't be gathered when the sun isn't shining.

A solar cell is usually made of silicon, a **semiconductor**. That means it can change sunlight into electricity. The cost of solar cells has been dropping in recent years. Large plants using solar-cell systems have been built in several countries, including Japan, Saudi Arabia, the United States, and Germany.

A solar power plant ▶

ENVIRONMENT

How much of your brain is water? ➤ page 70

WHAT IS THE ENVIRONMENT?

Everything that surrounds us is part of the environment. Not just living things like plants and animals, but also beaches and mountains, the air we breathe, the sunlight that provides warmth, and the water that we use in our homes, schools, and businesses.

PEOPLE AND THE ENVIRONMENT

Humans like ourselves may have lived on Earth for more than 300,000 years. For a long time people thought the Earth was so huge that it could easily absorb human wastes and pollution. And they thought that Earth's natural resources would never be used up.

In prehistoric times, people killed animals for food and built fires to cook food and keep themselves warm. They cut down trees for fuel, and their fires released pollution into the air. But there were so few people that their activities had little impact on the environment.

In modern times, the world's population has been growing very fast. In 1850 there were around a billion people in the world. In 1950 there were around 2.5 billion, and in 2002, there were more than six billion. Their activities have put a strain on the environment.

SHARING THE EARTH

We share the planet with trees, flowers, insects, fish, whales, dogs, and many other plants and animals. Each species (type) of animal or plant has its place on Earth, and each one is dependent on many others. Plants give off oxygen that animals need to breathe. Animals pollinate plants and spread their seeds. Animals eat plants and are in turn eaten by larger animals. When plants and animals die, they become part of the soil in which new plants, in their turn, take root and grow.

WATCHING OVER THE EARTH

People are becoming more aware that human activities can seriously damage the planet and the animals and plants on it. Sometimes this damage can be reversed or slowed down. But it is often permanent. On the following pages you'll learn about the damage, and about some things that can be done to help clean up and protect our planet.

You can learn more about the environment at:
WEB SITE *http://www.nwf.org/kids*

WHAT IS BIODIVERSITY?

Our planet, Earth, is shared by millions of species of living things. The wide variety of life on Earth, as shown by the many species, is called "biodiversity" (bio means "life" and diversity means "variety"). Human beings of all colors, races, and nationalities make up just one species, Homo sapiens.

SPECIES, SPECIES EVERYWHERE

This list is just a sampling of how diverse Earth is.

CONE BEARING "EVERGREEN" PLANTS: about 550 species

FLOWERING PLANTS: about 250,000 species

ROUNDWORMS: about 20,000 species

CRICKETS AND GRASSHOPPERS: about 20,000 species

FLIES: about 122,000 species

MOTHS & BUTTERFLIES: about 165,000 species

SCORPIONS: about 1,400 species

BIRDS OF PREY: 307 species

PARROTS: 353 species

PIGEONS: 309 species

TURTLES & TORTOISES: about 294 species

LIZARDS: about 4,500 species
► The Flying lizard of southeast Asia has "wings" of skin stretched over a special set of ribs. It can extend these skin wings to help it glide from tree to tree as it hunts for ants.

FROGS & TOADS: about 4,500 species
► The world's largest frog, the Goliath Frog of West Africa, grows up to 16 inches long and weighs as much as 7 pounds.

RODENTS: 1,702 species
► These "mouselike" creatures include rats, mice, voles, lemmings, hamsters, and gerbils. They make up one-quarter of all mammals on Earth. They are found on every continent but Antarctica.

SHARKS: about 330 species
► The biggest fish in the world is the whale shark, which can grow up to 46 feet long and weigh close to 12 tons.

WHALES & DOLPHINS: 83 species
► There are three species of dolphin that live in freshwater: the Ganges River dolphin (India), the Yangtze River dolphin (China), and the Pink River dolphin (which lives in the Amazon and Orinoco rivers in South America).

Some Threats to Biodiversity Plants and animals are harmed by pollution of the air, water, and land, and their habitats are often destroyed by deforestation. For example, in recent years, large areas of rain forests have been cleared for wood, farmland, and cattle ranches. People have become concerned that rain forests may be disappearing. Another threat is over-harvesting of animals, such as fish, for food or other products. For example, the number of catfish, salmon, and trout has been falling, and some species could eventually be wiped out entirely.

Protecting Biodiversity Efforts to reduce pollutants in air, water, and soil, to preserve rain forests, and to limit other deforestation and overharvesting can help preserve biodiversity. And there is some good news. A few species that were once endangered now will probably survive. The bald eagle, peregrine falcon, and gray wolf are three species that have been taken off the endangered species list.

HOME SWEET BIOME

A "biome" is a large natural area that is the home to a certain type of plant. The animals, climate, soil, and even the amount of water in the region also help distinguish a biome. There are more than 30 kinds of biomes in the world. But the following types cover most of Earth's surface.

FORESTS

Forests cover about one-third of Earth's land surface. Pines, hemlocks, firs, and spruces grow in the cool evergreen forests farthest from the equator. These trees are called **conifers** because they produce cones.

Temperate forests have warm, rainy summers and cold, snowy winters. Here **deciduous trees** (which lose their leaves in the fall and grow new ones in the spring) join the evergreens. Temperate forests are home to maple, oak, beech, and poplar trees, and to wildflowers and shrubs. These forests are found in eastern United States, southeastern Canada, northern Europe and Asia, and southern Australia.

Still closer to the equator are the **tropical rain forests**, home to the greatest variety of plants on Earth. The temperature never falls below freezing except on the mountain slopes. About 60 to 100 inches of rain fall each year. Tropical trees stay green all year. They grow close together, shading the ground. There are several layers of trees. The top, **emergent layer** has trees that can reach 200 feet in height. The **canopy**, which gets lots of sun, comes next, followed by the **understory**. The **forest floor**, covered with roots, gets little sun. Many plants cannot grow there.

Tropical rain forests are found mainly in Central America, South America, Asia, and Africa. They once covered more than 8 million square miles. Today, because of destruction by humans, fewer than 3.4 million square miles remain. More than half the plant and animal species in the world live there. Foods such as bananas and pineapples first grew there. Woods such as mahogany and teak also come from rain forests. Many kinds of plants there are used to make medicines.

When rain forests are burned, carbon dioxide is released into the air. This adds to the **greenhouse effect** (see page 72). As forests are destroyed, the precious soil is easily washed away by the heavy rains.

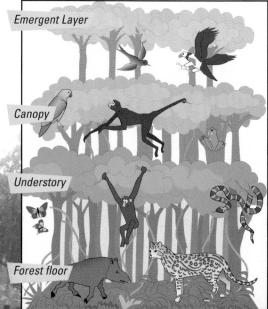

Emergent Layer

Canopy

Understory

Forest floor

A rain forest

TUNDRA AND ALPINE REGION

In the northernmost regions of North America, Europe, and Asia surrounding the Arctic Ocean are plains called the **tundra**. The temperature rarely rises above 45 degrees Fahrenheit, and it is too cold for trees to grow there. Most tundra plants are mosses and lichens that hug the ground for warmth. A few wildflowers and small shrubs also grow where the soil thaws for about two months of the year. This kind of climate and plant life also exists in the **alpine** region, on top of the world's highest mountains (such as the Himalayas, Alps, Andes, and Rockies), where small flowers also grow.

WHAT IS THE TREE LINE? On mountains in the north (such as the Rockies) and in the far south (such as the Andes), there is an altitude above which trees will not grow. This is the **tree line** or **timberline**. Above the tree line, you can see low shrubs and small plants, like Alpine flowers.

DESERTS

The driest areas of the world are the **deserts**. They can be hot or cold, but they also contain an amazing number of plants. Cactuses and sagebrush are native to dry regions of North and South America. The deserts of Africa and Asia contain plants called euporbias. Dates have grown in the deserts of the Middle East and North Africa for thousands of years. In the southwestern United States and northern Mexico, there are many types of cactuses, including prickly pear, barrel, and saguaro.

▲ *Arizona desert*

GRASSLANDS

▲ *Grassland in Alberta, Canada*

The areas of the world that are too dry to have green forests, but not dry enough to be deserts, are called **grasslands**. The most common plants found there are grasses. Cooler grasslands are found in the Great Plains of the United States and Canada, in the steppes of Europe and Asia, and in the pampas of Argentina. The drier grasslands are used for grazing cattle and sheep. In the **prairies**, where there is a little more rain, important grains, such as wheat, rye, oats, and barley are grown. The warmer grasslands, called **savannas**, are found in central and southern Africa, Venezuela, southern Brazil, and Australia. Most savannas have moist summers and cool, dry winters.

OCEANS

▼ *Coral reef*

Covering two-thirds of the earth, the **ocean** is by far the largest biome. Within the ocean are smaller biomes that include **coastal areas, tidal zones**, and **coral reefs**. Found in relatively shallow warm waters, the reefs are called the "rainforests of the ocean." Australia's Great Barrier Reef is the largest in the world. It is home to thousands of species of plant and animal life.

67

WHERE GARBAGE GOES

Most of the things around you will be replaced or thrown away someday. Skates, clothes, the toaster, furniture—they can break or wear out, or you may get tired of them. Where will they go when they are thrown out? What kinds of waste will they create, and how will it affect the environment?

LOOK AT WHAT iS NOW iN U.S. LANDFiLLS

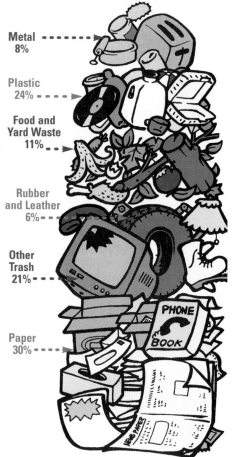

Metal ······▶ 8%

Plastic 24% ----▶

Food and Yard Waste 11% ..▶

Rubber and Leather 6%·-·

Other Trash 21%·-·

Paper 30%·----▶

What Happens to Things We Throw Away?

LANDFILLS
Most of our trash goes to places called landfills. A **landfill** (or dump) is a low area of land that is filled with garbage. Most modern landfills are lined with a layer of plastic or clay to try to keep dangerous liquids from seeping into the soil and ground water supply.

THE PROBLEM WITH LANDFILLS
More than half of the states in this country are running out of places to dump their garbage. Because of the unhealthful materials many contain, landfills do not make good neighbors, and people don't want to live near them. Many landfills are located in poor neighborhoods. But where can cities dispose of their waste? How can hazardous waste — material that can poison air, land, and water — be disposed of in a safe way?

INCINERATORS
One way to get rid of trash is to burn it. Trash is burned in a furnace-like device called an **incinerator**. Because incinerators can get rid of almost all of the bulk of the trash, some communities would rather use incinerators than landfills.

THE PROBLEM WITH INCINERATORS
Leftover ash and smoke from burning trash may contain harmful chemicals, called **pollutants**, and make it hard for some people to breathe. They can harm plants, animals, and people.

COASTAL CLEANUP *Every year on the third Saturday in September, the International Coastal Cleanup takes place along beaches, rivers, and waterways around the world. Much of the trash is harmful to marine life. In 2000, 850,000 volunteers collected 13.5 million pounds of trash—including over a million cigarette butts, 300,000 plastic bags, 72,000 ropes, 30,000 pieces of fishing line, and 15,000 plastic six-pack holders.*

Did You KNOW?

REDUCE, REUSE, RECYCLE

You can help reduce waste by reusing containers, batteries, and paper. You can also recycle newspaper, glass, and plastics to provide materials for making other products. Below are some of the things you can do.

	TO REDUCE WASTE	TO RECYCLE
PAPER	Use both sides of the paper. Use cloth towels instead of paper towels.	Recycle newspapers, magazines, comic books, and junk mail.
PLASTIC	Wash food containers and store leftovers in them. Reuse plastic bags.	Return soda bottles to the store. Recycle other plastics.
GLASS	Keep glass bottles and jars to store other things.	Recycle glass bottles and jars.
CLOTHES	Give clothes to younger relatives or friends. Donate clothes to thrift shops.	Cut unwearable clothing into rags to use instead of paper towels.
METAL	Keep leftovers in storage containers instead of wrapping them in foil. Use glass or stainless steel pans instead of disposable pans.	Recycle aluminum cans and foil trays. Return wire hangers to the dry cleaner.
FOOD/ YARD WASTE	Cut the amount of food you throw out. Try saving leftovers for snacks or meals later on.	Make a compost heap using food scraps, leaves, grass clippings, and the like.
BATTERIES	Use rechargeable batteries for toys and games, radios, tape players, and flashlights.	Find out about your town's rules for recycling or disposing of batteries.

What is made from RECYCLED MATERIALS?

► *From* **RECYCLED PAPER** we get newspapers, cereal boxes, wrapping paper, cardboard containers, and insulation.

► *From* **RECYCLED PLASTIC** we get soda bottles, tables, benches, bicycle racks, cameras, backpacks, carpeting, shoes, and clothes.

► *From* **RECYCLED STEEL** we get steel cans, cars, bicycles, nails, and refrigerators.

► *From* **RECYCLED GLASS** we get glass jars and tiles.

► *From* **RECYCLED RUBBER** we get bulletin boards, floor tiles, playground equipment, and speed bumps.

RECYCLE

PLASTIC

WATER, WATER EVERYWHERE

Earth is the water planet. More than two-thirds of its surface is covered with water, and every living thing on it needs water to live. Water is not only part of our life (cooking, cleaning, bathing), it's about 75% of our brains and 60% of our whole bodies! Humans can survive for about a month without food, but only for about a week without water. People also use water to cool machines in factories, to produce power, and to irrigate farmland.

HOW MUCH IS THERE TO DRINK? Seawater makes up 97% of the world's water. Another 2% of the water is frozen in ice caps, icebergs, glaciers, and sea ice. Half of the 1% left is too far underground to be reached. That leaves only 0.5% of freshwater for all the people, plants, and animals on Earth. This supply is renewable only by rainfall.

WHERE DOES DRINKING WATER COME FROM? Most smaller cities and towns get their freshwater from groundwater—melted snow and rain that seeps deep into the ground and is drawn out from wells. Larger cities usually rely on lakes or reservoirs for their water. Some areas of the world with little fresh water are turning to a process called **desalinization** (removing salt from seawater) as a solution. There is plenty of salt water to go around, but this process is slow and expensive.

THE HYDROLOGICAL CYCLE: WATER'S ENDLESS JOURNEY Water is special. It's the only thing on Earth that exists naturally in all three physical states: solid (ice), liquid, and gas (water vapor). It never boils naturally (except around volcanoes), but it evaporates (turns into a gas) easily into the air. These unique properties send water on a cycle of repeating events:

HOW DOES WATER GET INTO THE AIR? Sunlight causes surface water in oceans, lakes, swamps, and rivers to turn into water vapor. This is called **evaporation**. Plant photosynthesis releases water vapor into the air. Animals also release a little bit when they breathe. This is **transpiration**.

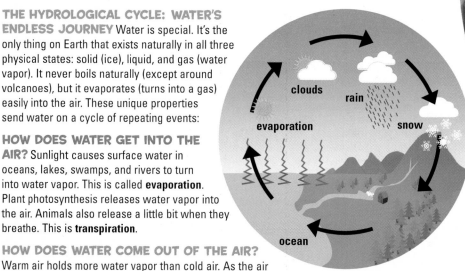

HOW DOES WATER COME OUT OF THE AIR? Warm air holds more water vapor than cold air. As the air rises into the atmosphere, it cools and the water vapor **condenses**— changes back into a tiny water droplets. These form clouds. As the drops get bigger, gravity pulls them down as **precipitation** (rain, snow, sleet, fog, and dew are all types of precipitation).

WHERE DOES THE WATER GO? Depending on where the precipitation lands, it can: **1.** evaporate back into the atmosphere; **2.** run off into streams and rivers; **3.** be absorbed by plants; **4.** soak down into the soil as ground water; **5.** fall as snow on a glacier and be trapped as ice for thousands of years.

WATER WOES

Pollution Polluted water can't be used for drinking, swimming, watering crops, or provide a habitat for plants and animals. Major sources of water pollutants are sewage, chemicals from factories, fertilizers and weed killers, and landfills that leak. In general, anything that anyone dumps on the ground finds its way into the water cycle. The United Nations has declared 2003 as the **"Year of Freshwater"** to remind people how important it is to protect precious freshwater. The UN estimates more than 5 million people a year die from illnesses caused by bad water.

Overuse Using water faster than nature can pass it through the hydrological cycle can create other problems. This may be one of the biggest problems of the 21st century. When more water is taken out of lakes and reservoirs (for drinking, bathing, and other uses) than is put back in, the water levels begin to drop. Combined with lower than normal rainfall, this can be devastating. In some cases, lakes become salty or dry up completely. Over-pumping of groundwater is causing severe problems in some parts of India and China.

TAKING ACTION

- ▶ In 2001, the U.S. Environmental Protection Agency ordered the largest river cleanup in history. About half a billion dollars will be spent over many years to dredge up 2.65 million cubic yards of mud from the bottom of New York's Hudson River. The mud is contaminated with PCBs, a chemical that can cause cancer.

- ▶ In January 2002, President George W. Bush signed a $21 million "Watershed Protection" bill to help protect and restore America's polluted waterways. A **watershed** is the network of rivers and streams that drain into a body of water.

- ▶ Read about the EPA's "Fifteen Things You Can Do to Make a Difference in Your Watershed," at *http://www.epa.gov/owow/watershed/earthday/earthday.html*

BE SMART ABOUT WATER USE!

Many states have water-use restrictions all the time. Other states restrict water use during times of drought, when there has been less rain than normal and water supplies are low. People in the U.S. use an average of 50+ gallons of water a day. Much of that is in the bathroom. Installing low-flow toilets and shower heads can greatly reduce that amount. Taking short showers helps. So does turning off the water while you brush your teeth. For more water saving-tips, go to *http://www.epa.gov/owm/resitips.htm*

THE DREADED DRIPPING FAUCET: Just one faucet, dripping very slowly (once a minute), can waste 38 gallons a year. Multiply that by several million houses and apartments, and you see a lot of water going down the drain!

Did You KNOW?

- ▶ *In the 1990s, New York City spent $295 million dollars to install 1.33 million low-flow toilets in 110,000 buildings. All together they save 70 to 90 million gallons of water a day!*

- ▶ *The watershed for the Amazon River in Brazil drains more than 5 million square miles—about 5% of Earth's land surface!*

WHAT IS AIR POLLUTION?

Air pollution is a dirtying of the air caused by toxic chemicals or other materials. The major sources of air pollution are cars, trucks and buses, waste incinerators, factories, and some electric power plants, especially those that burn fossil fuels, such as coal.

Because air is so basic to life, it is very important to keep the air clean by reducing or preventing air pollution. Air pollution causes lots of health problems and may help bring about **acid rain**, **global warming**, and a breakdown of the **ozone layer**.

TAKE A DEEP BREATH!
The air we breathe is made up mainly of gases: around 78% nitrogen, 21% oxygen, and 1% carbon dioxide, water vapor, and other gases. Humans breathe more than six quarts of air every minute.

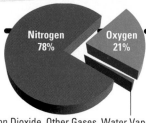

Nitrogen 78%

Oxygen 21%

Carbon Dioxide, Other Gases, Water Vapor 1%

WHAT IS ACID RAIN AND WHERE DOES IT COME FROM?

Acid rain is polluted rain or other precipitation that results from chemicals released into the air. The main sources of these chemicals are fumes, cars' exhaust pipes, and power plants that burn coal. When these chemicals mix with moisture and other particles, they create sulfuric acid and nitric acid. Winds often carry these acids many miles before they drop down in rain, snow, and fog, or even as dry particles. Acid rain can cause our eyes to sting and even make some people sick. It can also harm crops and trees.

GLOBAL WARMING

Many scientists believe that gases in the air are causing Earth's climate to gradually become warmer. This is called **global warming**. The hottest year on record was 1998. The second hottest was 2001. The third hottest was 1997, and 1999 was the sixth. If the climate becomes too warm, lots of ice near the North and South Poles could melt. More water would go into the oceans, and many areas along the coasts could be flooded.

In Earth's atmosphere there are tiny amounts of gases called **greenhouse gases**. These gases let the rays of the sun pass through to the planet, but they hold in the heat that comes up from the sun-warmed Earth—in much the same way as the glass walls of a greenhouse hold in the warmth of the sun.

As cities have increased in size and population, factories and businesses have also grown. People have needed more and more electricity, cars, and other things that must be manufactured. As industries in the world have grown, more greenhouse gases have been added to the atmosphere. These increase the thickness of the greenhouse "glass," causing more heat to be trapped than in the past. This is called the **greenhouse effect**.

FORESTS FOREVER?

Trees and forests are very important to the environment. In addition to holding water, trees hold the soil in place. Trees use carbon dioxide and give off oxygen, which animals and plants need for survival. And they provide homes and food for millions of types of animals.

Cutting down large numbers of trees, to use the land for something instead of a forest, is called **deforestation**. Although people often have good reasons for cutting down trees, deforestation can have serious effects. In the Amazon rain forest in South America, for example, thousands of plants and animal species are being lost before scientists can even learn about them. In the Pacific Northwest, there is a conflict between logging companies that want to cut down trees for lumber and people who want to preserve the ancient forests.

What Happens When Trees Are Cut Down?
Cutting down trees can affect the climate. After rain falls on a forest, mist rises and new rain clouds form. When forests are cut down, this cycle is disrupted. The area gets drier, causing a change in the climate.

If huge areas of trees are cut down, the carbon dioxide they would have used builds up in the atmosphere and contributes to the greenhouse effect. And without trees to hold the soil and absorb water, rain washes topsoil away, a process called **soil erosion**. Farming on the poorer soil that is left can be very hard.

What Are We Doing to Save Forests?
In many countries trees are being planted faster than they are being cut down. Foresting companies are working on more efficient methods of replacing and growing forests. In addition, communities and individuals are helping to save forests by recycling paper.

RAIN FOREST MAZE

START

FINISH

ANSWERS ON PAGES 314-317. FOR MORE PUZZLES GO TO WWW.WORLDALMANACFORKIDS.COM

GAMES & TOYS

BOARD GAMES

Most board games are part luck and part skill. Have you tried the ones below?

CHECKERS is a game for two, played on a board with 64 alternating light and dark squares (8 squares x 8 squares). To win, a player must capture (by jumping over them) all 12 of an opponent's pieces. The rules are simple, but play is more complicated than it looks!

Checkers is an American version of the British game draughts. Both are descended from "El-Quirkat," an ancient game from Egypt. Called Alquerque in Spanish, the game was brought to Spain by the Moors in the 1200s.

DID YOU KNOW? *In Canada and parts of Southeast Asia, draughts is played with 24 pieces on a 144-square board. Fanorona, a variation of Alquerque from the 1600s, is the national game of Madagascar.*

MONOPOLY® is a real estate trading game for two or more players, who move their pieces around by the throw of the dice. The object is to get "rich" and force your opponents into bankruptcy. You do it by trading or buying properties, building houses or hotels on them, and hoping your opponents will land on them and have to pay big rents. Landing on a hotel on Boardwalk costs $2,000.

Monopoly was first sold by Parker Brothers in the 1930s. Charles P. Darrow is known as its

inventor, but he actually got the idea from two earlier games, the Landlord Game, invented in 1904 by Elizabeth Magie Phillips, and a game about Atlantic City created by Charles Todd.

DID YOU KNOW? *World Monopoly championships are held every four years. In 2000, Yutaka Okada from Japan won the title. In 1999, Monopoly got its first new game piece in 40 years—a bag of money.*

PARCHEESI is board game for two, three, or four players. The object is to move four pawns from "start" to "home" in the center of the board. Dice determine the number of spaces a pawn can move. By landing on an occupied space, a player can "capture" an opponent's piece and send it back to start.

Parcheesi is an American version of an ancient game from India called pachisi. The name comes from the Indian word *pacis*, which means twenty-five, the highest score that can be rolled in that game. The game came to England in the 1860s under the name Ludo (Latin, for "I play"). It was first sold in the U.S. in the 1870s.

DID YOU KNOW? *In the 14th century, Indian Emperor Akbar I played chaupar (a version of pachisi) on great red and white marble courts. He used 16 women from his harem, dressed in different colors, as the game pieces.*

74

THE KING OF GAMES... THE GAME OF KINGS

Chess is a game of skill for two players. The aim is to "checkmate," or trap, the opponent's king. Chess was probably invented around the 6th or 7th century A.D. in India. From there it moved into Persia (now Iran); the word chess comes from the Persian word shah, which means "king". Today, there are national chess contests for children, and many schools have chess clubs. For further information, go to:

WEBSITE *http://www.uschess.org*

A chessboard has 64 squares, alternately light and dark, arranged in 8 rows of 8. Squares and chessmen are always called white or black. White moves first, then black and white take turns, moving one piece at a time. Each player begins with 16 chessmen: 8 pieces (a king, a queen, 2 bishops, 2 knights, and 2 rooks) and 8 pawns. Each piece moves differently. A chessman is captured, and removed, when an opponent's pawn or piece lands on its square.

When a player moves into position to capture the opponent's king, the opponent must block the move or move the king to safety. Otherwise, the king is "checkmated" and the game is over.

pawn   **rook**   **queen**   **king**   **bishop**   **knight**

A TIME-LINE OF VIDEO GAMES

1961—*Spacewar!*, played on an early microcomputer, is the first fully interactive video game.

1974—Atari's *Pong*, one of the first home video games, has "paddles" to hit a white dot back and forth on-screen.

1980—*Pac-Man*, *Space Invaders*, and *Asteroids* (first to let high scorers enter initials) invade arcades.

1985—Russian programmer Alex Pajitnov develops *Tetris* for play on a PC.

1986—Nintendo Entertainment System comes to the U.S. *Super Mario Bros.* is a huge hit!

1987—*Legend of Zelda* game released.

1989—Nintendo's hand-held video game system, Game Boy, debuts. *Adventures of Link* game released.

1990—The Sega Genesis system comes out.

1991—Sega's *Sonic the Hedgehog* makes his debut.

1996—Nintendo 64 is released.

1998—Game Boy Color and *Pokémon* hit the U.S.

2000—Sony's Playstation 2 arrives.

2001—Microsoft's XBOX and Nintendo's GameCube hit the shelves. *Luigi's Mansion* and *Super Smash Bros. Melee* make a big splash.

For more information about computer games, see page 55.

All About...
TRADING CARDS

WAGNER, PITTSBURG

Pick a card, any card! Trading cards have been around for a long time. Back in the 1870s, "trade cards" illustrated in color were printed as advertising. By the 1880s, collecting these cards was a popular hobby. Some favorite subjects were animals, birds, plants, nature, boats, Civil War generals, and famous scenes from history. Starting in the 1920s, movie star cards were big. But none have matched the popularity of baseball cards.

In the 1880s, baseball cards were sold in cigarette packs. From around 1914 to 1932 they were sold with candy, Cracker Jacks, and even ice cream. In 1933, three gum companies from Boston began issuing baseball cards.

A Brooklyn company called Topps started selling cards in 1950 to boost sales of their new Bazooka bubble gum. Their first cards were football and TV stars. Baseball cards followed in 1951. They didn't sell well at first, but Topps redesigned them in 1952, and the modern baseball card was born. Today, Topps, Fleer, and Upper Deck are the main sports cards companies.

The most famous baseball card in history is the 1909 Honus Wagner card, shown above. Only about 50 still exist. One was sold on eBay in July 2000 for $1.27 million!

All About...
ROBOT COMPETITIONS

Do you like robots? Would you like to watch them kick "bot"? Then check out these two cable TV shows full of remote-controlled, mechanical mayhem.

BattleBots, seen on Comedy Central, features high-tech robots by builders of all ages battling in boxing-style matches. These are held in a steel plated arena surrounded by bulletproof plastic. There are four weight classes: Lightweight, Middleweight, Heavyweight, and Super Heavyweight. Robots have 3 minutes to try to disable or damage their opponents. They have to watch out for the 6-inch metal spikes on the walls, the buzz saws that pop out of the floor, and the giant hammers.

Visit *http://www.battlebots.com* to find the rules and regulations for all the contests.

Robotica is on The Learning Channel. During each episode, viewers get to know the contestants and learn where they got their ideas and how their bots were built. The robot challenges include racetrack speed tests, target destruction, and complex mazes with hidden obstacles like oil slicks, walls of fire, rushing water, and punishing storms of hail.

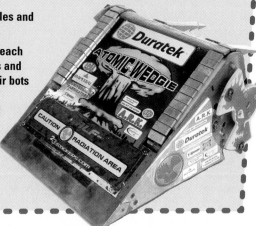

For more information on robots go to
WEB SITE *http://www.thetech.org*

TOP SELLING TOYS OF 2001

(ranked by sales in dollars, not including video games)

1. *Hot Wheels Basic Cars* by Mattel
2. *LeapPad* by LeapFrog
3. *LeapPad Books* by LeapFrog
4. *Barbie Cruisin' Jeep* by Fisher-Price (Mattel)
5. *Holiday Barbie* by Mattel
6. *Rumble Robots* by Trendmasters
7. *Kawasaki New Ninja* by Fisher-Price (Mattel)
8. *Hot Wheels 5-Car Gift Pack* by Mattel
9. *Barbie VW New Beetle* by Mattel
10. *Hitclips Micro Music* by Tiger Electronics (Hasbro)

CLASSIC AMERICAN TOYS ... YESTERDAY AND TODAY

The first half of the 20th century was a golden time for toy making. Some of the most popular toys in history were invented then, and are still going strong today. In 2002 the Teddy Bear had its 100th birthday! Matchbox cars and Mr. Potato Head celebrated their 50th.

LIONEL TRAINS started in 1901, after Joshua Lionel Cowen made a battery-powered train for a store window display. Customers just wanted the trains; they didn't care about the rest of the window. Lionel has sold over 50 million train sets since then.

In 1902, Rose Michtom made stuffed bears to sell in a store she ran with her husband in Brooklyn. She named them after President Teddy (Theodore) Roosevelt, and started a big trend. Stieff (1903) and Gund (1906) are the oldest **TEDDY BEAR** makers in business today.

Edwin Binney and C. Harold Smith made their first box of **CRAYOLA CRAYONS** in 1903. There were 8 colors—compared to 120 today. The Crayola factory in Easton, Pennsylvania, now produces nearly 3 billion crayons each year (12 million per day!).

► Britney Spears says her favorite color crayon is robin's egg blue. Tiger Woods likes wild strawberry, and President George W. Bush goes for magenta.

The **ERECTOR SET** was invented in 1913 by Dr. A.C. Gilbert. The nut-and-bolt metal construction sets were an American version of the British "Meccanics Made Easy" (later Meccano) sets from 1901. Erector Sets are now made by Meccano (in France).

▲ *Gold engine made for Lionel Train's 100th anniversary*

The next year, 1914, Charles Pajeau developed wooden **TINKER TOYS** for children too young for the Erector Set. Today they are made by OddzOn (a division of Hasbro).

LINCOLN LOGS were invented in 1916, by John Wright, son of architect Frank Lloyd Wright. He got the idea while watching his father design an earthquake-proof building in Japan. More than 100 million Lincoln Log sets have been sold since then.

Plastic **LEGO** bricks were invented in Denmark by Ole Kirk Christiansen in 1949. The company, whose name comes from the Danish words "LEg GOdt" (play well) has since made more than 206 billion of them! Imagine if you had to clean up that many in your room.

► Some other classic toys came a little later: Tonka trucks (1957), Barbie dolls (1959), GI Joe action figures (1965), Hot Wheels cars (1966), and Nerf toys (1969).

GEOGRAPHY

How many kinds of seaweed live in Australia's Great Barrier Reef? ➤page 81

LOOKING AT OUR WORLD

Did you ever travel on a spaceship? In a way, you're traveling around the Sun right now on a spaceship called Planet Earth.

THINKING GLOBAL

A globe is a small model of Earth. Like Earth, it is shaped like a ball or sphere. Earth isn't exactly a sphere because it gets flat at the top and bottom and bulges a little in the middle. This shape is called an oblate spheroid.

Because Earth is round, most flat maps that are centered on the equator do not show the shapes of the land masses exactly right. The shapes at the top and bottom usually look too big. For example, the island of Greenland, which is next to North America, may look bigger than Australia, though it is really much smaller.

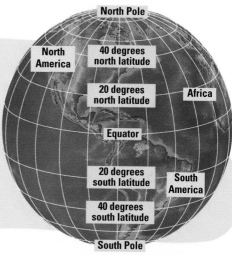

North Pole

North America

40 degrees north latitude

20 degrees north latitude

Africa

Equator

20 degrees south latitude

South America

40 degrees south latitude

South Pole

LATITUDE AND LONGITUDE

Imaginary lines that run east and west around Earth, parallel to the equator, are called parallels. They tell you the latitude of a place, or how far it is from the equator. The equator is at 0 degrees latitude. As you go farther north or south, the latitude increases. The North Pole is at 90 degrees north latitude. The South Pole is at 90 degrees south latitude.

Imaginary lines that run north and south around the globe, from one pole to the other, are called meridians. They tell you the degree of longitude, or how far east or west a place is from an imaginary line called the Greenwich meridian or prime meridian (0 degrees). That line runs through the city of Greenwich in England.

Which Hemispheres Do You Live In?

Draw an imaginary line around the middle of Earth. This is the equator. It splits Earth into two halves called hemispheres. The part north of the equator, including North America, is the northern hemisphere. The part south of the equator is the southern hemisphere.

You can also divide Earth into east and west. North and South America are in the western hemisphere. Africa, Asia, and most of Europe are in the eastern hemisphere.

READING A MAP

Below is a map of an imaginary place. Could you find your way around if you went there?

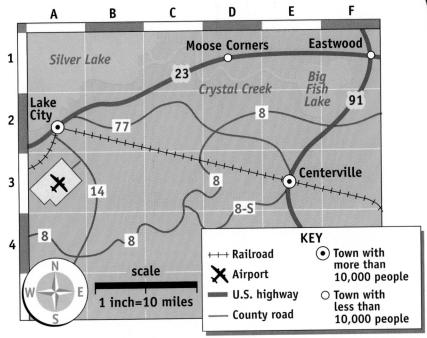

DIRECTION Maps usually have a **compass rose** that shows you which way is north. On most maps, like this one, north is straight up. When north is up, south is down, east is right, and west is left.

DISTANCE Of course the distances on a map are much shorter than the distances in the real world. The **scale** shows you how to estimate the real distance. In the map above, every inch on paper stands for a real distance of 10 miles.

PICTURES Maps usually have little pictures or symbols. The map **key** tells what they mean. Take a look at the key above. Which are the two smallest cities on the map? How would you get from the airport to Centerville by car?

FINDING PLACES Many maps have a list of places in alphabetical order, with a letter and number for each. In the map above, you can find Centerville (E3) by drawing a straight line down from the letter E on top, and another line going across from the number 3 on the side. Lines made like this form a **grid**. Centerville should be near the place on the grid where the lines for E and 3 meet.

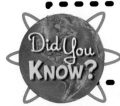

CALIFORNIA ISLAND? *Many early maps of North America showed California as a big island. Finally, in 1705, a Jesuit missionary proved that it was not an island by walking from New Mexico to the Pacific coast.*

THE SEVEN CONTINENTS

Almost two-thirds of Earth's surface is made up of water. The rest is land. Oceans are the largest areas of water. Continents are the biggest pieces of land.

	Area	2001 Population	Highest Point	Lowest Point
North America	8,300,000 square miles	486,000,000	Mount McKinley (Alaska), 20,320 feet	Death Valley (California), 282 feet below sea level
South America	6,800,000 square miles	351,000,000	Mount Aconcagua (Argentina), 22,834 feet	Valdes Peninsula (Argentina), 131 feet below sea level
Europe	8,800,000 square miles	729,000,000	Mount Elbrus (Russia), 18,510 feet	Caspian Sea (Russia, Azerbaijan; eastern Europe and western Asia), 92 feet below sea level
Asia	12,000,000 square miles	3,737,000,000	Mount Everest (Nepal, Tibet), 29,035 feet	Dead Sea (Israel, Jordan), 1,312 feet below sea level
Africa	11,500,000 square miles	823,000,000	Mount Kilimanjaro (Tanzania), 19,340 feet	Lake Assal (Djibouti), 512 feet below sea level
Australia & Oceania	3,200,000 square miles	31,000,000	Mount Kosciusko (New South Wales), 7,310 feet	Lake Eyre (South Australia), 52 feet below sea level
Antarctica	5,400,000 square miles	No permanent residents	Vinson Massif, 16,864 feet	Bentley Subglacial Trench, 8,327 feet below sea level

NOW THAT'S DEEP! *The deepest part of any ocean is the Marianas Trench, located just west of the Philippines in the Pacific Ocean. Its depth is 35,840 feet—almost 7 miles. That's greater than the height of the tallest mountain on earth!*

TALLEST, LONGEST, HIGHEST, DEEPEST

Longest River: Nile, in Egypt and Sudan (4,160 miles)

Highest Waterfall: Angel Falls, in Venezuela (3,212 feet)

Tallest Mountain: Mount Everest, in Tibet and Nepal (29,035 feet)

Deepest Lake: Lake Baykal, in Asia (5,315 feet)

Biggest Lake: Caspian Sea, in Europe and Asia (143,244 square miles)

Biggest Desert: The Sahara, in Africa (3,500,000 square miles)

Biggest Island: Greenland, in the Atlantic Ocean (840,000 square miles)

Deepest Cave: Lamprechtsofen-Vogelschacht, in Salzburg, Austria (5,354 feet deep)

▲ *Sahara Desert*

AMAZING GEOGRAPHY FACTS

SALTIEST SEA: The water in the Dead Sea, between Israel and Jordan, has about nine times more salts and minerals than the oceans. The sea gets its name from the fact that so much salt makes it impossible for marine life to live there. What is bad for fish is good for people. The dense water makes it easy to float.

LIVELIEST WATERS: The Great Barrier Reef off the northeast coast of Australia is the biggest structure made by living organisms. It is built from tiny marine polyps, called corals, and their skeletons. The largest coral reef in the world, it is home to 1,500 species of fish, 400 types of coral, 500 species of seaweed, 16 species of sea snake, and 6 species of sea turtle!

LOFTIEST LAKE: Lake Titicaca lies 12,580 feet above the ocean, along the mountainous border between Peru and Bolivia. It's the highest lake in the world that is big enough for large boats. Twenty-five rivers flow into the lake, which covers over 3,500 square miles. The ancient Incas built their capital next to the lake, which they considered sacred.

COOLEST ARCHES: Arches National Park in Arizona has more than 2,000 arches carved out of rock by 100 million years of erosion. The smaller arches are just 3 feet long. The largest, called Landscape Arch, spans 306 feet.

THE FOUR OCEANS

The facts about the oceans include their size and average depth.

PACIFIC OCEAN: 64,186,300 square miles; 12,925 feet deep

ATLANTIC OCEAN: 33,420,000 square miles; 11,730 feet deep

INDIAN OCEAN: 28,350,500 square miles; 12,598 feet deep

ARCTIC OCEAN: 5,105,700 square miles; 3,407 feet deep

Did You Know?

A FIFTH OCEAN? *The International Hydrographic Organization recently decided that the southern portions of the Atlantic, Pacific, and Indian oceans (a total of 7,848,300 square miles) should be counted as making up a separate ocean. They named it the Southern Ocean. Many countries agreed with this idea. If it catches on, we will all be learning about the world's five oceans in years to come.*

SOME EUROPEAN AND AMERICAN EXPLORERS

AROUND 1000 — **Leif Ericson**, from Iceland, explored "Vinland," which may have been the coasts of northeast Canada and New England.

1271-95 — **Marco Polo** (Italian) traveled through Central Asia, India, China, and Indonesia.

1488 — **Bartolomeu Dias** (Portuguese) explored the Cape of Good Hope in southern Africa.

1492-1504 — **Christopher Columbus** (Italian) sailed four times from Spain to America and started colonies there.

1497-98 — **Vasco da Gama** (Portuguese) sailed farther than Dias, around the Cape of Good Hope to East Africa and India.

1513 — **Juan Ponce de León** (Spanish) explored and named Florida.

1513 — **Vasco Núñez de Balboa** (Spanish) explored Panama and reached the Pacific Ocean.

1519-21 — **Ferdinand Magellan** (Portuguese) sailed from Spain around the tip of South America and across the Pacific Ocean to the Philippines, where he died. His expedition continued around the world.

1519-36 — **Hernando Cortés** (Spanish) conquered Mexico, traveling as far west as Baja California.

1527-42 — **Alvar Núñez Cabeza de Vaca** (Spanish) explored the southwestern United States, Brazil, and Paraguay.

1532-35 — **Francisco Pizarro** (Spanish) explored the west coast of South America and conquered Peru.

1534-36 — **Jacques Cartier** (French) sailed up the St. Lawrence River to the site of present-day Montreal.

1539-42 — **Hernando de Soto** (Spanish) explored the southeastern United States and the lower Mississippi Valley.

1603-13 — **Samuel de Champlain** (French) traced the course of the St. Lawrence River and explored the northeastern United States.

1609-10 — **Henry Hudson** (English), sailing from Holland, explored the Hudson River, Hudson Bay, and Hudson Strait.

1682 — **Robert Cavelier**, sieur de La Salle (French), traced the Mississippi River to its mouth in the Gulf of Mexico.

1768-78 — **James Cook** (English) charted the world's major bodies of water and explored Hawaii and Antarctica.

1804-06 — **Meriwether Lewis and William Clark** (American) traveled from St. Louis along the Missouri and Columbia rivers to the Pacific Ocean and back.

1849-59 — **David Livingstone** (Scottish) explored Southern Africa, including the Zambezi River and Victoria Falls.

VOLCANOES

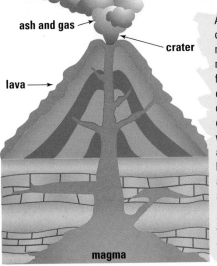

ash and gas

crater

lava

magma

A volcano is a mountain or hill with an opening on top known as a **crater**. Hot melted rock (**magma**), gases, ash, and other material from inside the earth mix together a few miles underground, rising up through cracks and weak spots in the mountain. Every once in a while, the mixture may blast out, or erupt, through the crater. The magma is called **lava** when it reaches the air. This red-hot lava may have a temperature of more than 2,000 degrees Fahrenheit. The hill or mountain is made of lava and other materials that come out of the opening, and then cool off and harden.

Some islands are really the tops of undersea volcanoes. The Hawaiian islands developed when volcanoes erupted under the Pacific Ocean.

Did You KNOW?

ICELAND is the "Land of Fire and Ice." The island nation, about the size of Ohio, was formed by lava flows from its many active volcanoes. In spite of all the volcanic heat, Iceland has the largest glaciers in Europe— covering 11% of the country.

SOME FAMOUS VOLCANIC ERUPTIONS

Year	Volcano (place)	Deaths (approximate)
79	Mount Vesuvius (Italy)	16,000
1586	Kelut (Indonesia)	10,000
1792	Mount Unzen (Japan)	14,500
1815	Tambora (Indonesia)	10,000
1883	Krakatau or Krakatoa (Indonesia)	36,000
1902	Mount Pelée (Martinique)	28,000
1980	Mount St. Helens (U.S.) ▼	57
1982	El Chichón (Mexico)	1,880
1985	Nevado del Ruiz (Colombia)	23,000
1986	Lake Nyos (Cameroon)	1,700
1991	Mt. Pinatubo (Philippines)	800

Where is the Ring of Fire?

The hundreds of active volcanoes found on the land near the edges of the Pacific Ocean make up what is called the **Ring of Fire**. They mark the boundary between the plates under the Pacific Ocean and the plates under the continents around the ocean. (The plates of the Earth are explained on page 84, with the help of a map.) The Ring of Fire runs all along the west coast of South and North America, from the southern tip of Chile to Alaska. The ring also runs down the east coast of Asia, starting in the far north in Kamchatka. It continues down past Australia.

EARTHQUAKES

Earthquakes may be so weak that they are hardly felt, or strong enough to do great damage. There are thousands of earthquakes each year, but most are too small to be noticed. About 1 in 5 can be felt, and about 1 in 500 causes damage.

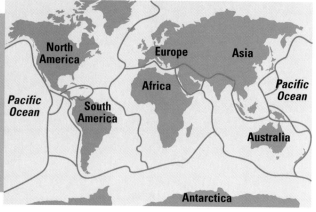

What Causes Earthquakes? The Earth's outer layer, its **crust**, is divided into huge pieces called **plates** (see map). These plates, made of rock, are constantly moving—away from each other, toward each other, or past each other. A crack in Earth's crust between two plates is called a **fault**. Many earthquakes occur along faults where two plates collide as they move toward each other or grind together as they move past each other. Earthquakes along the **San Andreas Fault** in California are caused by the grinding of two plates.

Measuring Earthquakes The Richter scale (see below) goes from 0 to more than 8. These numbers indicate the strength of an earthquake. Each number means the quake releases about 30 times more energy than the number below it. An earthquake measuring 6 on the scale is about 30 times stronger than one measuring 5 and 900 times stronger than one measuring 4. Earthquakes that are 4 or above are considered major. (The damage and injuries caused by a quake also depend on other things, such as whether the area is heavily populated and built up.)

The strength of an earthquake is registered on an instrument called a *seismograph* and is given a number on a scale called the *Richter scale.*

MAGNITUDE	EFFECTS
0-2	Earthquake is recorded by instruments but is not felt by people.
2-3	Earthquake is felt slightly by a few people.
3-4	People feel tremors. Hanging objects like ceiling lights swing.
4-5	Earthquake causes some damage; walls crack; dishes and windows may break.
5-6	Furniture moves; earthquake seriously damages weak buildings.
6-7	Furniture may overturn; strong buildings are damaged; walls and buildings may collapse.
7-8	Many buildings are destroyed; underground pipes break; wide cracks appear in the ground.
ABOVE 8	Total devastation, including buildings and bridges; ground wavy.

MAJOR EARTHQUAKES

The earthquakes listed here are among the largest and most destructive recorded in the past 100 years.

Year	Location	Magnitude	Deaths (approximate)
2002	Afghanistan (Northern)	6.1	1,000+
	Iran (Northern)	6.1	800+
2001	India (Western)	7.9	30,000+
1999	Taiwan (Taichung)	7.6	2,474
	Turkey (western)	7.4	17,200+
	Colombia (western)	6.0	1,185+
1998	Afghanistan (northeastern)	6.9	4,700+
	Afghanistan (northeastern)	6.1	2,323
1995	Russia (Sakhalin Island)	7.5	1,989
	Japan (Kobe)	6.9	5,502
1994	United States (Los Angeles area)	6.8	61
1993	India (southern)	6.3	9,748
1990	Iran (western)	7.7	40,000+
1989	United States (San Francisco area)	7.1	62
1988	Soviet Armenia	7.0	55,000
1985	Mexico (Michoacan)	8.1	9,500
1976	China (Tangshan)	8.0	255,000
	Guatemala	7.5	23,000
1970	Peru (northern)	7.8	66,000
1960	Chile (southern)	9.5	5,000
1939	Chile (Chillan)	8.3	28,000
1934	India (Bihar-Nepal)	8.4	10,700
1927	China (Nan-Shan)	8.3	200,000
1923	Japan (Yokohama)	8.3	143,000
1920	China (Gansu)	8.6	200,000
1906	Chile (Valparaiso)	8.6	20,000
	United States (San Francisco)	8.3	3,000+

THE BIG ONE In 1906, a major earthquake destroyed the city of San Francisco. At that time, many buildings in the city were built of wood, and fires set off by the earthquake burned almost 25,000 of them. No one knows exactly how many people were killed by the quake and fires, but it was probably more than 3,000. The quake ruptured the earth along a line 290 miles long and sent shockwaves that were felt from southern Oregon to Los Angeles. Today, scientists keep careful watch on the area around the city for warnings of future quakes.

HEALTH

Which three recent presidents were left-handed? ➤ page 89

INSIDE YOUR BODY

Your body is made up of many different parts that work together every minute of every day and night. It is more amazing than any machine or computer. Even though everyone's body looks different outside, people have the same parts inside.

DID YOU KNOW?

▶ You are constantly crying—even when tears aren't rolling down your cheeks. In a year, you will produce about a gallon of tears. But not because you are sad. About a dozen tubes above your eyelids make the tears to keep your eyes clean and moist. When you blink, the eyelids work like windshield wipers. The tears drain into the ducts below your eyes. But as you cry—from joy or pain—there is more fluid than the ducts can catch. The extra fluid runs down your cheek.

▶ Skin is made of layers of living cells. New cells are constantly being produced on the lower levels that push older cells to the surface of your skin. Every minute 30,000 to 40,000 dead skin cells fall off your body.

▶ The average adult has about 20 square feet of skin, and people shed about 40 pounds of skin during a lifetime.

▶ Trillions of bacteria and other tiny organisms live happily in your body. Right now there are probably about two million bacteria living on your face alone.

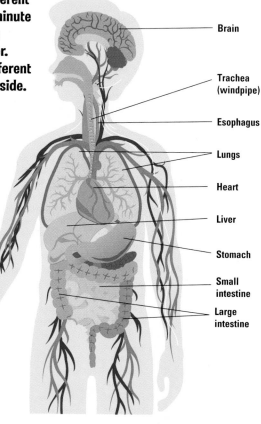

Brain

Trachea (windpipe)

Esophagus

Lungs

Heart

Liver

Stomach

Small intestine

Large intestine

What the Body's Systems Do

Each system of the body has its own job. Some of the systems also work together to keep you healthy and strong.

CIRCULATORY SYSTEM In the circulatory system, the **heart** pumps **blood**, which then travels through tubes, called **arteries**, to all parts of the body. The blood carries the oxygen and food that the body needs to stay alive. **Veins** carry the blood back to the heart.

DIGESTIVE SYSTEM The digestive system moves food through parts of the body called the **esophagus**, **stomach**, and **intestines**. As the food passes through, some of it is broken down into tiny particles called **nutrients**, which the body needs. Nutrients enter the bloodstream, which carries them to all parts of the body. The digestive system then changes the remaining food into waste that is eliminated from the body.

ENDOCRINE SYSTEM The endocrine system includes **glands** that are needed for some body functions. There are two kinds of glands. **Exocrine** glands produce liquids such as sweat and saliva. **Endocrine** glands produce chemicals called hormones. **Hormones** control body functions, such as growth.

MUSCULAR SYSTEM **Muscles** are made up of elastic fibers that help the body move. We use large muscles to walk and run, and small muscles to smile. Muscles also help protect organs.

SKELETAL SYSTEM The skeletal system is made up of the **bones** that hold your body upright. Some bones protect organs, such as the ribs that cover the lungs.

NERVOUS SYSTEM The nervous system enables us to think, feel, move, hear, and see. It includes the **brain**, the **spinal cord**, and **nerves** in all parts of the body. Nerves in the spinal cord carry signals back and forth between the brain and the rest of the body. The brain tells us what to do and how to respond. It has three major parts. The **cerebrum** controls thinking, speech, and vision. The **cerebellum** is responsible for physical coordination. The **brain stem** controls the respiratory, circulatory, and digestive systems.

RESPIRATORY SYSTEM The respiratory system allows us to breathe. Air comes into the body through the nose and mouth. It goes through the **windpipe** (or **trachea**) to two tubes (called **bronchi**), which carry air to the **lungs**. Oxygen from the air is taken in by tiny blood vessels in the lungs. The blood then carries oxygen to the cells of the body.

REPRODUCTIVE SYSTEM Through the reproductive system, adult human beings are able to create new human beings. Reproduction begins when a sperm cell from a man fertilizes an egg cell from a woman.

URINARY SYSTEM This system, which includes the **kidneys**, cleans waste from the blood and regulates the amount of water in the body.

SURPRISING FACTS ABOUT THE BODY

Your heart beats more than 100,000 times a day—or close to 3 billion times during an average lifetime.

Hiccups are caused by irritation of the **diaphragm** (the system of muscles between your chest and stomach that controls breathing). When the diaphragm contracts uncontrollably, it causes a sudden intake of breath, This suction causes the bit of tissue at the back of your throat, the **epiglotis**, to close rapidly— causing the "hic" in hiccups.

Your lungs are made up of about 300 million tiny air sacs called **alveoli**. If they could be laid flat, they would cover an area about the size of a tennis court.

Humans have been growing taller over the last 150 years: people in the industrialized world are on average 4 inches taller than they were in the mid-1800s.

A newborn's head accounts for one quarter of its weight.

Around two-thirds of a person's body weight is water. Blood is 92% water, and your brain is 75% water.

Fingernails grow four times faster than toenails.

The human head contains 22 bones.

While babies are born with over 300 bones, adults only have 206; many bones fuse together as people grow up.

STAY HEALTHY WITH EXERCISE

Daily exercise makes you feel good. It also helps you think better, sleep better, feel more relaxed, and stay at a healthy weight. Regular exercise will make you stronger and help you improve at physical activities. About three-quarters of ninth graders say they get enough exercise. Do you?

Breathing deeply during exercise gets more oxygen into your lungs with each breath. Your heart pumps more oxygen-filled blood all through your body with each beat. Muscles and joints get stronger and more flexible as you use them.

Here are some activities, with a rough idea of how many calories a 100-pound person would burn per minute while doing them:

ACTIVITY	CALORIES PER MINUTE
Jogging (6 miles per hour)	8
Jumping rope (easy)	7
Playing basketball	7
Playing soccer	6
Bicycling (9.4 miles per hour)	5
Skiing (downhill)	5
Raking the lawn	4
Rollerblading (easy)	4
Walking (4 miles per hour)	4
Bicycling (5.5 miles per hour)	3
Swimming (25 yards per minute)	3
Walking (3 miles per hour)	3

◀ *Lefty slugger Babe Ruth*

A FEW FACTS ABOUT LEFTIES

Three of the last four presidents were left-handed: Ronald Reagan, George H.W. Bush, and Bill Clinton. Other famous left-handers include Julius Caesar, Leonardo da Vinci, Queen Elizabeth II, Babe Ruth, Paul McCartney, and Julia Roberts.

About 13% of people are left-handed.

Throughout history left-handedness has been associated with evil or clumsiness. For sailors a "left-handed ship" means an unlucky ship. The Latin word for left is similar to the English word "sinister." Also, gauche, the word for "left" in French, is used to mean "awkward" in English.

Common household items such as scissors, can openers, coffee makers, telephones, even keyboards (the enter key and number pad are on the right) are made for right-handed people. Most power tools are made to be used with the right hand.

There are stores and Web sites that sell products made especially for left-handed people. For examples, go to (**WEB SITE**) *http://www.dmoz.org/shopping/Niche/Left-Handed_Products*

OLD WIVES' TALES

We get a lot of advice—even some we've heard a million times already. Some of it is good, but sometimes it's not quite true. Here are some common myths (or "old wives' tales") that are often repeated. You may want to take them with a grain of salt (have your doubts).

Don't swim for an hour after you eat. It's really OK to go in the water after you eat. But remember that some of your blood goes to the stomach area to help you digest your meal—leaving less blood to carry oxygen to your muscles, brain, and other organs. So don't overdo it. With less oxygen getting to your muscles, you could tire more easily. On land, you can stop to rest, but if you're in water over your head you might get into trouble. Also, it's definitely not a good idea to eat or chew gum *while* swimming because you could choke.

Eating carrots will improve your eyesight. Carrots do contain lots of Vitamin A, which helps keep your eyes healthy, but eating more than the recommended daily amount can't make your vision better.

Ice or butter will help a minor burn. Butter is greasy and thick like a medical ointment, but it won't help your burn or soothe your skin. If ice is left on your skin too long, it can cause frostbite, which damages skin tissue just like a burn. Try running cold water over a minor burn instead of putting butter or ice on it.

You'll get a cold if you go out in the cold with wet hair.
Viruses cause colds, not the weather.

Toads cause warts. The bumps on a toad's skin are not warts but glands. Some make mucous to help keep its skin moist. Others make a toxic, smelly liquid to help protect it from predators. Human warts are caused by a viral infection, and have nothing to do with toads.

We Are What We Eat

Have you ever noticed the labels on the packages of food you and your family buy? The labels provide information people need to make healthy choices about the foods they eat. Below are some terms you may see on labels.

NUTRIENTS ARE NEEDED

Nutrients are the parts of food the body can use. The body needs nutrients for growth, for energy, and to repair itself when something goes wrong. Carbohydrates, fats, proteins, vitamins, minerals, and water are different kinds of nutrients found in food. **Carbohydrates** and **fats** provide energy. **Proteins** aid growth and help maintain and repair the body. **Vitamins** help the body use food, help eyesight and skin, and aid in fighting off infections. **Minerals** help build bones and teeth and aid in such functions as muscle contractions and blood clotting. **Water** helps with growth and repair of the body. It also helps the body digest food and get rid of wastes.

CALORIES COUNT

A **calorie** is a measure of how much energy we get from food. The government recommends the number of calories that should be taken in for different age groups. The number of calories recommended for children ages 8 to 10 is about 1,900 a day. For ages 11 to 14, the government recommends around 2,200 calories a day for girls and 2,400 for boys.

To maintain a **healthy weight**, it is important to balance the calories in the food you eat with the calories used by the body every day. Every activity uses up some calories. The more active you are, the more calories your body burns. If you eat more calories than your body uses, you will gain weight.

Nutrition Facts

Serving Size 1/2 cup (1 oz.) = (30g)
Servings per container 14

Amount Per Serving	Cereal	Cereal w/ 1/2 cup Lowfat Milk
Calories	100	150
Calories from Fat	10	25
	% Daily Value**	
Total Fat 1g*	2%	4%
Saturated Fat 0g	0%	5%
Cholesterol 0mg	0%	3%
Sodium 50mg	2%	5%
Total Carbohydrates 20g	7%	9%
Dietary Fiber 2g	8%	8%
Sugars 5g		
Protein 4g		
Vitamin A	0%	6%
Vitamin C	0%	2%
Calcium	0%	15%
Iron	2%	4%

* Amount in Cereal. One half cup lowfat milk contributes an additional 50 calories, 1.5g total fat (1g saturated fat), 9 mg cholesterol, 60mg sodium, 6g total carbohydrates (6g sugars), and 3g protein.
** Percents (%) of a Daily Value are based on a 2,000 calorie diet. Your Daily Values may vary higher or lower depending on your calorie needs:

Nutrient	Calories	2,000	2,500
Total Fat	Less than	65g	80g
Sat Fat	Less than	20g	25g
Cholesterol	Less than	300mg	300mg
Sodium	Less than	2,400mg	2,400mg
Total Carbohydrates		300g	375g
Dietary Fiber		25g	30g

Calories per gram:
Fat 9 • Carbohydrate 4 • Protein 4

A LITTLE FAT GOES A LONG WAY

SOME LOWER-FAT FOODS

chicken or turkey hot dog
tuna fish canned in water
baked potato
pretzels
apple
plain popcorn (with no butter)
skim milk or 1% or 2% milk

SOME FATTY FOODS

beef or pork hot dog
fried hamburger
french fries
potato chips
tuna fish canned in oil
buttered popcorn
whole milk

A little bit of fat is important for your body. It keeps your body warm. It gives the muscles energy. It helps keep the skin soft and healthy. But the body needs only a small amount of fat to do all these things. Less than one-third of your calories should come from fat, if you're over two years old.

Cholesterol. Eating too much fat can make some people's bodies produce too much **cholesterol** (ka-LESS-ter-all). This waxy substance can build up over the years on the inside of arteries. Too much cholesterol keeps blood from flowing freely through the arteries and can cause serious health problems such as heart attacks.

To eat less fat, try eating lower-fat foods instead of fatty foods.

WHICH FOODS ARE THE RIGHT FOODS?

To stay healthy, it is important to eat the right foods and to exercise. To help people choose the right foods for good health and fitness, the U.S. government developed the food pyramid shown below. The food pyramid shows the groups of foods that everyone should eat every day.

FATS, OILS, AND SWEETS
Use sparingly

MILK, YOGURT, AND CHEESE GROUP
2 to 3 servings

1 serving = 1 cup of milk or yogurt; or 1 1/2 ounces of cheese

MEAT, POULTRY, FISH, DRY BEANS, EGGS, AND NUTS GROUP
2 to 3 servings

1 serving = 2 to 3 ounces of cooked lean meat, fish, or poultry; 1/2 cup of cooked dry beans; 2 eggs; 4 tablespoons of peanut butter; or 2/3 cup of nuts

VEGETABLE GROUP
3 to 5 servings

1 serving = 1 cup of raw, leafy green vegetables; 1/2 cup of other vegetables (cooked or chopped raw); or 3/4 cup vegetable juice

FRUIT GROUP
2 to 4 servings

1 serving = 1 medium apple, banana, or orange; 1/2 cup of cooked, chopped, or canned fruit; or 3/4 cup of fruit juice

BREAD, CEREAL, RICE, AND PASTA GROUP
6 to 11 servings

1 serving = 1 slice of bread; 1 ounce of ready-to-eat cereal; or 1/2 cup of cooked cereal, rice, or pasta

The foods at the bottom of the pyramid are the ones everyone needs to eat in the biggest amounts. At the top are the foods to be eaten in the smallest amounts. The number of servings needed depends on your age and body size. Younger, smaller people need fewer servings. Older, larger people need more.

Drugs, Alcohol, and Tobacco:
COOL WAYS TO SAY "NO"

Drugs, alcohol, and tobacco can do serious damage to people's bodies and minds. Most kids keep away from them. But some kids have a tough time saying "no" when they are offered harmful substances. Here are some ways to say "no." They're suggested by DARE, a U.S. government program. Add your own ideas to this list.

► Say "No thanks." (Say it again and again if you have to.)

► Give reasons. ("I don't like cigarettes" or "I'm going to soccer practice" or "My mom would kill me.")

► Change the subject or offer a better suggestion.

► Walk away. (Don't argue, don't discuss it. Just leave.)

► Avoid the situation. (If you are asked to a party where kids will be drinking, smoking, or using drugs, make plans to do something else instead.)

► Find strength in numbers. (Do things with friends who don't use harmful substances.)

Understanding AIDS

WHAT IS AIDS? AIDS is a disease that is caused by a virus called HIV. AIDS attacks the body's immune system. The immune system is important because it helps the body fight off infections and diseases.

HOW DO KIDS GET AIDS? A mother with AIDS may give it to her baby before the baby is born. Sometimes children (and adults, too) get AIDS from blood transfusions. But this happens less often, because blood banks now test all donations of blood for the AIDS virus.

HOW DO ADULTS GET AIDS? Adults get AIDS in two main ways: Having sex with a person who has AIDS, or sharing a needle used for drugs with a person who has AIDS.

HOW KIDS AND ADULTS DON'T GET AIDS. People don't get AIDS from everyday contact with infected people at school, at home, or other places. People don't get AIDS from clothes, telephones, or toilet seats, or from food prepared by someone with AIDS. Children don't get AIDS from sitting near AIDS victims or from shaking hands with them.

IS THERE A CURE FOR AIDS? There is no cure for AIDS. But researchers are working to develop a vaccine to prevent AIDS or a drug to cure it. And new treatments are beginning to increase the lifespan of many people with AIDS.

SUPER SNACKS

Hungry? Here are some treats you can make yourself.

APPLE SURPRISE

*You'll need: **apples, peanut butter, raisins***

Wash an apple and have an adult cut out the core (the center). Make sure to take out the seeds. Put a mixture of peanut butter and raisins in the middle.

MINI-PIZZAS

*You'll need: **a bagel, tomato sauce, shredded mozzarella cheese, any veggies or meat you want***

Have an adult cut the bagel in half. Then spread the sauce on each half of the bagel. Sprinkle on the cheese. Then put on any toppings you want. With adult supervision, stick it in the oven on low heat for 5 to 8 minutes or until the cheese starts to bubble. Let it cool down a couple of minutes, then you've got a miniature pizza!

DILL PICKLE ROLL-UPS

*You'll need: **dill pickles, thinly sliced ham, cream cheese***

Spread some cream cheese on a thinly sliced piece of ham and roll it around a dill pickle.

TRAIL MIX

*You'll need: **any kind of dry cereal (oat, corn, wheat); chocolate chips, raisins, or any kind of dried fruit pieces; peanuts or any kind of chopped nut***

For a great on-the-go snack, mix any combination of these ingredients (or other dry things you think might taste good) in equal amounts in a container. A small plastic bagful is easy to carry and will give you energy no matter where you go or what you're doing.

WHICH OF THE ITEMS BELOW DOESN'T BELONG IN THE GROUP?

ANSWERS ON PAGES 314-317. FOR MORE PUZZLES GO TO WWW.WORLDALMANACFORKIDS.COM

HOLIDAYS

What do Japanese kids do on the festival of "7-5-3"? ➤ page 95

HOLIDAYS IN THE UNITED STATES

There are no official holidays for the whole United States. The U.S. government decides which days will be federal holidays. (These are really just for Washington, D.C.) Each state picks its own holidays, but most states celebrate the ones listed here. On these holidays, most banks and schools are closed, and so are many offices. Washington's Birthday (or Presidents' Day), Memorial Day, and Columbus Day are usually celebrated on the nearest Monday.

NEW YEAR'S DAY Countries the world over celebrate the new year, although not always on January 1. For example, Chinese New Year falls between January 21 and February 19.

MARTIN LUTHER KING JR. DAY Observed on the third Monday in January, this holiday marks the birth (January 15, 1929) of the African-American civil rights leader Rev. Martin Luther King Jr. In 2003, it will be celebrated on January 20.

WASHINGTON'S BIRTHDAY OR PRESIDENTS' DAY On the third Monday in February (February 17, 2003), Americans celebrate the births of both George Washington (born February 22, 1732) and Abraham Lincoln (born February 12, 1809).

MEMORIAL DAY OR DECORATION DAY Memorial Day, observed on the last Monday in May (May 26, 2003), is set aside to remember men and women who died serving in the military.

FOURTH OF JULY OR INDEPENDENCE DAY July 4 is the anniversary of the day in 1776 when the American colonies signed the Declaration of Independence. Kids and grownups celebrate with bands and parades, picnics, barbecues, and fireworks.

LABOR DAY Labor Day, the first Monday in September, honors the workers of America. It was first celebrated in 1882. It falls on September 2 in 2002 and September 1 in 2003.

COLUMBUS DAY Celebrated on the second Monday in October, Columbus Day is the anniversary of October 12, 1492, the day Christopher Columbus was traditionally thought to have arrived in the Americas (on the island of San Salvador). It falls on October 14 in 2002 and October 13 in 2003.

ELECTION DAY Election Day, the first Tuesday after the first Monday in November (November 5 in 2002 and November 4 in 2003), is a holiday in some states.

VETERANS DAY Veterans Day, November 11, honors veterans of wars. First called Armistice Day, it marked the armistice (agreement) that ended World War I. This was signed on the 11th hour of the 11th day of the 11th month of 1918.

THANKSGIVING Thanksgiving was first observed by the Pilgrims in 1621 as a harvest festival and a day for thanks and feasting. In 1863, Abraham Lincoln revived the tradition. It comes on the fourth Thursday in November— November 28 in 2002 and November 27 in 2003.

CHRISTMAS Christmas is both a religious holiday and a legal holiday. It is celebrated on December 25.

OTHER SPECIAL HOLIDAYS

VALENTINE'S DAY February 14 is a day for sending cards or gifts to people you love.

MOTHER'S DAY AND FATHER'S DAY Mothers are honored on the second Sunday in May. Fathers are honored on the third Sunday in June.

HALLOWEEN In ancient Britain, Druids wore grotesque costumes on October 31 to scare off evil spirits. Today, "trick or treating" children collect candy and other sweets. Some also collect money for UNICEF, the United Nations Children's Fund.

KWANZAA This seven-day African-American festival begins on December 26. It celebrates seven virtues: unity, self-determination, collective work and responsibility, cooperative economics, purpose, creativity, and faith.

UNUSUAL HOLIDAYS

Did you celebrate **Be Nice to New Jersey Week**? It's held the first week of July every year. How about **International Pancake Day** (March 4)? Hundreds of little-known holidays are celebrated every year. Here are a few more (dates are for 2003):

Happy Mew Year For Cats Day (January 2)
Lost Penny Day (February 12)
National Pig Day (March 1)
Sorry Charlie Day (April 1)
Cartoonists Day (May 5)
Take Your Dog to Work Day (June 20)
National Ice Cream Day (July 20)
Hobbit Day (September 22)
World Hello Day (November 21)
Underdog Day (December 19)

Did You KNOW?

RED NOSE DAY *Every two years, people in Great Britain (and Australia) go bonkers on Red Nose Day. On March 16, 2001, millions of kids and adults in Britain wore red plastic noses and red clothes or wacky costumes. Bake sales, silly contests, wacky auctions, and a nationwide telethon were held. All the money raised went to the charity Comic Relief. The next Red Nose Day was planned for March 2003.*

WORLD HOLIDAYS AROUND THE WORLD

BOXING DAY December 26 is a holiday in Britain, and also in Australia, Canada, and New Zealand. On this day, at one time, Christmas gifts were given out in boxes to servants, trades-people, and the poor.

CANADA DAY Canada's national holiday, July 1, commemorates the union of Canadian provinces in 1867.

CHINESE NEW YEAR China's biggest holiday falls between January 21 and February 19 every year. Celebrations include parades, fireworks, and traditional meals. It comes on February 1 in 2003.

INDEPENDENCE DAY Mexico celebrates September 16 as its national holiday.

SHICHI-GO-SAN (SEVEN-FIVE-THREE) This Japanese festival is held near November 15, for boys ages 3 and 5, and girls ages 3 and 7. Dressed in fine clothes, they visit a shrine to give thanks for their health. Afterwards, their brightly colored paper bags—decorated with cranes and turtles, symbols of long life—are filled with candy and toys which they share.

INVENTIONS

Which came first, the telephone or the typewriter? ➤page 97

INVENTIONS CHANGE OUR LIVES

A lot of the world's inventions came before history was written. These include the wheel, pottery, many tools, and the ability to make fire. More recent inventions help us to travel faster, communicate better, and live longer.

Inventions Help Us Live Healthier and Longer Lives

YEAR	INVENTION	INVENTOR (COUNTRY)
1780	bifocal lenses for glasses	Benjamin Franklin (U.S.)
1819	stethoscope	René T.M.H. Laënnec (France)
1842	anesthesia (ether)	Crawford W. Long (U.S.)
1895	X ray	Wilhelm Roentgen (Germany)
1922	insulin	Sir Frederick G. Banting (Canada)
1929	penicillin	Alexander Fleming (Scotland)
1954	antibiotic for fungal diseases	R. F. Brown & E. L. Hazen (U.S.)
1955	polio vaccine	Jonas E. Salk (U.S.)
1973	CAT scanner	Godfrey N. Hounsfield (England)
1978	artificial heart	Robert K. Jarvik (U.S.)
1987	meningitis vaccine	Connaught Lab (U.S.)
2000	self-contained artificial heart	Robert K. Jarvik (U.S.)

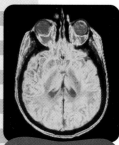

▲ A brain scan made with a CAT scanner

Inventions Take Us From One Place To Another

YEAR	INVENTION	INVENTOR (COUNTRY)
1785	parachute	Jean Pierre Blanchard (France)
1807	steamboat (practical)	Robert Fulton (U.S.)
1829	steam locomotive	George Stephenson (England)
1852	elevator	Elisha G. Otis (U.S.)
1885	bicycle	James Starley (England)
1885	motorcycle	Gottlieb Daimler (Germany)
1891	escalator	Jesse W. Reno (U.S.)
1892	automobile (gasoline)	Charles E. Duryea & J. Frank Duryea (U.S.)
1894	submarine	Simon Lake (U.S.)
1895	diesel engine	Rudolf Diesel (Germany)
1903	propeller airplane	Orville & Wilbur Wright (U.S.)
1939	helicopter	Igor Sikorsky (U.S.)
1939	jet airplane	Hans van Ohain (Germany)
1973	Jet Ski®	Clayton Jacobsen II (U.S)
1980	rollerblades	Scott Olson (U.S.)
2001	Segway Human Transport*	Dean Kamen (U.S.) ▶

*A computer-controlled electric scooter.

Inventions Help Us Communicate With One Another

YEAR	INVENTION	INVENTOR (COUNTRY)
105	paper	Ts'ai Lun (China)
1447	movable type	Johann Gutenberg (Germany)
1795	modern pencil	Nicolas Jacques Conté (France)
1837	telegraph	Samuel F.B. Morse (U.S.)
1845	rotary printing press	Richard M. Hoe (U.S.)
1867	typewriter	Christopher L. Sholes, Carlos Glidden, & Samuel W. Soulé (U.S.)
1876	telephone	Alexander G. Bell (U.S.)
1888	ballpoint pen	John Loud (U.S.)
1913	modern radio receiver	Reginald A. Fessenden (U.S.)
1937	xerography copies	Chester Carlson (U.S.)
1942	electronic computer	John V. Atanasoff & Clifford Berry (U.S.)
1944	auto sequence computer	Howard H. Aiken (U.S.)
1947	transistor	William Shockley, Walter H. Brattain, & John Bardeen (U.S.)
1955	fiber optics	Narinder S. Kapany (England)
1965	word processor	IBM (U.S.)
1979	cellular telephone	Ericsson Company (Sweden)
1987	laptop computer	Sir Clive Sinclair (England) ▶
1994	digital camera	Apple Computer, Kodak (U.S.)
2002	wind-up cell phone	Motorola (U.S.) & Freeplay Energy Group (England)

Inventions Make Our Lives Easier

YEAR	INVENTION	INVENTOR (COUNTRY)
1800	electric battery	Alessandro Volta (Italy)
1831	lawn mower	Edwin Budding & John Ferrabee (England)
1834	refrigeration	Jacob Perkins (England)
1846	sewing machine	Elias Howe (U.S.)
1851	cylinder (door) lock	Linus Yale (U.S.)
1879	practical light bulb	Thomas A. Edison (U.S.)
1886	dishwasher	Josephine Cochran (U.S.)
1891	zipper	Whitcomb L. Judson (U.S.)
1901	washing machine	Langmuir Fisher (U.S.)
1903	windshield wipers	Mary Anderson (U.S.)
1907	vacuum cleaner	J. Murray Spangler (U.S.)
1911	air conditioning	Willis H. Carrier (U.S.)
1924	frozen packaged food	Clarence Birdseye (U.S.)
1948	Velcro	Georges de Mestral (Switzerland)
1958	laser	A. L. Schawlow & C. H. Townes (U.S.) ▼
1963	pop-top can	Ermal C. Fraze (U.S.)
1969	cash machine (ATM)	Don Wetzel (U.S.)
1971	food processor	Pierre Verdon (France)
1980	Post-its	3M Company (U.S.)
1981	Polartec fabric	Malden Mills (U.S.)
2001	MET5 heat-generating jacket	Malden Ventures, Polartec, & North Face (U.S.)

Inventions Entertain Us

YEAR	INVENTION	INVENTOR (COUNTRY)
1709	piano	Bartolomeo Cristofori (Italy)
1877 ◀	phonograph	Thomas A. Edison (U.S.)
1877	microphone	Emile Berliner (U.S.)
1888	portable camera	George Eastman (U.S.)
1893	moving picture viewer	Thomas A. Edison (U.S.)
1894	motion picture projector	Charles F. Jenkins (U.S.)
1899	tape recorder	Valdemar Poulsen (Denmark)
1923	television*	Vladimir K. Zworykin* (U.S.)
1963	audiocassette	Phillips Corporation (Netherlands)
1963	steel tennis racquet	René Lacoste (France)
1969	videotape cassette	Sony (Japan)
1972	compact disc (CD)	RCA (U.S.)
1972	video game (Pong)	Noland Bushnell (U.S.)
1979	Walkman	Sony (Japan)
1995	DVD (digital video disk)	Matsushita (Japan)

Others who helped invent television include Philo T. Farnsworth (1926) and John Baird (1928).

Inventions Help Make Life Safer

YEAR	INVENTION	INVENTOR (COUNTRY)
1752	lightning rod	Benjamin Franklin (U.S.)
1815	safety lamp for miners	Sir Humphry Davy (England)
1863	fire extinguisher	Alanson Crane (U.S.) ▶
1923	automatic traffic signal	Garrett A. Morgan (U.S.)
1952	airbag	John Hetrick (U.S.)
1969	battery operated smoke detector	Randolph Smith & Kenneth House (U.S.)

All About...

THE SIGN LANGUAGE GLOVE

Seventeen-year-old Ryan Patterson got the idea in the summer of 2000. He saw another teen, who was deaf, trying to order lunch at Burger King. And he knew a non-speaking student who had a sign-language translator by his side all day at school. There had to be a better way! Ryan's invention, a Sign Translator, uses a leather golf glove, a small wireless receiver, and a screen. Sensors in the glove (using a technology he did not invent) pick up hand movements of the American Sign Language alphabet and change them into letters for the the screen. It would be hard to hold a long conversation this way. But for ordering lunch and other short messages, it could be just the thing.

NATIONAL INVENTORS HALL OF FAME

To learn more about inventions and the people who created them, or to make your own invention, visit

Inventure Place
National Inventors Hall of Fame
221 S. Broadway, Akron, Ohio 44308
Phone: (330) 762-4463.
E-mail: museum@invent.org
WEB SITE *http://www.invent.org*

Inventions Help Us Expand Our Universe

YEAR	INVENTION	INVENTOR (COUNTRY)
1250	magnifying glass	Roger Bacon (England)
1590	2-lens microscope	Zacharias Janssen (Netherlands)
1608	telescope	Hans Lippershey (Netherlands)
1714	mercury thermometer	Gabriel D. Fahrenheit (Germany)
1926	rocket engine	Robert H. Goddard (U.S.)
1930	cyclotron (atom smasher)	Ernest O. Lawrence (U.S.)
1943	Aqua Lung	Jacques-Yves Cousteau & Emile Gagnan (France)
1977	space shuttle	NASA (U.S.) ▶
2001	EZ-Rocket (reusable rocket engines)	Jeff Greason (U.S.)

GREAT IDEAS–BY ACCIDENT!

Ideas and discoveries often happen by accident, when people are looking for something else. Here's one that has saved many lives, and one that's just for fun!

▶ Scottish scientist Alexander Fleming was doing research on *staphylococcus* bacteria in 1928. He went away on vacation, leaving the bacteria growing in a glass dish in his laboratory. While he was gone, the dish was contaminated with a mold called *Penicillium notatum*. When Fleming came back, he found that the area around the mold didn't have any bacteria growing on it. That's how the infection-fighting drug **penicillin** got its start.

▶ One day, aerospace engineer Lonnie Johnson was working at home in Los Angeles. In his bathroom, he was testing a device called a heat pump. When a stream of water suddenly shot across the room, he realized it might make a great water gun. He teamed up with Bruce D'Andrade, and in 1991 the world first saw the **Super Soaker®**—launching a whole era in high-powered water squirters.

A BATTY IDEA?

Jacob Dunnack came up with the idea for "JD Batball" when he was six. On a visit to his grandmother's house, he brought his bat—but forgot the ball. He was very disappointed and decided it wouldn't happen again. So Jacob invented a hollow plastic baseball bat with a screw-on top so the balls can be stored inside. He showed everyone his creation at his school's "Invention Convention." His parents got someone to help him with the design. In November 2001, JD Batball hit the shelves at Toys "R" Us stores across the country!

Did You Know?

MARV JR. Researchers at Sandia National Laboratories have created the *Mini Autonomous Robot Vehicle Jr.* It's a robot that's smaller than a cherry! Powered by three watch batteries, "MARV Jr." can travel 20 inches per minute on rubber treads. Soon, mini-cameras, microphones, and sensors may be added. That would make it perfect for inspecting pipes and other hard-to-reach places, or for sneaking under doors to gather all kinds of information. Visit the lab's web site for more information about MARV Jr. and his big brother MARV: http://www.sandia.gov/isrc

LANGUAGE

Who said "The buck stops here"? ➤page 102

SHORT & SHORTER
ABBREVIATIONS & ACRONYMS

An abbreviation is a short form of a word or phrase used to save time or space. Here are some abbreviations:

etc. *et cetera* (and so forth)
FYI for your information
PC personal computer
rpm revolutions per minute
VCR video cassette recorder

An acronym is a kind of abbreviation. It is a word you can pronounce, formed from the first letters, or other parts, of each word in a group of words. Here are some acronyms:

NOW **N**ational **O**rganization for **W**omen
scuba **s**elf-**c**ontained **u**nderwater **b**reathing **a**pparatus
UNICEF **U**nited **N**ations **I**nternational **C**hildren's **E**mergency **F**und
yuppie **y**oung **u**rban **p**rofessional

New Words

The English language is always changing. New words become part of the vocabulary, while other words become outdated. Many new words come from the field of electronics and computers, from the media, even from slang.

dot-com: a company that sells its products or services online through a Web site. (*My brother started a new job at a **dot-com** that helps people who are moving to a new city find jobs, schools, and places to live.*)

duh: used to show something is really too obvious to need saying. (*Well, **duh**—the earth goes around the sun.*)

eye candy: something pretty to look at, but not anything more. (*The movie wasn't that good; it was just **eye candy**.*)

24-7: for twenty-four hours a day, seven days a week—all the time. (*The grocery store around the corner is open **24-7**.*)

wakeboard: a short board with foot bindings, used for pulling a rider along behind a motorboat. Riders do tricks and jumps off the boat's wake—the waves it makes going through the water. (*I fell off the **wakeboard** four times the first day I tried it.*)

PALINDROMES ƧƎMOЯbИI⅃Aꟼ

A **palindrome** is a word, verse, or sentence that reads the same backward and forward. If English were a very old language, the first words ever spoken could have been a palindrome: "Madam, I'm Adam." Or maybe, "Madam in Eden, I'm Adam." The answer Adam got could have been: "Eve." Here are some other palindromes to ponder.

A warning outside the veterinarian's office could read: **Step on no pets.**

If your aging cats act confused or strange, you may be dealing with **senile felines**.

Have you ever asked yourself: **Do geese see God?**

After trying unsuccessfully to lift a heavy rock, you might shout: **O, stone, be not so!**

You're making a drawing of your family, but you're not sure you have it right, so you could ask your brother: **Did I draw Della too tall, Edward? I did?**

Did You Know?

SOCCER *got its name in an odd way. In London in the 1860s, several clubs formed a group in order to agree to the same rules for football. Those who wanted to allow the ball to be carried left the group and started "rugby." The game played by the remaining clubs was called "Association Football," then "socca" for short, and later "soccer."*

All About...
EPONYMS

How would you like to have your name added as a word to the English language? A few people have been so lucky . . . or unlucky. An **eponym** is a word that comes from a person's name. Here are a few:

boycott: In 1880 a man in Ireland named Charles Boycott refused to lower rents. As a result, the public refused to have anything to do with him. The term **boycott** now means to avoid a person, organization, or company, or refuse to buy certain products, as a protest.

cardigan: The 7th earl of Cardigan (in Wales) had the soldiers in his military regiment wear knitted sweaters or jackets that fastened up the front. People then began to call this type of sweater a **cardigan**.

leotard: Julius Leotard was a French aerial gymnast who lived during the 19th century. His name became attached to the tight-fitting garment he wore when he performed.

sandwich: John Montagu, the 4th earl of Sandwich (in England) wanted something he could eat without having to get up from the table where he played games. The tasty, easy-to-hold **sandwich** fit the bill.

In Other Words: IDIOMS

Idioms are phrases that mean more than their words put together. If you take them word for word, they might not make much sense! Idioms are a little like puzzles: try imagining a picture or a situation that the phrase suggests, and guess at the meaning from there.

the buck stops here—"taking responsibility for something, instead of blaming someone else." President Harry S. Truman invented this phrase and had a sign made for his desk with those words. Truman liked to play poker, a popular card game. In poker a marker called a "buck" was placed in front of the player who would be the next to deal the cards. A player who didn't want to deal could pass the buck to the next player.

Harry Truman ▶

the fat's in the fire—"the damage is already done." This phrase probably came from a kitchen centuries ago. Fat was, and still is, often used in cooking. If it spills in the fire, it burns up right away, and there is nothing to be done about it.

a flash in the pan—"something that looks like it will be a big success, but does not work out." Flintlock muskets had a little pan to be filled with gunpowder. When the trigger was pulled, a spark from the flint would light that powder. It was supposed to burn through a hole in the barrel and light more powder behind the bullet. A "flash in the pan" made light and smoke for a second, but didn't fire the bullet.

footing the bill—"paying." The person who signs his or her name at the bottom, or "foot," of a bill or check (as at a restaurant) is the one who pays. Signing the foot, or "footing it," has come to mean paying.

hat trick—"scoring three times in a game." Used in hockey and soccer, this term came from the English game of cricket. In cricket, a bowler (sort of like a pitcher) tries to knock over three wooden stakes, or wickets, that are guarded by a player with a flat bat. Knocking down three wickets on three straight "pitches" was called a "hat trick." A long time ago, players who did it won a hat.

the jig is up—"the game or trick is exposed." In Shakespeare's time, "jig" was a slang for trick. When the "jig is up," the trick has been discovered.

the nick of time—"just before time is up." Years ago, the scores of some games (like soccer) were kept by cutting notches or "nicks" in each end of a wooden "tally stick." A winning goal that came just before the clock ran out was said to be a "nick in time."

pull the wool over someone's eyes—"trick or deceive." In the days when gentlemen wore powdered wigs, "wool" was a funny word for hair. Jokesters would knock a man's wig (his wool) down over his eyes so that he couldn't see what was happening.

raining cats and dogs—"raining very heavily." Centuries ago, people thought certain animals had magical powers. Sailors believed cats had something to do with rainstorms. Dogs and wolves were symbols of winds in Norse mythology.

Why did the turkey cross the road?
The chicken was out sick.

Why is 2 + 2 = 5 like your left foot?
It's not right.

What's the difference between a teacher and a railroad engineer?
One trains minds and the other minds trains.

What do you call a bee that hums quietly?
A mumblebee.

What did the mama broom say to the baby broom?
Go to sweep, little one.

Why was 6 afraid of 7?
Because 789.

Why is "b" such a hot letter?
Because it makes oil boil.

When is a door not a door?
When it's ajar.

What did the attorney wear when she appeared in court?
A lawsuit.

If it takes 12 men 6 days to dig a hole, how long will it take 6 men to dig half a hole?
There's no such thing as half a hole.

What did the pencil say to the paper?
I dot my "i" on you!

There were ten cats in a boat and one jumped out. How many were left?
None. They were copycats.

What do you call a black-and-blue Tyrannosaurus Rex?
A dino-sore.

What has four eyes but can't see?
Mississippi.

What starts with "t," ends with "t," and is full of "t" ?
A teapot.

Which side of the chicken has the most feathers?
The outside.

Why did the jelly roll?
It saw the apple turnover.

How do you make a witch scratch?
Take away her "w."

What do you call a sick alligator?
An illigator.

How do you make a hot dog stand?
Take away its chair.

Try these riddles. (The answers are upside down at the bottom.)

1. I know a word of letters three.
Add two, and fewer there will be.

2. I am always hungry, I must always be fed,
The finger I lick will soon turn red.

3. My life can be measured in hours,
I serve by being devoured.
Thin, I am quick
Fat, I am slow
Wind is my foe.

TOP TEN LANGUAGES

Would you have guessed that Mandarin, the principal language of China, is the most common spoken language in the world? You may find more surprises in the chart below, which lists languages spoken in 2000 by at least 100,000,000 native speakers (those for whom the language is their first language, or mother tongue) and some of the places where each one is spoken.

Hello!
(English)

Konnichi wa!
(Japanese)

¡Hola!
(Spanish)

LANGUAGE	WHERE SPOKEN	NATIVE SPEAKERS
Mandarin	China, Taiwan	874,000,000
Hindi	India	366,000,000
English	U.S., Canada, Britain	341,000,000
Spanish	Spain, Latin America	322,000,000
Arabic	Arabian Peninsula	207,000,000
Bengali	India, Bangladesh	207,000,000
Portuguese	Portugal, Brazil	176,000,000
Russian	Russia	167,000,000
Japanese	Japan	125,000,000
German	Germany, Austria	100,000,000

WHICH LANGUAGES ARE SPOKEN IN THE UNITED STATES?

Since the beginning of American history, immigrants have come to the United States from all over the world. They have brought their native languages with them.

¡Hola! That's how more than 17 million Americans say "hi" at home. Still, nearly 200 million Americans only speak English.

The table at right lists the other most frequently spoken languages in the United States, as of the 1990 census.

LANGUAGE USED AT HOME	SPEAKERS OVER 5 YEARS OLD
❶ English only	198,601,000
❷ Spanish	17,339,000
❸ French	1,702,000
❹ German	1,547,000
❺ Italian	1,309,000
❻ Chinese	1,249,000
❼ Tagalog	843,000
❽ Polish	723,000
❾ Korean	626,000
❿ Vietnamese	507,000
⓫ Portuguese	430,000
⓬ Japanese	428,000
⓭ Greek	388,000
⓮ Arabic	355,000
⓯ Hindi, Urdu, related languages	331,000
⓰ Russian	242,000
⓱ Yiddish	213,000
⓲ Thai	206,000
⓳ Persian	202,000
⓴ French Creole	188,000

Did You KNOW?

AHOY! *Using the word "hello" as a greeting is only as old as the telephone, which was invented in 1876. Alexander Graham Bell, the inventor of the telephone, suggested that people say "ahoy" when they answered a ring, but this didn't catch on. "Hello" caught on instead. It is related to "hallo," a cry of surprise used in the mid-19th century.*

LANGUAGE EXPRESS

Surprise your friends and family with your knowledge of words from other languages.

ENGLISH	SPANISH	FRENCH	GERMAN	CHINESE
January	enero	janvier	Januar	yi-yue
February	febrero	fevrier	Februar	er-yue
March	marzo	mars	Marz	san-yue
April	abril	avril	April	si-yue
May	mayo	mai	Mai	wu-yue
June	junio	juin	Juni	liu-yue
July	julio	julliet	Juli	qi-yue
August	agosto	aout	August	ba-yue
September	septiembre	septembre	September	jiu-yue
October	octubre	octobre	Oktober	shi-yue
November	noviembre	novembre	November	shi-yi-yue
December	diciembre	decembre	Dezember	shi er-yue
lion	león	lion	Lowe	shi
bird	pájaro	oiseau	Vogel	niao
horse	caballo	cheval	Pferd	ma
bear	oso	ours	Bar	xiong
blue	azul	bleu	blau	lan
red	rojo	rouge	rot	hong
green	verde	vert	grun	lu
yellow	amarillo	jaune	gelb	huang
black	negro	noir	schwarz	hei
white	blanco	blanc	weiss	bai
happy birthday!	¡feliz cumpleaños!	bonne anniversaire!	Glückwunsnch zum Geburtstag!	sheng-ri kuai le!
hello	¡hola!	bonjour!	hallo!	ni hao!
good-bye!	¡hasta luego!	au revoir!	auf Wiedersehen!	zai-jian!
one	uno	un	eins	yi
two	dos	deux	zwei	er
three	tres	trois	drei	san
four	cuatro	quatre	vier	si
five	cinco	cinq	funf	wu
six	seis	sex	sechs	liu
seven	siete	sept	sieben	qi
eight	ocho	huit	acht	ba
nine	nueve	neuf	neun	jiu
ten	diez	dix	zehn	shi

Bonne anniversaire!

SHENG-RI KUAI LE!

Glückwunsnch zum Geburtstag!

¡FELIZ CUMPLEAÑOS!

ANAGRAMS

An anagram takes all the letters of a word or phrase and switches them around in a way that still make sense. The best ones are funny, or surprising in some way. For example, one anagram for "school day" is "shady cool."

Easy ones:
glare   thicken
LARGE   **KITCHEN**

Harder:

lunch break
A BENCH LURK

cheerleader
DECLARE HERE

elementary school
A MOST LONELY CHEER
ENROLL A TOY SCHEME

middle school
SOME OLD CHILD
CLODDISH MOLE

pokemon cards
PANCAKE DORMS
SPACEMAN DORK
PACKMAN DOERS

Harry Potter
TRY PART HERO

Nintendo Gameboy
DOMINANT BOY GENE

Lord of the Rings
GOLD FORTH RISEN

Here's a really tough one:

The World Almanac for Kids
A MILD OWL RANSACKED FORTH
KIDS CALL EARTHWORM NO FAD (see pages 332-333)
ARMADILLO FETCH DARK SNOW

There are many websites to help you find anagrams for your name, or for any word or phrase you want. A good one is *http://www.anagram-engine.com*

LANGUAGE MAZE

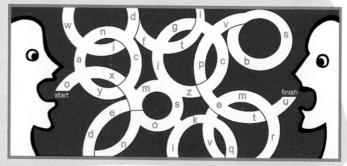

These two people are trying to have a conversation, but their speech is all jumbled. Can you help them? Try to get from "start" to "finish." If you trace the correct route, you'll pass all the letters you need. Write them down. Then unscramble the letters to see what they're trying to say.

ANSWERS ON PAGES 314-317. FOR MORE PUZZLES GO TO **WWW.WORLDALMANACFORKIDS.COM**

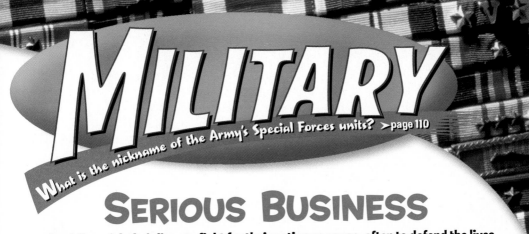

MILITARY

What is the nickname of the Army's Special Forces units? ➤ page 110

SERIOUS BUSINESS

Soldiers risk their lives to fight for their nation or cause, often to defend the lives and freedom of others. Since the beginning of the Revolutionary War, more than 2.6 million U.S. soldiers have been killed or wounded in wars (about as many people as now live in Arkansas). Today over 2.6 million American men and women serve in four major branches of the military, the Army, Navy, Air Force, and Marines.

Having more soldiers and weapons than the other side is an important advantage in war. So is military intelligence, or gaining secret information about an enemy, as well as such factors as deception, technology, and plain old stubbornness.

INTELLIGENCE During World War II, U.S. military intelligence broke a Japanese naval code used to send secret messages by radio. Americans thus learned of a planned attack on the U.S.-held island of Midway, northwest of Hawaii. Planes from U.S. aircraft carriers were able to ambush the Japanese fleet before it got in shooting range of the island.

DECEPTION During the Trojan War in the 12th century B.C., it is said that the Greeks built a large wooden horse, hid soldiers inside it, and left it outside Troy's main gate as a "gift." After the Trojans brought the horse inside the city, the soldiers slipped out and opened the gate so the Greek army could come in and burn the city.

TECHNOLOGY English forces in France used the longbow to defeat the French in the Battle of Agincourt, in 1415. Longbows, which were as tall as the archers themselves, could hurl heavy arrows 200 yards or more, or the length of two modern football fields.

COMMUNICATIONS Communications in the 19th century were not nearly as fast as they are today. When American and British armies fought the Battle of New Orleans in January 1815, neither side knew that a peace treaty "ending" the War of 1812 had been signed in Belgium two weeks earlier!

TACTICS The tactics of Confederate General Robert E. Lee led to a Southern victory in the Civil War Battle of Chancellorsville, Virginia, in May 1863. Trapped between two much larger Union forces, Lee divided his army into three parts and launched a surprise flanking attack that forced the Northerners to retreat.

STUBBORNNESS Soldiers and civilians in the Russian city of Stalingrad (Volgograd) held off an invading German army in 1942–43. The Russians refused to surrender the city despite terrible casualties and hardships. Eventually, Russian troops launched a counterattack, and the Germans retreated.

OUT OF THE ORDINARY

WHAT ARE SPECIAL OPERATIONS?

"Special operations" is a military term for missions not part of normal warfare. In war, two large forces usually face each other, with thousands of troops fighting at once. "Special Ops" take a special kind of soldier, working as part of a small unit, often deep inside enemy territory. They can fight anywhere, from baking deserts to steaming jungles to snow-covered mountains. Most are parachute-trained, and some are trained in underwater operations. They know foreign languages. They are some of the finest troops in any army.

U.S. SPECIAL OPERATIONS FORCES The U.S. has the most special-operation forces in the world. The Army, Navy, Air Force, and Marines have units. All are under the Defense Department's Special Operations Command at MacDill Air Force Base in Florida.

ARMY The Army's Special Forces (Green Berets, see page 110) and Rangers are the best known. The Rangers are part of the Army's 75th Regiment. Rangers specialize in larger-unit operations—like the raid on Taliban headquarters on October 19, 2001. More than 100 Rangers and other Special Forces troops took part in the first U.S. ground operations in Afghanistan. Their history goes back to "Roger's Rangers," a group of American frontiersmen who fought bravely in the French and Indian War (1754-63).

The Army's elite 160th Special Operations Aviation Regiment flies the famous MH-60K Black Hawk helicopters, often under enemy fire.

AIR FORCE The Air Force has a variety of units that provide transportation and air cover for U.S. commandos. These units include the 1st Special Operations Wing and two Special Operations Squadrons.

MARINES Every Marine Expeditionary Unit (of about 1,000 troops) has a Force Recon unit (about 150 troops) to act as its eyes and ears in the field.

NAVY Organized during World War II, the Navy's SEALs were originally called underwater demolition teams, or UDTs. SEAL stands for "Sea-Air-Land," reminding us that these Navy warriors can fight anywhere they are needed.

Navy SEALs ▶

IN THE AIR

Here are some of the aircraft used by the U.S. in the anti-terrorist war in Afghanistan known as Operation Enduring Freedom.

B-2A SPIRIT This is the long-range "stealth bomber." Its shape, high-altitude flight, and stealth technology make it almost impossible for enemy radar to detect it. The B-2 can fly 6,000 miles without refueling. Refueling in mid-air, it can fly 10,000 miles—from the U.S. to Afghanistan and back. That takes more than 40 hours! B-2s are part of the 509th Bomb Wing. All missions are flown from Whiteman Air Force Base in Missouri. The B-2 can travel close to the speed of sound (about 700 mph) and fly as high as 50,000 feet. It carries a crew of two: a pilot and a bombardier. It is 69 feet long, 17 feet high, and weighs 336,500 lbs. fully loaded. Its wingspan is 172 feet.

B-1B LANCER These are long-range, multi-role bombers. Each B-1B can carry up to 84 500-pound bombs or 20 Cruise missiles. It is difficult for enemy radar to detect. The plane's four turbo-fan engines can push it as high as 30,000 feet, at speeds over 900 miles per hour. The B-1B carries a crew of four: a commander, a co-pilot, plus offensive and defensive systems officers. It is 146 feet long, 34 feet high, and weighs 190,000 lbs. (empty). Its wingspan is 137 feet.

RQ-1 PREDATOR This unmanned, propeller-driven aircraft is used mostly for observation. It has video cameras, an infrared camera (for night vision), and radar. It can see through dense clouds and smoke. It may carry Hellfire missiles to strike targets on the ground. The Predator is 27 feet long, weighs 950 pounds, and has a wingspan of 27 feet. It has a cruising range of 424 miles, at 84 miles per hour, and can fly as high as 25,000 feet. It has a crew of zero.

WHO AM I?

I was born in 1336, in what is now Uzbekistan, in central Asia. I conquered many lands. Samarkand was the capital of my empire, which stretched east to India, north to Russia, and west to the Mediterranean Sea. I was cruel in war, but I loved scholarship and the arts. I died in 1405 while trying to conquer China.

Answer: Tamerlane

All About...
THE ARMY'S GREEN BERETS

TV news stories about the war in Afghanistan have showed bearded, heavily armed men in Afghan clothing trekking through the mountains in search of Osama bin Laden and his terrorists. Some of those bearded men were not Afghanis at all: they were disguised members of the U.S. Army's Special Forces.

Formed in 1952, the Special Forces "Green Berets" are among the best-known elite military units in the world. Their name comes from the caps they wear with their formal uniforms. They started wearing them in 1962, when John F. Kennedy was president. Today, the Army has four active-duty Special Forces Groups, made up of about 700 men each.

The basic unit of a Special Forces Group is the Alpha Detachment, or "A-Team." Each A-Team is made up of 12 men—a captain, a lieutenant, and 10 sergeants. Each member has a specialty (operations, intelligence, medicine, weapons, demolitions, or radio operations). And each member is also trained in a second specialty. For example, a Green Beret might be a radio operator and also trained in medicine or in using explosives.

Green Beret A-Teams have been very active in the war in Afghanistan. They have taken part in raids on Taliban strongholds. They have blown up bridges. They have called down bombing strikes from ground positions dangerously close to the targets. And they have searched hundreds of caves in the rugged Afghan mountains looking for hiding terrorists.

Perhaps the most important role for the A-Teams in Afghanistan has been training and advising friendly Afghan forces. Training and advising have been principal roles for the Green Berets since the creation of the service.

In Afghanistan, the Green Berets not only dressed like Afghans but also ate Afghan food, and lived among the Afghanis in very simple and harsh conditions. Special-operations troops must be able blend into their surroundings, no matter how difficult or dangerous the situation.

Army Staff Sergeant Barry Sadler, a Special Forces veteran of the Vietnam War, had a #1 song in 1966, "The Ballad of the Green Berets."

MONEY

Why are most coins round? ➤ page 112

HiSTORY of MONEY

Why Did People Start Using Money? At first, people bartered, which means they traded goods they had for things they needed. A farmer who had cattle might want to have salt to preserve meat, or cloth to make clothing. For this farmer, a cow became a "medium of exchange" — a way of getting things the farmer did not make or grow. Cattle became a form of money. Whatever people agreed to use for trade became the earliest kinds of money.

What Objects Have Been Used as Money?

▶ knives, rice, and spades in China around 3000 B.C.

▶ cattle and clay tablets in Babylonia around 2500 B.C.

▶ wampum (beads) and beaver fur by Native Americans of the northeast around A.D. 1500

▲ *Wampum used by Native Americans*

▶ tobacco by early American colonists around 1650

▶ whales' teeth by the Pacific peoples on the island of Fiji, until the early 1900s

Why Did Governments Start Issuing Money?
Governments were interested in issuing money because the money itself had value. If a government could gain control over the manufacture of money, it could increase its own wealth—often simply by making more money.

The first government to make coins that looked alike and use them as money is thought to be the Greek city-state of Lydia in the 7th century B.C. These Lydian coins were actually bean-shaped lumps made from a mixture of gold and silver.

By the Middle Ages (about A.D. 800-1100), gold had become a popular medium for trade in Europe. But gold was heavy and difficult to carry, and the cities and the roads of Europe at that time were dangerous places to carry large amounts of gold. So merchants and goldsmiths began issuing notes promising to pay gold to the person carrying the note. These "promissory notes" were the beginning of paper money in Europe. In the early 1700s, France's government became the first in Europe to issue paper money that looked alike. Paper money was probably also invented in China, where the explorer Marco Polo saw it in the 1280s.

Did You KNOW?

TWO CENTS WORTH *Up until the 1860s, the U.S. made coins worth a half cent, two cents, and three cents. One of the three-cent coins was even called a "nickel," because it was made of the metal called nickel. Five-cent pieces were made of silver until 1866, when they became nickels, too! The nickel coin we use today (Thomas Jefferson's image) was designed in 1938 and is still made partly of nickel.*

MAKING MONEY: THE U.S. MINT

WHAT IS THE U.S. MINT? The U.S. Mint, founded in 1792, makes all U.S. coins. It also safeguards the Treasury Department's stored gold and silver at Fort Knox, KY. The Bureau of Engraving and Printing designs and prints all U.S. paper money. Both the U.S. Mint and the Bureau of Engraving and Printing are part of the U.S. Treasury Department and have their headquarters in Washington, D.C.

WHAT KINDS OF COINS DOES THE MINT MAKE? Branches of the U.S. Mint in Denver and Philadelphia currently make coins for "circulation," or everyday use. A tiny "D" or "P" near the year, called a mint mark, tells you which one made the coin. A Lincoln cent or "penny" with no mint mark was probably made at the Philadelphia Mint, which has by tradition never marked pennies. The U.S. Mint also makes commemorative coins in honor of events, like the Olympics, or people, like Christopher Columbus.

WHOSE PORTRAITS ARE ON OUR MONEY? Presidents and other famous Americans appear on the front of all U.S. money. From 1999 to 2008, five new quarter designs are being minted each year. George Washington will stay on the front, but a design honoring one of the 50 states will appear on the back. The quarters for each state are coming out in the order in which the states joined the Union. By the end of 2001, these were Delaware, Pennsylvania, New Jersey, Georgia, Connecticut, Massachusetts, Maryland, South Carolina, New Hampshire, Virginia, New York, North Carolina, Rhode Island, Vermont, and Kentucky. In 2002, Tennessee, Ohio, Louisiana, Indiana, and Mississippi were joining the group. In 2003, look for Illinois, Alabama, Maine, Missouri, and Arkansas.

Denomination	Portrait	Denomination	Portrait
1¢	Abraham Lincoln, 16th President	$2	Thomas Jefferson, 3rd President
5¢	Thomas Jefferson, 3rd President	$5	Abraham Lincoln, 16th President
10¢	Franklin D. Roosevelt, 32nd President	$10	Alexander Hamilton, 1st Treasury Secretary
25¢	George Washington, 1st President		
50¢	John F. Kennedy, 35th President	$20	Andrew Jackson, 7th President
$1 (COIN)	Sacagawea, Native American woman	$50	Ulysses S. Grant, 18th President
$1 (BILL)	George Washington, 1st President	$100	Benjamin Franklin, inventor, U.S. patriot

Did You Know?

▶ The science and study of coins is called **numismatics**. When you look at old coins, you can learn about a nation's history—its kings, queens, war heroes, famous buildings, and symbols of power and authority, such as shields or coats of arms.

▶ We use coins to buy things. But they can also be beautiful works of art. For example, in 1907, the famous sculptor Augustus Saint-Gaudens designed a U.S. $20 gold coin showing a standing woman in a billowing robe who represented Liberty. On the reverse (back) a powerful flying eagle spreads its wings above the rays of the sun.

▶ Most coins are round rather than square or some other shape. Did you ever wonder why? Well, the round shape makes it easy for banks to wrap them into rolls. Also, the round shape helps protect coins made of gold or other valuable metals; crooks have a harder time cutting or scraping off parts of a round coin before spending it.

HOW MUCH MONEY IS IN CIRCULATION?

As of June 2001, the total amount of money in circulation in the United States came to $596,746,736,495 (almost 600 billion dollars). More than 30 billion dollars was in coins, the rest in paper money.

WHAT ARE EXCHANGE RATES?

When one country exports goods to another, the payment from the country buying the goods must be changed into the currency of the country selling them. An exchange rate is the price of one currency in terms of another. For example, in March 2002 one U.S. dollar could buy 1.6 Canadian dollars.

Here are the exchange rates in 1990 and 2002 between the U.S. dollar and the currency of some of the country's biggest trading partners.

What A U.S. Dollar Bought

COUNTRY	IN 1990	IN 2002
Canada	1.2 Canadian dollars	1.6 Canadian dollars
Great Britain	0.56 pound	0.71 pound
European Union*	—	1.16 euros
Japan	144.8 yen	133 yen
Mexico	2.8 pesos	9 pesos

United States   Japan

*The euro is used in Austria, Belgium, Finland, France, Germany, Greece, Ireland, Italy, Luxembourg, the Netherlands, Portugal, and Spain. Three EU countries—Denmark, Great Britain, and Sweden—have kept their own currencies.

all about...

THE EURO

Citizens of 12 countries in Europe (see above) were excited about the crisp new paper money and sparkling new coins they had starting in January 2002. This new currency, called the euro, is good in all 12 countries. Switching to the euro was a big job. In a short time banks had to get money worth 600 billion euros into the hands of 300 million people.

Many Germans were sad to see their marks disappear. People in France and Italy miss their francs and lire. But now money will flow easily from one country to another. This should make it easier to complete big financial deals between countries. And think how easy it will be for tourists. They can use the same kind of money to pay for a slice of pizza whether it's in Italy or in Belgium. Americans in Europe can easily figure what something costs because the euro and U.S. dollar are worth about the same—the euro equaled about 90 U.S. cents in spring 2002.

Some things didn't change. Criminals wasted no time pulling off the first euro theft. Right on January 1, two men robbed a bank in Spain of 90,000 euros.

Why Budgets Are Helpful

A budget is a plan that estimates how much money a person, a business, or a government will receive during a period of time, how much money will be spent and what it will be spent on, and how much money will be left over (if any).

A FAMILY BUDGET

Do you know what your family spends money on? Do you know where your family's income comes from? The chart below shows some sources of income and typical yearly expenses for a family's budget.

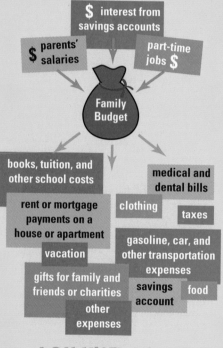

$ interest from savings accounts

$ parents' salaries

part-time jobs $

Family Budget

books, tuition, and other school costs

medical and dental bills

rent or mortgage payments on a house or apartment

clothing

taxes

vacation

gasoline, car, and other transportation expenses

gifts for family and friends or charities

savings account

food

other expenses

A BALANCED BUDGET

A budget is **balanced** when the amount of money you receive equals the amount of money you spend. A budget is **in deficit** when the amount of money you spend is greater than the amount of money you have.

MAKING YOUR OWN BUDGET

Imagine that you have a weekly allowance of $10. With this money you have to pay for things like snacks and magazines and also try to save up for special things. Planning a budget will help you manage your money. Here are some items you might want to put in your budget:

Possible Purchases and Cost:
Snacks: $.75 each
Collectible toy: $3.00
Book: $3.00

Savings:
For gifts: $.50–$2.00
For something special for yourself (like a basketball, a compact disc, a computer game, or concert tickets): $1.00 or more.

List the items you want along with their price. Add any other items that interest you—and their prices. Don't forget to add any money you want to save.

Item	Amount

Savings

Now total all your purchases and savings:

Is your budget balanced? Is the amount you plan to spend and save equal to the amount of your "income" ($10)? If not, try to reduce your planned savings or spending to make your budget balance.

WHAT DO YOU WANT TO BE?

More than 130 million people in the United States have jobs. You see many of them every day—teachers, bus drivers, or cashiers. Many jobs exist that you may not have ever heard of or thought of: aerospace engineer or actuary, for example. Although new jobs are constantly created, some jobs become unnecessary as different ways are found to do the work.

Here are just a few of the jobs people have today. Do you think any of them will interest you when you're ready to start your career?

COLLEGE PROFESSORS

College teachers, who are called professors, usually have a Ph.D., or a doctoral degree, in the subject they teach. That means they took courses and did special research for several years after graduating from college themselves. Professors teach students and grade papers and tests. They also do research and write about the subject they teach.

COMPUTER TECHNICIANS

As more and more people own or use computers, more workers are needed to repair the machines. Computer technicians also install and replace computer equipment.

NURSES

Caring for patients and helping doctors are two of the most important responsibilities nurses have. People are living longer and scientists are finding new ways to treat and cure diseases, so nurses are needed more and more.

FIREFIGHTERS

Fires can occur anywhere, such as in a city building or in a forest. A firefighter's most important job is to rescue people. Saving homes and other property from destruction is also important. Firefighters often use large trucks, tall ladders, and other heavy equipment. They have a dangerous job, and people regard them as heroes.

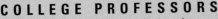

COIN TRIANGLE CHALLENGE

Arrange 10 pennies as shown. Moving one penny at a time, rearrange the triangle so that it points downward. If you can do it in 4 moves, you're good. If you can do it in 3, you're an expert!

ANSWERS ON PAGES 314-317. FOR MORE PUZZLES GO TO WWW.WORLDALMANACFORKIDS.COM

115

MOVIES & TV

What's the most popular animated kids' show on TV? ➤page 118

20 MOVIE HITS
(2001 AND EARLY 2002)

Diego, Sid, and Manny in Ice Age.

Atlantis: The Lost Empire (PG)
Big Fat Liar (PG)
Cats & Dogs (PG)
Dr. Dolittle 2 (PG)
Harry Potter and the Sorcerer's Stone (PG)
Ice Age (PG)

Jimmy Neutron: Boy Genius (G)
Jurassic Park III (PG-13)
Lord of the Rings: Fellowship of the Ring (PG-13)
The Mummy Returns (PG-13)
Monsters, Inc. (G)
Ocean's Eleven (PG-13)
Planet of the Apes (PG-13)
The Princess Diaries (G)
Rat Race (PG-13)
Return to Neverland (G)
Shrek (PG)
Snow Dogs (PG)
Spy Kids (PG)
The Time Machine (PG-13)

20 POPULAR KIDS VIDEOS OF 2001

102 Dalmatians
Barbie in the Nutcracker
Chicken Run
Dinosaur
Dr. Dolittle 2
Dr. Seuss' How the Grinch Stole Christmas
The Emperor's New Groove
The Kid
Lady and the Tramp II: Scamp's Adventure
The Land Before Time: The Big Freeze
Mary-Kate and Ashley: Holiday in the Sun

Mary-Kate and Ashley: Our Lips Are Sealed
Mary-Kate and Ashley: Winning London
Mickey's Magical Christmas: Snowed in at the House of Mouse
Pokémon: Mewtwo Returns
The Princess Diaries
Rugrats in Paris: The Movie
Shrek
Spy Kids
Toy Story 2

SOME POPULAR MOVIES

SNOW WHITE AND THE SEVEN DWARFS (1937) Walt Disney turned this classic fairy tale into the first-ever full-length animated film. It's still popular today.

THE WIZARD OF OZ (1939) As color came to the movies, Dorothy, played by Judy Garland, met a scarecrow, a tin woodsman, and a cowardly lion in the land of Oz.

NATIONAL VELVET (1944) In this exciting story, two kids train a dearly loved horse to compete in the Grand National Race.

SINGIN' IN THE RAIN (1952) In the most famous scene in this movie musical, the star, Gene Kelly, splashes through puddles as he dances down the street in the pouring rain.

THE SOUND OF MUSIC (1965) This musical tells the story of Maria Von Trapp, whose plans to become a nun change when she becomes the governess to seven motherless children and falls in love with their father.

STAR WARS (1977) Luke Skywalker, Princess Leia, and others battle Darth Vader and his dark Empire in a thriller set in outer space. The sequels *The Empire Strikes Back* **(1980)** and *The Return of the Jedi* **(1983)** were also huge hits. In 1999, a "prequel" was released, *Episode I: The Phantom Menace. Episode II: Attack of the Clones* opened in May 2002.

HARRY POTTER AND THE SORCERER'S STONE (2001) The adventures of Harry, Hermione, and Ron come to the big screen in this long-awaited movie, first in a series based on J. K. Rowling's Harry Potter books.

SHREK (2001) A big, green, moody ogre finds love and friendship in a very cracked fairy tale. This hilarious film uses the voices of Mike Myers, Eddie Murphy, Cameron Diaz, and John Lithgow.

LORD OF THE RINGS

"One Ring to rule them all, One Ring to find them,
One Ring to bring them all and in the darkness bind them."

English professor J.R.R. Tolkien wrote these ringing words years ago for his epic fantasy about the struggle between good and evil in another world. More than 100 million people have read, and loved, these books. In 2001, director Peter Jackson and a wonderful cast and crew brought the first part of Tolkien's story to the screen in *The Lord of the Rings: The Fellowship of the Ring*. It was a big hit.

The story is set in a place called Middle-earth. The dark Lord Sauron wants to get hold of a ring lost for centuries. He would use it to blot out civilization and cover the world in darkness. A young "hobbit" named Frodo Baggins has inherited the ring. With the help of a loyal fellowship including hobbits Sam, Merry, and Pippin; Gimli the dwarf; Legolas the elf; and humans Aragorn and Boromir, and with the guidance of the wizard Gandalf the Grey, Frodo must travel to the land of Mordor. There he must throw the ring into the flames of Mount Doom to destroy it. Opposing all of them are the evil wizard Saruman the White, as well as orcs, trolls, ringwraiths, and the monstrous mutant army called Uruk-hai.

The Lord of the Rings is really three movies. They were made together in the countryside of New Zealand. The second and third parts, *The Two Towers* and *The Return of the King*, are due out in December 2002 and December 2003.

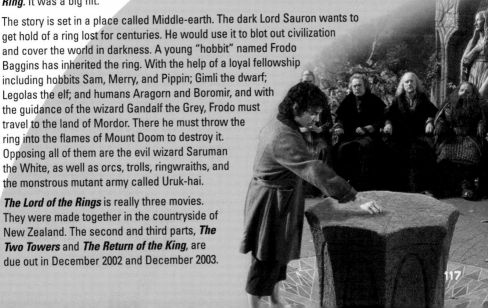

All About... SPONGEBOB

He's a talking yellow sponge who wears a tie and brown square pants. That's right, *sponge*. He looks sort of like a slice of Swiss cheese—not half bad for an invertebrate. He "works" as a fry cook, flipping Krabby Patties at the Krusty Krab. But you know this already if you're one of the 10 million kids—or 5 million adults—who watch *SpongeBob SquarePants* every week. It's the most popular animated kids' show on TV today.

The squeaky-voiced SpongeBob lives in a pineapple with his pet snail, Gary, in the town of Bikini Bottom (on the ocean floor). Although they live underwater, they still have bonfires and drive cars. Hey lighten up, its a cartoon!

SpongeBob's best friend is Patrick Starfish, a clueless, well, starfish. The two friends are often conjuring up any number of nutty schemes. Most of them do not seem to work. But they sure are fun to watch. Then there's SpongeBob's grumpy neighbor Squidward (an octopus). And a nemesis named Plankton, whose only goal is to get his hands on the secret recipe for the Krabby Patties.

Kids can enjoy the goofy slapstick comedy (and so can grownups).

POPULAR TV SHOWS IN 2001-2002
(Source: Nielsen Media Research; as of April 14, 2002)

AGES 6-11
1. *Survivor: Marquesas*
2. *Wonderful World of Disney*
3. *Survivor: Africa*
4. *Malcolm in the Middle*
5. *The Simpsons*

AGES 12-17
1. *Malcolm in the Middle*
2. *The Simpsons*
3. *Greg the Bunny*
4. *The Bernie Mac Show*
5. *Friends*

POWER   REW   PLAY   FF   PAUSE   CHANNEL   EJECT

POPULAR VIDEO GAMES IN 2001

Madden NFL 2002—Electronic Arts

Pokémon Crystal—Nintendo

Super Mario Advance—Nintendo

Gran Turismo 3: A-Spec—Sony

Pokémon Silver—Nintendo

Pokémon Stadium 2—Nintendo

Mario Party 3—Nintendo

Mario Tennis—Nintendo

Paper Mario—Nintendo

Super Smash Bros.—Nintendo

PEOPLE TO WATCH

Anne Hathaway

During her audition for Garry Marshall's movie *The Princess Diaries*, teenage actress Anne Hathaway accidentally fell off her chair. She was hired on the spot for the role of 15-year-old Mia Thermopolis, a geek who turns into a beautiful princess. Julie Andrews plays the grandmother who helps transform Mia. She also took Anne—who has been a fan of the former Mary Poppins since age 3—under her wing offscreen.

Anne was born on November 12, 1982, in Brooklyn, NY. She gained national attention as a troubled teen on the Fox network's short-lived 1999 series *Get Real*. Performing came naturally to Anne Hathaway. She is the daughter of stage actress Kate McCauley *(Les Miserables)*—and has the same name as William Shakespeare's wife! Also a trained soprano, she sang at Carnegie Hall—as a member of the All-Eastern U.S. High School Honors Chorus.

Anne ("Annie" to her friends) now goes to Vassar College in Poughkeepsie, New York. But fans can see her again on the big screen in the 2002 movie *The Other Side of Heaven*.

Hayden Christensen

By now the whole world knows Hayden Christensen is Anakin Skywalker, a.k.a. Darth Vader. But before May 12, 2000, almost nobody had ever heard of the Canadian teenager. He made headlines that day when director George Lucas picked him to co-star in *Star Wars Episode II: Attack of the Clones*. He's 21 now, and big news again as Episode II, co-starring Natalie Portman (Padmé Amidala) and Ewan McGregor (Obi-Wan Kenobi), hit theaters around the planet in May 2002.

Hayden was born in Vancouver, British Columbia, on April 19, 1981. But he grew up in Toronto. He's been acting in commercials, theater, and TV since he was seven. He got his start when his older sister did a Pringles commercial. There was no one to baby-sit for him, so he went along.

Hayden had a regular role in 2000 on Fox Family Channel's show *Higher Ground*. In between making Star Wars movies, Hayden played a troubled teenager in the 2001 film *Life as a House*. He was nominated for Golden Globe and Screen Actors Guild Awards as "Best Supporting Actor" for that movie. His career is on a rocket ride, so look for him in future films, especially *Star Wars Episode III*, due out in 2005.

MUSEUMS

Where can you see the plane flown by Orville Wright in 1903? ➤page 122

The word museum comes from a Greek word that means "temple of the Muses." Muses were the Greek goddesses of art and science.

The oldest museum in the U.S. is The Charleston Museum, founded in South Carolina in 1773. The U.S. now has more than 8,200 museums. Some are described here. For others, look in the Index under "Museums." You can also check out the Association of Children's Museums on the Internet at **WEB SITE** *http://www.aym.org*

KIDS' MUSEUMS

CAPITAL CHILDREN'S MUSEUM, Washington, D.C. • Exciting exhibits include an animation lab where you can create your own cartzs well as a life-sized maze and a science lab. In an imitation Mexican Village you can make and eat your own tasty tortillas.
WEB SITE *http://www.ccm.org*

CHILDREN'S DISCOVERY MUSEUM OF SAN JOSE, San Jose, California • Contains a hands-on bubble-world, a post office annex with 1950s furnishings, a bank, media studio, climbing tower, miniature city, and many interesting art and science exhibits.
WEB SITE *http://www.cdm.org*

THE CHILDREN'S MUSEUM OF UTAH, Salt Lake City, Utah • Let your imagination run wild in a "Willy Wonka-like" color factory, the cockpit of a Boeing airplane, a Wild West canyon, a rock climbing wall, a pioneer cabin, or a real-looking Indian cliff dwelling.
WEB SITE *http://www.childmuseum.org*

CURIOUS KIDS' MUSEUM, St. Joseph, Michigan In this place you can board and operate a model of a space shuttle that takes you to the moon and back, dig for dinosaur bones, make your own fossils, and climb to the top of a volcano.
WEB SITE *http://www.curiouskidsmuseum.org*

LYNN MEADOWS DISCOVERY CENTER, Gulfport, Mississippi • Here you can create your own video in a high-tech communications center, operate a crane, meet a robot, do gravity experiments in a science lab, and scramble up huge climbing tower.
WEB SITE *http://www.lmdc.org*

▲ The Children's Museum of Utah

LIVING HISTORY EXHIBITS

These places to visit have been restored or re-created to look the way they did many years ago. Museum staff wear costumes and show what life use to be like.

Jamestown Settlement, Williamsburg, Virginia. This re-created Indian village, fort, and settlement lets you experience the world of Pocahontas and the first permanent English settlers in America.

Yorktown Victory Center, Yorktown, Virginia. Witness life during the American Revolution in this re-created Continental Army camp and farm from the 1700s.

Historic Allaire Village, Wall, New Jersey. Blacksmiths, carpenters, and other workers demonstrate their trades in this restored village from the 1830s.

Agrirama (a-gri-RAH-mah), Tifton, Georgia. Travel back in time to rural Georgia in the late 1800s and visit a restored farmstead and town.

▲ *Jamestown blacksmith at work*

Somerville Manor, Lava Hot Springs, Idaho. This re-created medieval farm lets you experience the art, music, games, food, and work from Europe in the 1200s and 1300s.

Stuhr Museum of the Prairie Pioneer, Grand Island, Nebraska. This restored railroad town, Pawnee-Indian earth lodge, and pioneer settlement captures the flavor of life in Nebraska at the end of the 1800s.

ETHNIC MUSEUMS

These museums show the culture and history of different groups.

Freer Gallery of Art and Arthur M. Sackler Gallery, Washington, D.C. • Displays art from China, Japan, India, and other Asian countries.

The Jewish Museum, New York, New York • Has exhibits covering many centuries of Jewish history and culture.

The Balch Institute for Ethnic Studies, Philadelphia, Pennsylvania • Exhibits include the art, toys, tools, clothes, furniture, photographs, posters and other artifacts of over 60 ethnic groups in the U. S.

The Heard Museum, Phoenix, Arizona • Displays art by Native Americans, primarily from the southwestern U.S., such as the Apache, Hopi, and Navajo.

The Latin American Art Museum, Miami, Florida • Celebrates artwork, music, poetry, and dance performances by Hispanic and Latin American artists of today.

Charles H. Wright Museum of African American History, Detroit, Michigan • Features a large model of a slave ship, inventions by African Americans, music by black composers, and the space suit worn by the first U.S. black female astronaut.

Did You KNOW?

HISTORY WIRED *Superman first appeared in a comic book in 1938. You can see this book and hundreds of other fascinating objects at the National Museum of American History's new online museum. It's called "History Wired." Vivid pictures and lively histories go along with each exhibit, including Muhammad Ali's boxing gloves, Jacqueline Kennedy's inaugural gown, and George Washington's sword. Go to http://americanhistory.si.edu/ and click on "History Wired."*

ODD MUSEUMS

Leila's Hair Museum in Independence, Missouri, displays framed wreaths and more than 2,000 pieces of jewelry made from people's hair. The people all lived at least 100 years ago.

At the **Burlingame Museum of Pez Memorabilia** in Burlingame, California, you can find just about every plastic Pez candy dispenser ever made. They are all for sale. Prices range from $2.00 for Pez currently sold in stores to $1,300 for a special Mary Poppins dispenser.

The **Pretzel Museum** in Philadelphia, Pennsylvania, celebrates the art and history of pretzel-making, which dates back to Europe in the 6th century. Bakers demonstrate their craft. Best of all, visitors get to make and eat their own pretzels.

The **Mutter Museum** in Philadelphia, Pennsylvania, is filled with strange and disgusting medical wonders. One fascinating but gross exhibit shows coins, buttons, and other objects that have been removed from people's stomachs. Another displays brains, tumors, and other body parts of famous people.

The **Teddy Bear Museum** in Stratford-upon-Avon, England, is home to hundreds of stuffed teddy bears. Jim Henson's original Fozzie Bear Muppet is there. So is Christopher Robin Milne's bear, which inspired the stories of Winnie-the-Pooh.

The **American Sanitary Plumbing Museum** in Worcester, Massachusetts, may not be very glamorous. But its exhibits on the history of toilets, sinks, and pipes help prove how indoor plumbing has made our lives healthier and happier.

The **Cookie Jar Museum** in Lemont, Illinois, is devoted to cookie jars. There are no cookies, just jars—2,000 of them!

NATIONAL AIR AND SPACE MUSEUM

During 2002, the National Air and Space Museum celebrates its 25th birthday with a year-long party of special exhibits and events. There are paper airplane contests, kite-making workshops, and interviews with space shuttle astronauts. Even if you do not visit in 2002, there are amazing aircraft and spacecraft on display all the time, such as:

▲ The Wright Flyer

The Wright Flyer, the first successful airplane, flown by Orville Wright on December 17, 1903, at Kitty Hawk, North Carolina.

The Spirit of St. Louis, the aircraft flown by Charles A. Lindbergh on May 21, 1927, on the first nonstop flight across the Atlantic Ocean from New York to Paris. You can also check out lunar exploration vehicles or visit the Albert Einstein Planetarium.

Mercury Friendship 7, the first American-built spacecraft to orbit the Earth. It was flown for just under 5 hours by astronaut John H. Glenn Jr., on February 20, 1962.

Viking Lander, the first spacecraft to operate on Mars (July 20, 1976).

You can find these flying machines in the Milestones in Flight Gallery, but there are 22 other major galleries as well. The museum is at 7th and Independence Avenue, SW, Washington, D.C. Visit the museum online at **WEB SITE** *http://www.nasm.si.edu.*

MUSIC & DANCE

Who is the youngest perfomer to have a #1 song? ➤page 126

MUSICAL INSTRUMENTS

There are many kinds of musical instruments. Instruments in an orchestra are divided into four groups, or sections: string, woodwind, brass, and percussion.

PERCUSSION INSTRUMENTS make sounds when they are struck. This group includes drums, cymbals, triangles, gongs, bells, and xylophone. Keyboard instruments, like the piano, are sometimes thought of as percussion instruments.

▲ clarinet

WOODWINDS are long and round and hollow inside. They make sounds when air is blown into them through a mouth hole or a reed. The clarinet, flute, oboe, bassoon, and piccolo are woodwinds.

▲ trumpet

BRASSES are hollow inside. They make sounds when air is blown into a mouthpiece shaped like a cup or a funnel. The trumpet, French horn, trombone, and tuba are brasses.

▲ violin

STRINGED INSTRUMENTS make sounds when the strings are either stroked with a bow or plucked with the fingers. The violin, viola, cello, bass, and harp are used in an orchestra. The guitar, banjo, and mandolin are other stringed instruments.

▲ snare drum

INSTRUMENTS FROM ALL OVER

AFRICA—Sometimes called a "thumb piano," the **lamellophone** (also *sanza* or *mbira*) is an ancient instrument from central and southern Africa. It is played by plucking strips of metal or bamboo attached to a wooden plate or soundbox.

AUSTRALIA—The **didgeridoo** is a large tube of eucalyptus wood or bamboo. Players must breathe in through the nose while blowing out through the mouth. It has a deep, buzzing sound.

The didgeridoo ▶

INDIA—The **sitar** is a long-necked instrument with as many as 17 strings. The artist Ravi Shankar made Indian music popular in the West when he taught Beatle George Harrison how to play the sitar.

JAPAN—The **shakuhachi** is an ancient type of flute made from the root end of a bamboo stalk. With a simple structure and only five fingerholes, it produces a wide range of subtle musical tones.

MUSIC and MUSIC MAKERS

▶POP Pop music (short for popular music) puts more emphasis on melody (tune) than does rock and has a softer beat. **Famous pop singers:** Frank Sinatra, Barbra Streisand, Madonna, Michael Jackson, Mariah Carey, Brandy, 'N Sync, Destiny's Child, Jennifer Lopez, Britney Spears.

▶RAP and HIP-HOP In rap, words are spoken or chanted to a fast, hip-hop beat, with the emphasis on rhythm rather than melody. Rap was created in inner cities. The lyrics show strong feelings and may be about anger and violence. Hip-hop often includes "samples," which are pieces of music from other songs. **Famous rappers:** Coolio, LL Cool J, TLC, The Fugees, Will Smith, Nelly, Jay-Z. (For more about rap, see page 126).

▶JAZZ Jazz has its roots in the work songs, spirituals, and folk music of African-Americans. It began in the South in the early 1900s. **Famous jazz artists:** Louis Armstrong, Fats Waller, Jelly Roll Morton, Duke Ellington, Benny Goodman, Billie Holiday, Sarah Vaughan, Ella Fitzgerald, Dizzy Gillespie, Charlie Parker, Miles Davis, John Coltrane, Thelonious Monk, Wynton Marsalis.

▶ROCK (also known as Rock 'n' Roll) Rock music, which started in the 1950s, is based on black rhythm and blues and country music. It often uses electronic instruments and equipment. Folk rock, punk, heavy metal, and alternative music are types of rock music. **Famous rock musicians:** Elvis Presley, Bob Dylan, Chuck Berry, The Beatles, Janis Joplin, The Rolling Stones, Joni Mitchell, Bruce Springsteen, Pearl Jam, Matchbox 20.

▶BLUES The music called "the blues" developed from work songs and religious folk songs (spirituals) sung by African-Americans. It was introduced early in the 1900s by African-American musicians. Blues songs are usually sad. (A type of jazz is also called "the blues.") **Famous blues performers:** Ma Rainey, Bessie Smith, Billie Holiday, B. B. King, Muddy Waters, Robert Johnson, Howling Wolf, Etta James.

TOP ALBUMS of 2001

1. *1,* The Beatles
2. *Hotshot,* Shaggy
3. *Black & Blue,* Backstreet Boys
4. *Now 5,* Various Artists
5. *Chocolate Starfish and the Hot Dog Flavored Water,* Limp Bizkit
6. *Hybrid Theory,* Linkin Park
7. *Break the Cycle,* Staind
8. *A Day Without Rain,* Enya
9. *Celebrity,* 'N Sync
10. *Country Grammar,* Nelly

The Beatles in 1964 ▶

ROCK AND ROLL HALL OF FAME

The Rock and Roll Hall of Fame and Museum, located in Cleveland, Ohio, honors rock-and-roll musicians with exhibits and multi-media presentations. Musicians cannot be included until 25 years after their first record. Isaac Hayes, Brenda Lee, Tom Petty and the Heartbreakers, and the Talking Heads were among the performers added in 2002.

►**COUNTRY** American country music is based on Southern mountain music. Blues, jazz, and other musical styles have also influenced it. Country music became popular through the *Grand Ole Opry* radio show in Nashville, Tennessee, during the 1920s. **Famous country artists:** Hank Williams, Willie Nelson, Vince Gill, Reba McEntire, Tim McGraw, Faith Hill, Lee Ann Womack, Billy Gilman.

►**CLASSICAL** Often more complex than other types of music, classical music is based on European musical traditions that go back several hundred years. Common forms of classical music include the symphony, chamber music, opera, and ballet music. **Famous early classical composers:** Johann Sebastian Bach, Ludwig van Beethoven, Johannes Brahms, Franz Joseph Haydn, Wolfgang Amadeus Mozart, Franz Schubert, Peter Ilyich Tchaikovsky. **Famous modern classical composers:** Aaron Copland, Virgil Thomson, Igor Stravinsky.

►**OPERA** An opera is a play whose words are sung to music. The music is played by an orchestra. The words of an opera are called the libretto, and a long song sung by one character (like a speech in a play) is called an aria. **Famous operas:** *The Barber of Seville* (Gioacchino Rossini); *Madama Butterfly* (Giacomo Puccini); *Aida* (Giuseppe Verdi); *Porgy and Bess* (George Gershwin).

►**CHAMBER** Chamber music is written for a small group of musicians, often only three (a trio) or four (a quartet), to play together. In chamber music, each instrument plays a separate part. A string quartet (music written for two violins, viola, and cello) is an example of chamber music. Other instruments, such as a piano, are sometimes part of a chamber group.

SYMPHONY
A symphony is music written for an orchestra. The sections of a symphony are called movements.

VOICE
Human voices have a range in pitch from low to high. For men, the low end is called the bass (pronounced like base), followed by baritone, and tenor. The range for women goes from contralto (the lowest) up to alto, mezzo-soprano, and soprano. The next time you listen to a singer, try to figure out his or her range.

MUSICAL NOTATION
These are some of the symbols composers use when they write music.

treble clef	𝄞	half note	♩
bass clef	𝄢	quarter note	♩
sharp	♯	eighth note	♪
flat	♭	sixteenth note	♬
natural	♮	whole rest	▬
whole note	o	half rest	▬

AMERICAN MUSICALS

American musical theater uses singing, dancing, and music to tell stories in exciting ways. People come from all over to see musicals on Broadway, New York City's theater district. Musicals are also staged in many other places. Some musicals start as movies, or are made into movies. A few famous musicals are listed here. The date after the show's name is the year it opened on Broadway.

Aida (2000), a rock musical by Linda Wolverton, Tim Rice, and Elton John. In the Egyptian room of a modern museum, Amneris, once a queen of the ancient kingdom, brings the audience back to a time when war raged between Egypt and its southern neighbor, Nubia.

Annie (1977), by Charles Strouse and Martin Charnin. Here's how Little Orphan Annie was adopted by Daddy Warbucks. One featured song: "Tomorrow." Tony Award 1977.

Beauty and the Beast (1994), by Alan Menkin, Howard Ashman, and Tim Rice. First it was a story. Then it was a movie in French. Then it became an animated movie musical. Now the tale of Belle and the Beast she came to love is brought to life on a stage.

Cats (1982), by Andrew Lloyd Webber. Based on poems about all kinds of cats written by T.S. Eliot, this play closed in 2000 after a record 7,485 performances. Its best-known song was "Memory." Tony Award 1983.

Contact (2000), by Susan Stroman and John Weidman. The show consists of three short stories told mostly through dance. In each the main character hopes to find true love. A 2000 Tony Award winner.

The Lion King (1997), by Elton John, Tim Rice, Mark Mancina, Roger Allers, and Irene Meechi. Based on the animated Disney movie, this show uses masks and puppets to tell the story of animals progressing through "The Circle of Life." Tony Award 1998.

The Producers (2001), by Mel Brooks. What happens when you set out to make a flop? That's what the producers plan as a crazy way to get rich quick. Based on Mel Brooks's 1967 film of the same name, *The Producers* won a record 12 Tony Awards in 2001.

West Side Story (1957), by Leonard Bernstein and Stephen Sondheim. This groundbreaking show used music and dance to update the story of Romeo and Juliet to the West Side of Manhattan in New York City.

All About... HIP-HOP

Rap music with a hip-hop beat became popular in the mid-1970s among African American and Hispanic performers in New York City. It first went with an athletic style of dancing called breakdancing. The word *rap*, which comes from a slang word for "conversation," generally consists of chanted street poetry, often made up as you go along. Critics say rap music sometimes promotes violence. But many admire the clever way rappers like Public Enemy and KRS-1 use street talk to make people more aware of social issues. Lil' Romeo, an 11-year-old rapper, who is popular with kids, recently became the youngest artist in history to reach number one in the charts with his single "My Baby." In 2001, rappers Nas, Reverend Run of the group Run-DMC, and hundreds of others attended the world's first Hip-Hop Youth Summit in New York City.

DANCE

Dancers perform patterns of movement, usually to music or rhythm. Dance may be a form of art, or part of a religious ceremony. Or it may be done just for entertainment.

▶BALLET Ballet is a kind of dance based on formal steps. The movements are often graceful and flowing. Ballets are almost always danced to music, are performed for an audience, and often tell a story. In the 15th century, ballet was part of the elaborate entertainment performed for the rulers of Europe. In the 1600s, professional dance companies existed, but without women; women's parts were danced by men wearing masks. In the 1700s dancers wore bulky costumes and shoes with high heels. Women danced in hoopskirts—and so did men! In the 1800s ballet steps and costumes began to look the way they do now. Many of the most popular ballets today date back to the middle or late 1800s.

▶BALLROOM DANCING Ballroom, or social, dancing involves dances done for fun by ordinary people. Social dancing has been around since at least the Middle Ages, when it was popular at fairs and festivals. In the 1400s social dance was part of fancy court pageants. It developed into dainty ballroom dances like the minuet and the waltz during the 1700s. More recent new dances include the Charleston, lindy, twist, and tango, as well as disco dancing, break dancing, line dancing, and dances such as the macarena and electric slide.

▶MODERN DANCE Modern dance differs from classical ballet. It is often less concerned with graceful, flowing movement and with stories. Modern dance steps are often not performed in traditional ballet. Dancers may put their bodies into awkward, angular positions and turn their backs on the audience. Many modern dances are based on ancient art, such as Greek sculpture, or on dance styles found in Africa and Asia.

▶FOLK DANCE Folk dance is the term for a dance that is passed on from generation to generation and is part of the culture or way of life of people from a particular country or ethnic group. Virginia reel (American), czardas (Hungarian), jig, and the Israeli hora are some folk dances.

Some Famous Ballets

THE SLEEPING BEAUTY This 1890 ballet was the first ballet Anna Pavlova saw when she was a young girl in Russia, and it inspired her to become one the greatest ballerinas of all time. It carries the audience into a mystical world where spells are cast and a fairy comes to the aid of a handsome prince. Tchaikovsky composed the beautiful score.

SWAN LAKE First danced in St. Petersburg, Russia, in 1895 to music by Tchaikovsky. Perhaps the most popular ballet ever, *Swan Lake* is the story of a prince and his love for a maiden who was turned into a swan by an evil magician.

GISELLE *Giselle* is a classic romantic ballet that is as popular now as when it was first performed over 160 years ago (1841). It combines drama and dancing with mystery, romance, and magic. Adolphe Adam composed the music.

THE RIVER This 1970 ballet by Alvin Ailey is danced to music by the jazz musician Duke Ellington. It has been described as a celebration of life.

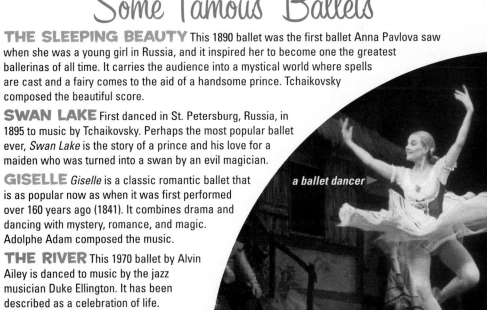

a ballet dancer ▶

NATIONS

What country lies inside the city of Rome? ➤page 165

KIDS AROUND THE WORLD

AFGHANISTAN

Under the Taliban, the Muslim fundamentalist group that ruled Afghanistan for 6 years, there were many strict rules. For example, girls were not allowed to go to school. When the Taliban were overthrown in 2001, life remained hard. Many families still live in crowded mud houses, with no heat in winter and not enough food. Many kids still can't go to school because they have to do chores like getting water or taking care of farm animals. Still, kids like the ones here riding a homemade Ferris wheel find time to have fun. They play games like hide and seek and *topay-danda*, a kind of stickball. Kite flying was forbidden under the Taliban but has become popular again.

CANADA

The first people in Canada were the Micmac Indians and the Inuit, or Eskimos, who came to Canada from Asia thousands of years ago. Like the kids in this picture, many native people still live there. In the 1600s, Canada was settled by French and British fur traders. Today it is a bilingual country. English and French are both official languages, and many Canadians can speak both languages. Canada is bigger than the United States but has only one-ninth as many people. Three out of four people live in urban areas, but there is plenty of open space. Most of the land is covered in snow all winter. Ice hockey, skiing, and curling are popular sports.

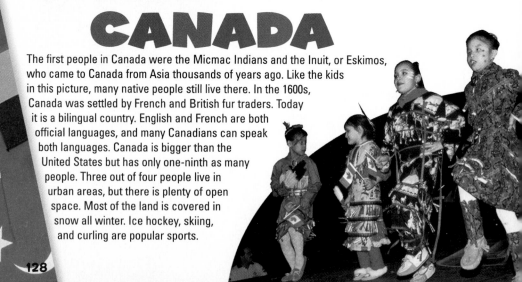

INDONESIA

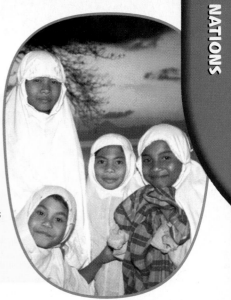

Indonesia is made up of more than 13,000 islands. It has people from many different ethnic groups. They speak over 250 languages. Most of Indonesia's 230 million people are Muslims, like these kids. Families in rural areas often live in small houses on platforms, with a ladder to get in and out. This helps protect from floods. Relatives usually live near each other and do lots of things together. Indonesian kids like video games, cartoons, and Harry Potter. Their favorite sports include soccer, badminton, and a kind of volleyball called *sepak takraw*.

JAMAICA

Jamaica is an island in the Caribbean Sea. Most Jamaicans are descendents of slaves brought from West Africa for Spanish and British colonists. Most of the people today speak a dialect, or local version, of English. It is a mixture of English with African languages, Spanish, and French. Storytelling is a big part of the traditional culture. Anansi the spider, who uses his cleverness to outsmart bigger opponents, is famous in Jamaican folklore. Jamaica enjoys warm weather all year round and is a popular vacation spot. Kids there like to play soccer, go snorkeling, and compete in track and field. Dominoes is a popular game.

PERU

The kids shown here live in the Andes Mountains. In all, four out of five people in Peru are native or part native in ancestry. Many speak local languages at home, such as Quechua, the language of the ancient Incas. Most Peruvians are Catholics, and seven out of ten live in urban areas. Peruvians often live in extended families, with aunts, uncles, cousins, and grandparents. Soccer and volleyball are popular sports. In some villages where electricity is scarce, there is a TV in the town plaza which everybody can watch.

MAPS AND FLAGS OF THE NATIONS OF THE WORLD

Maps showing the continents and nations of the world appear on pages 130 through 141. Flags of the nations appear on pages 142 through 145.

A map of the United States appears on pages 266-267.

AUSTRALIA

- ⍟ National Capital
- ★ State Capital
- • Other City

1:40,886,000

0   250   500 mi

0   250   500 km

Two-Point Equidistant Projection

©MAPQUEST.COM

PACIFIC ISLANDS

⊛ National Capital

★ Territorial Capital

● Other City

1:84,569,000

| 0 | 500 | 1,000 mi |

| 0 | 500 | 1,000 km |

Miller Projection

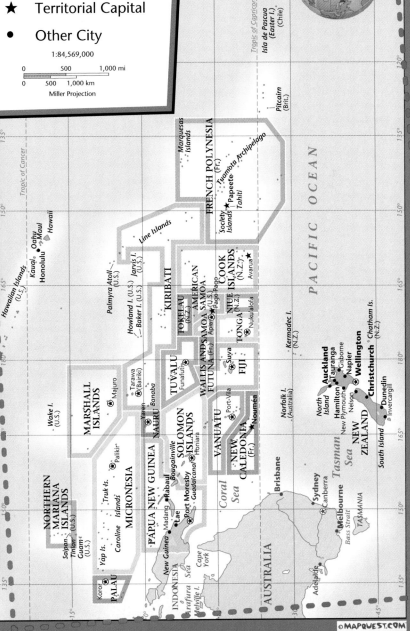

PACIFIC OCEAN

Tropic of Capricorn

Sala y Gomez (Chile)

Isla de Pascua (Easter I.) (Chile)

Pitcairn (Brit.)

Tropic of Cancer

Marquesas Islands

FRENCH POLYNESIA (Fr.)

Tuamotu Archipelago

Society Islands ★ Papeete Tahiti

Line Islands

Hawaiian Islands (U.S.)

Kauai Oahu Maui
Honolulu Hawaii

Palmyra Atoll (U.S.)

Howland I. (U.S.)
Baker I. (U.S.)

Jarvis I. (U.S.)

KIRIBATI

TOKELAU (N.Z.)

AMERICAN SAMOA (U.S.)
Pago Pago

COOK ISLANDS (N.Z.) ★ Avarua

NIUE (N.Z.)

Tarawa (Bairiki)

MARSHALL ISLANDS

Wake I. (U.S.)

Majuro

TUVALU
Funafuti

WALLIS AND FUTUNA (Fr.)

SAMOA ⊛ Apia

TONGA ⊛ Nuku'alofa

Kermadec I. (N.Z.)

NORTHERN MARIANA ISLANDS

Saipan
Tinian (U.S.)
Guam (U.S.)

Truk Is.
Caroline Islands

MICRONESIA

Yap Is.
Palikir

Banaba

Yaren NAURU

SOLOMON ISLANDS
Honiara

VANUATU
Port-Vila

FIJI
Suva

NEW CALEDONIA (Fr.)
★ Nouméa

Norfolk I. (Australia)

North Island
Auckland
Hamilton Tauranga
New Plymouth Gisborne
Nelson Napier
⊛ Wellington
Christchurch Chatham Is. (N.Z.)
Dunedin
Invercargill
South Island

NEW ZEALAND

Koror
PALAU

New Guinea

PAPUA NEW GUINEA
Rabaul
Madang Bougainville
Lae
Port Moresby Guadalcanal

Cape York

INDONESIA

Arafura Sea

Melville I.

Coral Sea

Brisbane

Tasman Sea

Sydney
Canberra ⊛

Melbourne

Bass Strait

TASMANIA

AUSTRALIA

Adelaide

© MapQuest.com

SWEDEN

NORWAY

GREAT BRITAIN

ICELAND

Spitsbergen

Greenland Sea

Denmark Strait

Cape Farewell

Arctic Circle

Tasiilaq

Nuuk (Godthaab)

GREENLAND (KALAALLIT NUNAAT) (Den.)

Labrador Sea

NEWFOUNDLAND

St. Anthony

Island of Newfoundland

St. John's

Corner Brook

St. Pierre & Miquelon Is. (Fr.)

Sydney

Anticosti I.

N.B.

NEW P.E.I.

BRUNS.

Happy Valley-Goose Bay

Labrador City

Scheffervile

QUÉBEC

Sept-Îles

Chibougamau

Chicoutimi

Hebron

Nord

Cape Morris Jessup

North Pole

Arctic Ocean

Knud Rasmussen Land

Qaanaaq (Thule)

Baffin Bay

Davis Strait

Pangnirtung

Iqaluit

Ungava Peninsula

Povungnituk

Belcher Is.

CANADIAN

SHIELD

ONTARIO

Alert

Ellesmere I.

Grise Fiord

Arctic Bay

Pond Inlet

Baffin Island

Repulse Bay

Hudson Strait

James Bay

Moosonee

Queen Elizabeth Islands

Resolute

Southampton I.

Hudson Bay

York Factory

Churchill

L. Winnipeg

Winnipeg

Banks I.

Victoria I.

Cambridge Bay

Holman

Kugluktuk

NUNAVUT

Yellowknife

Ft. Smith

Uranium City

MANITOBA

Thompson

Flin Flon

CANADA

Sachs Harbour

Great Bear L. (Grand lac de l'Ours)

Great Slave L. (Grand lac des Esclaves)

Fort Smith

Hay River

SASK.

Athabasca

La Loche

La Ronge

Prince Albert

Inuvik

Fort McPherson

Déline

NORTHWEST TERRITORIES

Ft. Simpson

L. Athabasca

Ft. McMurray

Edmonton

ALBERTA

Peace River

Saskatoon

Regina

Brandon

Mackenzie

Watson Lake

Fort Yukon

ALASKA

BROOKS RANGE

Point Barrow

Barrow

Kotzebue

Point Hope

Bering Strait

RUSSIA

Arctic Circle

Nome

Bethel

Yukon

Fairbanks

Dawson

Mayo

Carmacks

YUKON

Whitehorse

Skagway

Juneau

Sitka

Yakutat

Kenai

Seward

Kodiak

Valdez

Anchorage

Mt. McKinley 6,194 m. (20,320 ft.)

ALASKA RANGE

Gulf of Alaska

BRITISH COLUMBIA

Prince George

Jasper

Calgary

ROCKY

GREAT

Fraser

Columbia

COAST MOUNTAINS

Williams Lake

Prince Rupert

Queen Charlotte Is.

Kitimat

Ketchikan

Vancouver I.

Vancouver

Victoria

Seattle

Mt. Logan 5,959 m. (19,551 ft.)

Bering Sea

Arctic Circle

NORTH AMERICA

⊛ National Capital

★ Territorial Capital

• Other City

1:39,978,000

0   350   700 mi

0   350   700 km

Azimuthal Equal Area Projection

133

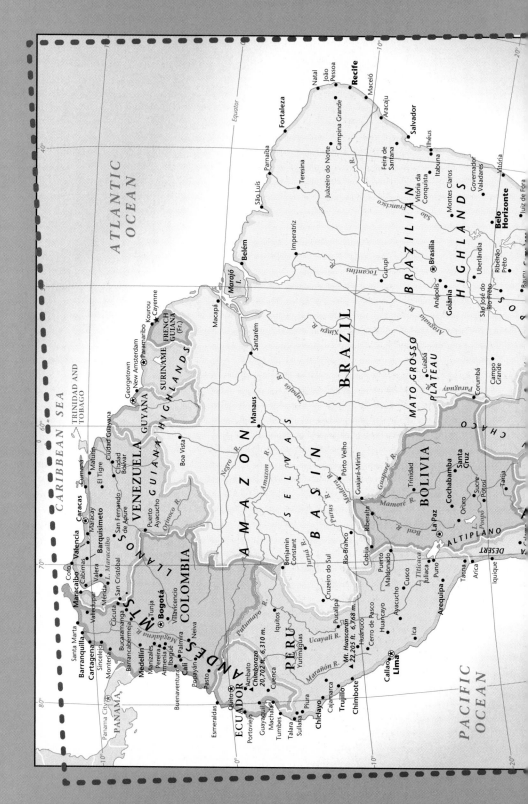

CARIBBEAN SEA

TRINIDAD AND
TOBAGO

ATLANTIC
OCEAN

PACIFIC
OCEAN

PANAMA

Panama City

Santa Marta
Barranquilla
Cartagena
Sincelejo
Montería

Coro
Maracaibo
Valencia
Cabimas
Valera
L. Maracaibo
Valledupar
Mérida
San Cristóbal

Caracas
Maracay
Barquisimeto
San Fernando de Apure

Cumaná
Maturín
El Tigre
Ciudad Guayana
Ciudad Bolívar

VENEZUELA

LLANOS

Puerto Ayacucho

Orinoco R.

Georgetown
New Amsterdam
Paramaribo
Cayenne
Kourou

SURINAME
FRENCH
GUIANA (Fr.)

GUIANA HIGHLANDS

Boa Vista

Macapá
Marajó I.

Belém

Santarém

Imperatriz

São Luís
Parnaíba
Teresina

Fortaleza

Natal
João Pessoa
Recife
Maceió
Aracaju

Campina Grande
Juazeiro do Norte

Salvador
Ilhéus
Itabuna

Feira de Santana
Vitória da Conquista
Montes Claros
Governador Valadares
Vitória

São Francisco R.

BRAZILIAN
HIGHLANDS

Belo Horizonte

Bucaramanga
Barrancabermeja
Medellín
Manizales
Pereira
Armenia
Ibagué
Cúcuta
Tunja
Bogotá
Villavicencio
Neiva

COLOMBIA

Magdalena R.

MTS.

Cali
Palmira
Popayán
Pasto
Buenaventura

ANDES

Esmeraldas
Quito
ECUADOR
Portoviejo
Ambato
Chimborazo 20,702 ft. 6,310 m.
Guayaquil
Machala
Cuenca
Tumbes
Talara
Sullana
Piura
Chiclayo
Cajamarca
Trujillo
Chimbote
Mt. Huascarán 22,205 ft. 6,768 m.

Putumayo R.

Iquitos
Yurimaguas
PERU
Huánuco
Cerro de Pasco
Huancayo
Ayacucho
Ica
Callao
Lima
Cusco
Puno
Arequipa
Tacna
Arica
Iquique

Pucallpa
Cruzeiro do Sul
Rio Branco
Cobija
Puerto Maldonado

Marañón R.
Ucayali R.

AMAZON

Manaus
Negro R.
Amazon R.

SELVAS
BASIN

Benjamin Constant
Juruá R.
Purus R.
Madeira R.
Pôrto Velho
Guajará-Mirim
Riberalta

Tapajós R.
Xingu R.
Tocantins R.
Araguaia R.

BRAZIL

Brasília
Anápolis
Goiânia
Uberlândia
Ribeirão Prêto
São José do Rio Prêto
Bauru

MATO GROSSO
PLATEAU

Cuiabá

Corumbá
Campo Grande

Paraguay R.

CHACO

Mamoré R.
Guaporé R.

Trinidad
BOLIVIA
Cochabamba
Santa Cruz
La Paz
Oruro
Sucre
Potosí
Tarija

Beni R.
Poopó

L. Titicaca
Juliaca

ALTIPLANO

DESERT

Equator

CENTRAL MTS.

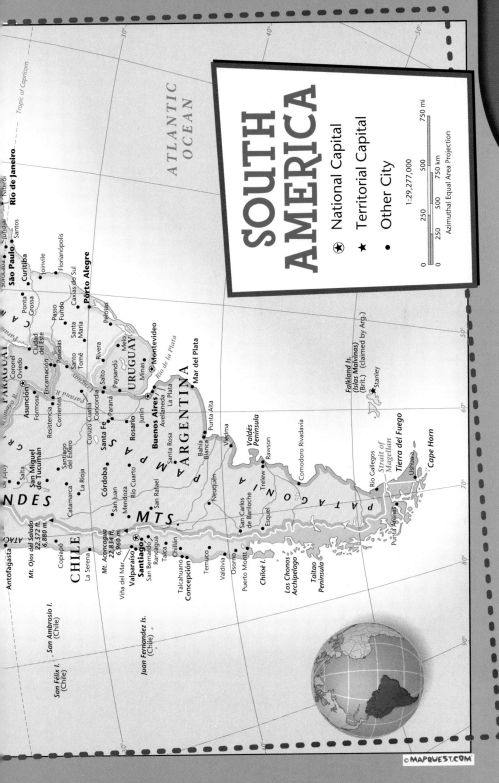

SOUTH AMERICA

⊛ National Capital

★ Territorial Capital

• Other City

1:29,277,000

| 0 | 250 | 500 | 750 km |
| 0 | 250 | 500 | 750 mi |

Azimuthal Equal Area Projection

ATLANTIC OCEAN

Tropic of Capricorn

Niterói
Rio de Janeiro
Santos
São Paulo
Sorocaba
Curitiba
Joinvile
Florianópolis
Ponta Grossa
Porto Alegre
Caxias do Sul
Passo Fundo
Santa Maria
Pelotas
PARAGUAY
Asunción
Coronel Oviedo
Ciudad del Este
Encarnación
Posadas
Santo Tomé
Rivera
Salto
Paysandú
Melo
URUGUAY
Minas
Montevideo
Formosa
Resistencia
Corrientes
Concordia
Paraná
La Plata
Mar del Plata
Santa Fe
Curuzú Cuatiá
Río de la Plata
Paraná R.
Uruguay R.
Bermejo R.
Pilcomayo R.
Paraná R.
Avellaneda
Buenos Aires
Rosario
Junín
San Miguel de Tucumán
Santiago del Estero
La Rioja
Río Cuarto
Santa Rosa
Punta Alta
Bahía Blanca
ARGENTINA
Córdoba
Catamarca
San Juan
Mendoza
San Rafael
Neuquén
Viedma
Valdés Peninsula
Rawson
Salta
G R A N   C H A C O
Antofagasta
ATAC.
Copiapó
La Serena
Mt. Ojos del Salado 22,572 ft. 6,880 m.
A N D E S   M T S.
Mt. Aconcagua 22,834 ft. 6,960 m.
CHILE
Viña del Mar
Valparaíso
San Bernardo
Rancagua
Santiago
Chillán
Talca
Curicó
Talcahuano
Concepción
Temuco
Valdivia
Osorno
Puerto Montt
Chiloé I.
Los Chonos Archipelago
Taitao Peninsula
San Carlos de Bariloche
Esquel
Trelew
Comodoro Rivadavia
P A T A G O N I A
Punta Arenas
Río Gallegos
Strait of Magellan
Tierra del Fuego
Ushuaia
Cape Horn
Falkland Is. (Islas Malvinas) (Brit.) (claimed by Arg.)
Stanley
San Ambrosio I. (Chile)
San Félix I. (Chile)
Juan Fernández Is. (Chile)

©MAPQUEST.COM

EUROPE

★ National Capital

• Other City

1:22,107,000

0   250   500 mi

0   250   500 km

Azimuthal Equal Area Projection

Reykjavík ·   Akureyri ·
ICELAND

Norwegian   *Sea*

Tromsø

Bodø

Faroe Is.
(Den.)

Trondheim

Shetland Is.
(Brit.)

NORWAY

Sundsvall

Bergen ·

Orkney
Is.

Stavanger ·

Oslo ★

SWEDEN

Uppsala ·

Hebrides

Aberdeen ·

Skagerrak

Linköping ·

Stockholm ★

Gotland

Glasgow ·
· Edinburgh

Belfast ·

GREAT BRITAIN
· Newcastle

Jutland   Århus ·

Göteborg ·

Öland

Dublin ·
IRELAND ★
Cork ·

Liverpool ·
(UNITED KINGDOM)
· Leeds
Manchester ·   · Sheffield

Irish
Sea

North
Sea

Copenhagen ★
DENMARK ·
Odense ·

· Helsingborg
· Malmö

Baltic

Birmingham ·

Cardiff ·
· Bristol

NETHERLANDS
Amsterdam ★

Gdańsk ·

Vistula

Hamburg ·

Szczecin ·

Land's End

Portsmouth ·

★ **London**

· Rotterdam

Bremen ·

Hannover ·

· Poznań

Berlin ★

GERMANY

Channel Is.
(Brit.)

English Channel
Le Havre ·

Antwerp ·
Brussels ★
Lille ·
BELGIUM · Liège

Essen ·
· Cologne
Bonn ·

Leipzig ·

· Dresden

Łódź

Brest ·

Rouen ·
LUXEMBOURG ·
Paris ★
Luxembourg ·

Frankfurt ·

Prague ★
CZECH REP.

· Wrocław

Katowice ★

Nantes ·

Loire

Strasbourg ·

Mannheim ·
Stuttgart ·

Brno ·
· Ostrava

Cape Finisterre

Gijón ·

Dijon ·

Bern ★
Zürich ·

Munich ·

Linz ·

SLOVAKIA

Vienna ★ Bratislava ·

Vigo ·

Bordeaux ·

FRANCE

Geneva ·
SWITZERLAND
Mt. Blanc
4807 m
(15,771 ft)

LIECHTENSTEIN

AUSTRIA

Graz ·

Budapest ★
HUNGARY

Porto ·

Bilbao ·

PORTUGAL

Valladolid ·

PYRENEES

Toulouse ·

Lyon ·

Verona ·
Milan ·
Turin ·

SLOVENIA
Ljubljana ·
Venice ·
Bologna ·

Pécs ·

DINARIC

Zagreb ·

CROATIA

IBERIAN

Zaragoza ·

Pico de Aneto
3404 m
(11,168 ft)

ANDORRA

Marseille ·
Toulon ·

Nice ·
MONACO
Genoa ·

Florence ·

Ligurian Sea

SAN
MARINO

BOSNIA &
HERZEGOVINA

Sarajevo ·

ALPS

Lisbon ★

Madrid ★

Cape
St. Vincent

Badajoz ·

Tagus

PENINSULA

Córdoba ·
· Sevilla

SPAIN

Valencia ·

Ebro

Barcelona ·

Balearic Sea

Majorca ·
Palma ·

Minorca ·

Corsica
(Fr.)

APENNINES

Elba

VATICAN
CITY

★ **Rome**

Split ·

Adriatic

Dubrovnik ·

Podgorica ·

Cádiz ·
Granada ·
· Alicante
· Málaga

Balearic Is.
(Sp.)

Sardinia
(It.)

Naples ·

ITALY

Bari ·

ATLANTIC
OCEAN

Cape
St. Vincent

Strait of
Gibraltar

GIBRALTAR (Brit.)

Mediterra

Cagliari ·

Tyrrhenian
Sea

Palermo ·

Salerno ·

Corfu

Ionian
Sea

Rabat ·
Casablanca ·

★ Algiers

MOROCCO

ATLAS

M O U N T A I N S

ALGERIA

Tunis ·

n *e* *a* *n*

Sea

Catania ·

Sicily

Mt. Etna
3323 m
(10,902 ft)

TUNISIA

Valletta ·
★ **MALTA**

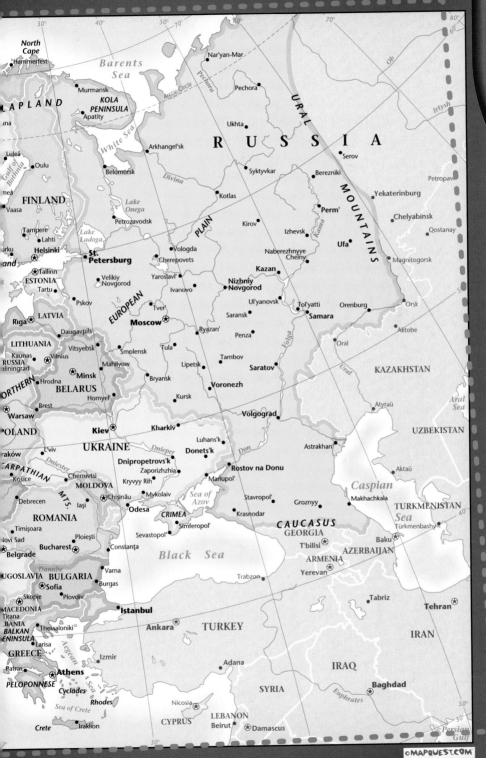

North Cape
Hammerfest
Barents Sea
Nar'yan-Mar
Ob
80°
60°
30°
40°
50°
70°
60°
70°

LAPLAND
Murmansk
KOLA PENINSULA
Apatity
Pechora
Pechora
URAL
Irtysh

una
White Sea
Ukhta
Petropavl

Luleå
Arkhangel'sk
R U S S I A
Arctic Circle
Serov

nea
Belomorsk
Syktyvkar
Berezniki
Yekaterinburg

FINLAND
Vaasa
Divina
Kotlas
Perm'
MOUNTAINS
Chelyabinsk

Tampere
Lahti
Lake Onega
Kirov
Izhevsk
Ufa
Kama
Qostanay

urku
Helsinki
Petrozavodsk
Naberezhnyye Chelny
Magnitogorsk

land
Lake Ladoga
Vologda
PLAIN
Kazan
5

Tallinn
St. Petersburg
Cherepovets
Nizhniy Novgorod

ESTONIA
Tartu
Velikiy Novgorod
Yaroslavl'
Ivanovo
Ul'yanovsk
Tol'yatti
Orenburg
Orsk

Pskov
EUROPEAN
Tver'
Samara

Riga
LATVIA
Moscow
Ryazan'
Saransk
Volga
Aktobe

Daugavpils
Penza

LITHUANIA
Vitsyebsk
Smolensk
Tula
Tambov
Oral

RUSSIA
Kaunas
Vilnius
Mahilyow
Lipetsk
Saratov
Ural
KAZAKHSTAN

aliningrad
Minsk
Bryansk
Voronezh

ORTHERN
Hrodna
BELARUS
Homyel'
Kursk
Atyraū
Aral Sea

Brest
Volgograd

Warsaw
Kiev
Kharkiv
Astrakhan
Aktaū
UZBEKISTAN

OLAND
Luhans'k
Don
Caspian

L'viv
UKRAINE
Dnieper
Donets'k

raków
Dniester
Dnipropetrovs'k
Zaporizhzhia
Makhachkala
TURKMENISTAN

ARPATHIAN
Chernivtsi
Kryyyy Rih
Rostov na Donu
Mariupol'
Sea
Türkmenbashy

Košice
MOLDOVA
Iași
Chişinău
Mykolaiv
Stavropol'
Groznyy
40°

Debrecen
Odesa
Sea of Azov
Krasnodar
CAUCASUS
GEORGIA
Baku

ROMANIA
CRIMEA
Simferopol'
T'bilisi
AZERBAIJAN

Timişoara
Sevastopol'
ARMENIA

ovi Sad
Bucharest
Constanța
Black Sea
Yerevan

Belgrade
Danube

UGOSLAVIA
BULGARIA
Varna
Trabzon
Tabriz

Sofia
Burgas
Tehran

Skopje
Plovdiv

MACEDONIA
Istanbul
IRAN

Tirana
Ankara
TURKEY

BANIA
Thessaloniki
IRAQ

ENINSULA
Larisa
Izmir
Adana

GREECE
SYRIA
Baghdad

Patras
Athens
Euphrates

PELOPONNESE
Cyclades
Rhodes
Nicosia
LEBANON
50°

Crete
Iraklion
Sea of Crete
CYPRUS
Beirut
Damascus
Persian Gulf
30°

©MAPQUEST.COM

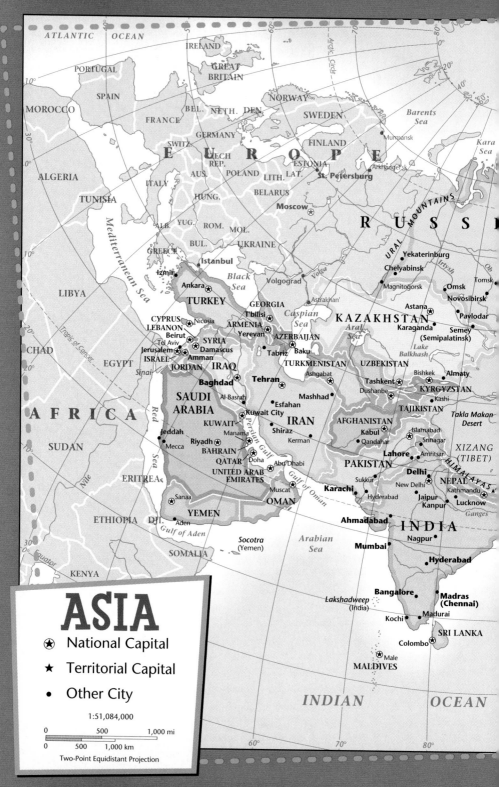

ATLANTIC OCEAN
IRELAND
PORTUGAL
GREAT BRITAIN
SPAIN
MOROCCO
FRANCE
BEL. NETH. DEN.
NORWAY
SWEDEN
Barents Sea
Murmansk
Kara Sea
ALGERIA
SWITZ.
GERMANY
CZECH REP.
FINLAND
ESTONIA
Arkhangel'sk
E U R O P E
AUS.
POLAND
LITH.
LAT.
St. Petersburg
ITALY
HUNG.
BELARUS
R U S S I
TUNISIA
ALB.
YUG.
ROM.
MOL.
Moscow
URAL MOUNTAINS
Yekaterinburg
LIBYA
GREECE
BUL.
UKRAINE
Istanbul
Chelyabinsk
Tomsk
Izmir
Black Sea
Volgograd
Volga
Magnitogorsk
Omsk
Novosibirsk
Mediterranean Sea
Ankara
Astrakhan'
Astana
Pavlodar
TURKEY
GEORGIA
T'bilisi
Caspian Sea
KAZAKHSTAN
CYPRUS
Nicosia
ARMENIA
Aral Sea
Karaganda
Semey (Semipalatinsk)
CHAD
LEBANON
Beirut
Tel Aviv
Yerevan
AZERBAIJAN
Lake Balkhash
Jerusalem
Damascus
Tabriz
Baku
TURKMENISTAN
UZBEKISTAN
Bishkek
Almaty
ISRAEL
SYRIA
Amman
Tehran
Tashkent
KYRGYZSTAN
EGYPT
JORDAN
IRAQ
Baghdad
Mashhad
Ashgabat
Dushanbe
Kashi
Sinai
Al-Basrah
Esfahan
TAJIKISTAN
Takla Makan Desert
SAUDI ARABIA
Kuwait City
IRAN
AFGHANISTAN
Islamabad
A F R I C A
Red Sea
KUWAIT
Manama
Shiraz
Kabul
Srinagar
XIZANG (TIBET)
SUDAN
Jeddah
Riyadh
Kerman
Qandahar
Lahore
Amritsar
Mecca
BAHRAIN
QATAR
Doha
PAKISTAN
Delhi
NEPAL
ERITREA
UNITED ARAB EMIRATES
Abu Dhabi
Gulf of Oman
Karachi
New Delhi
Kathmandu
Lucknow
Sanaa
Muscat
Hyderabad
Jaipur
ETHIOPIA
DJI.
Aden
OMAN
Ahmadabad
Kanpur
Ganges
Gulf of Aden
YEMEN
I N D I A
KENYA
Socotra (Yemen)
Arabian Sea
Nagpur
SOMALIA
Mumbai
Hyderabad
Lakshadweep (India)
Bangalore
Madras (Chennai)
Kochi
Madurai
SRI LANKA
Colombo
Male
MALDIVES
INDIAN OCEAN

Nile
Persian Gulf
Sukkur
Hyderabad

ASIA

⊛ National Capital

★ Territorial Capital

• Other City

1:51,084,000

0   500   1,000 mi

0   500   1,000 km

Two-Point Equidistant Projection

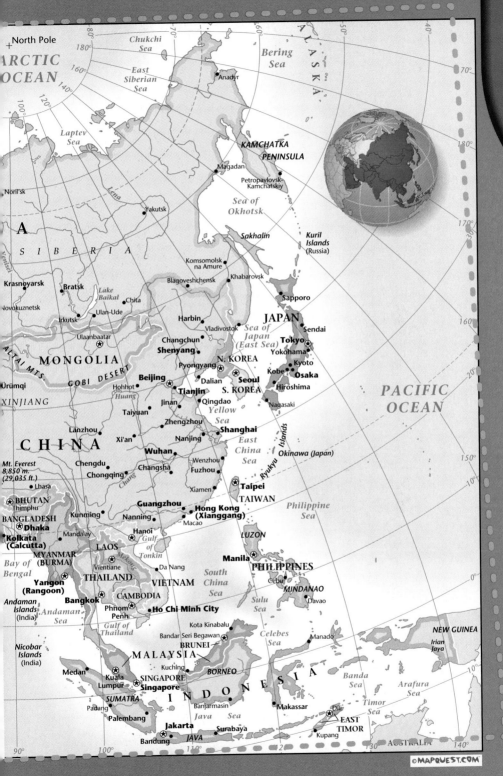

North Pole

ARCTIC OCEAN

Chukchi Sea

ALASKA

Bering Sea

East Siberian Sea

Anadyr

Laptev Sea

KAMCHATKA PENINSULA

Magadan

Petropavlovsk-Kamchatskiy

Noril'sk

Yakutsk

Sea of Okhotsk

A

SIBERIA

Sakhalin

Kuril Islands (Russia)

Krasnoyarsk

Bratsk

Lake Baikal

Chita

Komsomolsk na Amure

Khabarovsk

Sapporo

Novokuznetsk

Irkutsk

Ulan-Ude

Harbin

Vladivostok

JAPAN

Sendai

Ürümqi

Ulaanbaatar

Changchun

Sea of Japan (East Sea)

Tokyo

Yokohama

Kyoto

XINJIANG

MONGOLIA

GOBI DESERT

Shenyang

Pyongyang

N. KOREA

Kobe

Osaka

Beijing

Hohhot

Dalian

Seoul

Hiroshima

Huang

Tianjin

S. KOREA

Lanzhou

Taiyuan

Jinan

Qingdao

Nagasaki

CHINA

Xi'an

Zhengzhou

Yellow Sea

Shanghai

Nanjing

East China Sea

Mt. Everest 8,850 m. (29,035 ft.)

Chengdu

Wuhan

Wenzhou

Okinawa (Japan)

Lhasa

Chongqing

Changsha

Fuzhou

Ryukyu Islands

BHUTAN

Thimphu

Xiamen

Taipei

BANGLADESH

Dhaka

Kunming

Guangzhou

TAIWAN

Philippine Sea

Kolkata (Calcutta)

Mandalay

Nanning

Hong Kong (Xianggang)

Macao

LUZON

Bay of Bengal

MYANMAR (BURMA)

LAOS

Hanoi

Gulf of Tonkin

Manila

PHILIPPINES

Yangon (Rangoon)

THAILAND

Vientiane

VIETNAM

Da Nang

South China Sea

Cebu

MINDANAO

Andaman Islands (India)

Bangkok

CAMBODIA

Phnom Penh

Ho Chi Minh City

Sulu Sea

Davao

Andaman Sea

Gulf of Thailand

Kota Kinabalu

Manado

NEW GUINEA

Nicobar Islands (India)

MALAYSIA

Bandar Seri Begawan

BRUNEI

Celebes Sea

Irian Jaya

Medan

Kuching

BORNEO

INDONESIA

Banda Sea

Arafura Sea

Kuala Lumpur

SINGAPORE

Singapore

SUMATRA

Banjarmasin

Makassar

Timor Sea

Padang

Java Sea

Dili

Palembang

Jakarta

Surabaya

EAST TIMOR

Bandung

JAVA

Kupang

AUSTRALIA

PACIFIC OCEAN

©MAPQUEST.COM

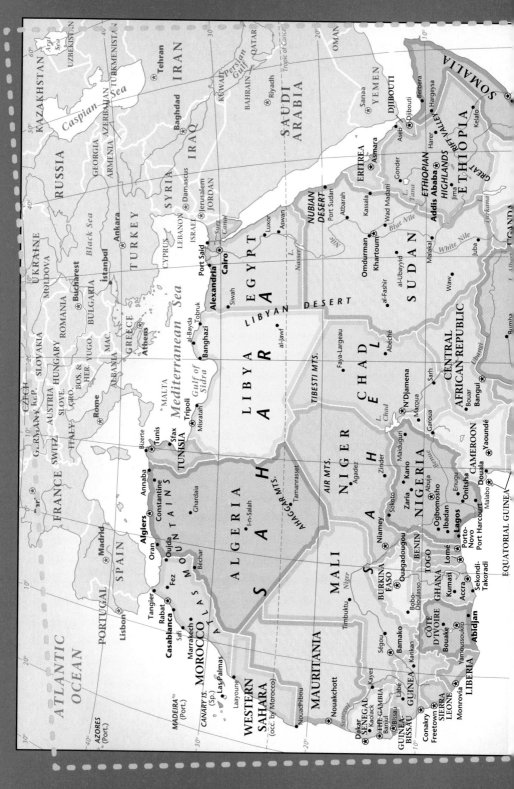

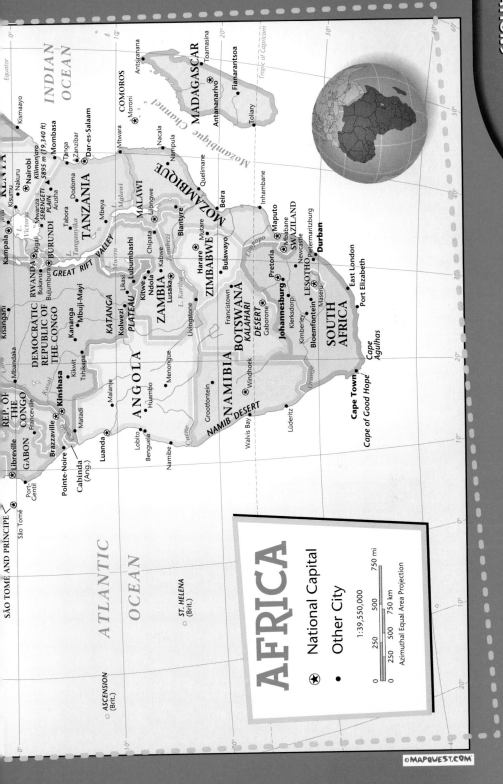

AFRICA

⊛ National Capital

• Other City

1:39,550,000

| 0 | 250 | 500 | 750 mi |
| 0 | 250 | 500 | 750 km |

Azimuthal Equal Area Projection

Map labels:

INDIAN OCEAN

Equator

Kismaayo

KENYA

Kampala ⊛ L. Victoria
Nakuru
Kisumu
Nairobi ⊛
Kilimanjaro ▲ 5895 m (19,340 ft)
Mombasa

COMOROS
Moroni ⊛
Mtwara

Dar-es-Salaam
Zanzibar
Tanga

MADAGASCAR
Antsiranana
Toamasina
Antananarivo ⊛
Fianarantsoa
Toliary
Tropic of Capricorn

Mozambique Channel

SERENGETI PLAIN
Mwanza
Arusha
Dodoma ⊛
TANZANIA
Tabora
Mbeya

RWANDA
Kigali ⊛
BURUNDI
Bujumbura ⊛
Bukavu
L. Tanganyika

Nacala
Nampula
Quelimane

MALAWI
Lilongwe ⊛
Blantyre
L. Malawi

MOZAMBIQUE
Beira
Inhambane
Maputo ⊛

GREAT RIFT VALLEY

DEMOCRATIC REPUBLIC OF THE CONGO
Kisangani
Mbandaka
L. Mweru
KATANGA PLATEAU
Kolwezi
Likasi
Lubumbashi
Ndola
Kitwe
Kabwe
ZAMBIA
Lusaka ⊛
L. Kariba
Livingstone
Kananga
Mbuji-Mayi

Kananga
Kikwit
Tshikapa
Kinshasa ⊛

REP. OF THE CONGO
Brazzaville ⊛
Franceville

GABON
Libreville ⊛
Port-Gentil

Pointe-Noire
Cabinda (Ang.)
Matadi

ANGOLA
Malanje
Luanda
Lobito
Benguela
Namibe
Huambo
Menongue

SÃO TOMÉ AND PRINCIPE
São Tomé

ATLANTIC OCEAN

ASCENSION (Brit.)

ST. HELENA (Brit.)

ZIMBABWE
Harare ⊛
Mutare
Bulawayo

BOTSWANA
Francistown
Gaborone ⊛
KALAHARI DESERT

NAMIBIA
Grootfontein
Windhoek ⊛
Walvis Bay
NAMIB DESERT
Lüderitz

Pretoria ⊛
Johannesburg ⊛
Klerksdorp
Newcastle
Kimberley
Bloemfontein ⊛
SOUTH AFRICA
SWAZILAND
Mbabane ⊛
Pietermaritzburg
Durban
LESOTHO
Maseru ⊛
East London
Port Elizabeth

Cape Town ⊛
Cape of Good Hope
Cape Agulhas

Limpopo
Orange

©MAPQUEST.COM

FLAGS of the NATIONS of the WORLD

(Afghanistan–Dominican Republic)

 AFGHANISTAN

 ALBANIA

 ALGERIA

 ANDORRA

 ANGOLA

 ANTIGUA AND BARBUDA

 ARGENTINA

 ARMENIA

 AUSTRALIA

 AUSTRIA

 AZERBAIJAN

 THE BAHAMAS

 BAHRAIN

 BANGLADESH

 BARBADOS

 BELARUS

 BELGIUM

 BELIZE

 BENIN

 BHUTAN

 BOLIVIA

 BOSNIA AND HERZEGOVINA

 BOTSWANA

 BRAZIL

 BRUNEI

 BULGARIA

 BURKINA FASO

 BURUNDI

 CAMBODIA

 CAMEROON

 CANADA

 CAPE VERDE

 CENTRAL AFRICAN REPUBLIC

 CHAD

 CHILE

 CHINA

 COLOMBIA

 COMOROS

 CONGO, DEMOCRATIC REP. OF THE

 CONGO, REP. OF THE

 COSTA RICA

 CÔTE D'IVOIRE

 CROATIA

 CUBA

 CYPRUS

 CZECH REPUBLIC

 DENMARK

DJIBOUTI

DOMINICA

DOMINICAN REPUBLIC

142

FLAGS of the NATIONS of the WORLD
(Ecuador–Lithuania)

 ECUADOR

 EGYPT

 EL SALVADOR

 EQUATORIAL GUINEA

 ERITREA

ESTONIA

 ETHIOPIA

 FIJI

FINLAND

FRANCE

GABON

THE GAMBIA

GEORGIA

GERMANY

 GHANA

GREECE

GRENADA

 GUATEMALA

GUINEA

 GUINEA-BISSAU

GUYANA

 HAITI

HONDURAS

HUNGARY

 ICELAND

 INDIA

INDONESIA

 IRAN

 IRAQ

 IRELAND

ISRAEL

ITALY

JAMAICA

JAPAN

 JORDAN

 KAZAKHSTAN

 KENYA

 KIRIBATI

 NORTH KOREA

 SOUTH KOREA

 KUWAIT

 KYRGYZSTAN

 LAOS

 LATVIA

 LEBANON

 LESOTHO

 LIBERIA

 LIBYA

 LIECHTENSTEIN

 LITHUANIA

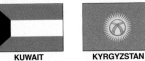

143

FLAGS of the NATIONS of the WORLD
(Luxembourg–Senegal)

 LUXEMBOURG

 MACEDONIA

 MADAGASCAR

 MALAWI

 MALAYSIA

 MALDIVES

 MALI

 MALTA

 MARSHALL ISLANDS

 MAURITANIA

 MAURITIUS

 MEXICO

 MICRONESIA

 MOLDOVA

 MONACO

 MONGOLIA

 MOROCCO

 MOZAMBIQUE

 MYANMAR (BURMA)

 NAMIBIA

 NAURU

 NEPAL

 NETHERLANDS

 NEW ZEALAND

 NICARAGUA

 NIGER

 NIGERIA

 NORWAY

 OMAN

 PAKISTAN

 PALAU

 PANAMA

 PAPUA NEW GUINEA

 PARAGUAY

 PERU

 PHILIPPINES

 POLAND

 PORTUGAL

 QATAR

 ROMANIA

 RUSSIA

 RWANDA

 ST. KITTS AND

 ST. LUCIA

 ST. VINCENT AND THE GRENADINES

 SAMOA

 SAN MARINO

 SÃO TOMÉ AND PRÍNCIPE

 SAUDI ARABIA

 SENEGAL

144

FLAGS of the NATIONS of the WORLD
(Seychelles–Zimbabwe)

SEYCHELLES

SIERRA LEONE

SINGAPORE

SLOVAKIA

SLOVENIA

SOLOMON ISLANDS

SOMALIA

SOUTH AFRICA

SPAIN

SRI LANKA

SUDAN

SURINAME

SWAZILAND

SWEDEN

SWITZERLAND

SYRIA

TAIWAN

TAJIKISTAN

TANZANIA

THAILAND

TOGO

TONGA

TRINIDAD AND TOBAGO

TUNISIA

TURKEY

TURKMENISTAN

TUVALU

UGANDA

UKRAINE

UNITED ARAB EMIRATES

UNITED KINGDOM (GREAT BRITAIN)

UNITED STATES

URUGUAY

UZBEKISTAN

VANUATU

VATICAN CITY

VENEZUELA

VIETNAM

YEMEN

YUGOSLAVIA

ZAMBIA

ZIMBABWE

FACTS ABOUT NATIONS

There are 193 nations in the world. The information for each of them goes across two pages. The left page gives the name and capital of each nation, its location, and its area. On the right page, the population column tells how many people lived in each country in 2001. The currency column shows the name of each nation's money and how much one United States dollar was worth there at the start of 2002. This column also shows which countries in Europe now use the euro, instead of their old currencies. The language column gives official languages and other common languages. The color next to the name of each nation matches the color for its continent on the map at right, and the background color for the corresponding map on pages 130-141.

NATION	CAPITAL	LOCATION OF NATION	AREA
Afghanistan	Kabul	Southern Asia, between Iran and Pakistan	250,000 sq. mi. (647,500 sq. km.)
Albania	Tiranë	Eastern Europe, between Greece and Yugoslavia	11,100 sq. mi. (28,750 sq. km.)
Algeria	Algiers	North Africa on the Mediterranean Sea, between Libya and Morocco	919,600 sq. mi. (2,381,740 sq. km.)
Andorra	Andorra la Vella	Europe, in the mountains between France and Spain	174 sq. mi. (450 sq. km.)
Angola	Luanda	Southern Africa on the Atlantic Ocean, north of Namibia	481,400 sq. mi. (1,246,700 sq. km.)
Antigua and Barbuda	St. John's	Islands on eastern edge of the Caribbean Sea	174 sq. mi. (440 sq. km.)
Argentina	Buenos Aires	Fills up most of the southern part of South America	1,068,300 sq. mi. (2,766,890 sq. km.)
Armenia	Yerevan	Western Asia, north of Turkey and Iran	11,500 sq. mi. (29,800 sq. km.)
Australia	Canberra	Continent south of Asia, between Indian and Pacific Oceans	2,967,910 sq. mi. (7,686,850 sq. km.)
Austria	Vienna	Central Europe, north of Italy	32,380 sq. mi. (83,860 sq. km.)
Azerbaijan	Baku	Western Asia, north of Iran	33,440 sq. mi. (86,600 sq. km.)
The Bahamas	Nassau	Islands in the Atlantic Ocean, east of Florida	5,380 sq. mi. (13,940 sq. km.)
Bahrain	Manama	In the Persian Gulf, near the coast of Qatar	240 sq. mi. (620 sq. km.)

POPULATION	CURRENCY	LANGUAGE	DID YOU KNOW?
27,755,775	$1 = 4,750 afghanis	Afghan Persian (Dari), Pashtu	Millions of landmines, buried during decades of war, litter the countryside.
3,544,841	$1 = 137 leks	Albanian, Greek	Mother Teresa of Calcutta was born here in 1910.
32,277,942	$1 = 76 dinars	Arabic, French, Berber Dialects	Algiers was a stronghold for Barbary pirates for 300 years.
68,403	$1 = 1.13 euros	Catalan, French, Castilian	Tiny Andorra is a major ski area in the Pyrenees Mountains.
10,593,171	$1 = 18 kwanzas	Portuguese, African dialects	In the 1400s, the Portuguese began trading slaves in Angola.
67,448	$1 = 2⅔ East Carribean dollars	English	Most of the people of the islands trace their roots to West Africa.
37,812,817	$1 = 1 peso	Spanish, English, Italian	Native cowboys, known as gauchos, are the folk heroes of Argentina.
3,330,099	$1 = 565 drams	Armenian	In 1988 an earthquake in Armenia killed 55,000 people.
19,546,792	$1 = 2 Australian dollars	English, aboriginal languages	Australia was founded as a British penal (prison) colony.
8,169,929	$1 = 1.13 euros	German	Most of Austria lies high in the eastern Alps of Europe.
7,798,497	$1 = 4,677 manats	Azeri, Russian, Armenian	Azerbaijan was once part of the Persian empire.
300,529	Bahamas dollar Same value as U.S. dollar	English, Creole	Only about 40 of the Bahamas' 700-plus islands are inhabited.
656,397	$1 = ⅜ dinars	Arabic, English, Farsi, Urdu	Bahrain was the center of a trading empire 3,000 years ago.

NATION	CAPITAL	LOCATION OF NATION	AREA
Bangladesh	Dhaka	Southern Asia, nearly surrounded by India	56,000 sq. mi. (144,000 sq. km.)
Barbados	Bridgetown	Island in the Atlantic Ocean, north of Trinidad	165 sq. mi. (430 sq. km.)
Belarus	Minsk	Eastern Europe, east of Poland	80,200 sq. mi. (207,600 sq. km.)
Belgium	Brussels	Western Europe, on the North Sea, south of the Netherlands	11,780 sq. mi. (30,510 sq. km.)
Belize	Belmopan	Central America, south of Mexico	8,860 sq. mi. (22,960 sq. km.)
Benin	Porto-Novo	West Africa, on the Gulf of Guinea, west of Nigeria	43,480 sq. mi. (112,620 sq. km.)
Bhutan	Thimphu	Asia, in the Himalaya Mountains, between China and India	18,000 sq. mi. (47,000 sq. km.)
Bolivia	La Paz	South America, in the Andes Mountains, next to Brazil	424,160 sq. mi. (1,098,580 sq. km.)
Bosnia and Herzegovina	Sarajevo	Southern Europe, on the Balkan Peninsula, west of Yugoslavia	19,740 sq. mi. (51,130 sq. km.)
Botswana	Gaborone	Southern Africa, between South Africa and Zambia	231,800 sq. mi. (600,370 sq. km.)
Brazil	Brasília	Occupies most of the eastern part of South America	3,286,490 sq. mi. (8,511,970 sq. km.)
Brunei	Bandar Seri Begawan	On the island of Borneo, northwest of Australia in the Pacific Ocean	2,230 sq. mi. (5,770 sq. km.)
Bulgaria	Sofia	Eastern Europe, on the Balkan Peninsula, bordering the Black Sea	42,820 sq. mi. (110,910 sq. km.)
Burkina Faso	Ouagadougou	West Africa, between Mali and Ghana	105,900 sq. mi. (274,200 sq. km.)
Burundi	Bujumbura	Central Africa, northwest of Tanzania	10,750 sq. mi. (27,830 sq. km.)
Cambodia	Phnom Penh	Southeast Asia, between Vietnam and Thailand	69,900 sq. mi. (181,040 sq. km.)
Cameroon	Yaoundé	Central Africa, between Nigeria and Central African Republic	183,570 sq. mi. (475,440 sq. km.)
Canada	Ottawa	Occupies the northern part of North America, north of the United States	3,851,810 sq. mi. (9,976,140 sq. km.)
Cape Verde (not on map)	Praia	Islands off the western tip of Africa	1,560 sq. mi. (4,030 sq. km.)
Central African Republic	Bangui	Central Africa, south of Chad	240,530 sq. mi. (622,984 sq. km.)

POPULATION	CURRENCY	LANGUAGE	DID YOU KNOW?
133,376,684	$1 = 57 takas	Bangla, English	Bangladesh declared independence from Pakistan in 1971.
276,607	$1 = 2 Barbados dollars	English	Barbados has about 5,000 so-called green monkeys that, when grown, have brownish-green fur.
10,335,382	$1 = 1,618 rubles	Byelorussian, Russian	For some 200 years, Belarus was a battleground in Polish-Russian wars.
10,274,595	$1 = 1.13 euros	Flemish (Dutch), French, German	Belgium is one of the wealthiest nations in the world.
262,999	$1 = 2 Belize dollars	English, Spanish, Mayan, Garifuna	Belize was Great Britain's last colony on the American mainland.
6,787,625	$1 = 732 CFA francs	French, Fon, Yoruba	Benin was the name of an African kingdom founded in the 12th century.
2,094,176	$1 = 46¾ ngultrums	Dzongkha, Tibetan	Bhutan has 770 species of birds, as well as tigers, elephants, and snow leopards.
8,445,134	$1 = 7 Bolivianos	Spanish, Quechua, Aymara	Bolivia's Lake Titicaca is the largest lake in South America.
3,964,388	$1 = 2 mark	Serbo-Croatian	Before its independence in 1992, the country was part of Yugoslavia.
1,591,232	$1 = 7 pula	English, Setswana	The Kalahari Desert covers most of southwestern Botswana.
176,029,560	$1 = 2 real	Portuguese, Spanish, English	Brazil, the world's 5th-largest country, spans nearly half of South America.
350,898	$1 = 2 Brunei dollars	Malay, English, Chinese	Tiny Brunei once ruled over all of Borneo and part of the Philippines.
7,621,337	$1 = 2 leva	Bulgarian	In the Middle Ages, Bulgaria became an important center of Slavic culture.
12,603,185	$1 = 732 CFA francs	French, tribal languages	The literacy rate in Burkina Faso (19%) is among the lowest in the world.
6,373,002	$1 = 851 francs	Kirundi, French, Swahili	The pygmy Twa people were the first people to live in this region.
12,775,324	$1 = 3,835 riels	Khmer, French	The ruined "lost city" of Angkor was discovered by the outside world in 1858.
16,184,748	$1 = 732 CFA francs	English, French	Mt. Cameroon is the highest mountain in West Africa.
31,902,268	$1 = 1½ Canadian dollars	English, French	The Canada/U.S. boundary is the world's longest undefended border.
408,760	$1 = 119 escudos	Portuguese, Crioulo	Pico do Cano is the only volcano still active on these volcanic islands.
3,642,739	$1 = 732 CFA francs	French, Sangho, Arabic, Hunsa, Swahili	The Central African Republic is one of Africa's least developed countries.

NATION	CAPITAL	LOCATION OF NATION	AREA
Chad	N'Djamena	North Africa, south of Libya	496,000 sq. mi. (1,284,000 sq. km.)
Chile	Santiago	Along the western coast of South America	292,260 sq. mi. (756,950 sq. km.)
China	Beijing	Occupies most of the mainland of eastern Asia	3,705,410 sq. mi. (9,596,960 sq. km.)
Colombia	Bogotá	Northwestern South America, southeast of Panama	439,740 sq. mi. (1,138,910 sq. km.)
Comoros	Moroni	Islands between Madagascar and the east coast of Africa	840 sq. mi. (2,170 sq. km.)
Congo, Democratic Republic of the	Kinshasa	Central Africa, north of Angola and Zambia	905,570 sq. mi. (2,345,410 sq. km.)
Congo, Republic of the	Brazzaville	Central Africa, east of Gabon	132,000 sq. mi. (342,000 sq. km.)
Costa Rica	San José	Central America, south of Nicaragua	19,700 sq. mi (51,100 sq. km.)
Côte d'Ivoire (Ivory Coast)	Yamoussoukro	West Africa, on the Gulf of Guinea, west of Ghana	124,500 sq. mi. (322,460 sq. km.)
Croatia	Zagreb	Southern Europe, south of Hungary	21,830 sq. mi. (56,540 sq. km.)
Cuba	Havana	In the Caribbean Sea, south of Florida	42,800 sq. mi. (110,860 sq. km.)
Cyprus	Nicosia	Island in the Mediterranean Sea, off the coast of Turkey	3,570 sq. mi. (9,250 sq. km.)
Czech Republic	Prague	Central Europe, south of Poland, east of Germany	30,350 sq. mi. (78,870 sq. km.)
Denmark	Copenhagen	Northern Europe, between the Baltic Sea and North Sea	16,640 sq. mi. (43,090 sq. km.)
Djibouti	Djibouti	North Africa, on the Gulf of Aden, across from Saudi Arabia	8,500 sq. mi. (22,000 sq. km.)
Dominica	Roseau	Island in the Caribbean Sea	290 sq. mi. (750 sq. km.)
Dominican Republic	Santo Domingo	On an island, along with Haiti, in the Caribbean Sea	18,810 sq. mi. (48,730 sq. km.)
East Timor	Dili	Part of an island in the South Pacific Ocean, north of Australia	5,740 sq. mi. (14,880 sq. km.)
Ecuador	Quito	South America, on the equator, bordering the Pacific Ocean	109,480 sq. mi. (283,560 sq. km.)
Egypt	Cairo	Northeastern Africa, on the Red Sea and Mediterranean Sea	386,660 sq. mi. (1,001,450 sq. km.)

POPULATION	CURRENCY	LANGUAGE	DID YOU KNOW?
8,997,237	$1 = 732 CFA francs	French, Arabic, Sara, Sango	Lake Chad, on the western border, grows smaller year by year.
15,498,930	$1 = 545 pesos	Spanish	Incas ruled northern Chile before the Spanish conquest in the 1600s.
1,284,303,705	$1 = 8¼ renminbis	Mandarin, Yue, Wu, Hakka	The giant panda, native to western China, is an endangered species.
41,008,227	$1 = 2,301 pesos	Spanish	Colombia is the world's principal source of emeralds.
614,382	$1 = 548 francs	Arabic, French, Comorian	Ylang-ylang, a major export, is a perfume made from a native tree.
55,225,478	$1 = 313 Congolese francs	French	In 2002, a volcanic eruption destroyed the large city of Goma.
2,958,448	$1 = 732 CFA francs	French, Lingala, Kikongo	Bantu peoples of the Congo have lived there since before A.D. 1000.
3,834,934	$1 = 342 colones	Spanish	More than 725 species of birds are native to Costa Rica.
16,804,784	$1 = 732 CFA francs	French, Dioula	The world's tallest cathedral was built in Yamoussoukro in the 1980s.
4,390,751	$1 = 8 kunas	Serbo-Croatian	One of Europe's oldest drugstores still stands today in the city of Dubrovnik.
11,224,321	$1 = 1 peso	Spanish	The U.S. has leased a naval base at Guantánamo Bay since 1903.
767,314	$1 = ⅗ pound	Greek, Turkish, English	Center of a kingdom in the 7th century B.C., Nicosia is one of the world's oldest cities.
10,256,760	$1 = 36 koruny	Czech, Slovak	The Czech Republic and Slovakia formed a single country, from 1918 to 1993.
5,368,854	$1 = 8³⁄₁₀ kronor	Danish, Faroese	"Little Mermaid" author Hans Christian Andersen was a Dane.
472,810	$1 = 170 Djibouti francs	French, Arabic, Afar, Somali	Djibouti is on a dangerous strait, the Bab al-Mandab ("gate of tears").
70,158	$1 = 2⅔ EC dollars	English, French patois	Dominica was sighted and named by Christopher Columbus in 1493.
8,721,594	$1 = 16½ pesos	Spanish	The country's Pico Duarte is the highest mountain in the West Indies.
871,000	U.S. dollar	English, Portuguese, Bahasa Indonesia, Tetum	Full independence for East Timor was scheduled for May 2002.
13,447,494	$1 = U.S. dollar	Spanish, Quechua	The Galápagos Islands in the Pacific make up a province of Ecuador.
70,712,345	$1 = 4½ pounds	Arabic, English, French	The pyramids at Giza are the oldest of the 7 wonders of the world.

NATION	CAPITAL	LOCATION OF NATION	AREA
El Salvador	San Salvador	Central America, southwest of Honduras	8,120 sq. mi. (21,040 sq. km.)
Equatorial Guinea	Malabo	West Africa, on the Gulf of Guinea, off the west coast of Cameroon	10,830 sq. mi. (28,050 sq. km.)
Eritrea	Asmara	Northeast Africa, north of Ethiopia	46,840 sq. mi. (121,320 sq. km.)
Estonia	Tallinn	Northern Europe, on the Baltic Sea, north of Latvia	17,460 sq. mi. (45,230 sq. km.)
Ethiopia	Addis Ababa	East Africa, east of Sudan	435,190 sq. mi. (1,127,130 sq. km.)
Fiji	Suva	Islands in the South Pacific Ocean, east of Australia	7,050 sq. mi. (18,270 sq. km.)
Finland	Helsinki	Northern Europe, between Sweden and Russia	130,130 sq. mi. (337,030 sq. km.)
France	Paris	Western Europe, between Germany and Spain	211,210 sq. mi. (547,030 sq. km.)
Gabon	Libreville	Central Africa, on the Atlantic coast, south of Cameroon	103,350 sq. mi. (267,670 sq. km.)
The Gambia	Banjul	West Africa, on the Atlantic Ocean, surrounded by Senegal	4,400 sq. mi. (11,300 sq. km.)
Georgia	Tbilisi	Western Asia, south of Russia, on the Black Sea	26,900 sq. mi. (69,700 sq. km.)
Germany	Berlin	Central Europe, northeast of France	137,890 sq. mi. (357,020 sq. km.)
Ghana	Accra	West Africa, on the southern coast	92,100 sq. mi. (238,540 sq. km.)
Greece	Athens	Southern Europe, in the southern part of the Balkan Peninsula	50,940 sq. mi. (131,940 sq. km.)
Grenada	Saint George's	Island on the eastern edge of the Caribbean Sea	130 sq. mi. (340 sq. km.)
Guatemala	Guatemala City	Central America, southeast of Mexico	42,040 sq. mi. (108,890 sq. km.)
Guinea	Conakry	West Africa, on the Atlantic Ocean, north of Sierra Leone	94,930 sq. mi. (245,860 sq. km.)
Guinea-Bissau	Bissau	West Africa, on the Atlantic Ocean, south of Senegal	13,950 sq. mi. (36,120 sq. km.)
Guyana	Georgetown	South America, on the northern coast, east of Venezuela	83,000 sq. mi. (214,970 sq. km.)
Haiti	Port-au-Prince	On an island, along with Dominican Republic, in the Caribbean Sea	10,710 sq. mi. (27,750 sq. km.)

POPULATION	CURRENCY	LANGUAGE	DID YOU KNOW?
6,353,681	$1 = 8¾ colones	Spanish	The country is the smallest and most populous in Central America.
498,144	$1 = 732 CFA francs	Spanish, French, Fang, Bubi	Malabo is located on an island in the Gulf of Guinea.
4,465,651	$1 = 13.5 nakfa	Tigrinya, Tigre, Kunama, Afar	Eritrea was once an important African colony of Italy.
1,415,681	$1 = 17½ kroons	Estonian, Russian	Estonia is the smallest and farthest north of the 3 Baltic States.
67,673,031	$1 = 8⅖ birr	Amharic, Tigrinya, Orominga	Ethiopia was once part of the ancient African Kingdom of Aksum.
856,346	$1 = 2⅛ Fiji dollars	English, Fijian, Hindustani	Only about 100 of Fiji's more than 300 islands and islets are inhabited.
5,183,545	$1 = 1.13 euros	Finnish, Swedish	Nearly one-third of Finland lies north of the Arctic Circle.
59,765,983	$1 = 1.13 euros	French	Known for its art, culture, and beauty, Paris is called the "City of Light."
1,233,353	$1 = 732 CFA francs	French, Bantu dialects	Three-quarters of Gabon is covered by a dense rain forest.
1,455,842	$1 = 17½ dalasi	English, Mandinka, Wolof	The Gambia is surrounded on three sides by the country of Senegal.
4,960,951	$1 = 2 laris	Georgian, Russian	Georgia is situated at the crossroads of Europe and Asia.
83,251,851	$1 = 1.13 euros	German	Hunters and gatherers lived in Germany 400,000 years ago.
20,244,154	$1 = 7,500 cedis	English, Akan, Ewe, Moshi-Dagomba, Ga	Ghana's Lake Volta is one of the largest man-made lakes in the world.
10,645,343	$1 = 1.13 euros	Greek, English, French	Ancient Greeks believed that Mt. Olympus was the home of the gods.
89,211	$1 = 2¾ EC dollars	English, French patois	Grenada is the smallest independent nation in the Western Hemisphere.
13,314,079	$1 = 8 quetzals	Spanish, Mayan languages	Guatemala was the center of the Mayan Empire (3rd-10th cent. AD).
7,775,065	$1 = 1,965 francs	French, tribal languages	More than one-third of the world's reserves of bauxite are in Guinea.
1,345,479	$1 = 732 CFA francs	Portuguese, Crioulo	Life-expectancy is 47 years for men and 51 for women.
698,209	$1 = 180 Guyana dollars	English, Amerindian dialects	Kaieteur Falls is one of the highest single-drop waterfalls in the world.
7,063,722	$1 = 26 gourdes	Haitian Creole, French	Haiti is the 2nd-oldest republic, after the U.S., in the Western Hemisphere.

NATION	CAPITAL	LOCATION OF NATION	AREA
Honduras	Tegucigalpa	Central America, between Guatemala and Nicaragua	43,280 sq. mi. (112,090 sq. km.)
Hungary	Budapest	Central Europe, north of Yugoslavia	35,920 sq. mi. (93,030 sq. km.)
Iceland	Reykjavik	Island off the coast of Europe, in the North Atlantic Ocean	40,000 sq. mi. (103,000 sq. km.)
India	New Delhi	Southern Asia, on a large peninsula on the Indian Ocean	1,269,350 sq. mi. (3,287,590 sq. km.)
Indonesia	Jakarta	Islands south of Southeast Asia, along the equator	705,190 sq. mi. (1,826,440 sq. km.)
Iran	Tehran	Southern Asia, between Iraq and Pakistan	636,000 sq. mi. (1,648,000 sq. km.)
Iraq	Baghdad	In the Middle East, between Syria and Iran	168,750 sq. mi. (437,070 sq. km.)
Ireland	Dublin	Off Europe's coast, in the Atlantic Ocean, west of Great Britain	27,140 sq. mi. (70,280 sq. km.)
Israel	Jerusalem	In the Middle East, between Jordan and the Mediterranean Sea	8,020 sq. mi. (20,770 sq. km.)
Italy	Rome	Southern Europe, jutting out into the Mediterranean Sea	116,310 sq. mi. (301,230 sq. km.)
Jamaica	Kingston	Island in the Caribbean Sea, south of Cuba	4,240 sq. mi. (10,990 sq. km.)
Japan	Tokyo	Four big islands and many small ones, off the east coast of Asia	145,880 sq. mi. (377,840 sq. km.)
Jordan	Amman	In the Middle East, south of Syria, east of Israel	35,300 sq. mi. (91,540 sq. km.)
Kazakhstan	Astana	Central Asia, south of Russia	1,049,200 sq. mi. (2,717,300 sq. km.)
Kenya	Nairobi	East Africa, on the Indian Ocean, south of Ethiopia	224,960 sq. mi. (582,650 sq. km.)
Kiribati	Tarawa	Islands in the middle of the Pacific Ocean, near the equator	280 sq. mi. (720 sq. km.)
Korea, North	Pyongyang	Eastern Asia, in the northern part of the Korean Peninsula	46,540 sq. mi. (120,540 sq. km.)
Korea, South	Seoul	Eastern Asia, south of North Korea, on the Korean Peninsula	38,020 sq. mi. (98,480 sq. km.)
Kuwait	Kuwait City	In the Middle East, on the northern end of the Persian Gulf	6,880 sq. mi. (17,820 sq. km.)
Kyrgyzstan	Bishkek	Western Asia, between Kazakhstan and Tajikistan	76,600 sq. mi. (198,500 sq. km.)

POPULATION	CURRENCY	LANGUAGE	DID YOU KNOW?
6,560,608	$1 = 16 lempiras	Spanish	About 90% of Hondurans are mestizo (of Spanish and Indian ancestry).
10,075,034	$1 = 272 forints	Hungarian (Magyar)	In 1872 the communities of Buda and Pest united as the city of Budapest.
279,384	$1 = 101 kronor	Icelandic (Islenska)	Iceland is home to more than 100 volcanoes and vast lava fields.
1,045,845,226	$1 = 48⅕ rupees	Hindi, English	More than 1,600 languages or dialects are spoken in India.
232,073,071	$1 = 10,415 rupiah	Bahasa Indonesian, English, Dutch	Indonesia is home to the komodo dragon, largest lizard in the world.
66,622,704	$1 = 1,750 rials	Persian (Farsi), Turkic, Luri	Many oases and forests enliven the great salt deserts of Iran.
24,001,816	$1 = ⅓ dinar	Arabic, Kurdish	In rural areas of Iraq, many people still live in tribal communities.
3,883,159	$1 = 1.13 euros	English, Gaelic	There are no serpents in Ireland, and the only reptile at all is the lizard.
6,029,529	$1 = 4½ new shekels	Hebrew, Arabic, English	The Dead Sea, on Israel's border, is almost 6 times as salty as the ocean.
57,715,625	$1 = 1.13 euros	Italian, German, French, Slovene	There are 2 independent countries inside Italy: San Marino and Vatican City.
2,680,029	$1 = 47 Jamaican dollars	English, Jamaican, Creole	Mountains cover four-fifths of Jamaica.
126,974,628	$1 = 131 yen	Japanese	More people live in Tokyo (26 million) than in any other city in the world.
5,307,470	$1 = ¾ dinar	Arabic, English	Philadelphia was the ancient name for Amman, Jordan's modern capital.
16,741,519	$1 = 151½ tenges	Kazakh, Russian	The shrinking Aral Sea was once the world's 4th-largest lake.
31,138,735	$1 = 79 shillings	Swahili, English	Kenya's diverse wildlife is protected in dozens of national parks.
96,335	$1 = 2 Australian dollars	English, Gilbertese	The nation's 33 islands are scattered over 2 million sq. mi. of ocean.
22,224,195	$1 = 2⅕ won	Korean	North Korea is rich in minerals but lacks enough food to feed its people.
48,324,000	$1 = 1,304 won	Korean	South Korea is known as one of East Asia's wealthy "Four Dragons."
2,111,561	$1 = ⅓ dinar	Arabic, English	The country gets its water supply by removing the salt from seawater.
4,822,166	$1 = 47⅖ soms	Kyrgyz, Russian	Ysyk Köl is the second-highest lake in the world, after Lake Titicaca.

NATION	CAPITAL	LOCATION OF NATION	AREA
Laos	Vientiane	Southeast Asia, between Vietnam and Thailand	91,400 sq. mi. (236,800 sq. km.)
Latvia	Riga	On the Baltic Sea, between Lithuania and Estonia	24,900 sq. mi. (64,590 sq. km.)
Lebanon	Beirut	In the Middle East, between the Mediterranean Sea and Syria	4,000 sq. mi. (10,400 sq. km.)
Lesotho	Maseru	Southern Africa, surrounded by the nation of South Africa	11,720 sq. mi. (30,350 sq. km.)
Liberia	Monrovia	Western Africa, on the Atlantic Ocean, southeast of Sierra Leone	43,000 sq. mi. (111,370 sq. km.)
Libya	Tripoli	North Africa, on the Mediterranean Sea, to the west of Egypt	679,360 sq. mi. (1,759,540 sq. km.)
Liechtenstein	Vaduz	Southern Europe, in the Alps between Austria and Switzerland	60 sq. mi. (160 sq. km.)
Lithuania	Vilnius	Northern Europe, on the Baltic Sea, east of Poland	25,200 sq. mi. (65,200 sq. km.)
Luxembourg	Luxembourg	Western Europe, between France and Germany	1,000 sq. mi. (2,590 sq. km.)
Macedonia	Skopje	Southern Europe, north of Greece	9,780 sq. mi. (25,330 sq. km.)
Madagascar	Antananarivo	Island in the Indian Ocean, off the east coast of Africa	226,660 sq. mi. (587,040 sq. km.)
Malawi	Lilongwe	Southern Africa, south of Tanzania and east of Zambia	45,750 sq. mi. (118,480 sq. km.)
Malaysia	Kuala Lumpur	Southeast tip of Asia and the north coast of the island of Borneo	127,320 sq. mi. (329,750 sq. km.)
Maldives	Male	Islands in the Indian Ocean, south of India	115 sq. mi. (300 sq. km.)
Mali	Bamako	West Africa, between Algeria and Mauritania	480,000 sq. mi. (1,240,000 sq. km.)
Malta	Valletta	Island in the Mediterranean Sea, south of Italy	120 sq. mi. (320 sq. km.)
Marshall Islands	Majuro	Chain of small islands in the middle of the Pacific Ocean	70 sq. mi. (181 sq. km.)
Mauritania	Nouakchott	West Africa, on the Atlantic Ocean, north of Senegal	398,000 sq. mi. (1,030,700 sq. km.)
Mauritius (not on map)	Port Louis	Islands in the Indian Ocean, east of Madagascar	720 sq. mi. (1,860 sq. km.)
Mexico	Mexico City	North America, south of the United States	761,610 sq. mi. (1,972,550 sq. km.)

POPULATION	CURRENCY	LANGUAGE	DID YOU KNOW?
5,777,180	$1 = 7,600 kip	Lao, French, English	Elephants are used as beasts of burden in Laos.
2,366,515	$1 = ⅗ lat	Lettish, Lithuanian	A moat, built in medieval times, surrounds the old section of Riga.
3,677,780	$1 = 1,513 pounds	Arabic, French, English, Armenian	Beirut is found in recorded history as early as the 15th century BC.
2,207,954	$1 = 12 maloti	English, Sesotho	Diamonds are Lesotho's chief export.
3,288,198	Same value as U.S. dollar	English, tribal languages	Liberia's pygmy hippopotamus is half the size of the common hippo.
5,368,585	$1 = ⅗ dinar	Arabic, Italian, English	Much of Libya lies within the great Sahara Desert.
32,842	$1 = 1⅗ Swiss francs	German, Alemanic dialect	Many international corporations have their headquarters in Liechtenstein.
3,601,138	$1 = 4 litas	Lithuanian, Polish, Russian	A Lithuanian-American, Valdas Adamkus, became president in 1998.
448,569	$1 = 1.13 euros	French, German	The duchy's capital city is located on the ruins of a Roman settlement.
2,054,800	$1 = 67⅓ denar	Macedonian, Albanian	The principal religion of Macedonia is Eastern Orthodox.
16,473,477	$1 = 6,364 francs	Malagasy, French	The island of Madagascar is the 4th largest in the world.
10,701,824	$1 = 67 kwacha	English, Chichewa	Lakes cover nearly one-fourth of Malawi.
22,662,365	$1 = 3⅘ ringgits	Malay, English, Chinese dialects	The Petronas Towers in the capital are the tallest buildings in the world.
320,165	$1 = 11¾ rufiyaas	Maldivian, Divehi, English	None of the more than 1,000 islands of the country is larger than 5 sq. mi.
11,340,480	$1 = 732 CFA francs	French, Bambara	The ancient empire of Mali extended as far west as the Atlantic Ocean.
397,499	$1 = ⅖ Maltese lira	Maltese, English	Malta is the 4th most densely populated country in the world.
73,630	U.S. dollar	English, Marshallese	More than 800 species of fish thrive in the waters of the Marshalls.
2,828,858	$1 = 269 ouguiya	Hasaniya Arabic, Wolof, Pular	Little plant life and few animals exist in the Sahara in northern Mauritania.
1,200,206	$1 = 30¼ Mauritian rupees	English, French, Creole, Hindi	The island of Mauritius is almost entirely enclosed by coral reefs.
103,400,165	$1 = 9⅕ new pesos	Spanish, Mayan dialects	Mexico City is built on the site of the Aztec settlement of Tenochtitlán.

NATION	CAPITAL	LOCATION OF NATION	AREA
Micronesia	Palikir	Islands in the western Pacific Ocean	270 sq. mi. (700 sq. km.)
Moldova	Chisinau	Eastern Europe, between Ukraine and Romania	13,000 sq. mi. (33,700 sq. km.)
Monaco	Monaco	Europe, on the Mediterranean Sea, surrounded by France	3/4 of a sq. mi. (2 sq. km.)
Mongolia	Ulaanbaatar	Central Asia between Russia and China	604,000 sq. mi. (1,565,000 sq. km.)
Morocco	Rabat	Northwest Africa, on the Atlantic Ocean and Mediterranean Sea	172,410 sq. mi. (446,550 sq. km.)
Mozambique	Maputo	Southeastern Africa, on the Indian Ocean	309,500 sq. mi. (801,590 sq. km.)
Myanmar (Burma)	Yangon (Rangoon)	Southern Asia, to the east of India and Bangladesh	262,000 sq. mi. (678,500 sq. km.)
Namibia	Windhoek	Southwestern Africa, on the Atlantic Ocean, west of Botswana	318,700 sq. mi. (825,420 sq. km.)
Nauru	Yaren district	Island in the western Pacific Ocean, just below the equator	8 sq. mi. (21 sq. km.)
Nepal	Kathmandu	Asia, in the Himalaya Mountains, between China and India	54,400 sq. mi. (140,800 sq. km.)
Netherlands	Amsterdam	Northern Europe, on the North Sea, to the west of Germany	16,030 sq. mi. (41,530 sq. km.)
New Zealand	Wellington	Islands in the Pacific Ocean east of Australia	103,740 sq. mi. (268,680 sq. km.)
Nicaragua	Managua	Central America, between Honduras and Costa Rica	50,000 sq. mi. (129,490 sq. km.)
Niger	Niamey	North Africa, south of Algeria and Libya	489,000 sq. mi. (1,267,000 sq. km.)
Nigeria	Abuja	West Africa, on the southern coast between Benin and Cameroon	356,670 sq. mi. (923,770 sq. km.)
Norway	Oslo	Northern Europe, on the Scandinavian Peninsula	125,180 sq. mi. (324,220 sq. km.)
Oman	Muscat	On the Arabian Peninsula, southeast of Saudi Arabia	82,030 sq. mi. (212,460 sq. km.)
Pakistan	Islamabad	South Asia, between Iran and India	310,400 sq. mi. (803,940 sq. km.)
Palau	Koror	Islands in North Pacific Ocean, southeast of Philippines	180 sq. mi. (460 sq. km.)
Panama	Panama City	Central America, between Costa Rica and Colombia	30,200 sq. mi. (78,200 sq. km.)

POPULATION	CURRENCY	LANGUAGE	DID YOU KNOW?
135,869	U.S. dollar	English, Trukese, Pohnpeian, Yapese	The U.S. is pledged to defend Micronesia, which has no army.
4,434,547	$1 = 13 leu	Moldovan, Russian	Moldova was at times part of Romania and the Soviet Union.
31,987	$1 = 1.13 euros	French, English, Italian	This rich but tiny country is the most densely populated in the world.
2,694,432	$1 = 1,102 tugriks	Khalkha Mongolian	Rugged Mongolia is the world's most sparsely populated country.
31,167,783	$1 = 11½ dirhams	Arabic, Berber dialects	Morocco has the broadest plains and highest mountains in North Africa.
19,607,519	$1 = 22,800 meticals	Portuguese, native dialects	The nation has 10 major ethnic groups, and none forms a majority.
42,238,224	$1 = 6¾ kyats	Burmese	Myanmar is widely known as the Land of Golden Pagodas.
1,820,916	$1 = 12 dollars	Afrikaans, English, German	Namibia is the second-most thinly populated country
12,329	$1 = 2 Australian dollars	Nauruan, English	Australian currency is the legal tender (money) used in Nauru.
25,873,917	$1 = 76⅗ rupees	Nepali, many dialects	A mysterious creature called the yeti is said to roam Nepal's mountain peaks.
16,067,754	$1 = 1.13 euros	Dutch	Much of the nation is below sea level and protected by dikes.
3,908,037	$1 = 2⅕ NZ dollars	English, Maori	Some 1,500 of the nation's plants grow nowhere else in the world.
5,023,818	$1 = 13¾ gold cordobas	Spanish	The country's Caribbean and Pacific coasts are more than 200 mi. long.
10,639,744	$1 = 742⅓ CFA francs	French, Hausa, Djerma	Niger was once part of noted ancient and medieval African empires.
129,934,911	$1 = 117 nairas	English, Hausa, Yoruba, Ibo	Once the capital, Lagos is Nigeria's largest and most important city.
4,525,116	$1 = 9 kroner	Norwegian	The Vikings were Norwegian sea rovers, traders, and explorers.
2,713,462	$1 = ⅜ rial Omani	Arabic	The average annual rainfall in Oman is generally less than 4 in. (100 mm.).
147,663,429	$1 = 60⅔ rupees	Urdu, English, Punjabi, Sindhi	K2, the world's 2nd-highest peak, is in the Hindu Kush in Pakistan.
19,409	U.S. dollar	English, Palauan	Palau has one of the smallest populations in the world.
2,882,329	$1 = 1 balboa	Spanish, English	Ships pay an average of $28,000 to pass through the Panama Canal.

NATION	CAPITAL	LOCATION OF NATION	AREA
Papua New Guinea	Port Moresby	Part of the island of New Guinea, north of Australia	178,700 sq. mi. (462,840 sq. km.)
Paraguay	Asunción	South America, between Argentina and Brazil	157,050 sq. mi. (406,750 sq. km.)
Peru	Lima	South America, along the Pacific coast, north of Chile	496,230 sq. mi. (1,285,220 sq. km.)
Philippines	Manila	Islands in the Pacific Ocean, off the coast of Southeast Asia	115,830 sq. mi. (300,000 sq. km.)
Poland	Warsaw	Central Europe, on the Baltic Sea, east of Germany	120,730 sq. mi. (312,680 sq. km.)
Portugal	Lisbon	Southern Europe, on the Iberian Peninsula, west of Spain	35,670 sq. mi. (92,390 sq. km.)
Qatar	Doha	Arabian Peninsula, on the Persian Gulf	4,420 sq. mi. (11,440 sq. km.)
Romania	Bucharest	Southern Europe, on the Black Sea, north of Bulgaria	91,700 sq. mi. (237,500 sq. km.)
Russia	Moscow	Stretches from Eastern Europe across northern Asia to the Pacific Ocean	6,592,800 sq. mi. (17,075,200 sq. km.)
Rwanda	Kigali	Central Africa, northwest of Tanzania	10,170 sq. mi. (26,340 sq. km.)
Saint Kitts and Nevis	Basseterre	Islands in the Caribbean Sea, near Puerto Rico	100 sq. mi. (260 sq. km.)
Saint Lucia	Castries	Island on eastern edge of the Caribbean Sea	240 sq. mi. (620 sq. km.)
Saint Vincent and the Grenadines	Kingstown	Islands on eastern edge of the Caribbean Sea, north of Grenada	150 sq. mi. (390 sq. km.)
Samoa (formerly Western Samoa)	Apia	Islands in the South Pacific Ocean	1,100 sq. mi. (2,860 sq. km.)
San Marino	San Marino	Southern Europe, surrounded by Italy	23 sq. mi. (60 sq. km.)
São Tomé and Príncipe	São Tomé	In the Gulf of Guinea, off the coast of West Africa	390 sq. mi. (1,000 sq. km.)
Saudi Arabia	Riyadh	Western Asia, occupying most of the Arabian Peninsula	756,990 sq. mi. (1,960,580 sq. km.)
Senegal	Dakar	West Africa, on the Atlantic Ocean, south of Mauritania	75,750 sq. mi. (196,190 sq. km.)
Seychelles (not on map)	Victoria	Islands off the coast of Africa, in the Indian Ocean	180 sq. mi. (460 sq. km.)
Sierra Leone	Freetown	West Africa, on the Atlantic Ocean, south of Guinea	27,700 sq. mi. (71,740 sq. km.)

POPULATION	CURRENCY	LANGUAGE	DID YOU KNOW?
5,172,633	$1 = 3⅔ kinas	English, Motu	More than 700 languages are spoken by hundreds of isolated tribes
5,884,491	$1 = 4,635 guarani	Spanish, Guarani	Paraguay named a state in honor of U.S. President Rutherford Hayes.
27,949,639	$1 = 3½ new soles	Spanish, Quechua, Aymara	Macchu Picchu, the "Lost City of the Incas," lies in the Peruvian Andes.
84,525,639	$1 = 43 pesos	Pilipino, English	The Philippine islands are the tops of an underwater mountain mass.
38,625,478	$1 = 4 zlotys	Polish	More than 9,300 lakes dot the Polish countryside.
10,084,245	$1 = 1.13 euros	Portuguese	Portugal is one of the world's largest producers of cork.
793,341	$1 = 3⅔ riyals	Arabic, English	Qatar is a flat desert region, where plant life of any kind is scarce.
22,317,730	$1 = 32,112 leu	Romanian, Hungarian	Bucharest was known as "the Paris of the East" for its beauty and culture.
144,978,573	$1 = 30½ rubles	Russian, many others	Lake Baykal, the world's deepest freshwater lake, is in Siberia.
7,398,074	$1 = 454 francs	French, English, Kinyarwanda,	The source of the Nile River has been located in Rwanda.
38,736	$1 = 2⅔ EC dollars	English	In 1493, Columbus named St. Kitts for his patron, St. Christopher.
160,145	$1 = 2⅔ EC dollars	English, French patois	Bananas are the principal export of this island country.
116,394	$1 = 2⅔ EC dollars	English, French patois	Soufrière, an active volcano in the north, last erupted in 1979.
178,631	$1 = 3½ tala	English, Samoan	Native tradition holds that the Polynesian race originated in Samoa.
27,730	$1 = 1.13 euros	Italian	San Marino is the 5th-smallest country in the world.
170,372	$1 = 8,937 dobras	Portuguese	Almost half the population of this country is under the age of 15.
23,513,330	$1 = 3¾ riyals	Arabic	More than half of the country is desert, and there are no permanent rivers.
10,589,571	$1 = 732 CFA francs	French, Wolof	Senegal is among the world's largest producers of peanuts.
80,098	$1 = 5⅔ rupees	English, French, Creole	French planters and their slaves first settled in the Seychelles in 1768.
5,614,743	$1 = 2,015 leones	English, Mende, Temne, Krio	Freetown was founded in 1787 as a haven for freed slaves.

NATION	CAPITAL	LOCATION OF NATION	AREA
Singapore	Singapore	Mostly on one island, off the tip of Southeast Asia	250 sq. mi. (650 sq. km.)
Slovakia	Bratislava	Eastern Europe, between Poland and Hungary	18,860 sq. mi. (48,850 sq. km.)
Slovenia	Ljubljana	Eastern Europe, between Austria and Croatia	7,820 sq. mi. (20,250 sq. km.)
Solomon Islands	Honiara	Western Pacific Ocean	10,980 sq. mi. (28,450 sq. km.)
Somalia	Mogadishu	East Africa, east of Ethiopia	246,200 sq. mi. (637,660 sq. km.)
South Africa	Pretoria (admin.) Cape Town (legisl.)	At the southern tip of Africa	471,010 sq. mi. (1,219,910 sq. km.)
Spain	Madrid	Europe, south of France, on the Iberian Peninsula	194,890 sq. mi. (504,780 sq. km.)
Sri Lanka	Colombo	Island in the Indian Ocean, southeast of India	25,330 sq. mi. (65,610 sq. km.)
Sudan	Khartoum	North Africa, south of Egypt, on the Red Sea	967,500 sq. mi. (2,505,810 sq. km.)
Suriname	Paramaribo	South America, on the northern shore, east of Guyana	63,040 sq. mi. (163,270 sq. km.)
Swaziland	Mbabane	Southern Africa, almost surrounded by South Africa	6,700 sq. mi. (17,360 sq. km.)
Sweden	Stockholm	Northern Europe, on the Scandinavian Peninsula	173,730 sq. mi. (449,960 sq. km.)
Switzerland	Bern (admin.) Lausanne (judicial)	Central Europe, in the Alps, north of Italy	15,940 sq. mi. (41,290 sq. km.)
Syria	Damascus	In the Middle East, north of Jordan and west of Iraq	71,500 sq. mi. (185,180 sq. km.)
Taiwan	Taipei	Island off southeast coast of China	13,890 sq. mi. (35,980 sq. km.)
Tajikistan	Dushanbe	Asia, west of China, south of Kyrgyzstan	55,300 sq. mi. (143,100 sq. km.)
Tanzania	Dar-es-Salaam	East Africa, on the Indian Ocean, south of Kenya	364,900 sq. mi. (945,090 sq. km.)
Thailand	Bangkok	Southeast Asia, south of Laos	198,000 sq. mi. (514,000 sq. km.)
Togo	Lomé	West Africa, between Ghana and Benin	21,930 sq. mi. (56,790 sq. km.)
Tonga	Nuku'alofa	Islands in the South Pacific Ocean	290 sq. mi. (750 sq. km.)

POPULATION	CURRENCY	LANGUAGE	DID YOU KNOW?
4,452,732	$1 = 1⅘ Singapore dollars	Chinese, Malay, Tamil, English	Singapore has one of the highest standards of living in Asia.
5,422,366	$1 = 48 koruny	Slovak, Hungarian	Slovakia was part of the kingdom of Hungary early in the 11th century.
1,932,917	$1 = 243 tolars	Slovenian, Serbo-Croatian	Slovenia is the most prosperous of the former Yugoslav republics.
494,786	$1 = 5⅔ Solomon dollars	English, Melanesian	The islands' mountains are of volcanic origin and heavily wooded.
7,753,310	$1 = 2,620 shillings	Somali, Arabic, Italian, English	Frankincense and myrrh are the major forestry products of Somalia.
43,647,658	$1 = 12 rand	Afrikaans, English, Ndebele, Sotho	South Africa mines more gold than any other country in the world.
40,077,100	$1 = 1.13 euros	Castilian Spanish, Catalan, Galician	Bullfighting is the national sport of Spain.
19,576,783	$1 = 93 rupees	Sinhala, Tamil, English	The Temple of the Tooth in Kandy is said to contain one of Buddha's teeth.
37,090,298	$1 = 2,560 pounds or $1 = 258 dinars	Arabic, Nubian, Ta Bedawie	The Nile River system is vital to the economy of Sudan.
436,494	$1 = 2,178 guilders	Dutch, Sranang Tongo	Most of Suriname's people are of East Indian origin.
1,123,605	$1 = 12 lilangeni	English, siSwati	Foreign people and companies own much of the country's land.
8,876,744	$1 = 10⅓ kronor	Swedish	An ice sheet covered Sweden until about 8,000 years ago.
7,301,994	$1 = 1⅗ francs	German, French, Italian, Romansch	The world's longest auto tunnel cuts through the Swiss Alps.
17,155,814	$1 = 49 pounds	Arabic, Kurdish, Armenian	Syria was once part of the empire of Alexander the Great.
22,548,009	$1 = 35 new Taiwan dollars	Mandarin Chinese, Taiwanese	Mainland China claims this country as one of its provinces.
6,719,567	$1 = 2,200 Tajik rubles	Tajik, Russian	The Nurek Dam in Tajikistan is the highest in the world.
37,187,939	$1 = 918 shillings	Swahili, English	Kilimanjaro, the highest mountain in Africa, is in northeast Tanzania.
62,354,402	$1 = 44 bahts	Thai, English	Thailand, once called Siam, is where the Siamese cat comes from.
5,285,501	$1 = 732 CFA francs	French, Ewe, Kabye	Togo is a leading world producer of phosphates.
106,137	$1 = 2 pa'angas	Tongan, English	Earthquakes in Tongo cause small islands to suddenly rise or sink.

NATION	CAPITAL	LOCATION OF NATION	AREA
Trinidad and Tobago	Port-of-Spain	Islands off the north coast of South America	1,980 sq. mi. (5,130 sq. km.)
Tunisia	Tunis	North Africa, on the Mediterranean, between Algeria and Libya	63,170 sq. mi. (163,610 sq. km.)
● Turkey	Ankara	On the southern shore of the Black Sea, partly in Europe and partly in Asia	301,380 sq. mi. (780,580 sq. km.)
Turkmenistan	Ashgabat	Western Asia, north of Afghanistan and Iran	188,500 sq. mi. (488,100 sq. km.)
Tuvalu	Funafuti Atoll	Chain of islands in the South Pacific Ocean	10 sq. mi. (26 sq. km.)
Uganda	Kampala	East Africa, south of Sudan	91,140 sq. mi. (236,040 sq. km.)
Ukraine	Kiev	Eastern Europe, south of Belarus and Russia	233,100 sq. mi. (603,700 sq. km.)
United Arab Emirates	Abu Dhabi	Arabian Peninsula, on the Persian Gulf	32,000 sq. mi. (82,880 sq. km.)
United Kingdom (Great Britain)	London	Off the northwest coast of Europe	94,530 sq. mi. (244,820 sq. km.)
United States	Washington, D.C.	In North America; 48 of 50 states between Canada and Mexico	3,717,810 sq. mi. (9,629,090 sq. km.)
Uruguay	Montevideo	South America, on the Atlantic Ocean, south of Brazil	68,040 sq. mi. (176,220 sq. km.)
Uzbekistan	Tashkent	Central Asia, south of Kazakhstan	172,740 sq. mi. (447,400 sq. km.)
Vanuatu	Port-Vila	Islands in the South Pacific Ocean	5,700 sq. mi. (14,760 sq. km.)
Vatican City		Surrounded by the city of Rome, Italy	1/5 sq. mi. (1/2 sq. km.)
Venezuela	Caracas	On the northern coast of South America, east of Colombia	352,140 sq. mi. (912,050 sq. km.)
Vietnam	Hanoi	Southeast Asia, south of China, on the eastern coast	127,240 sq. mi. (329,560 sq. km.)
Yemen	Sanaa	Asia, on the southern coast of the Arabian Peninsula	203,850 sq. mi. (527,970 sq. km.)
Yugoslavia	Belgrade, Podgorica	Europe, on Balkan Peninsula, west of Romania and Bulgaria	39,520 sq. mi. (102,350 sq. km.)
Zambia	Lusaka	Southern Africa, east of Angola	290,580 sq. mi. (752,610 sq. km.)
Zimbabwe	Harare	Southern Africa, south of Zambia	150,800 sq. mi. (390,580 sq. km.)

POPULATION	CURRENCY	LANGUAGE	DID YOU KNOW?
1,163,724	$1 = 6¼ Trinidad dollars	English, Hindi, French, Spanish	Trinidad gave birth to calypso, a popular folk music of the Caribbean.
9,815,644	$1 = 1⅜ dinar	Arabic, French	Most of Tunisia was once part of the Roman province called Africa.
67,308,928	$1 = 1,414,000 Turkish liras	Turkish, Kurdish, Arabic	Turkey is the site of Mt. Ararat, where Noah's ark was said to have come to rest.
4,688,963	$1 = 33¾ manats	Turkmen, Russian, Uzbek	The Kara Kum Desert occupies 80% of the area of Turkmenistan.
11,146	$1= 1¾ Australian dollars	Tuvaluan, English	Tuvalu has the world's 2nd-smallest population, after Vatican City.
24,699,073	$1 = 1,730 shillings	English, Luganda, Swahili	More than half the population of Uganda is under the age of 15.
48,396,470	$1 = 5⅓ hryvina	Ukrainian, Russian	Ukraine is a Slavic word meaning "borderlands".
2,445,989	$1 = 3⅔ dirhams	Arabic, Persian, English, Hindi	A hereditary ruler, or emir, governs each of the 7 states of this country.
59,778,002	$1 = ⅔ pound	English	The last successful invasion of England occurred in 1066.
280,562,489	U.S. dollar	English, Spanish	Lake Michigan is the only one of the Great Lakes entirely within the U.S.
3,386,575	$1 = 14¾ pesos	Spanish	More than 90% of Uruguay's people are of European descent.
25,563,441	$1 = 693 soms	Uzbek, Russian	The tomb of the Mongol conqueror Tamerlane is in Samarkand.
196,178	$1 = 145⅔ vatus	French, English, Bislama	Espiritu Santo, the largest island, was a key U.S. base during World War II.
870	$1 = 1.13 euros	Italian, Latin	This tiny country lies entirely inside the city of Rome.
24,287,670	$1 = 762½ bolivares	Spanish	The South American liberator Simón Bolívar, was born in Caracas.
81,098,416	$1 = 15,088 dong	Vietnamese, French, Chinese	In A.D. 39, two sisters—Trung Trac and Trung Nhi—led a successful revolt against foreign rule in the area.
18,701,257	$1 = 171 rials	Arabic	The city of Aden is Yemen's principal port and commercial center.
10,662,087	$1 = 66⅓ new dinars	Serbo-Croatian, Albanian	Present-day Yugoslavia is made up of the republics of Serbia and Montenegro.
9,959,037	$1 = 3,835 kwacha	English, native languages	The Zambezi, Africa's 4th-longest river, rises in Zambia.
11,376,676	$1 = 55½ Zimbabwe dollars	English, Shona, Sindebele	Zimbabwe is a leading world supplier of the metal chromium.

NUMBERS

How many digits are there in π? ➤page 169

NUMERALS IN ANCIENT CIVILIZATION

People have been counting since the earliest of times. This is what some numerals looked like in different cultures.

MODERN	1	2	3	4	5	6	7	8	9	10	20	50	100
Egyptian	I	II	III	IIII	III III	III III	IIII IIII	IIII IIII	IIII IIII	∩	∩∩	∩∩∩∩∩	9
Babylonian	Υ	ΥΥ	ΥΥΥ	ΥΥΤ	ΥΥΥΥ	ΥΥΥ	ΥΥΥ	ΥΥΥ	ΥΥΥΥ	<	«	≪≪	≪«
Greek	A	B	Γ	Δ	E	F	Z	H	θ	I	K	N	P
Mayan	•	••	•••	••••	—	⸫	••	•••	••••	=	☉	☱	☉
Chinese	一	二	三	四	五	六	七	八	九	十	二十	五十	百
Hindu	١	٢	٣	٤	٤	٢	﹀	﹤	٤	10	٢o	yo	100
Arabic	١	٢	٣	٤	٤	٤	v	٨	٩	١o	٢o	٤o	١oo

ROMAN NUMERALS

Roman numerals are still used today. The symbols used for different numbers are the letters I (1), V (5), X (10), L (50), C (100), D (500), and M (1,000). If one Roman numeral is followed by a larger one, the first is subtracted from the second. For example, IV means 5 – 1 = 4. Think of it as "one less than five." On the other hand, if one Roman numeral is followed by another that is equal or smaller, add them together. Thus, XII means 10 + 1 + 1 = 12. Can you put the year you were born in Roman numerals?

The Roman empire fell in A.D. 476. Can you put that year into Roman numerals?

ANSWERS ON PAGES 314-317. FOR MORE PUZZLES GO TO WWW.WORLDALMANACFORKIDS.COM

1 I	14 XIV	90 XC
2 II	15 XV	100 C
3 III	16 XVI	200 CC
4 IV	17 XVII	300 CCC
5 V	18 XVIII	400 CD
6 VI	19 XIX	500 D
7 VII	20 XX	600 DC
8 VIII	30 XXX	700 DCC
9 IX	40 XL	800 DCCC
10 X	50 L	900 CM
11 XI	60 LX	1,000 M
12 XII	70 LXX	2,000 MM
13 XIII	80 LXXX	3,000 MMM

▼The Colosseum

THE PREFIX TELLS THE NUMBER

▲ A tricycle

After each number are one or more prefixes used to form words that include that number. Knowing what the prefix stands for can help you understand the meaning of the word. For example, a **mono**rail has one track. A **pent**agon has five sides. **Sept**ember gets its name from the calendar used in Roman times, when it was the seventh month (the Roman year began in March). An **oct**opus has eight arms.

1	uni-, mon-, mono-	unicycle, unicorn, monarch, monorail
2	bi-	bicycle, binary, binoculars, bifocals
3	tri-	tricycle, triangle, trilogy, trio
4	quadr-, tetr-	quadrangle, quadruplet, tetrahedron
5	pent-, quint-	pentagon, pentathlon, quintuplet
6	hex-, sext-	hexagon, sextuplet, sextet
7	hept-, sept-	heptathlon, septuplet
8	oct-	octave, octet, octopus, octagon
9	non-	nonagon, nonet
10	dec-	decade, decibel, decimal
100	cent-	centipede, century
1000	kilo-	kilogram, kilometer, kilowatt
million	mega-	megabyte, megahertz
billion	giga-	gigabyte, gigawatt

BIG NUMBERS

Below are the words for some numbers, plus the number of zeros needed when each number is written out.

ten	1 zero	10
hundred	2 zeros	100
thousand	3 zeros	1,000
ten thousand	4 zeros	10,000
hundred thousand	5 zeros	100,000
million	6 zeros	1,000,000
ten million	7 zeros	10,000,000
hundred million	8 zeros	100,000,000
billion	9 zeros	1,000,000,000
trillion	12 zeros	1,000,000,000,000
quadrillion	15 zeros	1,000,000,000,000,000
quintillion	18 zeros	1,000,000,000,000,000,000
sextillion	21 zeros	1,000,000,000,000,000,000,000
septillion	24 zeros	1,000,000,000,000,000,000,000,000

There are words for even bigger numbers. For example, a **googol** has 100 zeros, and a **googolplex** is equal to the number 1 followed by a googol of zeros!

How Many SIDES and FACES Do They Have?

When a figure is flat (two-dimensional), it is a plane figure. When a figure takes up space (three-dimensional), it is a solid figure. The flat surface of a solid figure is called a face. Plane and solid figures come in many different shapes.

TWO-DIMENSIONAL

square   circle   triangle

THREE-DIMENSIONAL

cube   sphere   tetrahedron (pyramid)

The flat surface of a cube is a square.

WHAT ARE POLYGONS?

A polygon is a two-dimensional figure with three or more straight sides (called line segments). A square is a polygon. Polygons have different numbers of sides—and each has a different name. If the sides are all the same length and all the angles between the sides are equal, the polygon is called regular. If the sides are of different lengths or the angles are not equal, the polygon is called irregular. At right are some regular and irregular polygons.

NAME & NUMBER OF SIDES	REGULAR	IRREGULAR
TRIANGLE – 3		
QUADRILATERAL OR TETRAGON – 4		
PENTAGON – 5		
HEXAGON – 6		
HEPTAGON – 7		
OCTAGON – 8		
NONAGON – 9		
DECAGON – 10		

WHAT ARE POLYHEDRONS?

A polyhedron is a three-dimensional figure with four or more faces. Each face on a polyhedron is a polygon. Below are some polyhedrons with many faces.

 tetrahedron
4 faces

 hexahedron
6 faces

 octahedron
8 faces

 dodecahedron
12 faces

 icosahedron
20 faces

◀ *Great Pyramid of Khefren*

HOW DO YOU FIND THE AREA?

OF A SQUARE:

A square is a plane figure with four equal sides, like the figure you see here. To find the area for a square, use this formula:

SIDE x SIDE (**SIDE x SIDE** can also be written as S^2, pronounced "side squared").

The sides of this square are each 2 centimeters long. So the area is 2 x 2, or 4. These are no longer centimeters but **square centimeters**, like the smaller squares inside the big one.

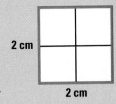

2 cm

2 cm

OF A TRIANGLE:

A triangle is a three-sided plane figure. The prefix "tri" means three, which refers to the three points where the sides of a triangle meet.

To find the area for a triangle use **½ x (BASE x HEIGHT)** (first multiply the base by the height, then multiply that number by ½).

This triangle has a base of 2 centimeters and a height of 3 centimeters. So the area will be 3 square centimeters.

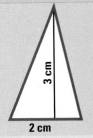

3 cm

2 cm

OF A CIRCLE:

The distance around a circle is called its **circumference**. All the points on the circumference are an equal distance from the center. That distance from center to circumference is called the **radius**. A **diameter** is any straight line that has both ends on the circle and passes through its center. It's twice as long as the radius.

To find the area for a circle you need to use π—a number called **pi** that is always the same, about 3.14. The formula for area is:

π x **RADIUS** x **RADIUS** (or π x **RADIUS SQUARED**).

For instance, this circle has a radius of 2 centimeters, so its area = π x 2 x 2, or π x 2^2; that is, 3.14 x 4. This comes to 12.56 square centimeters.

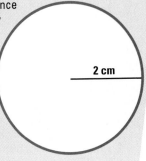

2 cm

--- *All About...* **3.14 (π)** ---

In math, π, the Greek letter pi, stands for the number you get when you divide the circumference of a circle by its diameter. This number, about 3.14, is always the same, no matter how big the circle is! The Babylonians discovered this relationship in 2000 B.C.

Actually, no one can say *exactly* what the value of π is. When you divide the circumference by the diameter it does not come out even, and you can keep going as many places as you want: 3.14159265.... it goes on forever. The most accurate calculation of π so far was made by Dr. Yasumasa Kanada of the University of Tokyo in 1999. He used a super computer to figure out the value 206,158,430,000 places to the right of the decimal point. He beat the previous record by more than 150,000,000,000 digits. It took the computer more than 37 hours to run the program! In 1995, Hiroyuki Goto of Tokyo, Japan, set a record by memorizing the most digits of π (42,195).

Multiplication Table

x	0	1	2	3	4	5	6	7	8	9	10	11	12
0	0	0	0	0	0	0	0	0	0	0	0	0	0
1	0	1	2	3	4	5	6	7	8	9	10	11	12
2	0	2	4	6	8	10	12	14	16	18	20	22	24
3	0	3	6	9	12	15	18	21	24	27	30	33	36
4	0	4	8	12	16	20	24	28	32	36	40	44	48
5	0	5	10	15	20	25	30	35	40	45	50	55	60
6	0	6	12	18	24	30	36	42	48	54	60	66	72
7	0	7	14	21	28	35	42	49	56	63	70	77	84
8	0	8	16	24	32	40	48	56	64	72	80	88	96
9	0	9	18	27	36	45	54	63	72	81	90	99	108
10	0	10	20	30	40	50	60	70	80	90	100	110	120
11	0	11	22	33	44	55	66	77	88	99	110	121	132
12	0	12	24	36	48	60	72	84	96	108	120	132	144

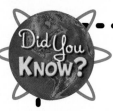

Did You Know?

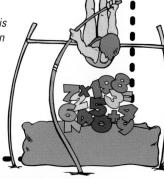

THE INTERNATIONAL MATHEMATICAL OLYMPIAD *(IMO) is a World Championship Mathematics Competition for high school students. It is held in a different country every year. The first IMO was held in 1959 in Romania, with students from 7 countries competing. Today contestants come from over 80 countries from 5 continents. Visit the official web site of the IMO at:* **http://imo.math.ca/IMO/** *or the American Mathematics Competition web site at:* **http://www.unl.edu/amc.**

Who Am I?

I was born in Syracuse, a Greek seaport in Sicily, in 287 B.C. I am one of history's greatest mathematicians. In fact, I am credited with calculating the most commonly used value of π (pi)—3.14. I was also a great inventor. One of my designs, a screw used for raising water, is still used for irrigation. I also invented war machines, such as catapults and cranes.

Answer: Archimedes

NUMBER PUZZLES

1 Divide the face of the clock into three parts with two lines so that the sum of the numbers in the three parts are equal. Can you divide the clock face into six parts so that the numbers in each section have the same sum?

2 One morning grasshopper fell down a hole 2 meters deep. He would climb .25 of a meter every day but at night he slid down .125 of a meter. At this rate, how many days until the grasshopper gets out?

3 An ice cream stand has nine different flavors. A group of children come to the stand and each buys a double scoop cone with two flavors of ice cream. If none of the children chooses the same combination of flavors, and every different combination of flavors is chosen, how many children are there?

FLAVORS

Vanilla	Peach	Chocolate	Pistachio	Fudge Swirl
Strawberry	Coffee	Chocolate Chip	Cherry Vanilla	

4 A math student interviewed 50 fifth graders. Of the students interviewed, 41 said they like peanut butter on their sandwiches, 35 liked jam on their sandwiches, and 30 liked both. How many students liked neither?

5 ## NUMBER MAZE

Start in the top left square and try to get to the END square. The numbers tell you how many squares you can move. You can only move horizontally or vertically—not diagonally.

Hint: Your first move can be down two squares to the "2" or to the right two squares to the "3."

2	1	3	1
3	2	1	2
2	1	2	3
1	3	2	END

ANSWERS ON PAGES 314-317. FOR MORE PUZZLES GO TO
WWW.WORLDALMANACFORKIDS.COM

POPULATION

Which state in the U.S. has the fewest people? >page 173

WHERE DO PEOPLE LIVE?

Our planet is growing—not in size, but in population. In 1959, Earth had five billion people. Forty years later, in 1999, the number of people on Earth hit six billion. By 2050, the world population is expected to grow to more than nine billion people. Much of that growth will be in the world's poorest nations. (Despite the worldwide population growth, some nations are actually losing population, such as Russia and Ukraine.)

LARGEST CITIES IN THE WORLD

Here are the ten cities in the world that have the most people, as of 2000. Numbers include people from the whole built-up area around each city (the metropolitan area).

CITY, COUNTRY	POPULATION
Tokyo, Japan	26,444,000
Mexico City, Mexico	18,131,000
Mumbai (Bombay), India	18,066,000
São Paulo, Brazil	17,755,000
New York City, U.S.	16,640,000
Lagos, Nigeria	13,427,000
Los Angeles, U.S.	13,140,000
Kolkata (Calcutta), India	12,918,000
Shanghai, China	12,887,000
Buenos Aires, Argentina	12,560,000

LARGEST COUNTRIES
(Most People, 2002)

POPULATION	COUNTRY
1,284,304,000	China
1,045,845,000	India
287,041,000	United States
232,073,000	Indonesia
176,030,000	Brazil
147,663,000	Pakistan
144,979,000	Russia
133,377,000	Bangladesh
129,935,000	Nigeria
126,975,000	Japan
103,400,000	Mexico
84,526,000	Philippines
83,252,000	Germany
81,098,000	Vietnam
70,712,000	Egypt
67,673,000	Ethiopia
67,309,000	Turkey
66,623,000	Iran
65,354,000	Thailand
59,778,000	Great Britain
59,766,000	France
57,716,000	Italy
55,225,000	Congo Republic
48,396,000	Ukraine
48,324,000	South Korea

SMALLEST COUNTRIES
(Fewest People, 2002)

POPULATION	COUNTRY
880	Vatican City
11,146	Tuvalu
12,329	Nauru
19,409	Palau
27,730	San Marino
31,987	Monaco
32,842	Liechtenstein

Population of the UNITED STATES 2001

Estimated U.S. Population on July 1, 2001: 284,796,887.

Rank & State Name	Population	Rank & State Name	Population
1 California	34,501,130	27 Oregon	3,472,867
2 Texas	21,325,018	28 Oklahoma	3,460,097
3 New York	19,011,378	29 Connecticut	3,425,074
4 Florida	16,396,515	30 Iowa	2,923,179
5 Illinois	12,482,301	31 Mississippi	2,858,029
6 Pennsylvania	12,287,150	32 Kansas	2,694,641
7 Ohio	11,373,541	33 Arkansas	2,692,090
8 Michigan	9,990,817	34 Utah	2,269,789
9 New Jersey	8,484,431	35 Nevada	2,106,074
10 Georgia	8,383,915	36 New Mexico	1,829,146
11 North Carolina	8,186,268	37 West Virginia	1,801,916
12 Virginia	7,187,734	38 Nebraska	1,713,235
13 Massachusetts	6,379,304	39 Idaho	1,321,006
14 Indiana	6,114,745	40 Maine	1,286,670
15 Washington	5,987,973	41 New Hampshire	1,259,181
16 Tennessee	5,740,021	42 Hawaii	1,224,398
17 Missouri	5,629,707	43 Rhode Island	1,058,920
18 Wisconsin	5,401,906	44 Montana	904,433
19 Maryland	5,375,156	45 Delaware	796,165
20 Arizona	5,307,331	46 South Dakota	756,600
21 Minnesota	4,972,294	47 Alaska	634,892
22 Louisiana	4,465,430	48 North Dakota	634,448
23 Alabama	4,464,356	49 Vermont	613,090
24 Colorado	4,417,714	50 District of Columbia	571,822
25 Kentucky	4,065,556	51 Wyoming	494,423
26 South Carolina	4,063,011		

▼ New York City, the largest city in the U.S.

LARGEST CITIES IN THE UNITED STATES

Cities grow and shrink in population. At right is a list of the largest cities in the United States in 2000 compared with their populations in 1950. Which seven cities increased in population? Which three decreased?

RANK & CITY	2000	1950
1 New York, NY	8,008,278	7,891,957
2 Los Angeles, CA	3,694,820	1,970,358
3 Chicago, IL	2,896,016	3,620,962
4 Houston, TX	1,953,631	596,163
5 Philadelphia, PA	1,517,550	2,071,605
6 Phoenix, AZ	1,321,045	106,818
7 San Diego, CA	1,223,400	334,387
8 Dallas, TX	1,188,580	434,462
9 San Antonio, TX	1,144,646	408,442
10 Detroit, MI	951,270	1,849,568

Taking the Census: Everyone Counts

Were you counted during Census 2000? The United States takes a census every 10 years. It tries to count everyone. But in every census, some people get missed. In Census 2000, census-takers tried to track down and count people who did not send back forms, so that this census would be as accurate as possible. Census officials believe that this census was one of the most accurate ever, but that it missed about 1 out of 100 people.

Why is the census needed?

▶ The population of a state determines how many representatives it has in the U.S. House.

▶ Census information helps the federal government in Washington, D.C., decide which public services must be provided and where.

▶ The census provides a picture of the people. Where do they live? How old are they? What do they do? How much do they earn? How many kids do they have? What is their background?

When was the first U.S. census taken?

It was in 1790 just after the American Revolution. That year census-takers counted 3,929,200 people lived in what was then the United States. Most of them lived on farms or in small towns. (Today, three out of every four Americans live in or near cities.)

News from Census 2000

▶ In the U.S. and around the world, more people are living longer. In about 25 years, say census officials, the world's elderly population (people age 65 and over) will be almost double what it is today. Meanwhile, there will be roughly the same number of children then as there are now. The number of Americans over 65 will grow 80%. Growth in all other age groups will average 15%. Improved health care and changing attitudes towards family planning help explain the trend.

▶ About 33.1 million Americans (or about 12%) claimed Irish ancestry on the 2000 Census form. That's almost nine times the population of Ireland itself!

Who Are We?

Census 2000 was the first time a census allowed Americans to identify themselves as being of more than one race. Almost seven million people made that choice. That is about two percent of the total population of the United States. This list shows the percentage of Americans that felt they belonged in each of the racial groups listed here.

▶ Hispanics are the fastest-growing minority in the United States, up almost 58% since the 1990 census.

▶ One out of every 10 Americans was born in another country. This is the first time since the 1930s that this has been true.

▶ Thanks to the Child Citizenship Act of 2000, all children adopted overseas by Americans will automatically become U.S. citizens. Every year, Americans adopt about 20,000 children from other nations.

RACE	PERCENT OF POPULATION
One race	97.6%
White	75.1%
Black or African American	12.3%
American Indian and Alaska Native	0.9%
Asian	3.6%
Native Hawaiian and Other Pacific Islander	0.1%
Some other race	5.5%
Two or more races	2.4%
Hispanic or Latino	12.5%
Not Hispanic or Latino	87.5%
(Hispanics may be of any race.)	

COUNTING THE FIRST AMERICANS

American Indians, also called Native Americans, lived in North and South America long before the first European explorers arrived. Their ancestors are thought to have arrived more than 20,000 years ago, probably from Northeast Asia. American Indians are not one people, but many different peoples, each with their own traditions.

How many American Indians were here in the 1400s? About 850,000 Native Americans lived in what is now the United States before Columbus arrived.

How many American Indians are in the U.S. now? During the 17th, 18th, and 19th centuries, disease and wars with white settlers and soldiers caused the deaths of thousands of American Indians. By 1910 there were only about 220,000 left in the United States. Since then, the American Indian population has increased dramatically. According to Census 2000, the total number of Native Americans was about 2.5 million.

In 1924, the U.S. Congress approved a law giving citizenship to all Native Americans.

WHERE DO NATIVE AMERICANS LIVE?

Below are the states with the largest Native American populations according to Census 2000. The states are numbered in the map below.*

①	California	333,346	⑨	New York	82,461
②	Oklahoma	273,230	⑩	South Dakota	62,283
③	Arizona	255,879	⑪	Michigan	58,479
④	New Mexico	173,483	⑫	Montana	56,068
⑤	Texas	118,362	⑬	Minnesota	54,967
⑥	North Carolina	99,551	⑭	Florida	53,541
⑦	Alaska	98,043	⑮	Wisconsin	47,228
⑧	Washington	93,301	⑯	Oregon	45,211

* Figures do not include people who said they were of more than one race.

175

The Many Faces of America:
IMMIGRATION

You have probably heard it said that America is a nation of immigrants. Many Americans are descended from Europeans, Africans, or Asians.

COMING TO AMERICA

Millions of people have immigrated to the United States from all over the world—more than 40 million since 1820. Today the U.S. is experiencing a period of high immigration. Immigrants come for various reasons, such as to live in freedom, to escape poverty or oppression, and to make better lives for themselves and their children. But some people were brought here by force. In the 1600s, the British began shipping Africans to the American colonies to work as slaves. One out of every three people living in the southern colonies in the 1700s was a slave.

▲ Immigrants entering the U.S. at Ellis Island, early 1900s

WHAT COUNTRIES DO IMMIGRANTS COME FROM?

Immigrants come to the United States from many countries. Below are some of the countries immigrants came from in 2000. The name of the country is followed by the number of immigrants. In 2000, immigration from all countries to the United States totaled 849,807.

Mexico	173,919
China	45,652
Philippines	42,474
India	42,046
Vietnam	26,747
Nicaragua	24,029
El Salvador	22,578
Haiti	22,364
Cuba	20,831
Dominican Republic	17,536
Russia	17,110
Canada	16,210
Jamaica	16,000
North and South Korea	15,830
Ukraine	15,810

Where Do Immigrants Settle?

In 2000, more than two-thirds of the immigrants from Mexico went to live in California or Texas, while almost half of the immigrants from China went to two states: California and New York. About 75 percent of the immigrants from Cuba went to live in Florida.

This bar chart shows the states that received the highest number of immigrants in 2000.

California
217,753

New York
106,061

Florida
98,391

Texas
63,840

New Jersey
40,013

Illinois
36,180

BECOMING AN AMERICAN CITIZEN

When a foreign-born person becomes a citizen of the United States, we say the person has become naturalized. To apply for American citizenship, a person:

► Must be at least 18 years old.

► Must have lived legally in the United States for at least five years.

► Must be able to understand English if under the age of 55.

► Must be of good moral character.

► Must show knowledge of the history and form of government of the United States.

A CITIZENSHIP TEST

When immigrants wanting to be United States citizens are interviewed, they may be asked any of 100 questions. Here are some of them. How many can you answer correctly?

❶ How many stripes are there in the flag?

❷ What do the stripes on the flag mean?

❸ Who is the president of the United States today?

❹ Who elects the president of the United States?

❺ Can the Constitution be changed?

❻ What is Congress?

❼ Who elects Congress?

❽ What are the duties of the Supreme Court?

❾ What is the capital of your state?

❿ In what month do we vote for the president?

Answers are on pages 314-318.

THE STATUE OF LIBERTY

Many of the immigrants who crossed the Atlantic Ocean and steamed into New York Harbor passed by the Statue of Liberty. Set on her own island, the "Lady With the Lamp" was given to the United States by France and has served as a welcome to Americans-to-be since she was erected in 1886. In 1903, a poem by the U.S. poet Emma Lazarus was inscribed at the base of the statue. Two of its lines read:

"Give me your tired, your poor,
Your huddled masses yearning to breathe free...."

177

PRIZES & CONTESTS

Who won the New Artist Grammy for 2001? ➤ page 180

NOBEL PRIZES

The Nobel Prizes are named after Alfred B. Nobel (1833–1896), a Swedish scientist who invented dynamite, and left money to be given every year to people who have helped humankind. The Nobel Peace Prize goes to people who the judges think did the most during the past year to help achieve peace. Prizes are also given for physics, chemistry, medicine-physiology, literature, and economics. In 2001 the peace prize went in two equal portions, to the United Nations (UN) and to its secretary-general, Kofi Annan, for their work for a better organized and more peaceful world.

Kofi Annan

Past winners of the Nobel Peace Prize include:

Kim Dae Jung

2000 Kim Dae Jung, South Korean president, for championing human rights and efforts toward peace with North Korea

1999 Médecins Sans Frontières (Doctors Without Borders), a pioneering organization that gives medical help to disaster victims

1994 Yasir Arafat, Palestinian leader; Shimon Peres, foreign minister of Israel; Yitzhak Rabin, prime minister of Israel

1993 Nelson Mandela, leader of South African blacks; Frederik Willem de Klerk, president of South Africa

1986 Elie Wiesel, U.S. holocaust survivor and author

1979 Mother Teresa, India, leader of the Order of the Missionaries of Charity, who care for the sick and dying

1973 Henry Kissinger, U.S. secretary of state; Le Duc Tho, of North Vietnam (declined the prize)

1964 Martin Luther King Jr., leader of the Southern Christian Leadership Conference

1952 Albert Schweitzer, missionary, surgeon

1906 Theodore Roosevelt, president of the United States

1905 Baroness Bertha von Suttner, an early advocate of peace through international cooperation; the first woman to win the prize

Other winners of Nobel Prizes have included:

John Nash, 1994 Nobel Prize in Economics John Nash Jr. was born in Bluefield, West Virginia, in 1928. Although he struggled with mental illness for much of his career, he made many important contributions to game theory and mathematics. After many years he won recognition in 1994 when he shared the Nobel Prize in Economics with John Harsanyi and Reinhard Selten. His story is told in the Oscar-winning movie *A Beautiful Mind*.

Toni Morrison, 1993 Nobel Prize in Literature Born in Lorain, Ohio, in 1931, Toni Morrison is known for writing both fiction and nonfiction on African-American themes. Her books include *Beloved, The Song of Solomon,* and *Tar Baby.*

Francis Crick, James Watson, and Maurice Wilkins, 1962 Nobel Prize in Medicine These scientists won a Nobel Prize in 1962, for discovering the double helix structure of DNA. They made the discovery in 1953.

▲ *Nobel Peace Prize medal*

Albert Einstein, 1921 Nobel Prize in Physics Albert Einstein was born in Germany in 1879 and later immigrated to the United States. He won the Nobel Prize *not* for his famous theory of relativity, but for his 1905 work on the photoelectric effect.

THE MEDAL OF HONOR

The Medal of Honor is given by the United States government for bravery in war against an enemy. The first medals were awarded in 1863. Since that time, nearly 3,400 people have received the award.

PULITZER PRIZES

The Pulitzer Prizes are named after Joseph Pulitzer (1847–1911), a journalist and publisher, who gave the money to set them up. The prizes are given yearly in the United States for journalism, drama, literature, and music.

SPINGARN MEDAL

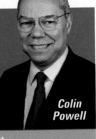
Colin Powell

The Spingarn Medal was set up in 1914 by Joel Elias Spingarn, leader of the National Association for the Advancement of Colored People (NAACP). It is awarded every year by the NAACP for achievement by a black American. Here are some winners:

2002: U.S. Representative John Lewis	**1991:** General Colin Powell
2000: Oprah Winfrey	**1985:** Actor Bill Cosby
1999: Publisher Earl Graves	**1979:** Civil rights activist Rosa Parks
1998: Civil rights activist Myrlie Evers-Williams	**1975:** Baseball player Hank Aaron
1994: Writer and poet Maya Angelou	**1957:** Martin Luther King Jr.

WHO AM I?

I was born on April 28, 1926, in Monroeville, Alabama. I wrote only one novel, but it won the Pulitzer Prize in 1961 and became one of the best selling books of all time. In fact, in 2001, Chicago officials started a campaign to have everyone read it at the same time. It was also made into a popular film, in 1962. Gregory Peck won a Best Actor Oscar for it.

Answer: Harper Lee, author of "To Kill a Mockingbird".

Entertainment Awards

The Oscar ceremonies are watched on TV by millions of people all over the world. Among other awards given every year for the best in entertainment are the Grammys and the MTV Video Music Awards.

◀ *Halle Berry and Denzel Washington at the Oscars ceremony*

ACADEMY AWARDS

The Oscars are awarded every year by the Academy of Motion Picture Arts and Sciences for the best in movies. Here are some of the films and people that won Oscars for 2001.

Best Picture: *A Beautiful Mind*

Best Actor: Denzel Washington, *Training Day*

Best Actress: Halle Berry, *Monster's Ball*

Best Supporting Actor: Jim Broadbent, *Iris*

Best Supporting Actress: Jennifer Connelly, *A Beautiful Mind*

Best Director: Ron Howard, *A Beautiful Mind*

Best Original Screenplay: Julian Fellowes, *Gosford Park*

MTV VIDEO MUSIC AWARDS

The MTV Video Music Awards are presented each year in a variety of music video categories. Here are some winners for 2001:

Best Video of the Year: Pink, Christina Aguilera, Lil' Kim, Mya, and Missy Elliott, "Lady Marmalade"

Best New Artist: Alicia Keys, "Fallin'"

Best Male Video: Moby featuring Gwen Stefani, "South Side"

Best Female Video: Eve featuring Gwen Stefani, "Let Me Blow Ya Mind"

Best Group Video: 'N Sync, "Pop"

Best Pop Video: 'N Sync, "Pop"

GRAMMY AWARDS

Grammys are given out each year by the National Academy of Recording Arts and Sciences. Some of the winners for 2001 were:

Record of the Year (single): "Walk On," U2

Album of the Year: *O Brother, Where Art Thou?* (various artists)

Song of the Year: "Fallin'," Alicia Keys

New artist: Alicia Keys

Rock Duo or Group: "Elevation," U2

Rock album: *All That You Can't Leave Behind*, U2

Rock song: "Drops of Jupiter," written by Charlie Colin, Rob Hotchkiss, Pat Monahan, & Scott Underwood (of Train)

Pop Vocal Album: *Lovers Rock*, Sade

Rhythm and Blues Song: "Fallin'," Alicia Keys

Rap Soloist: "Get Ur Freak On," Missy "Misdemeanor" Elliot

Rap Album: *Stankonia*, Outkast

Country Album: *Timeless—Hank Williams Tribute* (various artists)

Spoken Word Album for Children: *Mama Don't Allow*, Tom Chapin

Musical Album for Children: *Elmo and The Orchestra*

Film or TV Song: "Boss of Me," from "Malcolm in the Middle," John Flansburgh & John Linnell, songwriters

CONTESTS

If you have a special talent or interest and you like to compete, why not enter a contest? Here are a few examples:

HOW DO YOU SPELL "WINNER"?

After finishing second in 2000, eighth-grader Sean Conley from Anoka, Minnesota, won the 2001 National Spelling Bee. If you're good at spelling, maybe you could be a future winner. Newspapers across the U.S. run local spelling bees for kids ages 15 and under. Winners may qualify for the Scripps Howard National Spelling Bee held in Washington, D.C., in late May or early June every year. If you're interested, ask you school principal to contact your local newspaper.

Sean received a $10,000 cash prize and a $1,000 U.S. savings bond after spelling "succedaneum" (SUX-ah-DAY-nee-um) in the 16th round. *Succedaneum* is defined as "one that comes next, after, or replaces another in an office position or role."

Here are all the words Sean had to spell correctly. How many would you have gotten right?

ROUND	SPELLING WORD	ROUND	SPELLING WORD
1	auriferous	9	pilchard
2	eradicate	10	zetetic
3	impecuniously	11	concinnity
4	inesculent	12	epexegesis
5	tropophilous	13	aleatoric
6	palynological	14	irenicism
7	schadenfreude	15	gallimaufry
8	zarzuela	16	succedaneum

WEB SITE *http://www.spellingbee.com*

WHERE CAN YOU FIND GEOGRAPHY LOVERS?

Kyle Haddad-Fonda, 14, of Shoreline, Washington, won the 2001 National Geographic Bee. His prize was a $25,000 college scholarship.

To win, he had to answer this question: **Below the equilibrium line of glaciers there is a region of melting, evaporation, and sublimation. Name this zone.**

Answer: **zone of ablation**

This was Kyle's third trip to the National Geographic Bee finals, as he was also the Washington state champion in 1999 and 2000. He said the best part of the competition was meeting other children from around the country. Besides geography, Kyle is interested in protecting all sites of antiquity. He also plays the classical harp and runs track.

Nick Jachowski, 14, of Makawao, Hawaii, finished second and won a scholarship of $15,000. The third-place winner was Jason Ferguson, 13, of Dallas, Texas. He won a $10,000 scholarship.

If you want to enter this contest, you must be a fourth- through eighth-grader. School-level bees are followed by state-level bees and then the national competition. For more information, ask your school principal to write to: National Geographic Bee; National Geographic Society; 1145 17th Street NW; Washington, D.C. 20036-4688. The registration deadline each year is October 15. You can also visit the web site:

WEB SITE *http://www.nationalgeographic.com*

GO FLY A KITE!

Children of all ages are invited to enter their own handmade kites into the Smithsonian Kite Festival, which is held every year in Washington, D.C., at cherry blossom time (late March to early April) on the National Mall.

The event is sponsored by The Smithsonian Associates and the National Air and Space Museum. Kite fliers from across the U.S. and all over the world participate. The sky is filled with all kinds of kites, from bowed to box/cellular to fighter and delta kites. There is even a category for UFOs—Unclassified Flying Objects. There are also demonstrations by kite-flying masters, as well as a traditional battle of Japanese rokkaku (six-sided) kites. For more information, visit

WEBSITE *http://www.kitefestival.org*

P-U! THE GROSSEST SNEAKERS WIN!

Danny DeNault of New Milford, Connecticut, won the 2002 Odor-Eaters Rotten Sneaker Contest. It's held in Montpelier, Vermont, which calls itself the "Rotten Sneaker Capital of the World." Nine-year-old Danny beat competitors from across the country. And it's no wonder, since he lives and works on a farm, steps in cow pies, and keeps his sneakers in a plastic bag on the porch! He won a $500 savings bond, the Golden Sneaker trophy, and a year's supply of Odor-Eaters products. His sneakers are now enshrined in the Odor-Eaters Hall of Fumes. The contest is held in mid-March each year. For more information, visit the Odor-Eaters web site:

WEBSITE *http://www.kitefestival.org*

CASTLES IN SAND

Everyone who's been to the beach has felt the urge to play in the sand—to dig holes in it, pile it into towers, even build sand castles. Some people like it so much that they travel all over the world to compete in contests. Professional teams have built towers more than 33 feet high!

But you don't have to live near the ocean (or be a professional). Most contests have separate divisions for kids and/or families, and many are held on lakeshores, or anywhere that water and sand can be found—or brought in.

The secret is to pile up and pack a big mound of wet sand, then carve it using tools. Sticks or shells from the beach make good tools and so do plastic forks, spoons, and knives. You can make animals, cartoon characters, or almost anything. All it takes (besides water and sand) is imagination and practice. For more information, visit

WEBSITE *http://sandcastlecentral.com*

RELIGION

Whose birth is celebrated on Mawlid? ➤ page 185

How did the universe begin? Why are we here on Earth? What happens to us after we die? For many people, religion is a way of answering questions like these. Believing in a God or gods, or in a Divine Being, is one way of making sense of the world around us. Religions can also help guide people's lives.

About six billion people all over the world are religious believers. Different religions have different beliefs. For example, Christians, Jews, and Muslims all believe in one God, while Hindus believe in many gods. On this page and the next are some facts about the world's major religions.

BUDDHISM

WHO STARTED BUDDHISM? Gautama Siddhartha (the Buddha), around 525 B.C.

WHAT IS THE RELIGIOUS WRITING? The three main collections of Buddhist writings are called the **Tripitaka**, or "Three Baskets."

WHAT DO BUDDHISTS BELIEVE? Buddha taught that life is filled with suffering. In order to be free of that suffering, believers have to give up worldly possessions and worldly goals and try to achieve a state of perfect peace known as *nirvana*.

HOW MANY ARE THERE? In 2001, there were more than 360 million Buddhists, mostly in Asia.

WHAT KINDS ARE THERE? There are two main kinds of Buddhists. **Theravada** ("Path of the Elders") **Buddhism**, the older kind, is more common in the southern part of Asia. **Mahayana** ("Great Vessel") **Buddhism** is more common in northern Asia.

CHRISTIANITY

WHO STARTED CHRISTIANITY? Jesus Christ, in the first century. He was born in Bethlehem between 8 B.C. and 4 B.C. and died about A.D. 29.

WHAT IS THE RELIGIOUS WRITING? The **Bible**, including the Old Testament and New Testament, is the main religious writing of Christianity.

WHAT DO CHRISTIANS BELIEVE? That there is one God. That Jesus Christ is the Son of God, who came on Earth, died to save humankind, and rose from the dead.

HOW MANY ARE THERE? Christianity is the world's biggest religion. In 2001 there were more than two billion Christians, in nearly all parts of the world. More than one billion of the Christians were **Roman Catholics**, who follow the leadership of the pope in Rome. Other groups of Christians include **Orthodox Christians**, who accept most of the same teachings as **Roman Catholics** but follow different leadership, and **Protestants**, who often disagree with Catholic teachings. Protestants rely especially on the Bible itself. They belong to many different group or "denominations."

183

HINDUISM

WHO STARTED HINDUISM?
Aryan beliefs spread into India, around 1500 B.C. These beliefs were mixed with the beliefs of the people who already lived there.

WHAT IS THE RELIGIOUS WRITING?
The **Bhagavad Ghita**, part of a long poem about war, is one of several Hindu religious writings.

WHAT DO HINDUS BELIEVE?
That there are many gods and many ways of worshipping. That people die and are reborn many times as other living things. That there is a universal soul or principle known as **Brahman**. That the goal of life is to escape the cycle of birth and death and become part of the **Brahman**. This is achieved by leading a pure and good life.

HOW MANY ARE THERE?
In 2001, there were about 820 million Hindus, mainly in India and places where people from India have gone to live.

WHAT KINDS ARE THERE?
There are many kinds of Hindus, who worship different gods or goddesses.

ISLAM

WHO STARTED ISLAM?
Muhammad, the Prophet, in A.D. 610.

WHAT IS THE RELIGIOUS WRITING?
The **Koran** (al-Qur'an in Arabic) sets out the main beliefs and practices of Islam, the religion of Muslims.

People who believe in Islam are known as Muslims. The word "Islam" means submission to God. Muslims believe that there is no other god than the one God; that Muhammad is the prophet and lawgiver of his community; that they should pray five times a day, fast during the month of Ramadan, give to the poor, and once during their life make a pilgrimage to Mecca in Saudi Arabia if they can afford it.

HOW MANY ARE THERE?
In 2001, there were more than one billion Muslims, mostly in parts of Africa and Asia. The two main branches are: **Sunni Muslims**, who make up over 80 percent of all Muslims today, and **Shiite Muslims**, who broke away in a dispute over leadership after Muhammad died in 632.

JUDAISM

WHO STARTED JUDAISM?
Abraham is considered to be the founder of Judaism. He lived around 1300 B.C.

WHAT IS THE RELIGIOUS WRITING?
The most important is the **Torah**, the first five books of the Old Testament of the Bible.

WHAT DO JEWS BELIEVE?
That there is one God who created the universe and rules over it. That they should be faithful to God and carry out God's commandments.

HOW MANY ARE THERE?
In 2001, there were about 14½ million Jews living around the world. Many live in Israel or the United States.

WHAT KINDS ARE THERE?
In the United States there are three main kinds: **Orthodox**, **Conservative**, and **Reform**. Orthodox Jews are the most traditional. Traditional means that they follow strict laws about how they dress, what they can eat, and how they conduct their lives. Conservative Jews follow many of the traditions. Reform Jews are the least traditional.

MAJOR HOLY DAYS FOR
CHRISTIANS, JEWS, AND MUSLIMS

CHRISTIAN HOLY DAYS

	2002	2003	2004
Ash Wednesday	February 13	March 5	February 25
Good Friday	March 29	April 18	April 9
Easter Sunday	March 31	April 20	April 11
Easter for Orthodox Churches	May 5	April 27	April 11
Christmas	December 25	December 25	December 25

JEWISH HOLY DAYS
The Jewish holy days begin at sundown the night before the first full day of the observance. The dates of these evenings are listed below.

	2002 (5762)	2003 (5763)	2004 (5764)
Passover	March 27	April 16	April 6
Rosh Hashanah (New Year)	September 16	September 26	September 16
Yom Kippur	September 15	October 5	September 25
Hanukkah	November 29	December 19	December 8

ISLAMIC (MUSLIM) HOLY DAYS

	2002 (1423)	2003 (1424)	2004 (1425)
Muharram 1 (New Year)	March 15	March 4	February 22
Mawlid (Birthday of Muhammad)	May 24	May 13	May 1
Ramadan 1	November 6	October 26	October 16
Id al-Adha Dhu al-Hijjah 10	February 22	February 11	January 21

MAJOR HOLY DAYS FOR
BUDDHISTS AND HINDUS

BUDDHIST HOLY DAYS
Not all Buddhists use the same calendar to determine religious holidays and festivals. Here are some well-known Buddhist observances and the months (on the Gregorian calendar) in which they may fall:

Nirvana Day, mid-February: Marks the death of Siddhartha Gautama (the Buddha).

Vesak, April/May: Buddha's Birthday.

Khao Pansa, begins on full moon in July: Three-month observance similar to Christian Lent.

Bodhi Day, November/December: Celebrates the Buddha's achieving a "blessed state" in 596 B.C.

HINDU HOLY DAYS
Hindu festivals happen throughout the year. Different Hindu groups use different calendars. Here are a few of the many Hindu festivals and the months (on the Gregorian calendar) in which they may fall:

Maha Shivaratri, February/March: festival dedicated to Shiva, creator and destroyer.

Holi, March/April: festival of spring.

Ramanavami, March/April: anniversary of the birth of Rama, who is Vishnu in human form.

Diwali, October/November: Hindu New Year, the "Festival of Lights."

RELIGIOUS MEMBERSHIP IN THE UNITED STATES

Did you know that Protestants are the largest religious group in the United States, and that Catholics are the second largest? The pie chart below shows how many people belong to the largest religious groups. These numbers are recent estimates; no one knows exactly how many people belong to each group.

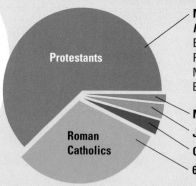

More than 100 million
Including:

Baptists	28 million	Methodists	12 million
Pentecostals	11 million	Lutherans	9 million
Mormon	5 million	Presbyterians	4 million
Episcopalians	2 million	Reformed Churches	2 million

Muslims ....4 million

Jews ....6 million

Orthodox Christians .....6 million

62 million

There were also an estimated 2 million Buddhists and 1 million Hindus.

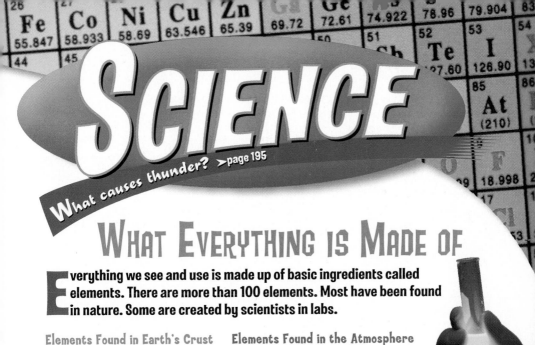

What causes thunder? ➤page 195

WHAT EVERYTHING IS MADE OF

Everything we see and use is made up of basic ingredients called elements. There are more than 100 elements. Most have been found in nature. Some are created by scientists in labs.

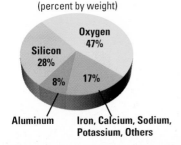

Elements Found in Earth's Crust
(percent by weight)

Oxygen 47%
Silicon 28%
Aluminum 8%
17%
Iron, Calcium, Sodium, Potassium, Others

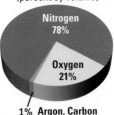

Elements Found in the Atmosphere
(percent by volume)

Nitrogen 78%
Oxygen 21%
1% Argon, Carbon Dioxide, Others

IT ALL STARTS WITH AN ATOM

The smallest possible piece of an element that has all the properties of the original element is called an **atom**. Each tiny atom is made up of even smaller particles called **protons**, **neutrons**, and **electrons**. These are made up of even smaller particles called **quarks**.

To tell one element from another, scientists count the number of protons in an atom. The total number of protons is called the element's **atomic number**. All of the atoms of an element have the same number of protons and electrons, but some atoms have a different number of neutrons. For example, carbon-12 has six protons and six neutrons, and carbon-13 has six protons and seven neutrons.

We call the amount of matter in an atom its atomic mass. Carbon-13 has a greater atomic mass than carbon-12. The average atomic mass of all of the different atoms of the same element is called the element's **atomic weight**. Every element has a different atomic number and a different atomic weight.

CHEMICAL SYMBOLS ARE SCIENTIFIC SHORTHAND

When scientists write the names of elements, they often use a symbol instead of spelling out the full name. The symbol for each element is one or two letters. Scientists write O for oxygen and He for helium. The symbols usually come from the English name for the element (C for carbon). The symbols for some of the elements come from the element's Latin name. For example, the symbol for gold is Au, which is short for Aurum, the Latin word for gold.

How Elements are Named

How many of these elements have you heard of?

NAME	SYMBOL	WHAT IT IS	WHEN FOUND	NAMED FOR
Aluminum	Al	metal	1825	*alumen*, Latin word for "alum"
Helium	He	gas	1868	the Greek word *helios*, meaning sun
Mercury	Hg	liquid metal	B.C.	the Roman god Mercury
Neon	Ne	gas	1898	the Greek word *neon*, meaning new
Palladium	Pd	transitional metal	1803	asteroid Pallas (a name for Greek goddess of wisdom)
Strontium	Sr	alkaline earth metal	1808	Strontian, town in Scotland
Uranium	U	radioactive metal	1789	the planet Uranus
Zirconium	Zr	transitional metal	1789	*zargun*, Persian word for "gold-like"

Elements are named after places, scientists, myths, or properties of the element. But no element gets a name until the International Union of Pure and Applied Chemistry (IUPAC) accepts it. In all, 109 elements have been named. Several others have been reported, but not named and not yet confirmed. Can you think of a few names to suggest?

All About...
COMPOUNDS

Carbon, hydrogen, nitrogen, and oxygen are the most common chemical elements in the human body. Many other elements may be found in small amounts. These include calcium, iron, phosphorous, potassium, and sodium.

When elements join together, they form compounds. Water is a compound made up of hydrogen and oxygen. Salt is a compound made up of sodium and chlorine.

Common Name	Contains the Compound	Contains the Elements
Aspirin	acetylsalicylic acid	carbon, oxygen, hydrogen
Baking soda	sodium bicarbonate	sodium, hydrogen, carbon, oxygen
Bleach (liquid)	sodium hypochlorite	sodium, chlorine, oxygen
Chalk	calcium carbonate	calcium, carbon, oxygen
Iron pyrite (fool's gold)	iron disulfide	iron, sulfur
Marble	calcium carbonate	calcium, carbon
Rubbing alcohol	isopropyl alcohol	carbon, hydrogen, oxygen

MINERALS, ROCKS, and GEMS

WHAT ARE MINERALS?

Minerals are solid materials that were never alive. All the land on our planet—even the ocean floor—rests on a layer of rock made up of minerals. Minerals have also been found on other planets, on our moon, and in meteorites that landed on Earth. Some minerals, such as **gold** and **silver**, are made up entirely of one element. But most are formed from two or more elements joined together.

The most common mineral is **quartz**, which is made of silicon and oxygen and is found all over the world. **Sand** is made up mostly of quartz. **Graphite**, which is used in pencils, is another common mineral. Other minerals, like **diamonds**, are very rare and valuable. Diamonds and graphite are different forms of the same element—carbon!

WHAT ARE ROCKS?

Rocks are combinations of minerals. There are three kinds:

1 IGNEOUS ROCKS—rocks that form from melted minerals deep in the Earth that cool and become solid. Granite is an igneous rock made from quartz, feldspar, and mica.

2 SEDIMENTARY ROCKS—rocks that usually form in the beds of seas, lakes, and rivers from tiny pieces of other rocks, sand, and shells packed together. It takes millions of years to form sedimentary rocks. Limestone is a kind of sedimentary rock.

3 METAMORPHIC ROCK—Over millions of years, the heat and pressure inside Earth can change the minerals in igneous and sedimentary rocks. When these minerals change, the new rock is called a **metamorphic rock**. Marble is a metamorphic rock formed from limestone.

WHAT ARE GEMS?

Most **gems** are minerals that have been cut and polished to be used as jewelry or other kinds of decoration. Some gems are not minerals. A pearl is not a mineral; it comes from an oyster, which is a living thing. The most valued gems—diamonds, emeralds, rubies, and sapphires—are minerals called **precious stones**. Here are some popular gems:

GEM NAME	MINERAL	ELEMENT IT IS MADE OF	USUAL COLORS
Topaz	aluminum, fluosilicate	aluminum, silicon, oxygen, fluorine, hydrogen	red, pink
Diamond	carbon	carbon	bluish white
Emerald	beryl	beryllium, silicon, aluminum, oxygen	green
Aquamarine	beryl	beryllium, silicon, aluminum, oxygen iron	blue-green
Ruby	corundum	aluminum, oxygen	red
Sapphire	corundum	aluminum, oxygen	blue

Did You KNOW?

TINY ORGANISMS CALLED EXTREMOPHILES get their energy by taking in dissolved substances and changing them to solids. These organisms are widely used in pollution cleanup. One kind of extremophile "eats" dissolved gold near hot water vents deep in the ocean. But you can't get rich by making solid gold this way. It would cost more than the value of the gold.

WHAT IS DNA?

Every cell in every living thing (or organism) has DNA, a molecule that contains all the information about that organism. Lengths of connected DNA molecules, called genes, are like tiny pieces of a secret code. They determine what each organism is like in great detail.

Genes are passed on from parents to children, and no two organisms (except identical twins) have the same DNA. Many things about us—the color of our eyes or hair, whether we're tall or short, the size of our feet—depend on the genes we inherited from our parents.

DNA "FINGERPRINTS"

DNA is located in each of your cells, including your blood, saliva, hair follicles, and skin. No one else has a DNA pattern exactly like yours. Using skin or hair collected at a crime scene and samples from a suspect, scientists can analyze the makeup of the two sets of DNA. If they match and no error was made collecting the material, they are almost surely from the same person. Cells from a person at a crime scene can be evidence that the person was present at the crime. DNA evidence is also used to show that some convicted people are innocent.

WHAT MAKES US HUMAN

The human genome is the DNA code for our species—it's what makes us human beings. In 2000, the U.S. Human Genome Project reached a milestone. It identified the 3.1 billion separate codes in human DNA. In 2001, researchers reported that the human genome contains about 30,000 to 40,000 genes. For the first time, we got an outline of the genetic code for the human race.

Surprisingly, humans don't have that many more genes than the roundworm, which has about 20,000! But we do have three times as many kinds of proteins as the fly or worm, because of a process in humans called "alternative splicing." This means that the same gene can produce more than one kind of protein. By studying genes scientists can learn more about hereditary diseases and get a better idea of how human beings evolved.

All About... CLONING

A clone is an organism that has developed from a cell of just one other organism. This means it has the exact same DNA as its parent. Scientists have been able to clone mammals artificially. The most famous clone was a sheep named Dolly, born in Scotland in 1996. Dolly has now developed arthritis sooner than most sheep do. Scientists don't know whether this is because she was cloned or for some other reason. But labs that have cloned cattle, sheep, and goats say the animals that survive to adulthood are normal in every way they can measure.

In February 2002, researchers in Texas announced the birth of "CC" (carbon copy), the world's first cloned cat. CC has exactly the same DNA as Rainbow, the cat she was cloned from. But these two cats look different. This is because calico patterns on cats are caused by random changes during their growth in the womb, rather than by genes.

Human cloning may also be possible one day. But many people believe human cloning would be wrong.

"CC," a cloned cat ▶

Some Famous Scientists

Tim Berners-Lee (1955–), a British computer whiz who radically changed the history of computing and communication when he invented the World Wide Web in 1989. Since then he has worked to make the web grow as a source of information about everything under the sun. He works at a laboratory in Massachusetts.

Nicolaus Copernicus (1473–1543), a Polish scientist known as the founder of modern astronomy. He came up with the theory that Earth and other planets revolve around the sun. At the time most people thought Earth was the center of the universe, and not much attention was paid to his theory.

Marie Curie (1867–1934), a Polish-French physical chemist known for discovering radium, which is used to treat some diseases. She won the Nobel Prize for chemistry in 1911. She and her husband, Pierre Curie, also won the Nobel Prize for physics in 1903 for their work in radiation.

Charles Darwin (1809–1882), a British scientist best known for his theory of evolution. According to this theory, living creatures slowly developed over millions of years into the forms they have today.

Thomas Edison (1847–1931), Ohio-born inventor who only attended school for three months. He created devices that transformed society, such as a reliable electric lightbulb, the electric generator, phonograph, wireless telegraph, motion-picture projector, and alkaline, iron-nickel batteries.

Albert Einstein (1879–1955), a German-American physicist who developed a revolutionary theory about the relationships between time, space, matter, and energy. He won a Nobel Prize in 1921.

Frederick Jones (1892–1961), changed our eating habits by inventing refrigerated trucks, eliminating the problem of food spoilage.

Johannes Kepler (1571–1630), German astronomer who developed three laws of planetary motion. He was the first to propose a force (later named gravity) that governs planets' orbits around the sun.

Ada Lovelace (1815–1852), British mathematical genius who is considered the first computer programmer. She designed a "language" for the first computing machine (invented by Charles Babbage).

Lise Meitner (1878–1968), physicist who first discovered nuclear fission. She later predicted the chain reaction, which eventually led to the development of the atomic bomb, along with other nuclear energies.

Louis Eugene Neel (1904–2000), a French physicist who discovered that certain materials that do not conduct electricity can still be magnetized. This allowed the development of the silicon computer chip. His work on magnetism also led to the theory of plate tectonics.

Sir Isaac Newton (1642–1727), a British scientist famous for many revolutionary discoveries. He worked out the basic laws of motion and gravity. He also showed that sunlight is made up of all the colors of the rainbow. He invented the branch of mathematics called calculus, but he kept this discovery quiet. Soon after, a German philosopher and mathematician named Gottfried von Leibniz (1646–1716) also worked out a system of calculus, and made it widely known.

Wolfgang Pauli (1900–1958), Austrian-American physicist who invented a famous rule of physics. It says two electrons cannot occupy the same energy state in an atom at the same time. This helps explain why objects do not blend into each other. In 1931 he proposed the existence of a tiny particle, called a neutrino. Scientists confirmed 25 years later that it exists.

SCIENCE MUSEUMS

If you like exhibits you can touch and interact with, here are a few museums that you might like to visit:

Franklin Institute Science Museum, Philadelphia, Pennsylvania.
Benjamin Franklin has his own exhibit hall where visitors can experiment with some of his inventions. The bioscience exhibit invites visitors to listen to their own heartbeats and experience what it's like inside a human heart. "It's All in the Brain" helps visitors experience how the brain reacts to the outside world.

WEB SITE *http://www.fi.edu*

Did You KNOW?

BENJAMIN FRANKLIN first suggested the idea of "daylight saving" time in an essay published in 1784.

The Science Museum of Minnesota, St. Paul, Minnesota,
gives visitors the chance to gaze at one of the world's only complete mounted Triceratops, create and destroy a (pretend) tornado, examine a (real) Egyptian mummy, and enjoy exciting films like *Pathway to the Stars* and *Island of the Sharks*.

WEB SITE *http://www.smm.org*

A kid at Chicago's Museum of Science and Industry ▼

The Museum of Science, Boston,
Massachusetts, invites visitors to become explorers in the world of natural mysteries, check out the action on the Science Live! Stage, get wired in at the Cahners Computer Place, take a dip in the Virtual Fish Tank, and find out why "Seeing is Deceiving" at the Light House in the Investigate activity center.

WEB SITE *http://www.mos.org*

The Museum of Science and Industry, Chicago, Illinois, is the
largest science museum in a single building in the Western Hemisphere. It has more than 800 exhibits. Among these is an interactive hip-hop exhibit and the new "Science of the SuperCroc" display, which includes a 40-foot skeleton of the ancient croc.

WEB SITE *http://www. msi.chicago.org*

SOLAR-POWERED RAINMAKER

Did you ever wonder where rain comes from? Most of it comes from the sea. About 208 cubic miles of water evaporates from the world's oceans every day, to fall down as rain. But the sea is salty and rainwater is fresh. Why is that? You can build a solar still to purify saltwater, and see for yourself. (Just to be safe, and not too messy, have an adult around while you do this.)

THE MATERIALS:

▶ a **clean** jar (either glass or plastic is OK), with a wide opening and a lid

▶ a container that will hold water and is small enough to fit upright inside the jar

▶ salt, water, and a spoon

THE SETUP:

1 Fill the small container about three-quarters full of water.

2 Stir in a couple of teaspoons of salt (taste it).

3 Place the lid upside-down on the table or counter.

4 Stand the container of saltwater inside the upside-down lid.

5 Turn the big jar over and carefully screw it onto the lid, over the water container.

6 Put your new solar still in a sunny window for a few hours.

Note: If you don't have a jar, you can use a large bowl and cover the top with plastic wrap. You can use tape or a rubber band to seal it tightly.

WHAT HAS HAPPENED:

After your solar still is in the sun for a while, you should notice droplets forming on the inside of the jar. The heat from the sun caused water to evaporate (turn from liquid to gas) from the saltwater solution, leaving the salt where it was. As some of the fast-moving water vapor molecules came in contact with the sides of the jar, which were exposed to cooler air outside, they slowed down. When the molecules slowed enough, they condensed, changing from gas back to liquid form. (If you put the jar in the refrigerator for a while, it would speed up the condensation.)

TEST THE WATER YOURSELF:

Carefully open the jar and use your finger to taste any water droplets that collected in the lid or on the insides of the jar. Are they fresh or salty? Taste the saltwater again for comparison.

Would this experiment work if you mixed dirt in with the saltwater? Try it and see.

To learn more about evaporation and the hydrological cycle, see page 70.

SCIENCE Q & A

WHY DO LEAVES CHANGE COLOR IN THE FALL? Tree leaves contain a chemical called *chlorophyll*, which makes them look green in spring and summer. Chlorophyll helps capture light energy from the Sun and change it to a chemical form, like sugar, as food for the tree. The leaves also contain yellow and orange *carotenoids* (the substance that makes carrots orange), but the green chlorophyll in spring and summer masks those other colors. In the fall, as days get shorter and colder, the chlorophyll breaks down and the yellow and orange show up. If the temperature falls below 45 degrees at night, sugar made during the day gets trapped in the leaves. This is what makes sugar maple leaves look red.

WHY IS IT COLD IN THE WINTER AND HOT IN THE SUMMER? Imagine a line running through the center of Earth from the north pole to the south pole. Earth rotates around this line (its *axis*). Because Earth's axis is tilted (23.5 degrees), either the Northern or Southern Hemisphere points toward the Sun as the planet orbits around it. When the Northern Hemisphere points toward the Sun in June, July, and August, the Southern Hemisphere points away. In December, January, and February, these positions are reversed (Australia has its summer during North America's winter!) Tilting away from the Sun in winter means that the light comes in at an angle. The heat energy from the Sun is less intense because it is spread out over more area.

WHY DOES SHAKING A CAN OF SODA MAKE IT SPRAY ALL OVER? A can of soda contains *carbon dioxide gas* under pressure. The pressure makes it dissolve in the soda. Molecules in a liquid have a strong attraction for each other (called *surface tension*). It takes energy to separate them, so it is hard for the carbon dioxide inside the can to form bubbles. Once a bubble is formed, it takes less energy for the gas molecules to join the existing bubble.

When you open a soda can, the gas escapes slowly and the soda takes a long time to go flat. But if you shake the can first, the little bit of gas above the soda seeps into the liquid as small bubbles. This gives the gas many "starting points" to get out—in a hurry.

WHAT CAUSES RAINBOWS? The light we usually see (visible light) is made up of different frequencies, or colors, in a certain range, called the *spectrum*. The colors of the visible spectrum are red, orange, yellow, green, blue, indigo, and violet. White light is a mixture of all these colors. A *prism* can separate the frequencies mixed in a beam of white light. When you see a rainbow, the tiny water droplets in the air act as many tiny prisms, separating the Sun's white light into the colors of the spectrum.

WHY DO DIVERS GET "THE BENDS"?

The air we breathe is 78% *nitrogen* and 21% oxygen. Our bodies can't use nitrogen and we normally get rid of it when we breathe out. Underwater, the pressure on a diver's body increases. The diver is also breathing pressurized air—which is mostly nitrogen—from tanks. More and more nitrogen gets into the body as the diver goes deeper. This is OK until the diver starts back up. Rising fast makes the nitrogen form bubbles. This can cause a rash, coughing, dizziness, unconsciousness, and death. It also makes it hard to bend at the joints—that's why we call it the "bends." To avoid this, a diver must rise very slowly. Then the nitrogen can escape through the lungs, molecule by molecule—the only safe way.

WHY DOES CHOPPING ONIONS MAKE YOUR EYES WATER?

It isn't the smell. The knife breaks open the onion's cells, letting out enzymes that react with other substances from the broken cells. A *gas* is formed which reacts with water on the surface of your eyes to form a mild *sulfuric acid*. The front of the eye (cornea) has many sensitive *nerve endings*. They detect the irritation and alert the brain. The brain tells the tear ducts (*lachrymal glands*) to produce more water to clean the eyes.

WHAT CAUSES THUNDER? *Lightning* does. In an instant,

a bolt of lightning can heat the air around it up to 60,000°F. The heated air expands violently, like an explosion. As the air expands it also cools quickly and starts to contract. This quick expansion and contraction air creates the shock waves we hear as thunder.

Think of popping a balloon. When you blow it up, you are putting the air under pressure. Why? Because air molecules in the balloon are packed more tightly than they are in the air around it. The rubber keeps the air inside the balloon from spreading out. When the balloon breaks, the air expands rapidly (like the air superheated by lightning). The molecules from inside the balloon push against those on the outside—creating a shock wave that you hear as a "pop."

WHY IS THE SKY BLUE? *Sunlight* makes the sky blue. Light from the Sun is actually

white until it reaches Earth's atmosphere. Then it hits water vapor, dust, and other particles in the air and scatters in different directions. White light is made up of all the colors of the spectrum. Since blue is scattered much more than any other color, blue is what we see when we look up at a clear sky. During sunrises and sunsets, we see red and orange because the Sun is closer to the horizon, scattering blue light out of our line of sight.

CAN A BASEBALL PITCHER REALLY MAKE A BALL CURVE?

Pitchers can make a ball curve as much as 17 1/2 inches from its path. A snap of the wrist puts extra *spin* on the ball. As it spins, the stitches on one side move with the airflow around it. The stitches on the other side move against the airflow. When stitches and air move together, the flow is faster. The increased speed reduces the air pressure on that side. On the opposite side, the air pressure is increased. The ball moves—curves—toward the side of the ball with the lower pressure.

SIGNS & SYMBOLS

What were "whales" and "turtles" in World War II? ➤ page 197

Signs and symbols give us information at a glance. In the days when most people could not read, pictures helped them find their way around. Today, many of the same symbols are used the world over.

ROAD SIGNS

Stop	One Way	No Entry	No U-Turn	No Parking
Right Turn	No Left Turn	Hill	Signal Ahead	School Zone
Pedestrian Crossing	Deer Crossing	Railroad Crossing	Road Work Ahead	Cross Road
Winding Road	Slippery Road	Divided Highway	Yield	Merging Traffic

SOME USEFUL SYMBOLS

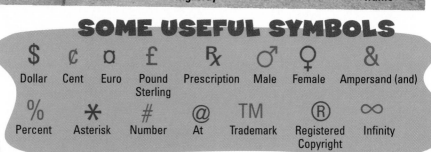

$	¢	₡	£	℞	♂	♀	&
Dollar	Cent	Euro	Pound Sterling	Prescription	Male	Female	Ampersand (and)

%	✻	#	@	TM	®	∞
Percent	Asterisk	Number	At	Trademark	Registered Copyright	Infinity

THE ZODIAC

The zodiac is an imaginary belt that goes around the sky. The orbits of the sun, moon, and most planets are within it. It crosses parts of 21 constellations. Below are the symbols for the 12 constellations most commonly associated with the zodiac.

ARIES (Ram)
March 21–April 19

TAURUS (Bull)
April 20–May 20

GEMINI (Twins)
May 21–June 21

CANCER (Crab)
June 22–July 22

LEO (Lion)
July 23–August 22

VIRGO (Maiden)
August 23–Sept. 22

LIBRA (Balance)
Sept. 23–Oct. 23

SCORPIO (Scorpion)
Oct. 24–Nov. 21

SAGITTARIUS
(Archer)
Nov. 22–Dec. 21

CAPRICORN (Goat)
Dec. 22–Jan. 19

AQUARIUS
(Water Bearer)
Jan. 20–Feb. 18

PISCES (Fishes)
Feb. 19–March 20

All About...
NATIVE AMERICAN CODE TALKERS

In 1918, during the final days of World War I, an American Army captain overheard two soldiers speaking in their native Choctaw language. He didn't understand the words, but he understood something more important. The Germans, who had broken all the U.S. radio codes used so far, would be just as puzzled by Choctaw as he was. The captain's idea led to a secret program of the U.S. military. In World War II, Navajo Indian "code talkers" used a coded form of their language to send secret U.S. military messages in the Pacific. The Japanese could not understand this double code. Comanche soldiers in Europe talked right past the Germans, and other tribes used their languages as codes too. When there were no Native American words for a military term or the name of a country, the code talkers used other words instead. To talk about tanks, the Comanches used their word for *turtle*. The Navajo used their word for *whale* to refer to a battleship. A fighter plane was a "humming bird," and a bomber was a "buzzard."

In 2001, 29 Navajo code talkers were awarded the Congressional Gold Medal. President George W. Bush personally presented the medals to four of the five code talkers still living.

Navajo code talkers at a field radio, 1943 ▶

197

BRAILLE

Many blind people read with their fingers, using a system of raised dots called Braille. Braille was developed by Louis Braille (1809-1852) in France in 1826, when he was still a teenager.

The Braille alphabet, numbers, punctuation, and speech sounds are shown by 63 different combinations of 6 raised dots arranged in a grid like this:

```
1  4
2  5
3  6
```

All the letters in the basic Braille alphabet are lowercase. Special symbols are added to show that what follows is a capital letter or a number. The white circles on the grid below show the raised dots.

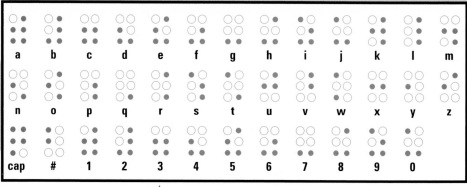

▲ *Braille alphabet and numbers*

SIGN LANGUAGE

Many people who are deaf or hearing-impaired, and cannot hear spoken words, talk with their fingers instead of their voices. To do this, they use a system of manual signs (the manual alphabet), or finger spelling, in which the fingers are used to form letters and words. Originally developed in France by Abbe Charles Michel De l'Epee in the late 1700s, the manual alphabet was later brought to the United States by Laurent Clerc (1785-1869), a Frenchman who taught people who were deaf.

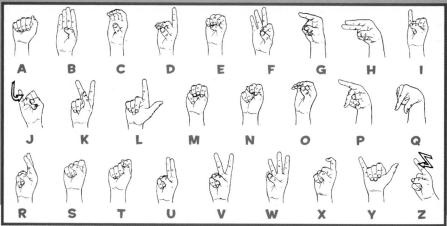

▲ *American Manual Alphabet*

THE STORY OF & *The ampersand (&) comes from the Latin word et, which means "and." Think of a curly capital E followed by a lowercase t whose bar slants down to the right, and you may begin to see the word behind the symbol. The @ symbol comes from Latin, too. It was a handwritten version of the Latin word ad (meaning "to") that developed in the Middle Ages. By turning the d's vertical part into a circle, and by combining the two letters, the monks who were doing the writing saved ink, time, and parchment.*

JBEYQ NYZNANP SBE XVQF

No, that's not a mistake. In order to figure out what it says, take a look at the "Split Alphabet" code below. This is one simple way to create a secret code.

SPLIT ALPHABET

To solve this secret code, you need a key. The key is created by writing out the alphabet until the halfway point (just after the letter M), and then writing out the rest of the alphabet so that each letter is underneath a letter from the first half. The key looks like this:

A B C D E F G H I J K L M
N O P Q R S T U V W X Y Z

When you want to encode a letter, simply use the letter that it is paired up with. For example, "A" becomes "N," and "O" becomes "B." The title on this page uses the Split Alphabet code. Can you figure out what it says? Here's another hidden message. Can you decode it?

V UNIR ARJF SBE LBH

THREE-ROW BLOCK

To put messages into this code, first write them out in a block with three rows (or as close to three rows as you can) and then read downward. It helps if you count the letters first, then divide by 3, so that you know how long each row should be. For example, let's encode the message "I can come over tomorrow." The message has 20 letters. Divided by 3, that equals more than 6, so we'll use 7 letters in the first two rows. Here's what our box will look like:

I C A N C O M
E O V E R T O
M O R R O W

Reading downward, you can create the encoded message:

IEM COO AVR NER CRO OTW MO

To decode a message, simply put the letters back into a three-row box, going down each column before moving to the next one. The hardest part is gussing where the spaces should be so that the decoded message isn't just one long word!

Can you tell people your full name using the three-row block?

ANSWERS ON PAGES 314-317. FOR MORE PUZZLES GO TO WWW.WORLDALMANACFORKIDS.COM

What temperature is it in space? ➤page 206

The SOLAR SYSTEM

Nine planets, including Earth, travel around the Sun. These planets, together with the Sun, make up the solar system.

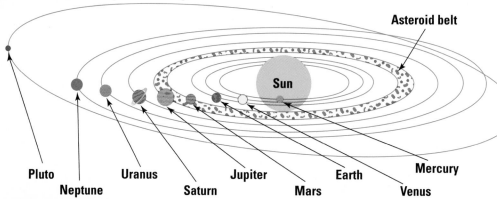

Asteroid belt

Sun

Pluto
Neptune
Uranus
Saturn
Jupiter
Mars
Earth
Venus
Mercury

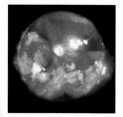

THE SUN IS A STAR

Did you know that the Sun is a star, like the other stars you see at night? It is a typical, medium-size star. But because the Sun is much closer to our planet than any other star, we can study it in great detail. The diameter of the Sun is 864,000 miles—more than 100 times Earth's diameter. The gravity of the Sun is nearly 28 times the gravity of Earth.

How Hot Is the Sun? The surface temperature of the Sun is close to 10,000°F, and it is believed that the sun's inner core may reach temperatures near 35 million degrees! The Sun provides enough light and heat energy to support all forms of life on our planet.

The Planets are in Motion

The planets move around the Sun along oval-shaped paths called **orbits**. One complete path around the Sun is called a **revolution**. Earth takes one year, or 365¼ days, to make one revolution around the Sun. Planets that are farther away from the Sun take longer. Some planets have one or more **moons**. A moon orbits a planet in much the same way that the planets orbit the Sun.

Each planet also spins (or rotates) on its axis. An **axis** is an imaginary line running through the center of a planet. The time it takes Earth to rotate on its axis equals one day. Here are some other facts about the planets.

The Planets

1 MERCURY

Average distance from the Sun: 36 million miles
Diameter: 3,032 miles
Temperature: 333 degrees F
Surface: silicate rock
Time to revolve around the Sun: 88 days
Time to rotate on its axis:
  58 days, 15 hours, 30 minutes
Number of moons: 0

DID YOU KNOW? *Four billion years ago a gigantic asteroid hit Mercury, creating a 1,300-mile-wide crater on the surface—so big that the entire state of Texas could fit in it.*

2 VENUS

Average distance from the Sun: 67 million miles
Diameter: 7,521 miles
Temperature: 867 degrees F
Surface: silicate rock
Time to revolve around the Sun: 224.7 days
Time to rotate on its axis: 243 days
Number of moons: 0

DID YOU KNOW? *Even though Venus is farther away from the Sun than Mercury, it is the hottest planet because the high level of carbon dioxide in the atmosphere creates an extreme greenhouse effect, trapping in the Sun's heat.*

3 EARTH

Average distance from the Sun: 93 million miles
Diameter: 7,926 miles
Temperature: 59 degrees F
Surface: water, basalt and granite rock
Time to revolve around the Sun: 365 ¼ days
Time to rotate on its axis: 23 hours, 56 minutes, 4.2 seconds
Number of moons: 1

DID YOU KNOW? *The Earth is moving around the Sun at approximately 67,000 miles an hour.*

4 MARS

Average distance from the Sun: 142 million miles
Diameter: 4,213 miles
Temperature: −81 degrees F
Surface: iron-rich basaltic rock
Time to revolve around the Sun: 687 days
Time to rotate on its axis:
  24 hours, 37 minutes, 22 seconds
Number of moons: 2

DID YOU KNOW? *Many features on Mars seem to have been shaped by water, although the only water left on Mars is frozen underneath layers of dust at the north and south poles.*

5 JUPITER

Average distance from the Sun: 484 million miles
Diameter: 88,732 miles
Temperature: −162 degrees F
Surface: liquid hydrogen
Time to revolve around the Sun: 11.9 years
Time to rotate on its axis: 9 hours, 55 minutes, 30 seconds
Number of moons: 16

DID YOU KNOW? *Jupiter is so big that all the other planets in the solar system could fit inside it at the same time.*

6 SATURN

Average distance from the Sun: 888 million miles
Diameter: 74,975 miles
Temperature: −218 degrees F
Surface: liquid hydrogen
Time to revolve around the Sun: 29.5 years
Time to rotate on its axis: 10 hours, 30 minutes
Number of moons: at least 18

DID YOU KNOW? *Using the world's first telescope, Galileo discovered what turned out to be rings around Saturn.*

7 URANUS

Average distance from the Sun: 1.8 billion miles

Diameter: 31,763 miles

Temperature: −323 degrees F

Surface: liquid hydrogen and helium

Time to revolve around the Sun: 84 years

Time to rotate on its axis: 17 hours, 14 minutes

Number of moons: 18

DID YOU KNOW? *Viewed from a telescope on Earth, Uranus appears to rotate on its side because its poles are tilted 98 degrees.*

8 NEPTUNE

Average distance from the Sun: 2.8 billion miles

Diameter: 30,603 miles

Temperature: −330 degrees F

Surface: liquid hydrogen and helium

Time to revolve around the Sun: 164.8 years

Time to rotate on its axis: 16 hours, 6 minutes

Number of moons: 8

DID YOU KNOW? *Winter on Triton, Neptune's largest satellite, is thought to be the coldest place in the solar system, with temperatures routinely plummeting to −390 degrees Fahrenheit.*

9 PLUTO

Average distance from the Sun: 3.6 billion miles

Diameter: 1,413 miles

Temperature: −369 degrees F

Surface: rock with methane, nitrogen, and carbon dioxide gas

Time to revolve around the Sun: 247.7 years

Time to rotate on its axis: 6 days, 9 hours, 18 minutes

Number of moons: 1

DID YOU KNOW? *Every 228 years, Pluto's elliptical orbit brings it closer to the Sun than Neptune, for 20 years.*

FACTS ABOUT THE PLANETS

Largest planet: Jupiter

Smallest planet: Pluto

Planet closest to the Sun: Mercury

Planet closest to Earth: Venus (Every 19 months, it gets closer than any other planet ever does.)

Fastest-moving planet: Mercury (107,000 miles per hour)

Slowest planet: Pluto (10,600 mph)

Warmest planet: Venus

Coldest planet: Pluto

Tallest mountain: Mars

Deepest ocean: Jupiter

Did You Know?

*To say something happens "once in a blue moon" means that it rarely occurs. References have been made to a blue moon as far back as the 1500s, and at one time, it meant "never." But today, people say that a "blue moon" is the second full moon in a calendar month. This happens about every 2½ years (the next one will be in July 2004). Interestingly, the moon really **can** look blue, but only rarely, when dust or smoke (such as from a big volcano or huge forest fires) fills the air over a wide area.*

THE MOON

The moon is about 238,900 miles from Earth. It is 2,160 miles in diameter and has no atmosphere. The dusty surface is covered with deep craters. It takes the same time for the moon to rotate on its axis as it does to orbit Earth (27 days, 7 hours, 43 minutes). This is why one side of the moon is always facing Earth. The moon has no light of its own, but reflects light from the Sun. The fraction of the lighted part of the moon that we see is called a *phase*. It takes the moon about 29½ days to go through all its phases.

Phases of the Moon

New Moon

Crescent Moon

First Quarter

Full Moon

Last Quarter

Crescent Moon

New Moon

EXPLORING *Space*

American space exploration began in January 1958, when the Explorer I satellite was launched into orbit. In 1958, NASA (the National Aeronautics and Space Administration) was formed.

SEARCHING for LIFE

For years scientists have tried to discover whether there is life on other planets in our solar system or elsewhere. They look for signs of what is needed for life on Earth—basics like water and proper temperature.

NASA is searching for signs of life on Mars. This search will continue until at least 2013. Some spacecraft will fly around Mars taking pictures. Others will land there to study soil and rocks and look for living things. Mars Pathfinder and Mars Global Surveyor, launched in 1996, reached Mars in 1997. (Unfortunately, two later missions to Mars failed.)

In 1996, scientists examined two meteorites that may have come from Mars and found evidence that some form of life may have existed there billions of years ago.

NASA has a new telescope mission planned for 2005 called the Terrestrial Planet Finder. It will look for planets similar to Earth in other solar systems through a giant, space-based telescope.

Outside of NASA, another program is looking for life on other worlds. It is called SETI (Search for Extraterrestrial Intelligence). Most often it uses powerful radio telescopes to detect signs of life. Recently, however, astronomers began searching for light signals as signs of extraterrestrial life.

In the last few years, astronomers have found over 70 planets outside our solar system. There could be life on one of those planets, or on a planet we have not found yet.

UNMANNED MISSIONS IN THE SOLAR SYSTEM

1962 — Mariner 2 First successful flyby of Venus.

1964 — Mariner 4 First probe to reach Mars, 1965.

1972 — Pioneer 10 First probe to reach Jupiter, 1973.

1973 — Mariner 10 Only U.S. probe to Mercury, 1974.

1975 — Viking 1 and 2 Landed on Mars in 1976.

1977 — Voyager 1 Reached Jupiter in 1979 and Saturn in 1980.

1977 — Voyager 2 Reached Jupiter in 1979, Saturn in 1981, Uranus in 1986, Neptune in 1989.

1978 — Pioneer Venus 1 Operated in Venus orbit 14 years.

1989 — Magellan Orbited and mapped Venus.

1989 — Galileo Reached Jupiter, 1995.

1996 — Mars Pathfinder Landed on Mars, sent a roving vehicle (Sojourner) to explore the surface.

1997 — Cassini Expected to reach Saturn in 2004.

1998 — Lunar Prospector Began yearlong orbit.

1999 — Stardust Expected to reach Comet Wild-2 in 2004 to collect dust samples and return them to Earth in 2006.

2001 — Mars Odyssey Launched in April 2001 to study mineralogy and radiation of the planet's surface.

2002 — Mars Odyssey settles into mapping orbit around Mars to study the chemical composition of the red planet.

◄ *Mars Odyssey*

NOT JUST PLANETS
What else is in the solar system besides planets?

COMETS are fast-moving chunks of ice, dust, and rock that form huge gaseous heads as they move nearer to the Sun. One of the most well-known is **Halley's Comet**. It can be seen about every 76 years and will appear in the sky again in the year 2061.

ASTEROIDS (or minor planets) are solid chunks of rock or metal that range in size from small boulders to hundreds of miles across. **Ceres**, the largest, is about 600 miles long. Thousands of asteroids orbit the Sun between Mars and Jupiter.

SATELLITES are objects that move in an orbit around a planet. Moons are natural satellites. Satellites made by humans are used as space stations and observatories. They are also used to take pictures of Earth's surface and to transmit communications signals.

METEOROIDS are small pieces of stone or metal traveling in space. Most meteoroids are fragments from comets or asteroids that broke off from crashes in space with other objects. A few are actually chunks that blew off the Moon or Mars after an asteroid hit. When a meteoroid enters the Earth's atmosphere, it usually burns up completely. This streak of light is called a **meteor**, or "shooting star." If a piece of a meteoroid survives its trip through our atmosphere and lands on Earth, it is called a **meteorite**.

WHAT IS AN ECLIPSE

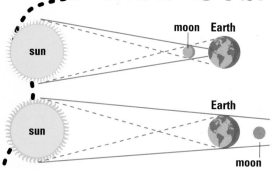

sun — moon — Earth

sun — Earth — moon

During a **solar eclipse**, the moon casts a shadow on Earth. A total solar eclipse is when the Sun is completely blocked out. When this happens, a halo of gas can be seen around the Sun. This is called the **corona**.

Sometimes Earth casts a shadow on the moon. During a total **lunar eclipse**, the moon remains visible, but it looks dark, often with a reddish tinge (from sunlight bent through Earth's atmosphere).

UPCOMING TOTAL SOLAR ECLIPSES

DECEMBER 4, 2002
Will be seen in southern Africa, over the Indian Ocean, and in Australia.

AUGUST 21, 2017
Will be seen from Oregon to South Carolina.

APRIL 8, 2024
Will be seen from Mexico to the Northeastern United States and Canada.

UPCOMING TOTAL LUNAR ECLIPSES

MAY 16, 2003
Will be seen in North, Central, and South America.

NOVEMBER 8-9, 2003
Will be seen from Africa to Europe and western Asia and eastern North America.

MAY 4, 2004
Will be seen in eastern Asia, eastern Africa, and the southern Pacific Ocean.

CONSTELLATIONS

Ancient cultures used myths to explain how constellations came to be. The constellation of Cassiopeia looks like the letter "W" in the sky. In Greek mythology, Cassiopeia was an Ethiopian queen. She was the wife of Cepheus and the mother of Andromeda. According to tradition, when she died, she was changed into the constellation that is named after her.

Andromeda

Cassiopeia

Cepheus

POLARIS
(North Star)

Ursa Minor
(Little Dipper)

Big Dipper

Ursa Major

BIG QUESTIONS

WHAT IS A LIGHT-YEAR?

A **LIGHT-YEAR** is a measure of distance, not time. It is the distance light travels in a year going 186,000 miles a second—which is the fastest speed anything travels. Alpha Centauri, the nearest star that we can see in the sky, is a little over four light-years away. When we see this star in the night sky, the light we see is from four years ago!

HOW FAR AWAY ARE THE STARS?

The stars are all different distances from Earth. Our Sun is about 93 million miles away. The next closest star is Proxima Centauri, which is part of the triple star system of Alpha Centauri. Proxima is about 25 trillion miles, or 4.2 light-years, away (see above) and cannot be seen by the unaided eye. But on a clear night you can see some stars much farther—up to 2.7 million light-years-—away, even without a telescope or binoculars. And with NASA's powerful Hubble Telescope you could see star explosions, called **SUPERNOVAS**, up to 12 billion light-years away!

WHAT IS A GALAXY?

A **GALAXY** is a group of billions of stars held together by gravity. Galaxies also contain interstellar gas and dust. The universe may have about 50 billion galaxies. The one we live in is called the **MILKY WAY**. The Sun and most stars we see are just a few of the 200 billion stars in the Milky Way. Light from a star along one edge of the galaxy would take about 100,000 years to reach the other edge.

Andromeda galaxy

WHAT IS THE TEMPERATURE IN SPACE?

Space itself doesn't have a temperature because it is a vacuum. Things in space do have temperatures. Their temperature depends on how much radiation they receive from planets and stars. If you put something in space and shielded it from all outside radiation, it would eventually cool to about 3 degrees Kelvin, or –468 degrees Fahrenheit.

WHY DOES THE RISING MOON LOOK SO BIG?

Believe it or not, the moon looks bigger when it's rising because of an optical illusion. The moon isn't any closer to us when it comes over the horizon but it looks close and big because we see it next to familiar objects such as buildings, trees, or mountains. If you want to test this, extend your arm and put your thumb over the moon when you see it on the horizon. It will look a little smaller than your fingernail. When the moon is high in the sky, do this again and you'll notice that it looks the same size.

HOW OLD IS THE UNIVERSE?

Scientists estimate the universe began about 13 to 15 billion years ago. Many experts believe it formed from the **BIG BANG**. According to this theory, everything—all matter and energy—was packed together into a tiny space. This blew apart in a huge explosion, and the universe was born. Ever since, the universe has been expanding. Some astronomers believe the universe will eventually get so big it will start to collapse on itself. (They call that collapse "The Gnab Gib," "Big Bang" spelled backwards.) Others expect it to expand forever. Maybe *The World Almanac for Kids 2999* will have the answer!

FIRST ASTRONAUTS IN SPACE

The start of the U.S. space program in 1958 was a response to the Soviet Union's launching of its satellite SPUTNIK I into orbit on October 4, 1957. In 1961, three years after NASA was formed, President John F. Kennedy promised Americans that the United States would land a person on the moon by the end of the 1960s. NASA landed men on the moon in July 1969. Since then, more than 400 astronauts have made trips into outer space. This time line shows some of the early flights of astronauts into space.

1961 — On April 12, Soviet cosmonaut Yuri Gagarin, in Vostok 1, became the **first human to orbit Earth**. On May 5, U.S. astronaut Alan B. Shepard Jr. of the Mercury 3 mission became the **first American in space**.

1962 — On February 20, U.S. astronaut John H. Glenn Jr. of Mercury 6 became the **first American to orbit Earth**.

1963 — From June 16 to 19, the Soviet spacecraft Vostok 6 carried the **first woman in space**, Valentina V. Tereshkova.

1965 — On March 18, Soviet cosmonaut Aleksei A. Leonov became the **first person to walk in space**. He spent 10 minutes outside the spaceship. On December 15, U.S. Gemini 6A and 7 (with astronauts) became the **first vehicles to rendezvous** (approach and see each other) **in space**.

1966 — On March 16, U.S. Gemini 8 became the **first craft to dock with** (become attached to) **another vehicle** (an unmanned Agena rocket).

1967 — On January 27, a fire in a U.S. Apollo spacecraft on the ground killed astronauts Virgil I. Grissom, Edward H. White, and Roger B. Chaffee. On April 24, Soyuz 1 crashed to the Earth, killing Soviet cosmonaut Vladimir Komarov.

1969 — On July 20, after successful flights of Apollo 8, 9, and 10, U.S. Apollo 11's **lunar module *Eagle* landed on the moon's surface** in the area known as the Sea of Tranquility. Neil Armstrong became the **first person ever to walk on the moon**.

1970 — In April, Apollo 13 astronauts returned safely to Earth after an explosion damaged their spacecraft and prevented them from landing on the moon.

1971 — In July and August, U.S. Apollo 15 astronauts tested the **Lunar Rover** on the moon.

1972 — In December, Apollo 17 was the sixth and **final U.S. space mission to land successfully on the moon**.

1973 — On May 14, the U.S. put its **first space station, Skylab, into orbit**. The last Skylab crew left in January 1974.

1975 — On July 15, the U.S. launched Apollo 18 and the U.S.S.R. launched Soyuz 19. Two days later, the **American and Soviet spacecraft docked**, and for several days their crews worked and spent time together in space. This was NASA's last space mission with astronauts until the space shuttle.

SHUTTLES and SPACE STATIONS

In the 1970s, NASA developed the space shuttle program. Earlier space capsules could not be used again after returning to Earth.

In 1986, the Soviet Union launched its MIR space station. By the mid-1990s, the United States and Russia were sharing projects in space. Now they have joined other nations in building an International Space Station.

1977 — The first shuttle, **Enterprise**, took off from the back of a 747 jet airliner.

1981 — **Columbia** was launched and became the first shuttle to reach Earth's orbit.

1983 — In April, NASA began using a third shuttle, **Challenger**. Two more **Challenger** flights in 1983 included astronauts Sally K. Ride and Guion S. Bluford Jr., the first American woman and first African-American man in space. In November, **Columbia** was launched carrying Spacelab, a European scientific laboratory.

1984 — In August, the shuttle **Discovery** was launched for the first time.

1985 — In October, the shuttle **Atlantis** was launched for the first time.

1986 — On January 28, after 24 successful missions, **Challenger** exploded 73 seconds after takeoff. Astronauts Dick Scobee, Michael Smith, Ellison Onizuka, Judith Resnik, Greg Jarvis, and Ron McNair, and teacher Christa McAuliffe died. In February, the Soviet space station **Mir** was launched into orbit.

1988 — In September new safety procedures led to a successful launch of **Discovery**.

1990 — On April 24, the **Hubble Space Telescope** was launched from **Discovery**.

1992 — In May, NASA launched a new shuttle, **Endeavour**.

1995 — In March, astronaut Norman Thagard became the first American to travel in a Russian spacecraft; he joined cosmonauts on **Mir**. In June, **Atlantis** docked with **Mir** for the first time.

1996 — In March, Shannon Lucid joined the **Mir** crew. She spent 188 days in space, setting the record for all American and all female astronauts.

1998 — In October astronaut John Glenn was launched into space a second time, aboard the shuttle **Discovery**. In December, **Endeavour** was launched with **Unity**, a U.S.-built part of the International Space Station. The crew attached it to the Russian-built **Zarya** control module.

1999 — In July, Eileen Collins became the first woman to command a shuttle, the **Columbia**.

2000 — The first crew, Expedition One, arrived at the International Space Station in November.

2001 — In February, **Atlantis** carried the lab module **Destiny** to the International Space Station (see page 209). **Mir** parts splashed down in the Pacific Ocean east of New Zealand in March, ending the 15-year Russian program.

2002 — In March, **Columbia** astronauts repaired the **Hubble Space Telescope**. In May, **Endeavour** was scheduled to carry the Expedition 5 crew to the Space Station and return Expedition 4 to Earth.

March 8, 2002: Astronaut John M. Grunsfeld does repairs on the giant Hubble Space Telescope temporarily hosted in the Space Shuttle's cargo bay

INTERNATIONAL SPACE STATION

The International Space Station (ISS) is being built by 16 countries, including the U.S. and Russia. By the time it is completed in 2004, more than 40 space missions—carrying crews and supplies—will have been flown there. The first crew of three astronauts lived and worked aboard the ISS for about four months starting in October 2000. The fourth crew was scheduled to return to Earth at the end of May 2002, after almost six months in space. A fifth ISS crew was slated to follow immediately, with a sixth going up in September.

During construction, crews are expected to make 160 space walks in all, for a total of 960 hours outside the ISS. That's 40 days! When it's finished, the ISS will weigh over 1 million pounds. It will be about a hundred yards square (356 feet wide and 290 feet long). That's four times bigger than the Russian *Mir* space station. There will be almost an acre of solar panels to supply electricity to the 52 computers and six scientific laboratories on board.

The ISS is orbiting the Earth at an altitude of 250 miles. To find out when you might be able to see it over your town, go to **WEB SITE** *http://spaceflight.nasa.gov*

A DAY ABOARD THE INTERNATIONAL SPACE STATION

Daily life in space has many challenges that Earth-bound beings will never experience.

First of all, a "day" in space is artificial: as the Space Station orbits the Earth, astronauts go through 15 dawns in 24 hours. In order to avoid permanent jet lag, astronauts still wake up in the "morning" and begin their day as do humans on Earth.

Almost everything must be recycled—including food, air, and water from the shower. In fact, the only thing that doesn't get recycled is human waste, which is thrown out through a suction device connected to the space toilet. Lack of gravity affects everything. Food must be kept inside bags or weighted down by magnets or it will float away and possibly get caught in the controls for the Space Station. Astronauts must exercise or they will lose their bone and muscle mass. They must also sleep with their sleeping bag attached to a wall, or they will free-float and possibly get sucked into an air vent.

Astronauts work hard all day performing experiments, doing medical tests, checking equipment, and doing repairs. At the end of the day, they get free time to write e-mails, watch DVDs, or simply watch the Earth rotate, which they say is the most fun of all.

...All About... SPACE CAMP

Since 1982, U.S. Space Camp has given over 400,000 kids a taste of life in space. The space education program, based in Huntsville, Alabama, lets them feel what it is like to experience zero-gravity, moonwalks, and space shuttle landings. They get to ride in a G-Force Accelerator, where they spin at a force of three times normal gravity.

In October 2001 the popular program took to the road on its "Mission to Malls" tour. A total of 16 malls across America are on its schedule through 2003. The space camp may be landing at a mall near you. So aspiring astronauts should head to the mall if they want to shoot for the stars. For more information go to

WEB SITE *http://www2.spacecamp.com/spacecamp/mission_malls_schedule.asp*

SPORTS

What did President Grover Cleveland do in 1893? ➤page 217

BASEBALL

In 2001 the Arizona Diamondbacks beat the New York Yankees 4 games to 3 to win their first-ever World Series. The "Fall Classic" was one of the most exciting in history. The Yankees won Games 4 and 5 in a very dramatic way. In both games, they trailed by two runs with two outs in the bottom of the ninth inning. Each time, a two-run homer tied the game and New York went on to win in extra innings. But in Game 7, Arizona mounted a rally of their own. With the Yankees leading 2-1 in the bottom of the ninth, the Diamondbacks struck for 2 runs to take the game … and the championship!

2001 MAJOR LEAGUE LEADERS

MVP AWARD
AL: Ichiro Suzuki, Seattle
NL: Barry Bonds, San Francisco

CY YOUNG AWARD (top pitcher)
AL: Roger Clemens, New York
NL: Randy Johnson, Arizona

ROOKIE OF THE YEAR
AL: Ichiro Suzuki, Seattle
NL: Albert Pujols, St. Louis

BATTING CHAMPS
AL: Ichiro Suzuki, Seattle, .350
NL: Larry Walker, Colorado, .350

HOME RUN LEADERS
AL: Alex Rodriguez, Texas, 52
NL: Barry Bonds, San Francisco, 73

EARNED RUN AVERAGE LEADERS
AL: Freddy Garcia, Seattle, 3.05
NL: Randy Johnson, Arizona, 2.49

COOL FEATS, FACTS, AND FIRSTS

▶ With 64 homers in 2001, Sammy Sosa became the only player ever to hit more than 60 in a season three times.

▶ The youngest major leaguer in the modern era was Cincinnati Reds pitcher Joe Nuxhall, who made his debut in 1944 at the age of only 15 years, 10 months, and 11 days.

▶ The youngest player in the modern era to hit a home run was Tommy Brown (17 years, 4 months, 14 days) of the Brooklyn Dodgers. He hit it against the Pirates in 1945.

▶ The most total runs ever scored in a game is 49. The Chicago Cubs beat the Philadelphia Phillies 26-23 in 1922.

▶ Joel Youngblood is the only major leaguer to get a hit for two different teams on the same day. In 1982, while playing for the Mets in an afternoon game in Chicago, he was told he'd been traded to the Expos. He left during the game and flew to Philadelphia, where he went into the game that evening in the sixth inning.

▶ Cal Hubbard is the only member of both the Pro Football Hall of Fame and the Pro Baseball Hall of Fame. He was an NFL lineman before becoming a Major League umpire.

LITTLE LEAGUE

Little League Baseball is the largest youth sports program in the world. It began in 1939 in Williamsport, Pennsylvania, with 45 boys playing on three teams. Now nearly three million boys and girls ages 5 to 18 play on 200,000 Little League teams in more than 80 countries.

WEB SITE http://www.littleleague.org

All About... **BARRY BONDS**

Who can forget 1998, when Mark McGwire and Sammy Sosa chased Roger Maris's home run record of 61? McGwire won the race, smashing 70 round-trippers. But Barry Bonds did even better in 2001—smashing an unbelievable 73 homers. The San Francisco Giants outfielder moved into seventh place on the all-time home run list with 567.

After his record-breaking season, you'd think Barry would be happy. But the slugger was disappointed because the Giants missed the playoffs. He's used to records—he's the only player in the 400 homers/400 stolen bases club.

Bonds has been around baseball all of his life. His father Bobby was a star player in the 1970s, and Willie Mays is his godfather! What Barry wants is to win the World Series. In the meantime, he won a record fourth MVP Award in 2001. He gave the first three to his mother and two oldest kids. He said he'll give this one to his 3-year-old daughter, Alisha.

THE NEGRO LEAGUES

Willie Mays (left) Roy Campanella

In the early 20th century Major League Baseball, like America, was segregated. Black and Latino players weren't allowed in the majors. They formed their own teams and traveled around, playing exhibition games against each other and any other teams they could find. This was called "barnstorming." In the 1920s and 1930s, pro leagues such as the Negro National League, the Eastern Colored League, and the Negro American League were formed. The Homestead Grays (Pennsylvania), Pittsburgh Crawfords, and Kansas City Monarchs were some of the more successful teams. Famous players included Josh Gibson, a powerful home run hitter called the "black Babe Ruth"; James "Cool Papa" Bell, a base-stealer said to be so fast he could "turn out the light and get in bed before the room got dark"; and the legendary Leroy "Satchel" Paige, who pitched into his 50s. Hall of Fame players like Hank Aaron, Roy Campanella, and Willie Mays got their start in the Negro Leagues.

BASEBALL HALL OF FAME

The National Baseball Hall of Fame and Museum opened in 1939, in Cooperstown, New York. To be eligible for membership, players must be retired from baseball for five years.

Address: 25 Main Street, PO Box 590, Cooperstown, NY 13326

Phone: (607) 547-7200; toll-free: (888) 425-5633

WEB SITE http://www.baseballhalloffame.org

Hall of Fame plaque for Hank Aaron, the all-time leader in home runs ▶

211

BASKETBALL

Basketball began in 1891 in Springfield, Massachusetts, when Dr. James Naismith invented it, using peach baskets as hoops. At first, each team had nine players instead of five. Big-time pro basketball started in 1949, when the National Basketball Association (NBA) was formed. The Women's National Basketball Association (WNBA) began play in 1997.

HIGHLIGHTS OF THE 2001–2002 NBA SEASON

SCORING LEADER:
Allen Iverson,
Philadelphia 76ers

Games: 60
Points: 1,883
Average: 31.4

REBOUNDING LEADER:
Ben Wallace,
Detroit Pistons

Games: 80
Rebounds: 1,039
Average: 13.0

ASSISTS LEADER:
Andre Miller,
Cleveland Cavaliers

Games: 81
Assists: 882
Average: 10.9

STEALS LEADER:
Jason Kidd,
New Jersey Nets

Games: 82
Steals: 175
Average: 2.1

BLOCKED SHOTS LEADER:
Ben Wallace,
Detroit Pistons

Games: 80
Blocks: 278
Average: 3.5

Most Valuable Player:
Tim Duncan, San Antonio Spurs

Defensive Player of the Year:
Ben Wallace, Detroit Pistons

Rookie of the Year:
Pau Gasol, Memphis Grizzlies

Coach of the Year:
Rick Carlisle, Detroit Pistons

NBA Hall of Fame

The Naismith Memorial Basketball Hall of Fame was founded in 1959 to honor great basketball players, coaches, referees, and others important to the history of the game.

Address: 1150 W. Columbus Ave., Springfield, MA 01105.

Phone: (413) 781-6500. **WEB SITE** http://www.hoophall.com

TRULY A WIZARD

As a Chicago Bull, Michael Jordan won six NBA Championships and dazzled the world with his magic. And at 39, his "Airness" is now a genuine Wizard—a Washington Wizard, that is. The superstar played his first official game as a Wizard on October 11, 2001.

In order to play he had to give up his position as a part owner of the Wizards. He was also the team's president of basketball operations. He didn't regret his decision. "I feel there is no better way of teaching young players than to be on the court with them as a fellow player," he said.

Jordan did become a big inspiration to his young teammates—the Wizards won almost twice as many games as the year before. And even though MJ was slowed by a knee injury, he proved he could still play. On January 4, 2002, he became only the fourth NBA player to surpass 30,000 career points. He also was chosen as an All-Star Game starter for the 13th time in his career.

The Harlem Globetrotters

When Abe Saperstein founded the Globetrotters in Chicago in 1927, they were a serious team. The fun-loving style of today's Globetrotters didn't develop until 1939. One night, with a 107-point lead, players clowned around and the crowd loved it! They began to work comic sketches and displays of basketball wizardry into their games every night. In the 1940s Reece "Goose" Tatum developed many routines and the role of the "Clown Prince"—later played by "Meadowlark" Lemon, then "Geese" Ausbie. Another famous trotter was "Curly" Neal, one of the world's greatest dribblers. Now in their 75th year, the Trotters have entertained more than 100 million fans in 115 countries. On November 13, 2000, Michigan State beat the Trotters, 72-68, snapping a 1,270-game winning streak. For the record, the Globetrotters once won 8,829 games in a row! Among sports stars who once played for the Globetrotters were NBA Hall of Famers Wilt Chamberlain and Connie Hawkins, baseball Hall of Fame pitcher Bob Gibson, and boxing great Sugar Ray Robinson.

HIGHLIGHTS OF THE 2001 WNBA SEASON

Most Valuable Player: Lisa Leslie, Los Angeles Sparks

Defensive Player of the Year: Debbie Black, Miami Sol

Rookie of the Year: Jackie Stiles, Portland Fire

Coach of the Year: Dan Hughes, Cleveland Rockers

Scoring Leader: Katie Smith, Minnesota Lynx
Games: 32   Points: 739   Average: 23.1

Rebounding Leader:
Yolanda Griffith, Sacramento Monarchs
Games: 32   Rebounds: 357   Average: 11.2

Assists Leader:
Ticha Penicheiro, Sacramento Monarchs
Games: 23   Assists: 172   Average: 7.5

All About... LISA LESLIE

In 2001, Lisa Leslie led the Los Angeles Sparks all the way to the WNBA title. On the way, the 6-foot-5 center was named MVP of the All-Star Game, regular season, and championship playoffs. She's the first player to sweep all three awards in a season.

Lanky Lisa has long been one of the world's finest woman basketball players. As a high-school senior in Inglewood, California, she once scored an unbelievable 101 points in the first half (her opponents declined to play the second half). After college, she went on to lead the USA Women to gold medals in the 1996 and 2000 Olympics. Lisa has played for the Sparks since the first WNBA season in 1997. She's the WNBA's all-time leader in points and rebounds. Off the court she has worked as a fashion model, and in 1999 she received a trophy for her charitable work with foster children. This Spark truly sparkles!

COLLEGE BASKETBALL

The men's National Collegiate Athletic Association (NCAA) Tournament began in 1939. Today, it is a spectacular 65-team extravaganza. The Final Four weekend, when the semi-finals and finals are played, is one of the most-watched sports competition in the U.S. The Women's NCAA Tournament began in 1982. Since then, the popularity of the women's game has grown by leaps and (re)bounds.

THE 2002 NCAA TOURNAMENT RESULTS

MEN'S FINAL FOUR

SEMI-FINALS:
Indiana 73, Oklahoma 64
Maryland 97, Kansas 88

FINALS:
Maryland 64, Indiana 52

MOST OUTSTANDING PLAYER:
Juan Dixon, Maryland

WOMEN'S FINAL FOUR

SEMI-FINALS:
Oklahoma 86, Duke 71
Connecticut 79, Tennessee 56

FINALS:
Connecticut 82, Oklahoma 70

MOST OUTSTANDING PLAYER:
Swin Cash, Connecticut

NAISMITH AWARD WINNERS 2001-2002

Presented by the Atlanta Tipoff Club to honor the nation's best in college basketball.

MEN Player of the Year: Jason Williams, Duke Coach of the Year: Ben Howard, Pittsburgh

WOMEN Player of the Year: Sue Bird, Connecticut Coach of the Year: Geno Auriemma, Connecticut

THE JOHN R. WOODEN AWARD

Awarded to the nation's outstanding male college basketball player by the Los Angeles Athletic Club.
2002 winner: Jason Williams, Duke

THE WADE TROPHY

Awarded to the nation's outstanding female college basketball player by the National Association for Girls and Women in Sport.
2002 winner: Sue Bird, Connecticut

SUE BIRD... FLYING HIGH

In March 2002, 5-foot-9 guard Sue Bird led the undefeated Connecticut Huskies to their second national championship in three years. Along the way she won a few awards for being the best women's college basketball player: the Naismith, Honda Sports, Associated Press Player of the Year, and the Wade Trophy. Oh, and she was named First Team All-America and led the nation in free-throw shooting at 89.2%!

Sue is used to being the best. She was the New York City and New York State Player of the Year in high school. In 1997-98, she led Christ the King High to a national title and a 27-0 record. She was First Team All-America back then, too. So when the 2002 WNBA draft rolled around on April 19, who do you think was the first guard ever to be the #1 pick? That's right, number 10, Sue Bird. (She wears that number because her birthday is in October—the 10th month, get it?)

Her new team, the Seattle Storm, and just about everyone else, is sure Sue will continue her winning ways in the pros.

FOOTBALL

American football began as a college sport. The first game that was like today's football took place between Yale and Harvard in New Haven, Connecticut, on November 13, 1875. The National Football League started in 1922. The rival American Football League began in 1960. The two leagues played the first Super Bowl in 1967. In 1970, the leagues merged. In 2002, the Houston Texans were set to begin play, and the NFL was scheduled for realignment. The AFC and NFC will each have four divisions of four teams.

PATRIOT-IC SUPER BOWL

At Super Bowl XXXVI in New Orleans, the AFC's New England Patriots upset the NFC's St. Louis Rams, 20-17. After intercepting a pair of passes from the Rams' star quarterback Kurt Warner—Cornerback Ty Law returned one for a TD—the Pats led 14-3 at the half. St. Louis scored two fourth-quarter TDs to tie the score at 17 with 1:21 left to go. But New England quarterback Tom Brady, the game's MVP, led a drive to the Rams' 30-yard line. With only 7 seconds left, Adam Vinitieri's 48-yard field goal gave the Patriots their first Super Bowl win!

2001 NFL LEADERS & AWARDS

RUSHING YARDS: Priest Holmes, Kansas City Chiefs • 1,555
RUSHING TDs: Shaun Alexander, Seattle Seahawks • 14
RECEPTIONS: Rod Smith, Denver Broncos • 113
RECEIVING YARDS: David Boston, Arizona Cardinals • 1,598
RECEIVING TDs: Terrell Owens, San Francisco 49ers • 16
PASSING YARDS: Kurt Warner, St. Louis Rams • 4,830
PASSER RATING: Kurt Warner, St. Louis Rams • 101.4
PASSING TDs: Kurt Warner, St. Louis Rams • 36
PASS INTERCEPTIONS: (tie) Ronde Barber, Tampa Bay Buccaneers; Anthony Henry, Cleveland Browns • 10
SACKS: Michael Strahan, New York Giants • 22.5 (NFL record)

2001 ASSOCIATED PRESS AWARDS

Most Valuable Player: Kurt Warner, St. Louis Rams ▶
Offensive Player of the Year: Marshall Faulk, St. Louis Rams
Defensive Player of the Year: Michael Strahan, New York Giants
Coach of the Year: Dick Jauron, Chicago Bears
Offensive Rookie of the Year: Anthony Thomas, Chicago Bears
Defensive Rookie of the Year: Kendrell Bell, Pittsburgh Steelers
Comeback Player of the Year: Garrison Hearst, San Francisco 49ers

WEB SITE http://www.nfl.com

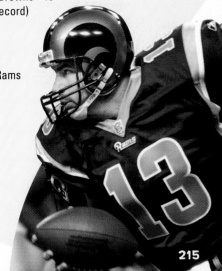

215

FANTASTIC FINISHES

"The Greatest Game Ever Played" **December 28, 1958, NFL Championship, New York, New York (Yankee Stadium):** Baltimore Colts 23, New York Giants 17 With a 14-3 lead in the 3rd quarter, the Colts had the ball on the Giants' 1-yard line and seemed to be on their way to an easy win. But the Giants made a determined goal-line stand, got the ball on their own 5-yard line, and drove downfield for a TD. In the 4th quarter, Frank Gifford caught a TD pass to give the Giants a 17-14 lead. But Colts star quarterback Johnny Unitas passed his team down the field, completing 3 to Ray Berry for 62 yards. With 7 seconds left, the Colts kicked a field goal to force the first post-season overtime. In the extra period, the Giants punted and Unitas went to work. He took the Colts 80 yards before fullback Alan "The Horse" Ameche bulled into the end zone from the 1-yard line, to end what many still call "the greatest game ever played."

"The Immaculate Reception" **December 23, 1972, AFC Divisional Playoffs, Pittsburgh, Pennsylvania**: Pittsburgh Steelers 13, Oakland Raiders 7 Down 7-6, with just over a minute left, the Steelers' Terry Bradshaw fired a pass downfield to halfback John Fuqua, who was hit hard by Raiders defender Jack Tatum just as the ball arrived. It hit one of the players and bounced in the air and, luckily for the Steelers, into the hands of rookie running back Franco Harris. After his "immaculate reception," Harris ran 42 yards to score with 5 seconds left.

"The Catch" **January 10, 1982, NFC Championship Game, San Francisco, California: San Francisco 49ers 28, Dallas Cowboys 27** The 49ers and Cowboys traded the lead six times. With less than five minutes to go and behind 27-21, the 49ers got the ball on their own 11-yard line. Led by quarterback Joe Montana, the Niners were able to move the ball to the Cowboys' six-yard line with 58 seconds left. Montana connected with receiver Dwight Clark, whose now-famous leaping catch for the winning TD sent the 49ers to their first Super Bowl.

"The Comeback" **January 3, 1993, AFC Wild Card Game, Orchard Park, New York: Buffalo Bills 41, Houston Oilers 38 (OT)** Down 35-3 early in the third quarter, Buffalo backup quarterback Frank Reich (starter Jim Kelly was injured) went to work. The Bills scored an amazing five straight TDs to go ahead 38-35. Reich threw four TD passes, three of them to wide receiver Andre Reed. Houston's Al Del Greco tied the game with a field goal as the fourth quarter ended. In overtime, Buffalo's Nate Odomes picked off a Warren Moon pass. That set up Steve Christie's field goal, to end one of the NFL's greatest comebacks.

DID YOU KNOW?

▶ Every time Oakland Raiders wide receiver Jerry Rice catches a pass or scores a TD he sets a new record. Rice has scored 196 TDs in his 17-year career, including a record 185 receiving TDs. At the end of the 2001 season, he had caught 1,364 passes, 271 more than any other receiver. Rice played 16 years with the San Francisco 49ers before signing with the Raiders in 2001.

▶ The NFL will welcome a 32nd team into its ranks in 2002: the Houston Texans. The city of Houston, Texas, lost its original franchise, the Oilers, after the 1996 season, when they moved to Tennessee (they're now called the Titans).

PRO FOOTBALL HALL OF FAME

Football's Hall of Fame was founded in 1963 by the National Football League to honor outstanding players, coaches, and contributors.

Address: Pro Football Hall of Fame, 2121 George Halas Drive NW, Canton, OH 44708.

Phone: (330) 456-8207.

WEBSITE *http://www.profootballhof.com*

COLLEGE FOOTBALL

College football is one of America's most colorful and exciting sports. The National Collegiate Athletic Association (NCAA), founded in 1906, oversees college football today.

The Miami Hurricanes beat the Nebraska Cornhuskers, 37-14, in the Rose Bowl on January 3, 2002, to complete an undefeated season and win the national championship.

2001 TOP 5 COLLEGE TEAMS

Chosen by the Associated Press Poll and the USA Today/ESPN Poll

Rank	AP	USA Today/ESPN
①	Miami	Miami
②	Oregon	Oregon
③	Florida	Florida
④	Tennessee	Tennessee
⑤	Texas	Texas

DID YOU KNOW? *One of the oldest college football rivalries is between Army and Navy. The two military academies began playing each other way back in 1890. President Grover Cleveland banned the Army-Navy game in 1893, after observing a very rough contest that Navy won 6-4. In 1897, future President Theodore Roosevelt urged that the teams start playing again. Two years later the contest resumed, and the Army-Navy game has been played ever since. Army currently leads the series with a record of 49 wins, 46 losses, and 7 ties.*

HEISMAN TROPHY

The Heisman Trophy goes to the most outstanding U.S. college football player. The 2001 winner was quarterback **Eric Crouch** of the University of Nebraska. The 23-year-old led his team to a spot in the national championship Rose Bowl game against Miami and an 11-2 record. The 6'1", 200-pound senior passed for 1,510 yards and threw seven touchdown passes. Even more impressive, the quick-footed Crouch rushed for 1,115 yards and 18 touchdowns. And he even caught a TD pass in a big Nebraska win during the 2001 season.

GREAT COLLEGE FOOTBALL MOMENTS

Jan. 2, 1984, Orange Bowl: Miami 31, Nebraska 30 The underdog Miami Hurricanes led the top-ranked, undefeated Nebraska Cornhuskers, 17-0. But the 'Huskers didn't give up—they even scored a TD on a trick play known as the "fumblerooski." The quarterback put the ball on the ground, where it was picked up by a lineman who ran it into the end zone. Miami still led 31-17 in the fourth quarter, but Nebraska scored two more TDs to pull within a point of the 'Canes. After their final score, Nebraska tried a two-point conversion that would have given them the win. But the quarterback's pass was blocked, and Miami got the victory and a national championship.

Jan. 2, 1987, Fiesta Bowl: Penn State 14, Miami 10 The heavily favored Miami Hurricanes were ranked No. 1, and Penn State Nittany Lions were No. 2. Both teams had perfect 11-0 records going into the game, which would decide the national champion. Miami's offense outgained Penn State's 445 yards to 162. But Miami quarterback Vinny Testaverde was sacked four times and threw five interceptions, including one at the Penn State six-yard line with less than 20 seconds left.

Nov. 9, 2001, Arkansas Razorbacks 58, Mississippi Rebels 56 It took a record seven overtime periods and more than four hours to end the longest game in the history of college football. The game was tied 17-17 at the end of four quarters, but the two teams traded six TDs during overtime. Arkansas finally won after Mississippi tight end Doug Ziegler was stopped a yard short of the goal line during a two-point conversion attempt. Three Arkansas players rushed for at least 100 yards, including freshman quarterback Matt Jones, who didn't enter the game until the fourth quarter.

GOLF

Golf began in Scotland as early as the 1400s. The first golf course in the U.S. opened in 1888 in Yonkers, NY. The sport has grown to include both men's and women's professional tours. And millions play golf just for fun.

The men's tour in the U.S. is run by the Professional Golf Association (PGA).

The four major championships (with the year first played) are:

British Open (1860)
United States Open (1895)
PGA Championship (1916)
Masters Tournament (1934)

The women's tour in the U.S. is guided by the Ladies Professional Golf Association (LPGA).

The four major championships are:

United States Women's Open (1946)
McDonalds LPGA Championship (1955)
Nabisco Championship (1972)
*Women's British Open (1976)

*Replaced the du Maurier Classic as a major in 2001.

THAT KID CAN PLAY

In December 2001, high school junior William Augustus Tryon IV—make that "Ty," please!—became the youngest golfer ever to qualify for the PGA Tour. The 17-year-old shot a sizzling 66 in the final round of the "Q-school" tournament to earn the right to turn pro. But he's under 18, so he can only play a limited schedule. At 16, he was the youngest player since 1956 to make it to the final round of a PGA tournament. His dad gave him the nickname "Ty," after the Chevy Chase character from the hit movie *Caddyshack,* a comedy about golf. 2002 didn't start off so well for Ty. He had tonsillitis and mononucleosis, and had to miss several tournaments. But you can bet that he'll Ty, try again.

Did You KNOW?

TIGERIFFIC!

Tiger Woods won the Masters for the third time in his career in April 2002. That gave him seven major tournament victories by the age of 26! Tiger's idol, the legendary Jack Nicklaus, didn't win his seventh until he was 28 years old. Nicklaus won 18 majors in all.

GYMNASTICS

It takes strength, coordination, and grace to become a top gymnast. Although the sport goes back to ancient Greece, modern-day gymnastics began in Sweden in the early 1800s. The sport has been part of the Olympics since 1896.

Men today compete in the All-Around, High Bar, Parallel Bars, Rings, Vault, Pommel Horse, Floor Exercises, and Team Combined. The women's events are the All-Around, Uneven Parallel Bars, Balance Beam, Floor Exercises, and Team Combined. In rhythmic gymnastics, women compete in All-Around, Rope, Hoop, Ball, Clubs, and Ribbon.

At the 2001 World Gymnastic Championships in Ghent, Belgium, Katie Heenan of Burke, Virginia, won a bronze medal in the uneven bars. It was the first medal for a U.S. woman at the World Championships since 1996. Sean Townsend, of Houston, Texas, won the first individual men's gold for the U.S. since 1979. He won it on the parallel bars.

ICE H CKEY

Ice hockey began in Canada in the mid-1800s. The National Hockey League (NHL) was formed in 1916. In 2002, the NHL had 30 teams—24 in the U.S. and 6 in Canada.

In 2001, the Colorado Avalanche won their second Stanley Cup, defeating the defending champion New Jersey Devils 4 games to 3. Colorado goaltender Patrick Roy earned his third Conn Smythe Trophy (Playoff MVP). At right is a list of Stanley Cup winners since 1990.

SEASON	WINNER	RUNNER-UP
1990-91	Pittsburgh Penguins	Minnesota North Stars
1991-92	Pittsburgh Penguins	Chicago Black Hawks
1992-93	Montreal Canadiens	Los Angeles Kings
1993-94	New York Rangers	Vancouver Canucks
1994-95	New Jersey Devils	Detroit Red Wings
1995-96	Colorado Avalanche	Florida Panthers
1996-97	Detroit Red Wings	Philadelphia Flyers
1997-98	Detroit Red WIngs	Washington Capitals
1998-99	Dallas Stars	Buffalo Sabres
1999-2000	New Jersey Devils	Dallas Stars
2000-2001	Colorado Avalanche	New Jersey Devils

The Adventures of LORD STANLEY'S CUP

In 1892, Lord Stanley, the British governor general of Canada, bought a silver cup (actually a bowl) as an annual prize for the best amateur hockey team in Canada.

Today, NHL champions have their names engraved on one of the silver rings around the cup's base. When all the bands are filled, the oldest one is retired to the Hockey Hall of Fame and a new ring is added.

The Stanley Cup is the only professional sports trophy that each player on the winning team gets to take home. The Cup has had many interesting adventures:

► In 1997, Darren McCarty of the Red Wings took the cup to Bob's Big Boy for breakfast, and for a round of golf in the afternoon.

► In 2000, New Jersey's Scott Gomez rode with the cup to his hometown of Anchorage, Alaska, on a dogsled. Later that summer, Gomez's teammate, goalie Martin Brodeur, brought it to the movies and filled it with popcorn.

► In 2001, Mark Waggoner (Avalanche vice president of finance) took the trophy to new heights. With a special backpack, he carried the 35-pound cup up 14,433 feet to the top of Colorado's highest mountain (Mount Elbert).

IGINLA IGNITES

Calgary Flames forward Jarome Iginla made history in the 2001-2002 season. He became the first black player to win the NHL's Art Ross trophy for most total points (96), and also the first black to win the Maurice Richard trophy for most goals (52).

Jarome's father, Elvis, is originally from Nigeria, and Iginla means "big tree" in the Yoruba language. Born and raised in Canada, Jarome began playing hockey as a youngster growing up in Edmonton and is now among the NHL's best players. At the Winter Olympics in Salt Lake City in February, the African-Canadian star won a gold medal as a member of the Canadian team. In the title game, he netted two goals for Team Canada as they defeated the U.S. 5-2.

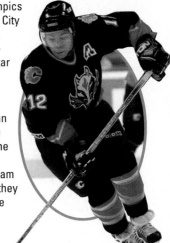

HOCKEY HALL OF FAME
The Hockey Hall of Fame was opened in 1961 to honor hockey greats. **Address:** BCE Place, 30 Yonge Street, Toronto, Ontario, Canada M5E 1X8. **Phone:** (416) 360-7735 **WEB SITE** *http://www.hhof.com*

THE OLYMPIC GAMES

The first Olympics were held in Greece more than 2,500 years ago. In 776 B.C. they featured just one event—a footrace. Boxing, wrestling, chariot racing, and the pentathlon (which consists of five different events) came later. The Olympic Games were held every four years for more than 1,000 years, until A.D. 393, when a Roman emperor stopped them.

SALT LAKE 2002

2002 WINTER OLYMPICS: SALT LAKE CITY

About 3,500 athletes and officials from 80 countries took part in the Winter Olympics in Salt Lake City, Utah, from February 8 to February 24, 2002. There were 78 medals awarded in 7 sports. Germany won the most medals—35—but the United States was close behind. The U.S., which had never before won more than 13 medals at the Winter Olympics, won a whopping 34. The mascots for the 2002 Games, symbolizing the Olympic motto of "Citius, Altius, Fortius"—Swifter, Higher, Stronger—were Powder, the snowshoe hare; Copper, the coyote; and Coal, the black bear. The next Olympics will be held in Athens, Greece (Summer 2004), and Turin, Italy (Winter 2006).

Highlights from SALT LAKE CITY

▶ A judging scandal in the pairs figure skating was one of the biggest news stories of the Games. It was finally resolved by giving gold medals to both the Russians, Yelena Berezhnaya and Anton Sikharulidze, and the Canadians, Jamie Sale and David Pelletier.

▶ Canada won both men's and women's ice hockey tournaments. It was Canada's first gold medal in men's hockey in 50 years. The U.S. men's and women's teams each claimed silver medals.

▶ In the first Olympic skeleton competition since 1948, American Jim Shea took the gold. It was an emotional win for the third-generation Olympian, whose grandfather (a speed skating double medalist in 1932) was killed in an auto accident just before the 2002 Games.

▶ Janica Kostelic of Croatia won four medals (three gold, one silver) in the women's downhill events. Hers were the first and only Winter Olympics medals ever won by Croatia.

▶ In a huge upset, 16-year-old Sarah Hughes won the figure skating gold medal, outskating both Russia's Irina Slutskaya (silver) and fellow American Michelle Kwan (bronze).

▶ Americans Jill Bakken and Vonetta Flowers won the first women's bobsled competition in Olympic history. Flowers was also the first black U.S. athlete ever to win winter gold.

The figure skaters who shared the gold medal. Front: Yelena Berezhnaya and Jamie Sale. Back: Anton Sikharulidze and David Pelletier. ▶

SOME MODERN OLYMPIC FIRSTS

1896 — **The first modern Olympic Games were held in Athens, Greece.** A total of 312 athletes from 13 nations participated in nine sports.

1900 — **Women competed in the Olympic Games for the first time.**

1908 — **For the first time, medals were awarded to the first three people to finish each event**—a gold for first, a silver for second, and a bronze for third.

1920 — **The Olympic flag was raised for the first time, and the Olympic oath was introduced.** The five interlaced rings of the flag represent: Africa, America, Europe, Asia, and Australia.

1924 — **The first Winter Olympics, featuring skiing and skating events, were held.**

The Olympic flame was introduced at the Olympic Games. A relay of runners carries a torch with the flame from Olympia, Greece, to the site of each Olympics.

1994 — **Starting with the 1994 Winter Olympics, the winter and summer Games have alternated every two years,** instead of being held in the same year, every fourth year.

2002 Winter Olympic Sports

Alpine Skiing
(downhill, slalom, giant slalom, super-G, Alpine combined)

Biathlon
(cross-country skiing, rifle marksmanship)

Bobsled

Curling

Figure Skating

Freestyle Skiing
(moguls, aerials)

Ice Hockey

Luge

Nordic Skiing
(cross-country skiing, ski jumping, Nordic combined)

Skeleton

Snowboarding
(parallel giant slalom, halfpipe)

Speed Skating
(long track, short track)

...All About... SNOWBOARDING

The U.S. dominated the snowboarding halfpipe competition at the 2002 Olympics. Vermont's Kelly Clark, 18, won the women's competition, making her the first American gold medalist of the Games. In the men's event, Ross Powers, Danny Kass, and Jarret Thomas stomped the competition. Their tricks were sick, their air was big, and they took gold, silver, and bronze! In the men's parallel giant slalom, American Chris Klug took a bronze medal just 19 months after he had a life-saving liver transplant.

The history of snowboards goes back to 1965, when Sherman Poppen produced a "Snurfer." It was just 2 skis bolted together, with a rope on the front to hold on to. Jake Burton had a Snurfer when he was a teenager, and in 1977 he started a company—Burton Snowboards—to improve on the concept. It took more than 100 different designs before Burton got the "snowboard" he wanted. Out west, another pioneering "snow-surfer," Tom Sims—of Sims Snowboards—was building boards as well. But it wasn't until 1983, when Stratton Mountain Resort in Vermont finally allowed snowboards on the slopes, that the sport really began to grow. Other resorts soon followed, and today, resorts that don't allow snowboards are rare.
Snowboarding became an Olympic sport in 1998.

SKATING

Recreational skating began with highly waxed wooden blades. The first all-steel skate was invented by E.W. Bushnell of Philadelphia around 1850. There are two types of competitive ice skating today: figure skating and speed skating.

FIGURE SKATING

Figure skating, which is almost like ballet, is judged by the way the skaters perform certain turns and jumps and by the creative difficulty of their programs. There are singles competitions for both men and women, pairs skating, and ice dancing.

2002 WORLD CHAMPIONSHIPS

	WOMEN'S SINGLES	MEN'S SINGLES
Gold Medal:	Irina Slutskaya, Russia	Alexei Yagudin, Russia
Silver Medal:	Michelle Kwan, United States	Timothy Goebel, United States
Bronze Medal:	Fumie Suguri, Japan	Takeshi Honda, Japan

- - - All About... SARAH HUGHES

Figure skater Sarah Hughes made history at the 2002 Winter Olympics. She was the first woman athlete to land two triple-triple jump combinations in one program— the triple Salchow-triple loop and the triple toe-triple loop. She was also the first Olympic skater to fight her way from fourth after the short program to first overall and a gold medal. And she was only 16!

The fourth of six children, Sarah began skating at age 3 when she saw her two older brothers and sister on the ice. Unlike many top skaters, she trains close to home. In her spare time (she doesn't have much), she enjoys reading, tennis, and playing the violin.

When she returned home after the Olympics, New York City Mayor Michael Bloomberg presented her with a key to the city. Sarah says she feels a strong responsibility as a role model. An honor student, she will graduate with her high school class at Great Neck, New York, in June 2003. She plans to go on to college and study medicine.

AMERICA'S OLYMPIC CHAMPIONS
(for figure skating in singles competition)

MEN: Dick Button (1948, 1952), Hayes Alan Jenkins (1956), David Jenkins (1960), Scott Hamilton (1984), Brian Boitano (1988)

WOMEN: Tenley Albright (1956), Carol Heiss (1960), Peggy Fleming (1968), Dorothy Hamill (1976), Kristi Yamaguchi (1992), Tara Lipinski (1998), Sarah Hughes (2002)

SPEED SKATING

Speed skating is divided into two types: long track and short track. In long track, competitors race the clock skating around a 400-meter oval. This became an Olympic sport for men in 1942, for women in 1960. Short track skating became an official Olympic sport in 1992. The track is much smaller (111 meters), with a pack of four to six skaters racing against each other instead of the clock.

WEB SITE http://www.usspeedskating.org

222

SOCCER

Soccer, also called football outside the U.S., is the number one sport worldwide, played by the most people, and in almost every country. More than 240 million people play organized soccer, according to a 2000 survey done by FIFA (Fédération Internationale de Football Association), the sport's international governing body. That's one out of every 25 people on the planet. The survey also found that more than 20 million women play soccer. Countries with the highest number of regular adult soccer players were the United States, 18 million; Indonesia, 10 million; Mexico, 7.4 million; China, 7.2 million; Brazil, 7 million; and Germany, 6.3 million.

THE WORLD CUP

Held every four years, the Men's World Cup is the biggest soccer tournament in the world. The first World Cup was held in Uruguay in 1930. The most recent World Cup competition, in 1998, was held in France. It was estimated that more than 2 billion people— one out of every 3 people on Earth—watched the final game that year between Brazil and France, which won 3-0.

Qualifying for the 2002 World Cup began in March 2000 with 198 teams from 180 countries and 19 other regions such as England, Scotland, and Wales. By November 2001, that number was down to 32—including co-hosts Japan and Korea, and current champ France, who all got into the finals automatically. All 32 were scheduled to compete in the World Cup finals, held May 31 through June 30.

Led by exciting players like Clint Mathis and 20-year-old rising star Landon Donavan (*at right*), Team USA hoped to redeem themselves for their last-place finish in 1998 and make it to the second round.

The U.S. women's team (champs in 1991 and 1999) will play in the 2003 Women's World Cup, to be held in China, September 28–October 16. The 2006 Men's World Cup is set for Germany.

WUSA–WOMEN'S UNITED SOCCER ASSOCIATION

The WUSA kicked off its first season in 2001. There were 20 players from the U.S. national team, including World Cup stars Brandi Chastain, Julie Foudy, Mia Hamm, and Briana Scurry. On August 25, 2001, the Bay Area CyberRays defeated the Atlanta Beat on penalty kicks (4-2) to win the first Founder's Cup. Julie Murray (CyberRays) was named MVP of the Championship game. New York's Tiffany Millbrett was the WUSA MVP and Offensive Player of the Year.

WEB SITE *http://www.wusa.com*

MLS–MAJOR LEAGUE SOCCER

On October 21, 2001, the San Jose Earthquakes won the MLS Cup, 2-1, over the Los Angeles Galaxy. Dwanye DeRosario's goal in sudden-death overtime earned him Championship MVP honors. Earthquake forward Landon Donavan, who earlier in the year scored a record 4 goals in the MLS All-Star Game, had tied the match just before the half with his fifth post-season goal.

WEB SITE *http://www.mlsnet.com*

SPECIAL OLYMPICS

The Special Olympics is dedicated to "empowering individuals with mental retardation." It is the world's largest program of sports training and athletic competition for children and adults with special needs. Founded in 1968, Special Olympics International has offices in all 50 U.S. states and Washington, D.C., and throughout the world. The organization offers training and competition to 1.5 million athletes in 150 countries.

The first Special Olympics competition took place in Chicago in 1968. After national events in individual countries, Special Olympics International holds World Games. These alternate between summer and winter sports every two years. In March 2001, more than 2,500 athletes and coaches from 80 countries gathered in Anchorage, Alaska, for the World Winter Games. More than 7,000 athletes from 160 countries were expected at the 2003 World Summer Games in Dublin, Ireland, the first to be held outside of the U.S.

SPECIAL OLYMPICS OFFICIAL SPORTS

▶ **Winter:** alpine and cross-country skiing, figure and speed skating, floor hockey, snowshoeing, snowboarding

▶ **Summer:** aquatics (swimming and diving), athletics (track and field), basketball, bowling, cycling, equestrian, golf, gymnastics, powerlifting, roller skating, soccer, softball, tennis, volleyball

▶ **Demonstration sports:** badminton, bocce, sailing

For more information, contact Special Olympics International Headquarters, 1325 G Street NW, Suite 500, Washington, D.C. 20005. Phone: (202) 628-3630.

WEB SITE *http://www.specialolympics.org*

Swimming

When the modern Olympic Games began in Athens, Greece, in 1896, the only racing stroke was the breaststroke. Today, men and women at the Olympics swim the backstroke, breaststroke, butterfly, and freestyle, in events ranging from 50 meters to 1,500 meters.

SOME GREAT U.S. OLYMPIC SWIMMERS

Mark Spitz made history by winning seven gold medals at the 1972 Games in Munich. He won 11 medals—nine gold—in his Olympic career.

Matt Biondi won seven medals—five gold—at the 1988 Olympics in Seoul. He won eight gold medals, 11 overall, in his Olympic career from 1984 to 1992.

Janet Evans, at age 17, won three golds at the 1988 Olympics in Seoul. In 1992 she won another gold and a silver at Barcelona.

Dara Torres won five golds at the 2000 Games in Sydney, the most by a U.S. woman at one Olympiad. Seven years after retiring, she returned to become the first American to swim in four Olympics (1984, 1988, 1992, 2000).

TENNIS

Modern tennis began in 1873. It was based on court tennis. In 1877 the first championships were held in Wimbledon, near London. In 1881 the first official U.S. men's championships were held at Newport, Rhode Island. Six years later, the first women's championships took place, in Philadelphia. The four most important ("grand slam") tournaments today are the Australian Open, the French Open, the All-England (Wimbledon) Championships, and the U.S. Open.

Grand Slam Tournaments

ALL-TIME GRAND SLAM SINGLES WINNERS

MEN	Australian	French	Wimbledon	U.S.	Total
Pete Sampras (b. 1971)	2	0	7	4	13
Roy Emerson (b. 1936)	6	2	2	2	12
Bjorn Borg (b. 1956)	0	6	5	0	11
Rod Laver (b. 1938)	3	2	4	2	11
Bill Tilden (1893-1953)	*	0	3	7	10
WOMEN					
Margaret Smith Court (b. 1942)	11	5	3	5	24
Steffi Graf (b. 1969)	4	6	7	5	22
Helen Wills Moody (1905-1998)	*	4	8	7	19
Chris Evert (b. 1954)	2	7	3	6	18
Martina Navratilova (b. 1956)	3	2	9	4	18

Never played in tournament.

DID YOU KNOW? **DRAMA DOWN UNDER** *Jennifer Capriati's 4-6, 7-6 (7), 6-2 win over Martina Hingis in the January 2002 Australian Open was the greatest comeback in the history of women's tennis. In a tough match held in 95-degree heat (January means summer in Australia), Capriati was down 4-6, 0-4, before she fought off a record four match points.*

Venus Rising... to #1

On February 25, 2002, 21-year-old Venus Williams reached the spot her father said she'd be all along—number 1! Venus was only the 10th woman to reach the top since the computer rankings began in 1975. She lost the ranking for 2 weeks to Jennifer Capriati, who won the 2002 Australian Open. But Venus went back on top in late April, and was hoping for a great year ahead.

Her brightly beaded hair is rarely a topic of conversation these days. It's her winning ways and 120-mile-per-hour serves that grab most people's attention. Venus was *Sports Illustrated's* Sportswoman of the Year in 2000, her breakout year. She won singles titles at Wimbledon, the U.S. Open, and the 2000 Summer Olympics. In 2001, she followed up on her great success, defending her Wimbledon and U.S. Open titles. In the U.S. Open, she defeated her sister, Serena, 6-2, 6-4. It was the first Grand Slam final between sisters in 117 years. It was also the first U.S. Open women's final to be held in prime time. Nearly 23 million people watched it.

Serena was the first Williams sister to win a Grand Slam singles title (1999 U.S. Open), but after that, big sister Venus led the way.

X GAMES

The X Games, founded by ESPN television executive Ron Semiao, were first held in June 1995 in Newport, Rhode Island. They originally featured skateboarding and BMX biking events. Considered the Olympics of action sports, the X Games include both summer and winter competitions, each held annually in the United States. Star athletes include skateboarder Tony Hawk, street luger Biker Sherlock, and BMX (bicycle) freestyler Dave Mirra.

2002 WINTER X GAMES

The sixth annual Winter X Games took place January 17-20 in Aspen, Colorado, with 267 athletes representing 25 states and 16 countries. Events held were Motocross "Big Air" (motorcycles), Skiing, Snowboarding, and Snowmobiling. Highlights included first-place finishes by Brian Deegan in the Big Air event, and by snowboarders Jarret Thomas and Kelly Clark. At the 2002 Winter Olympics a month later, Thomas won bronze in the Men's Halfpipe, and Clark took the gold in the Women's.

SUMMER X GAMES

The Summer X Games have been held annually since 1995, featuring sports such as Skateboarding, BMX (bicycles) and Motocross (motorcycle), In-Line Skating, Wakeboarding, Street Luging, and Speed Climbing. At the 2001 Games, in Philadelphia, BMX biker Dave Mirra added another gold medal to his collection. He now had 13 medals in all (10 gold, 3 silver), making him the most decorated athlete in X Games history. Philadelphia was also set to host the 2002 Summer X Games, August 15-19.

WEB SITE *http://expn.go.com*

All About... TONY HAWK

Born in Carlsbad, California, in 1968, Tony Hawk is probably the world's most famous skateboarder. Since 1978, he's won many championships, as well as nine Summer X Games medals (5 gold, 3 silver, 1 bronze). Tony also invented nearly 50 maneuvers. He was ESPN's Alternative Athlete of the Year in 1999. That was the year he did "The 9" (a 900 degree aerial spin—that's 2.5 times around) at the X Games in San Francisco. It's a move that was once thought to be impossible!

Tony's hard work and dedication helped change skateboarding from an obscure sport to a multimillion dollar enterprise, with many fans and heavy TV coverage. He currently serves as the CEO for three skateboarding-related companies.

TRANSPORTATION

Who were the first humans to fly? ➤ page 229

What would people from the 1600s, or the 1800s, think if they could come back and look at the world today? They would get lots of surprises. One surprise would be how fast people can travel to distant places.

HOW LONG DID IT TAKE?

1620 — *The Mayflower* took 66 days to sail across the Atlantic from Plymouth, England, to present-day Provincetown, Massachusetts.

1819 — The first Atlantic Ocean crossing by a ship powered in part by steam (*Savannah*, from Savannah, Georgia, to Liverpool, England) took 27 days.

1845 — A trip from Missouri to California by "wagon train" (covered wagons, usually pulled by oxen) took 4-5 months.

1854 — The clipper ship *Flying Cloud* sailed from New York to San Francisco (going around the tip of South America) in a record 89 days, 8 hours.

1876 — The *Transcontinental Express*, celebrating the U.S. centennial, crossed the country by rail from New York to San Francisco, in a record 83 hours, 39 minutes.

1927 — Charles Lindbergh flew from New York to Paris in 33½ hours. It was the first nonstop flight made across the Atlantic by one person.

1952 — The passenger ship *United States* set a record when it crossed the Atlantic in 3 days, 10 hours, and 40 minutes.

1969 — *Apollo 11*, averaging 3,417 mph, took just under four days to reach the moon (about 70 times the distance from London to New York).

1981 — At a speed of about 17,500 miles per hour, space shuttle *Columbia* circled the globe in 90 minutes.

1990 — A U.S. Air Force SR-71 "Blackbird" flew coast-to-coast in 1 hour, 7 minutes, and 54 seconds (at an average speed of 2,124 miles per hour).

1995 — Two Air Force B-1B bombers flew around the world nonstop (refueling in flight) in 36 hours and 13 minutes.

1996 — A British Airways Concorde jet flew from New York to London in 2 hours, 53 minutes. ▶

1999 — Bertrand Piccard and Brian Jones completed the first around-the-world balloon flight in the *Breitling Orbiter 3*. It took 19 days, 21 hours, 55 minutes.

2002 — Steve Fossett sailed across the Atlantic from New York to Cornwall, England. It took 4 days, 17 hours, 28 minutes.

TRAINS

The first successful steam locomotive was built in England in 1804. Richard Trevithick's engine pulled 24,000 pounds of iron, 70 men, and 5 wagons along a 9.5-mile track. In 1830 the **Baltimore and Ohio** introduced America's first steam locomotive, the **"Tom Thumb,"** to haul both passengers and freight. America's first transcontinental railroad was built from 1862 to 1869 (see page 230). Other railroad lines followed quickly over the next decades. In 1893, the first **electrified rail line** went into service, in Baltimore. **Diesel engines** were introduced in 1928, and **streamlined** trains began to appear in 1934.

▲ Bullet trains, Tokyo Station

The most famous modern high-speed train is the **Shinkansen (Bullet Train)**, introduced in Japan in 1964. It can go as fast as 130 miles per hour. In 1981 France launched the **Train à Grande Vitesse (TGV),** which runs commercially at speeds of up to 186 mph. In the U.S. in 2000, Amtrak introduced **Acela Express** 150-mph high-speed service between Boston and Washington, D.C. Japan Railway is testing **Maglev** (MAGnetic LEVitation) trains. These use huge magnetic forces to lift trains above the track and send them forward on electical currents. The lack of friction helps them cruise at speeds of around 280 mph, and they have reached a record speed of 343 mph.

AUTOS

In 1886 **Gottlieb Daimler** patented a three-wheeled motor carriage in Germany. That same year, **Karl Benz** produced his first successful gasoline-powered vehicle. **John W. Lambert** of Ohio made the first gas-powered automobile in the U.S. in 1891.

Five years later, the **Duryea Brothers** of Springfield, Massachusetts, started the first car manufacturing company in the U.S. **Henry Ford** came soon after. His production of the Model T using an assembly line in 1913 revolutionized the automobile industry, making cars affordable for large numbers of people. Many improvements were made over the years, such as the first aerodynamically designed car, the **Chrysler Airflow** (1934), and air-conditioning, introduced by the Packard company in 1940. Ferdinand Porsche's **Volkswagen** "beetle," mass-produced after World War II, was one of the most popular cars in history.

Today's cars have computer-run features that make them safer and more efficient. Some even have the Global Positioning System to help you get where you want to go. But the main focus for developing the car of the future is fuel efficiency. Scientists all over the world are working on designing alternative-fuel cars. **Zero Emission Vehicles** (ZEVs) that use hydrogen cells to make electricity are one promising possibility.

◄ 1911 Ford Model T

 AIR

EARLY AIRCRAFT In 1783, the **Montgolfier brothers** flew the first hot air balloon over Paris. Another Frenchman, **Henri Giffard**, flew the first **dirigible** (blimp) in 1852. It was powered by steam.

The first **heavier-than-air flying machine** was also steam-powered. **Samuel P. Langley** of the Smithsonian Institution in Washington, D.C., built a model plane with a 12-foot wingspan that flew nearly a mile in 1896. **Wilbur and Orville Wright** had been experimenting with heavier-than-air machines at the same time. In 1903 they traveled from their bicycle shop in Dayton, Ohio, to Kitty Hawk, North Carolina. Here they made four successful manned flights on December 17, launching the air age.

MILESTONES IN AVIATION

Airlines were first developed in the U.S. to carry mail. Transcontinental service was launched in 1921, bringing mail from San Francisco to New York in 33 hours—3 times faster than by train. By 1926, regular airmail service was in place, and a pilot named Charles A. Lindbergh was flying the Chicago-to-St. Louis route. Passenger service was well under way by 1930.

Aircraft continued to get bigger and faster. In 1936, the **DC-3** set a record flying from Los Angeles to Newark, New Jersey, in 13 hours and 4 minutes. In 1959 the **Boeing 707** was launched. It was the first successful passenger jet. The Boeing 707 could carry 180 passengers at 550 miles per hour—about 225 mph faster than propeller-powered airliners. One of the most famous airliners to be developed was the **Boeing 747** "jumbo jet," introduced in 1969. Cruising at 566 mph, it can carry about 500 passengers. By around 2005, Boeing hopes to introduce the **Sonic Cruiser**. This radically designed jet would carry 225 passengers up to 11,500 miles nonstop at speeds of 725 mph.

 SEA

Ships are used for many activities, from fishing, to vacationing, to exploration, to war. But their most important job has always been carrying cargo. The Egyptians were building reed and wooden sailboats some 5,000 years ago. They also built wooden **barges** over 200 feet long that could carry close to 2,000,000 pounds of cargo.

By the 1500s, huge sailing ships called **galleons** were hauling cargo around the world. Spanish galleons carried gold, spices, and other riches back to Europe from South America. These ships had to be big and needed cannons to defend themselves from pirates. Later cargo ships did without cannons. **Packet ships** began regularly scheduled passenger service across the Atlantic in 1818. In the 1840s, the U.S. built the first **clipper ships**. With a slender hull and many sails, they were the fastest ships of the pre-steam era.

The world's biggest ship today is the supertanker *Jahre Viking*. It's 1,502 feet long. That's longer than the Empire State building is tall. The *Jahre Viking* can carry 4.2 million barrels of oil. The *Queen Mary 2*, scheduled to be finished in 2003, will be the largest passenger ship ever. It will be 23 stories high and 1,131 feet long. That's almost 150 feet longer than the height of Eiffel Tower.

Star Clipper *cruise ship*

A SHORT HISTORY OF TRANSPORTATION
WIND, WHEELS, AND WATER

◀ Sagres Two, three-masted bark, Portugal

5000 B.C.
People harness animal-muscle power. Oxen and donkeys carry heavy loads.

3500 B.C.
Egyptians create the first sailboat. Before this, people made rafts or canoes and paddled them with poles or their hands.

1450s
Portuguese build fast ships with three masts. These plus the compass usher in an age of exploration.

1730s
Stagecoach service begins in the U.S.

5000 B.C.

3500 B.C.
In Mesopotamia (modern-day Iraq), people invent vehicles with wheels. But the first wheels are made of heavy wood, and the roads are terrible.

1100 B.C.
Chinese invent the magnetic compass. It allows them to sail long distances.

1660s
Horse-drawn stagecoaches begin running in France. They stop at stages to switch horses and passengers—the first mass transit system.

1769
James Watt patents the first successful steam engine.

All About...

THE TRANSCONTINENTAL RAILROAD

The California Gold Rush of 1849 made people realize the need to build a railroad to speed the trip from California to the east. In 1862 Congress authorized funds to build the railroad. The Union Pacific was to build west from Omaha, Nebraska, and the Central Pacific east from Sacramento, California. From 1866 to 1869, the two companies struggled to overcome rugged terrain, desert heat, freezing winters, and Indian attacks. Chinese, Irish, and other immigrant workers were brought in to complete the task. Finally, in 1869, the two roads were joined at Promontory Point in Utah. A golden spike was driven into the last tie to commemorate this milestone.

◀ Replica of Union Pacific's Locomotive No. 119

AGE OF MACHINES

1807
Robert Fulton patents a highly efficient steamboat.

1903
At Kitty Hawk, North Carolina, Orville Wright pilots the first powered heavier-than-air machine on a 12-second flight.

1939
The first practical helicopter and first jet plane are invented. The jet flies up to 434 mph. Jet passenger service began in 1958.

1981
The Space Shuttle *Columbia* is the first reusable spacecraft with a human crew.

1997
British driver Andy Green breaks the sound barrier on land for the first time, going 763 mph.

1839
Kirkpatrick Macmillan of Scotland invents the first pedaled bicycle.

1908
Henry Ford builds the first Model T, a practical car for the general public.

1961
Russian cosmonaut Yuri Gagarin orbits the Earth in a spaceship.

1830
Passenger rail service begins in England with the *Rocket,* a steam train built by George Stephenson. It goes about 24 miles an hour.

1862
Étienne Lenoir of Belgium builds the first car with an internal-combustion engine.

1947
Flying 700 mph, U.S. Air Force Capt. Charles "Chuck" Yeager breaks the sound barrier in the jet-powered Bell X-1.

1969
U.S. astronauts aboard *Apollo 11* land on the Moon.

2000
Amtrak runs its northeast high-speed *Acela* train. It can go 150 miles an hour.

Did You KNOW?

FLYING PRESIDENTS *Franklin D. Roosevelt had the first presidential airplane, the* Sacred Cow. *John F. Kennedy's plane was the first to be known as* Air Force One. *There are actually two* Air Force One *planes today. Both are specially outfitted Boeing 747s. Each has a presidential office and bedroom with a dressing room, bathroom, and shower. There's also a dining/conference room and accommodations for guests and staff. Two galleys provide meals made for up to 100 people at a time.*

TRAVEL

Where is the world's biggest amusement park? ➤ page 234

THERE'S NO PLACE LIKE HOME— OR AT LEAST THESE HOMES!

Pack your suitcase. It's vacation time! How would you like to visit some of these cool places where people lived long ago?

BILTMORE (ASHEVILLE, NC) If there had been a hide-and-seek world championship in the time of George Vanderbilt, then his mansion, built in 1895, would have been the place to hold it. Located in the beautiful Blue Ridge Mountains of North Carolina, it has 250 rooms in all. In its day it was the largest private home in the United States. You can visit it today.

HEARST CASTLE (SAN SIMEON, CA) Newspaper magnate William Randolph Hearst called it "La Cuesta Encantada"—the enchanted hill—and it's easy to see why. His castle and its surroundings are like fantasies made real. Feast your eyes on the rich tapestries and fireplaces brought over from Gothic castles, or tour the gardens, terraces, and pools outside, all with a view of the Pacific Ocean.

MESA VERDE CLIFF DWELLINGS (MESA VERDE NATIONAL PARK, MANCOS, CO) How about a visit to a thousand-year-old home... built into a cliff? These elaborate remains of stone buildings and courtyards, protected by cliff overhangs above, give you a close look at how Native Americans lived long ago. Around A.D. 1300 the cliff dwellers suddenly left their homes. Nobody knows why, but maybe you can come up with your own guess as you explore the place.

▲ *Mesa Verde*

MONTICELLO (CHARLOTTESVILLE, VA) You probably know Thomas Jefferson wrote the Declaration of Independence—but did you know he was also a very good architect? He designed his beautiful home, Monticello, and spent a good 40 years fixing it up. There are many clever gadgets, including a new kind of plow and a "wheel cipher," for putting messages in code. The staircases are mostly hidden, and his bed allowed him to roll out in two different rooms. If you visit Monticello you will also hear about sad things, since it was a working plantation, with most of the work done by slaves.

ST. SIMONS ISLAND LIGHTHOUSE (ST. SIMONS ISLAND, GA) Lighthouses aren't just lights—they're houses! Until it became automated in 1950, this 19th-century treasure was the home of the keeper, the assistant keeper, and their families. You can see their rooms today. You'll love the view after climbing all 129 of the tower's steps.

Monticello ▶

WORLD CITIES

AMSTERDAM Ride your way through a maze of **canals** on a pedal boat called a "canal bike," or rent a regular bicycle on streets that are great for cycling. The **Anne Frank House**, where the Frank family went into hiding from the Nazis in World War II, is now a world-renowned museum.

LONDON Ride the **double-decker buses**—on the left side of the street!—from the ancient **Tower of London** to the sleek new Ferris wheel called the **London Eye**. And don't forget to visit some of the city's beautiful green spaces, such as **St. James's Park**.

NEW YORK Take the elevator to the top of the **Empire State Building** for a bird's-eye view of this huge city. Get a look at the past when you walk through **South Street Seaport**. See the dinosaurs at the **Museum of Natural History**. Pet the real live zoo animals in **Central Park** and ride on the carousel. And don't forget the ferry to the **Statue of Liberty**.

Empire State Building

PARIS A short walk from the medieval cathedral of **Notre Dame** are the lively cafés of the **Left Bank.** After climbing the steps of Sacre Coeur in hilly **Montmartre**, enjoy a boat ride along the **Seine**, or visit the **Eiffel Tower** and get a bird's-eye view of where you've been.

Eiffel Tower

ROME Pretend you're a gladiator at the **Colosseum** or explore the underground **Catacombs**. Back on the street, local artists are waiting to sketch your portrait at the **Piazza Navona**.

SAN FRANCISCO Check out the **sea lions** at Pier 39, ride the **cable car** up through **Chinatown** and past the needle-like **Transamerica Pyramid**. Try the interactive exhibits at **Exploratorium**, a great museum of science, art, and technology. Finally, cross the bay on the **Golden Gate Bridge** and look back at the dramatic skyline.

Golden Gate Bridge

TOKYO If you're ready for an early-morning adventure, go for a dawn visit to the **Tsukiji Fish Market**. There are hundreds of fish types to see, and a bowl of steaming noodles will make a fun breakfast. Later in the day, see singing, dancing, and beautiful costumes at a **Kabuki theater**. There are also many beautiful **Buddhist temples** and **Shinto shrines** to visit.

WASHINGTON, D.C., is another great U.S. city to visit. For information about things to see there, go to page 285.

TREEHOUSE HOTELS *Move over, birds: A new breed of hotel is taking hold, high up in the branches! Travelers of all budgets are choosing to sleep in treehouses. Some of them are very simple—almost like pitching your tent on a platform in the air. Others have nice furniture and include washers, driers, and television sets! There are even treehouse hotels with fireplaces—makes you wonder, doesn't it?*

Did You Know?

AMUSEMENT PARKS: THEN & NOW

Amusement parks today are filled with bright lights, food, fun, and thrilling rides. But the earliest amusement parks, which appeared in Europe more than 400 years ago, were very different. Some of the attractions were flower gardens, bowling, music, and a few simple rides.

By 1884, amusement parks began to get more exciting. That's when the Switchback Gravity Pleasure Railway came to Coney Island in Brooklyn, New York. In 1893, the George Ferris Great Wheel was introduced in Chicago. The "Ferris" Wheel weighed more than four million pounds and stood 264 feet high. A year later, Chutes Park opened in Chicago. It was the first park to charge admission.

In the 1920s, some of the best roller coasters of all time were built. Many large cities had as many as six amusement parks. But the stock market crash and the Great Depression in the 1930s caused many parks to close.

In 1955, Disneyland opened in Anaheim, California. Different sections of the park, such as Tomorrowland and the Magic Kingdom, had their own themes. Disneyland became known as the country's first theme park.

These days amusement parks are more popular than ever, with thrill-seekers flocking to places like Six-Flags Great Adventure in New Jersey. Those with strong stomachs can brave the sleek, ultramodern, gravity-defying rides like Medusa, while others can stick to less scary kinds of fun.

POPULAR PARKS

PARK	LOCATION
Blackpool Pleasure Beach	England
Cedar Point	Ohio, USA
Disneyland	California, USA
Everland, Kyunggi-Do	South Korea
Lotte World	South Korea
Ocean Park, Hong Kong	China
Six Flags Great Adventure	New Jersey, USA
Tokyo Disneyland	Japan
Walt Disney World	Florida, USA
Yokohama Hakkejima Sea Paradise	Japan

FABULOUS FACTS

Largest amusement park: Walt Disney World, Lake Buena Vista, Florida, 28,000 acres

Park with the most rides: Blackpool Pleasure Beach, Blackpool, United Kingdom, 58 (41 major rides, 17 kiddie rides)

Park with the most roller coasters: Six Flags Magic Mountain, Valencia, California, 15

Oldest operating ferris wheel: Wonderland, Gaultier, Mississippi (The wheel opened in New Jersey in 1895 and moved to Wonderland in 1990.)

Oldest operating water ride: The Old Mill, Kennywood, West Mifflin, Pennsylvania. Built in 1901, it was rebuilt in 1926.

Oldest operating merry-go-round: Flying Horses, Martha's Vineyard, Oak Bluff, Massachusetts, built in 1876

TALK LIKE AN EXPERT

Amusement parks have their own lingo.

AIRTIME: the feeling of rising out of your seat while riding on a roller coaster

HYPER COASTER: a roller coaster with at least one drop of over 200 feet

INVERSION: part of a roller coaster ride that turns riders upside down

INVERTED COASTER: a roller coaster that travels underneath the track

MULTI-LOOPER: a roller coaster with several inversions

THEME PARK: a place in which the rides, attractions, shows, and buildings all have the same theme or subject, such as Sea World

IT'S NOT ALWAYS ABOUT THE RIDES

Ah, the thrill of riding on a roller coaster: the sick stomach, the shriek we let out as we start to plunge down the steepest slope! Some of us love it...and some of us hate it. But many amusement parks have other fun features along with the rides.

► **The Africa Safari Park** near Baton Rouge, LA, lets you get a look at exotic species from all over the world. While riding in your car along the gravel road, you can stop to meet and even feed the animals.

► **Bonfante Gardens Theme Park** in Gilroy, CA, has a collection of weird "circus trees." Their trunks might form the shape of a basket, or a lightning bolt, or a huge piece of jewelry. This is done by pruning, grafting, and bending the trees as they grow. Each tree is really several trees that have grown together to look like one.

► At **Legoland** in Carlsbad, CA (and in Europe), Lego blocks are used to make everything from cities to cars to driver's licenses. It's a whole new world made out of blocks just like the ones you might have at home.

► **SeaWorld** (with locations in San Antonio, TX, San Diego, CA, and Orlando, FL) is the home of all kinds of exciting marine life, from friendly porpoises to killer whales!

▲ *SeaWorld*

DID YOU KNOW? *AMERICA'S FIRST ROLLER COASTER wasn't supposed to be fun at all! It was built in 1827 to carry coal from a Pennsylvania mountaintop mine to boats on the canal below. But the speeding coal carts of "Gravity Road" soon attracted crowds. The owners agreed to let people (including commuters) ride in the afternoons, with mornings still reserved for coal. Gravity Road's rails are gone now, but they ran for 18 miles and dropped a total of more than 1,200 feet, more than any roller coaster built just for fun.*

WORLD'S FASTEST ROLLER COASTERS
1. **Dodonpa:** 107 mph, Gotemba City, Japan
2. **Superman: The Escape:** 100 mph, Valencia, California
3. **Steel Dragon 2000:** 95 mph, Mie, Japan
4. **Millennium Force:** 92 mph, Sandunsky, Ohio
5. **Goliath:** 85 mph, Valencia, California
   Titan: 85 mph, Arlington, Texas

WORLD'S LONGEST ROLLER COASTERS
1. **Steel Dragon 2000:** 8,133 ft, Mie, Japan
2. **The Ultimate:** 7,498 ft, North Yorkshire, England
3. **The Beast:** 7,400 ft, Cincinnati, Ohio
4. **Son of Beast:** 7,032 ft, Cincinnati, Ohio
5. **Millennium Force:** 6,595 ft, Sandusky, Ohio

WORLD'S TALLEST ROLLER COASTERS
1. **Superman: The Escape:** 415 ft, Valencia, California
2. **Tower of Terror:** 380 ft, Gold Coast, Australia
3. **Steel Dragon 2000:** 318 ft, Mie, Japan
4. **Fujiyama:** 259 ft, Yamanashi, Japan
5. **Millennium Force:** 310 ft, Sandusky, Ohio

UNITED NATIONS

How many countries belong to the UN? ➤page 236

A COMMUNITY OF NATIONS

The United Nations (UN) was started in 1945 after World War II. The first members of the UN were 50 nations that met in San Francisco, California. They signed an agreement known as the UN Charter. By early 2002, the UN had 189 independent countries as members—not counting East Timor, which was moving close to independence, and Switzerland, which finally, in 2002, voted to seek membership.

Flags fly at the UN

The UN Charter lists these purposes:
- ▶ to keep worldwide peace and security
- ▶ to develop friendly relations among countries
- ▶ to help countries cooperate in solving problems
- ▶ to promote respect for human rights and basic freedoms
- ▶ to be a center that helps countries achieve their goals

FAST FACTS ABOUT THE UN

UN Day is celebrated every year on October 24, the day the UN Charter was ratified by a majority of nations.

- ▶ The UN has its own fire department, security force, and postal service. Its UN post office sells stamps that can be used only to send mail from the UN.

- ▶ The flags of all member nations fly in front of UN headquarters. They are in alphabetical order, from Afghanistan to Zimbabwe.

- ▶ The secretary-general (chief officer) of the UN is Kofi Annan of Ghana. In June 2001 the General Assembly unanimously reelected him to a second five-year term.

- ▶ The United Nations and Kofi Annan shared the Nobel Peace Prize in 2001. It wasn't the first time for the UN. The UN Peacekeeping Forces won it in 1988 and the UN High Commissioner for Refugees in 1954 and 1981. UNICEF (United Nations Children's Fund) won it in 1965, and the International Labor Organization, a special agency associated with the UN, received it in 1969.

- ▶ Kofi Annan wasn't the first secretary-general to win the Peace Prize. Dag Hammarskjold was named to win it in 1961, shortly after he died in a plane crash while on a peace mission.

Did You KNOW?

BIG BUCKS *In 1945, John D. Rockefeller Jr., drawing from the Rockefeller family fortune, bought a six-block site along New York City's East River for $8.5 million, and donated it to the UN for its headquarters. He also built Rockefeller Center in New York and gave most of the money to create Colonial Williamsburg in Virginia.*

UN PEACEKEEPERS

The Security Council sets up and directs UN peacekeeping missions, to try to stop people from fighting while the countries or groups try to work out their differences. The map below shows the location of 15 peacekeeping missions that were operating in January 2002. These peacekeepers wear blue helmets or berets with white UN letters. In December 2001 the United Nations approved a special peacekeeping force in Afghanistan, with troops or the support from 18 countries. These troops work under UN authority but do not wear UN berets.

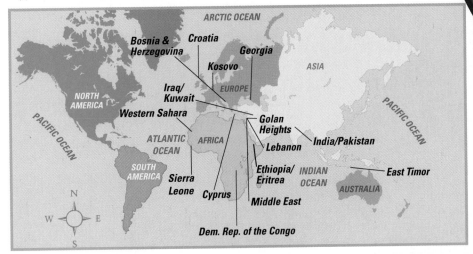

HOW THE UN IS ORGANIZED

GENERAL ASSEMBLY What It Does: discusses world problems, admits new members, appoints the secretary-general, decides the UN budget **Members:** All members of the UN belong to the General Assembly; each country has one vote.

SECURITY COUNCIL What It Does: discusses questions of peace and security **Members:** Five permanent members (China, France, Great Britain, Russia, and the United States), and ten members elected by the General Assembly for two-year terms. In early 2002 the ten were Colombia, Ireland, Mauritius, Norway, and Singapore (ending that year) and Bulgaria, Cameroon, Guinea, Mexico, and Syria (ending in 2003).

ECONOMIC AND SOCIAL COUNCIL What It Does: deals with issues related to trade, economic development, industry, population, children, food, education, health, and human rights **Members:** Fifty-four member countries elected for three-year terms.

INTERNATIONAL COURT OF JUSTICE (WORLD COURT) located at The Hague, Netherlands **What It Does:** highest court for disputes between countries **Members:** Fifteen judges, each from a different country, elected to nine-year terms.

SECRETARIAT What It Does: carries out day-to-day operations of the UN **Members:** UN staff, headed by the secretary-general.

CHILDREN'S SUMMIT In May 2002, some 3,000 delegates, including more than 250 kids, from over 180 nations met at the UN for a special Children's Summit. They reviewed progress made in dealing with children's needs around the world.

UNITED STATES

What branch of government has its own special handshake? ➤page 254

UNITED STATES: FACTS & FIGURES

AREA:	LAND	WATER	TOTAL
50 states and Washington, D.C.	3,536,278 square miles	181,518 square miles	3,717,796 square miles

POPULATION (2002): 287,041,000   **CAPITAL:** Washington, D.C.

LARGEST, HIGHEST, AND OTHER STATISTICS

▲ Old Faithful geyser in Yellowstone National Park

Largest state: Alaska (615,230 square miles)
Smallest state: Rhode Island (1,231 square miles)
Northernmost city: Barrow, Alaska (71°17' north latitude)
Southernmost city: Hilo, Hawaii (19°44' north latitude)
Easternmost city: Eastport, Maine (66°59'05" west longitude)
Westernmost city: Atka, Alaska (174°12' west longitude)
Highest settlement: Climax, Colorado (11,360 feet)
Lowest settlement: Calipatria, California (184 feet below sea level)
Oldest national park: Yellowstone National Park (Idaho, Montana, Wyoming), 2,219,791 acres, established 1872
Largest national park: Wrangell-St. Elias, Alaska (8,323,618 acres)
Longest river system: Mississippi-Missouri-Red Rock (3,710 miles)
Deepest lake: Crater Lake, Oregon (1,932 feet)
Highest mountain: Mount McKinley, Alaska (20,320 feet)
Lowest point: Death Valley, California (282 feet below sea level)
Rainiest spot: Mount Waialeale, Hawaii (average annual rainfall, 460 inches)
Tallest building: Sears Tower, Chicago, Illinois (1,450 feet)
Tallest structure: TV tower, Blanchard, North Dakota (2,063 feet)
Longest bridge span: Verrazano-Narrows Bridge, New York (4,260 feet)
Highest bridge: Royal Gorge, Colorado (1,053 feet above water)

INTERNATIONAL BOUNDARY LINES OF THE U.S.

U.S.-Canadian border . . . . 3,987 miles
(excluding Alaska)
Alaska-Canadian border . . . . . 1,538 miles
U.S.-Mexican border . . . . 1,933 miles
(Gulf of Mexico to Pacific Ocean)

Atlantic coast . . . . 2,069 miles
Gulf of Mexico coast . . . . 1,631 miles
Pacific coast . . . . 7,623 miles
Arctic coast, Alaska . . . . 1,060 miles

Did You KNOW?

THE SMALLEST PARK in the U.S.—and the world—is in Portland, Oregon. Mill Ends Park is a circle 2 feet across, in the middle of Front Avenue. It was originally meant for a light pole. Newspaper columnist Dick Fagan pulled out the weeds in it and planted flowers. It was dedicated in 1948 and became an official city park in 1976.

SYMBOLS of the United States

THE GREAT SEAL

The Great Seal of the United States shows an American bald eagle with a ribbon in its mouth bearing the Latin words "e pluribus unum" (out of many, one). In its talons are the arrows of war and an olive branch of peace. On the back of the Great Seal is an unfinished pyramid with an eye (the eye of Providence) above it. The seal was approved by Congress on June 20, 1782.

THE FLAG

The flag of the United States has 50 stars (one for each state) and 13 stripes (one for each of the original 13 states). It is called unofficially the "Stars and Stripes."

The first U.S. flag was commissioned by the Second Continental Congress in 1777 but did not exist until 1783, after the American Revolution. Historians are not certain who designed the Stars and Stripes. Many different flags are believed to have been used during the American Revolution.

The flag of 1777 was used until 1795. In that year Congress passed an act ordering that a new flag have 15 stripes, alternate red and white, and 15 stars on a blue field. In 1818, Congress directed that the flag have 13 stripes and that a new star be added for each new state of the Union. The last star was added in 1960 for the state of Hawaii.

1777 **1795** **1818**

There are many customs for flying the flag and treating it with respect. For example, it should not touch the floor and no other flag should be flown above it, except for the UN flag at UN headquarters. When the flag is raised or lowered, or passes in a parade, or during the Pledge of Allegiance, people should face it and stand at attention. Those in military uniform should salute. Others should put their right hand over their heart. The flag is flown at half staff as a sign of mourning.

PLEDGE OF ALLEGIANCE TO THE FLAG

"I pledge allegiance to the flag of the United States of America and to the republic for which it stands, one nation under God, indivisible, with liberty and justice for all."

THE NATIONAL ANTHEM

"The Star-Spangled Banner" was a poem written in 1814 by Francis Scott Key as he watched British ships bombard Fort McHenry, Maryland, during the War of 1812. It became the National Anthem by an act of Congress in 1931. The music to "The Star-Spangled Banner" was originally a tune called "Anacreon in Heaven."

THE U.S. CONSTITUTION
THE FOUNDATION OF AMERICAN GOVERNMENT

The Constitution is the document that created the present government of the United States. It was written in 1787 and went into effect in 1789. It establishes the three branches of the U.S. government, which are the executive (headed by the president), the legislative (the Congress), and the judicial (the Supreme Court and other federal courts). The first 10 amendments to the Constitution (the Bill of Rights) explain the basic rights of all American citizens.

You can find the constitution on-line at:

WEBSITE *http://www.nara.gov/exhall/charters/constitution*

THE PREAMBLE TO THE CONSTITUTION

The Constitution begins with a short statement called the Preamble. The Preamble states that the government of the United States was established by the people.

> "We, the people of the United States, in order to form a more perfect Union, establish justice, insure domestic tranquility, provide for the common defense, promote the general welfare, and secure the blessings of liberty to ourselves and our posterity do ordain and establish this Constitution for the United States of America."

THE ARTICLES

The original Constitution contained seven articles. The first three articles of the Constitution establish the three branches of the U.S. government.

Article 1, Legislative Branch Creates the Senate and House of Representatives and describes their functions and powers.

Article 2, Executive Branch Creates the office of the President and the Electoral College and lists their powers and responsibilities.

Article 3, Judicial Branch Creates the Supreme Court and gives Congress the power to create lower courts. The powers of the courts and certain crimes are defined.

Article 4, The States Discusses the relationship of the states to one another and to the citizens. Defines the states' powers.

Article 5, Amending the Constitution Describes how the Constitution can be amended (changed).

Article 6, Federal Law Makes the Constitution the supreme law of the land over state laws and constitutions.

Article 7, Ratifying the Constitution Establishes how to ratify (approve) the Constitution.

AMENDMENTS TO THE CONSTITUTION

The writers of the Constitution understood that it might need to be amended, or changed, in the future. Article 5 describes how the Constitution can be amended.

In order to pass, an amendment must be approved by a two-thirds majority in the House of Representatives and a two-thirds majority in the Senate. The amendment must then be approved by three-fourths of the states (38 states). So far, the Constitution has been amended 27 times.

The Bill of Rights: The First Ten Amendments

The first ten amendments were adopted in 1791 and contain the basic freedoms Americans enjoy as a people. These amendments are known as the Bill of Rights. They are summarized below.

1 Guarantees freedom of religion, speech, and the press.

2 Guarantees the right of the people to have firearms.

3 Guarantees that soldiers cannot be lodged in private homes unless the owner agrees.

4 Protects citizens against being searched or having their property searched or taken away by the government without a good reason.

5 Protects rights of people on trial for crimes.

6 Guarantees people accused of crimes the right to a speedy public trial by jury.

7 Guarantees people the right to a trial by jury for other kinds of cases.

8 Prohibits "cruel and unusual punishments."

9 Says that specific rights listed in the Constitution do not take away rights that may not be listed.

10 Establishes that any powers not given specifically to the federal government belong to states or the people.

Other Important Amendments

13 (1865): Ends slavery in the United States.

14 (1868): Establishes the Bill of Rights as protection against actions by a state government; guarantees equal protection under the law for all citizens.

15 (1870): Guarantees that a person cannot be denied the right to vote because of race or color.

19 (1920): Gives women the right to vote.

22 (1951): Limits the president to two four-year terms of office.

24 (1964): Outlaws the poll tax (a tax people had to pay before they could vote) in federal elections. (The poll tax had been used to keep African Americans in the South from voting.)

25 (1967): Gives the president the power to appoint a new vice president, with the approval of Congress, if a vice president dies or leaves office in the middle of a term.

26 (1971): Lowers the voting age to 18 from 21.

THE EXECUTIVE BRANCH:
The PRESIDENT and the CABINET

The executive branch of the federal government is headed by the president. It also includes the vice president, people who work for the president or vice president, the major departments of the federal government, and special agencies. The cabinet is made up of the vice president, heads of the major departments, and other top officials. It meets when the president asks for its advice. As head of the executive branch, the president is responsible for enforcing the laws passed by Congress and is commander in chief of U.S. armed forces. The chart at right shows cabinet departments in the order in which they were created.

PRESIDENT

VICE PRESIDENT

CABINET DEPARTMENTS

1. State
2. Treasury
3. Defense
4. Justice
5. Interior
6. Agriculture
7. Commerce
8. Labor
9. Housing and Urban Development
10. Transportation
11. Energy
12. Education
13. Health and Human Services
14. Veterans Affairs

HOW LONG DOES THE PRESIDENT SERVE?
The president serves a four-year term, starting on January 20. No president can be elected more than twice.

WHAT HAPPENS IF THE PRESIDENT DIES?
If the president dies in office or cannot complete the term, the vice president becomes president. If the president is disabled, the vice president can become acting president until the president is able to work again. The next person to become president after the vice president would be the Speaker of the House of Representatives. A person who finishes more than two years of a president's term can be elected to only one more term.

The White House has an address on the World Wide Web especially for kids. It is:

WEBSITE *http://www.whitehousekids.gov*

You can send e-mail to the president at:

EMAIL *president@whitehouse.gov*

DID YOU KNOW? *The White House has its own tennis court, jogging track, swimming pool, movie theater, and bowling lane. It has 5 chefs, who can serve dinner to up to 140 guests.*

The White House, home of the U.S. president

ELECTIONS
Electing the President and Vice President

Every four years on the first Tuesday after the first Monday in November, American voters go to the polls and elect a president and vice president. Right? Well, sort of. The president and vice president are the only elected U.S. officials who are not actually chosen by a direct vote of the people. They are really elected by the 538 members of the Electoral College.

The Electoral College is not really a college, but a group of people chosen in each state. In 1787 the men writing the Constitution did not agree on how a president should be selected. Some did not trust ordinary people to make a good choice. So they compromised and agreed to have the Electoral College do it.

In the early days before political parties became important, electors voted for whomever they wanted. In modern times the political parties hold primary elections and conventions to choose candidates for president and vice president. When voters choose the candidates of a particular party, they are actually choosing electors from that party. The electors have agreed to vote for their party's candidate, and except in very rare cases this is what they do.

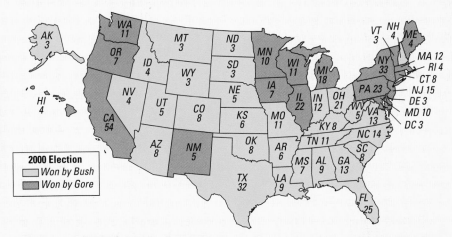

2000 Election
- Won by Bush
- Won by Gore

THE ELECTORAL COLLEGE STATE BY STATE

The number of electors for each state and the District of Columbia is equal to the total number of senators and representatives each has in Congress. For example, Minnesota has eight representatives and two senators, for a total of ten. (In the 2004 election, numbers of representatives will change because of 2000 Census results.) The electors chosen in November meet in state capitals in December. In almost all states, the party that got the most votes in November wins all the electors and electoral votes for the state. This happens even if the results of the election in the state are very close.

In early January the electors' votes are officially opened during a special session of Congress. If no presidential candidate wins a majority (at least 270) of the electoral votes, the House of Representatives chooses the president. This happened in 1800, 1824, and 1877.

Can a candidate who didn't win the most popular votes still win a majority of electoral votes? Yes. That's what happened in 1876, 1888, and again in 2000.

PRESIDENTS AND VICE PRESIDENTS OF THE UNITED STATES

PRESIDENT / VICE PRESIDENT	YEARS IN OFFICE
❶ George Washington	1789–1797
John Adams	1789–1797
❷ John Adams	1797–1801
Thomas Jefferson	1797–1801
❸ Thomas Jefferson	1801–1809
Aaron Burr	1801–1805
George Clinton	1805–1809
❹ James Madison	1809–1817
George Clinton	1809–1812
Elbridge Gerry	1813–1814
❺ James Monroe	1817–1825
Daniel D. Tompkins	1817–1825
❻ John Quincy Adams	1825–1829
John C. Calhoun	1825–1829
❼ Andrew Jackson	1829–1837
John C. Calhoun	1829–1832
Martin Van Buren	1833–1837
❽ Martin Van Buren	1837–1841
Richard M. Johnson	1837–1841
❾ William H. Harrison	1841
John Tyler	1841
❿ John Tyler	1841–1845
No Vice President	
⓫ James Knox Polk	1845–1849
George M. Dallas	1845–1849
⓬ Zachary Taylor	1849–1850
Millard Fillmore	1849–1850
⓭ Millard Fillmore	1850–1853
No Vice President	
⓮ Franklin Pierce	1853–1857
William R. King	1853
⓯ James Buchanan	1857–1861
John C. Breckinridge	1857–1861
⓰ Abraham Lincoln	1861–1865
Hannibal Hamlin	1861–1865
Andrew Johnson	1865
⓱ Andrew Johnson	1865–1869
No Vice President	
⓲ Ulysses S. Grant	1869–1877
Schuyler Colfax	1869–1873
Henry Wilson	1873–1875
⓳ Rutherford B. Hayes	1877–1881
William A. Wheeler	1877–1881
⓴ James A. Garfield	1881
Chester A. Arthur	1881
㉑ Chester A. Arthur	1881–1885
No Vice President	

PRESIDENT / VICE PRESIDENT	YEARS IN OFFICE
㉒ Grover Cleveland	1885–1889
Thomas A. Hendricks	1885
㉓ Benjamin Harrison	1889–1893
Levi P. Morton	1889–1893
㉔ Grover Cleveland	1893–1897
Adlai E. Stevenson	1893–1897
㉕ William McKinley	1897–1901
Garret A. Hobart	1897–1899
Theodore Roosevelt	1901
㉖ Theodore Roosevelt	1901–1909
Charles W. Fairbanks	1905–1909
㉗ William Howard Taft	1909–1913
James S. Sherman	1909–1912
㉘ Woodrow Wilson	1913–1921
Thomas R. Marshall	1913–1921
㉙ Warren G. Harding	1921–1923
Calvin Coolidge	1921–1923
㉚ Calvin Coolidge	1923–1929
Charles G. Dawes	1925–1929
㉛ Herbert Hoover	1929–1933
Charles Curtis	1929–1933
㉜ Franklin D. Roosevelt	1933–1945
John Nance Garner	1933–1941
Henry A. Wallace	1941–1945
Harry S. Truman	1945
㉝ Harry S. Truman	1945–1953
Alben W. Barkley	1949–1953
㉞ Dwight D. Eisenhower	1953–1961
Richard M. Nixon	1953–1961
㉟ John F. Kennedy	1961–1963
Lyndon B. Johnson	1961–1963
㊱ Lyndon B. Johnson	1963–1969
Hubert H. Humphrey	1965–1969
㊲ Richard M. Nixon	1969–1974
Spiro T. Agnew	1969–1973
Gerald R. Ford	1973–1974
㊳ Gerald R. Ford	1974–1977
Nelson A. Rockefeller	1974–1977
㊴ Jimmy Carter	1977–1981
Walter F. Mondale	1977–1981
㊵ Ronald Reagan	1981–1989
George Bush	1981–1989
㊶ George Bush	1989–1993
Dan Quayle	1989–1993
㊷ Bill Clinton	1993–2001
Al Gore	1993–2001
㊸ George W. Bush	2001–
Richard B. Cheney	2001–

PRESIDENTS
of the United States

GEORGE WASHINGTON Federalist Party   **1789-1797**
Born: Feb. 22, 1732, at Wakefield, Westmoreland County, Virginia
Married: Martha Dandridge Custis (1731-1802); no children
Died: Dec. 14, 1799; buried at Mount Vernon, Fairfax County, Virginia
Early Career: Soldier; head of the Virginia militia; commander of the
   Continental Army; chairman of Constitutional Convention (1787)

JOHN ADAMS Federalist Party   **1797-1801**
Born: Oct. 30, 1735, in Braintree (now Quincy), Massachusetts
Married: Abigail Smith (1744-1818); 3 sons, 2 daughters
Died: July 4, 1826; buried in Quincy, Massachusetts
Early Career: Lawyer; delegate to Continental Congress; signer of the
   Declaration of Independence; first vice president

THOMAS JEFFERSON Democratic-Republican Party   **1801-1809**
Born: Apr. 13, 1743, at Shadwell, Albemarle County, Virginia
Married: Martha Wayles Skelton (1748-1782); 1 son, 5 daughters
Died: July 4, 1826; buried at Monticello, Albemarle County, Virginia
Early Career: Lawyer; member of the Continental Congress; author of the
   Declaration of Independence; governor of Virginia; first secretary of
   state; author of the Virginia Statute on Religious Freedom

JAMES MADISON Democratic-Republican Party   **1809-1817**
Born: Mar. 16, 1751, at Port Conway, King George County, Virginia
Married: Dolley Payne Todd (1768-1849); no children
Died: June 28, 1836; buried at Montpelier Station, Virginia
Early Career: Member of the Virginia Constitutional Convention (1776);
   member of the Continental Congress; major contributor to the U.S.
   Constitution; writer of the *Federalist Papers*; secretary of state

JAMES MONROE Democratic-Republican Party   **1817-1825**
Born: Apr. 28, 1758, in Westmoreland County, Virginia
Married: Elizabeth Kortright (1768-1830); 2 daughters
Died: July 4, 1831; buried in Richmond, Virginia
Early Career: Soldier; lawyer; U.S. senator; governor of Virginia;
   secretary of state

JOHN QUINCY ADAMS Democratic-Republican Party   **1825-1829**
Born: July 11, 1767, in Braintree (now Quincy), Massachusetts
Married: Louisa Catherine Johnson (1775-1852); 3 sons, 1 daughter
Died: Feb. 23, 1848; buried in Quincy, Massachusetts
Early Career: Diplomat; U.S. senator; secretary of state

ANDREW JACKSON Democratic Party　　　**1829-1837**
Born: Mar. 15, 1767, in Waxhaw, South Carolina
Married: Rachel Donelson Robards (1767-1828); 1 son
Died: June 8, 1845; buried in Nashville, Tennessee
Early Career: Lawyer; U.S. representative and senator; soldier in the
　　U.S. Army

MARTIN VAN BUREN Democratic Party　　　**1837-1841**
Born: Dec. 5, 1782, at Kinderhook, New York
Married: Hannah Hoes (1783-1819); 4 sons
Died: July 24, 1862; buried at Kinderhook, New York
Early Career: Governor of New York; secretary of state; vice president

WILLIAM HENRY HARRISON Whig Party　　　**1841**
Born: Feb. 9, 1773, at Berkeley, Charles City County, Virginia
Married: Anna Symmes (1775-1864); 6 sons, 4 daughters
Died: Apr. 4, 1841; buried in North Bend, Ohio
Early Career: First governor of Indiana Territory; superintendent of
　　Indian affairs; U.S. representative and senator

JOHN TYLER Whig Party　　　**1841-1845**
Born: Mar. 29, 1790, in Greenway, Charles City County, Virginia
Married: Letitia Christian (1790-1842); 3 sons, 5 daughters
　　Julia Gardiner (1820-1889); 5 sons, 2 daughters
Died: Jan. 18, 1862; buried in Richmond, Virginia
Early Career: U.S. representative and senator; vice president

JAMES KNOX POLK Democratic Party　　　**1845-1849**
Born: Nov. 2, 1795, in Mecklenburg County, North Carolina
Married: Sarah Childress (1803-1891); no children
Died: June 15, 1849; buried in Nashville, Tennessee
Early Career: U.S. representative; Speaker of the House; governor
　　of Tennessee

ZACHARY TAYLOR Whig Party　　　**1849-1850**
Born: Nov. 24, 1784, in Orange County, Virginia
Married: Margaret Smith (1788-1852); 1 son, 5 daughters
Died: July 9, 1850; buried in Louisville, Kentucky
Early Career: Indian fighter; general in the U.S. Army

MILLARD FILLMORE Whig Party　　　**1850-1853**
Born: Jan. 7, 1800, in Cayuga County, New York
Married: Abigail Powers (1798-1853); 1 son, 1 daughter
　　Caroline Carmichael McIntosh (1813-1881); no children
Died: Mar. 8, 1874; buried in Buffalo, New York
Early Career: Farmer; lawyer; U.S. representative; vice president

FRANKLIN PIERCE Democratic Party   **1853-1857**
Born: Nov. 23, 1804, in Hillsboro, New Hampshire
Married: Jane Means Appleton (1806-1863); 3 sons
Died: Oct. 8, 1869; buried in Concord, New Hampshire
Early Career: U.S. representative, senator

JAMES BUCHANAN Democratic Party   **1857-1861**
Born: Apr. 23, 1791, Cove Gap, near Mercersburg, Pennsylvania
Married: Never
Died: June 1, 1868, buried in Lancaster, Pennsylvania
Early Career: U.S. representative; secretary of state

ABRAHAM LINCOLN Republican Party   **1861-1865**
Born: Feb. 12, 1809, in Hardin County, Kentucky
Married: Mary Todd (1818-1882); 4 sons
Died: Apr. 15, 1865; buried in Springfield, Illinois
Early Career: Lawyer; U.S. representative

ANDREW JOHNSON Democratic Party   **1865-1869**
Born: Dec. 29, 1808, in Raleigh, North Carolina
Married: Eliza McCardle (1810-1876); 3 sons, 2 daughters
Died: July 31, 1875; buried in Greeneville, Tennessee
Early Career: Tailor; member of state legislature; U.S. representative;
    governor of Tennessee; U.S. senator; vice president

ULYSSES S. GRANT Republican Party   **1869-1877**
Born: Apr. 27, 1822, in Point Pleasant, Ohio
Married: Julia Dent (1826-1902); 3 sons, 1 daughter
Died: July 23, 1885; buried in New York City
Early Career: Army officer; commander of Union forces during Civil War

RUTHERFORD B. HAYES Republican Party   **1877-1881**
Born: Oct. 4, 1822, in Delaware, Ohio
Married: Lucy Ware Webb (1831-1889); 5 sons, 2 daughters
Died: Jan. 17, 1893; buried in Fremont, Ohio
Early Career: Lawyer; general in Union Army; U.S. representative;
    governor of Ohio

JAMES A. GARFIELD Republican Party   **1881**
Born: Nov. 19, 1831, in Orange, Cuyahoga County, Ohio
Married: Lucretia Rudolph (1832-1918); 5 sons, 2 daughters
Died: Sept. 19, 1881; buried in Cleveland, Ohio
Early Career: Teacher; Ohio state senator; general in Union Army;
    U.S. representative

21 **CHESTER A. ARTHUR** Republican Party   **1881-1885**
Born: Oct. 5, 1829, in Fairfield, Vermont
Married: Ellen Lewis Herndon (1837-1880); 2 sons, 1 daughter
Died: Nov. 18, 1886; buried in Albany, New York
Early Career: Teacher; lawyer; vice president

22 **GROVER CLEVELAND** Democratic Party   **1885-1889**
Born: Mar. 18, 1837, in Caldwell, New Jersey
Married: Frances Folsom (1864-1947); 2 sons, 3 daughters
Died: June 24, 1908; buried in Princeton, New Jersey
Early Career: Lawyer; mayor of Buffalo; governor of New York

23 **BENJAMIN HARRISON** Republican Party   **1889-1893**
Born: Aug. 20, 1833, in North Bend, Ohio
Married: Caroline Lavinia Scott (1832-1892); 1 son, 1 daughter
           Mary Scott Lord Dimmick (1858-1948); 1 daughter
Died: Mar. 13, 1901; buried in Indianapolis, Indiana
Early Career: Lawyer; general in Union Army; U.S. senator

24 **GROVER CLEVELAND**   **1893-1897**
See 22, above

25 **WILLIAM MCKINLEY** Republican Party   **1897-1901**
Born: Jan. 29, 1843, in Niles, Ohio
Married: Ida Saxton (1847-1907); 2 daughters
Died: Sept. 14, 1901; buried in Canton, Ohio
Early Career: Lawyer; U.S. representative; governor of Ohio

26 **THEODORE ROOSEVELT** Republican Party   **1901-1909**
Born: Oct. 27, 1858, in New York City
Married: Alice Hathaway Lee (1861-1884); 1 daughter
      Edith Kermit Carow (1861-1948); 4 sons, 1 daughter
Died: Jan. 6, 1919; buried in Oyster Bay, New York
Early Career: Assistant secretary of the Navy; cavalry leader in Spanish-American War; governor of New York; vice president

27 **WILLIAM HOWARD TAFT** Republican Party   **1909-1913**
Born: Sept. 15, 1857, in Cincinnati, Ohio
Married: Helen Herron (1861-1943); 2 sons, 1 daughter
Died: Mar. 8, 1930; buried in Arlington National Cemetery, Virginia
Early Career: Reporter; lawyer; judge; secretary of war

28 **WOODROW WILSON** Democratic Party   **1913-1921**
Born: Dec. 28, 1856, in Staunton, Virginia
Married: Ellen Louise Axson (1860-1914); 3 daughters
      Edith Bolling Galt (1872-1961); no children
Died: Feb. 3, 1924; buried in Washington, D.C.
Early Career: College professor and president; governor of New Jersey

WARREN G. HARDiNG Republican Party 1921-1923
Born: Nov. 2, 1865, near Corsica (now Blooming Grove), Ohio
Married: Florence Kling De Wolfe (1860-1924); 1 daughter
Died: Aug. 2, 1923; buried in Marion, Ohio
Early Career: Ohio state senator; U.S. senator

CALViN COOLiDGE Republican Party 1923-1929
Born: July 4, 1872, in Plymouth, Vermont
Married: Grace Anna Goodhue (1879-1957); 2 sons
Died: Jan. 5, 1933; buried in Plymouth, Vermont
Early Career: Massachusetts state legislator; lieutenant governor and governor; vice president

HERBERT HOOVER Republican Party 1929-1933
Born: Aug. 10, 1874, in West Branch, Iowa
Married: Lou Henry (1875-1944); 2 sons
Died: Oct. 20, 1964; buried in West Branch, Iowa
Early Career: Mining engineer; secretary of commerce

FRANKLiN DELANO ROOSEVELT Democratic Party 1933-1945
Born: Jan. 30, 1882, in Hyde Park, New York
Married: Anna Eleanor Roosevelt (1884-1962); 4 sons, 1 daughter
Died: Apr. 12, 1945; buried in Hyde Park, New York
Early Career: Lawyer; New York state senator; assistant secretary of the Navy; governor of New York

HARRY S. TRUMAN Democratic Party 1945-1953
Born: May 8, 1884, in Lamar, Missouri
Married: Elizabeth Virginia "Bess" Wallace (1885-1982); 1 daughter
Died: Dec. 26, 1972; buried in Independence, Missouri
Early Career: Farmer; haberdasher (ran men's clothing store); judge; U.S. senator; vice president

DWiGHT D. EiSENHOWER Republican Party 1953-1961
Born: Oct. 14, 1890, in Denison, Texas
Married: Mary "Mamie" Geneva Doud (1896-1979); 2 sons
Died: Mar. 28, 1969; buried in Abilene, Kansas
Early Career: Commander, Allied landing in North Africa and later Supreme Allied Commander in Europe during World War II; president of Columbia University

JOHN FiTZGERALD KENNEDY Democratic Party 1961-1963
Born: May 29, 1917, in Brookline, Massachusetts
Married: Jacqueline Lee Bouvier (1929-1994); 2 sons, 1 daughter
Died: Nov. 22, 1963; buried in Arlington National Cemetery, Virginia
Early Career: U.S. naval commander; U.S. representative and senator

LYNDON BAINES JOHNSON Democratic Party 1963-1969
Born: Aug. 27, 1908, near Stonewall, Texas
Married: Claudia "Lady Bird" Alta Taylor (b. 1912); 2 daughters
Died: Jan. 22, 1973; buried in Johnson City, Texas
Early Career: U.S. representative and senator; vice president

RICHARD MILHOUS NIXON Republican Party 1969-1974
Born: Jan. 9, 1913, in Yorba Linda, California
Married: Thelma "Pat" Ryan (1912-1993); 2 daughters
Died: Apr. 22, 1994; buried in Yorba Linda, California
Early Career: Lawyer; U.S. representative and senator; vice president

GERALD R. FORD Republican Party 1974-1977
Born: July 14, 1913, in Omaha, Nebraska
Married: Elizabeth "Betty" Bloomer (b. 1918); 3 sons, 1 daughter
Early Career: Lawyer; U.S. representative; vice president

JIMMY (JAMES EARL) CARTER Democratic Party 1977-1981
Born: Oct. 1, 1924, in Plains, Georgia
Married: Rosalynn Smith (b. 1927); 3 sons, 1 daughter
Early Career: Peanut farmer; Georgia state senator; governor
of Georgia

RONALD REAGAN Republican Party 1981-1989
Born: Feb. 6, 1911, in Tampico, Illinois
Married: Jane Wyman (b. 1914); 1 son, 1 daughter
Nancy Davis (b. 1923); 1 son, 1 daughter
Early Career: Film and television actor; governor of California

GEORGE BUSH Republican Party 1989-1993
Born: June 12, 1924, in Milton, Massachusetts
Married: Barbara Pierce (b. 1925); 4 sons, 2 daughters
Early Career: U.S. Navy pilot; businessman; U.S. representative; U.S.
ambassador to the United Nations; vice president

BILL (WILLIAM JEFFERSON) CLINTON Democratic Party 1993-2001
Born: Aug. 19, 1946, in Hope, Arkansas
Married: Hillary Rodham (b. 1947); 1 daughter
Early Career: College professor; Arkansas state attorney general;
governor of Arkansas

GEORGE W. BUSH Republican Party 2001-
Born: July 6, 1946, in New Haven, Connecticut
Married: Laura Welch (b. 1946); 2 daughters
Early Career: Political adviser; businessman; governor of Texas

PRESIDENTIAL FACTS

Tallest president Abraham Lincoln. He was 6 feet, 4 inches.

Shortest president James Madison. He was 5 feet, 4 inches, and weighed only about 100 pounds.

Longest-living president John Adams (1735-1826). He lived 90 years, 247 days.

Born on the 4th of July Calvin Coolidge, on July 4, 1872.

Died on the 4th of July Two presidents died on the exact same day—July 4, 1826: John Adams and Thomas Jefferson. Both had signed the Declaration of Independence exactly 50 years before. James Monroe also died on July 4—in 1831.

Only president to serve more than two terms Franklin Delano Roosevelt.

Only president to serve two terms that were not back to back Grover Cleveland.

Only president who was unmarried James Buchanan. His niece, Harriet Lane, acted as White House hostess for her uncle.

MEET THE FIRST LADIES

MARTHA WASHINGTON
was the first First Lady. A wealthy widow when she married George Washington, she helped his position as a Virginia planter.

ELEANOR ROOSEVELT,
wife of Franklin D. Roosevelt, was an important public figure. She urged her husband to support civil rights and the rights of workers. After his death she served as a delegate to the UN.

DOLLEY MADISON,
James Madison's wife, was famous as a hostess and for saving a portrait of George Washington during the War of 1812, when the British were about to burn the White House.

JACQUELINE KENNEDY,
wife of John F. Kennedy, was known for her elegance and style. She restored the White House and made it a symbol the country could be proud of.

MARY TODD LINCOLN,
wife of Abraham Lincoln, was a well-educated Southerner who strongly opposed slavery. She had a sad life. Her husband was assassinated and three of her four children died young.

LAURA BUSH,
wife of George W. Bush, was a librarian and teacher. She is interested in books, history, art, and the well-being of children. She and her husband have twin daughters, both college students.

251

THE LEGISLATIVE BRANCH

CONGRESS

The Congress of the United States is the legislative branch of the federal government. Congress's major responsibility is to pass the laws that govern the country and determine how money collected in taxes is spent. It is the president's responsibility to enforce the laws. Congress consists of two parts—the Senate and the House of Representatives.

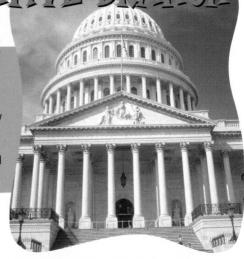

The Capitol, where Congress meets ▶

THE HOUSE OF REPRESENTATIVES

The number of members of the House of Representatives for each state depends on its population according to a recent census. But each state has at least one representative, no matter how small its population. A term lasts two years.

The first House of Representatives in 1789 had 65 members. As the country's population grew, the number of representatives increased. Since the 1910 census, however, the total membership has been kept at 435. After the results of Census 2000 were added up, 7 states gained seats and 9 states lost seats.

THE SENATE

The Senate has 100 members, two from each state. The Constitution says that the Senate will have equal representation (the same number of representatives) from each state. Thus, small states have the same number of senators as large states. Senators are elected for six-year terms. There is no limit on the number of terms a senator can serve.

The Senate also has the responsibility of approving people the president appoints for certain jobs: for example, cabinet members and Supreme Court justices. The Senate must approve all treaties by at least a two-thirds vote. It also has the responsibility under the Constitution of putting on trial high-ranking federal officials who have been impeached (see next page) by the House of Representatives.

You can reach the Senate
and the House on-line at:

WEB SITE *http://www.senate.gov*
http://www.house.gov

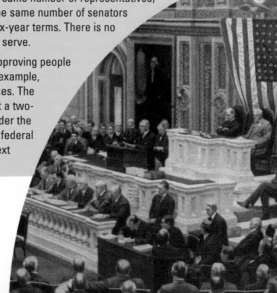

THE HOUSE OF REPRESENTATIVES, BY STATE

Here are the numbers of representatives each state will have by 2003, compared with 10 years earlier and 30 years earlier:

State	2003	1993	1973	State	2003	1993	1973
Alabama	7	7	7	Montana	1	1	2
Alaska	1	1	1	Nebraska	3	3	3
Arizona	8	6	4	Nevada	3	2	1
Arkansas	4	4	4	New Hampshire	2	2	2
California	53	52	43	New Jersey	13	13	15
Colorado	7	6	5	New Mexico	3	3	2
Connecticut	5	6	6	New York	29	31	39
Delaware	1	1	1	North Carolina	13	12	11
Florida	25	23	15	North Dakota	1	1	1
Georgia	13	11	10	Ohio	18	19	23
Hawaii	2	2	2	Oklahoma	5	6	6
Idaho	2	2	2	Oregon	5	5	4
Illinois	19	20	24	Pennsylvania	19	21	25
Indiana	9	10	11	Rhode Island	2	2	2
Iowa	5	5	6	South Carolina	6	6	6
Kansas	4	4	5	South Dakota	1	1	2
Kentucky	6	6	7	Tennessee	9	9	9
Louisiana	7	7	8	Texas	32	30	24
Maine	2	2	2	Utah	3	3	2
Maryland	8	8	8	Vermont	1	1	1
Massachusetts	10	10	12	Virginia	11	11	10
Michigan	15	16	19	Washington	9	9	7
Minnesota	8	8	8	West Virginia	3	3	4
Mississippi	4	5	5	Wisconsin	8	9	9
Missouri	9	9	10	Wyoming	1	1	1

Washington, D.C., Puerto Rico, American Samoa, Guam, and the Virgin Islands each have one nonvoting member of the House of Representatives.

WHAT IMPEACHMENT MEANS

"Impeachment" means charging a high-ranking U.S. government official (such as a president or federal judge) with serious crimes — "high crimes and misdemeanors" — in order to possibly remove the person from office. Only the House of Representatives can vote to impeach officials. Once it does, there is a trial in the Senate.

The chief justice of the Supreme Court presides. A two-thirds vote is needed to remove the person from office.

In 1868, President Andrew Johnson (above) was impeached. He was found not guilty in a Senate trial. In 1974, a House committee recommended the impeachment of President Richard Nixon, but he resigned before the whole House could vote. On December 19, 1998, the House voted to impeach President Bill Clinton (left) for perjury and obstructing justice. On February 12, 1999, after a Senate trial, he was found not guilty of perjury, 55-45, and of obstructing justice, by a 50-50 vote.

THE JUDICIAL BRANCH
The SUPREME COURT

The highest court in the United States is the Supreme Court. It has nine justices who are appointed for life by the president with the approval of the Senate. Eight of the nine members are called associate justices. The ninth is the chief justice, who presides over the Court's meetings.

What Does the Supreme Court Do? The Supreme Court's major responsibilities are to judge cases that involve reviewing federal laws, actions of the president, treaties of the United States, and laws passed by state governments to be sure they do not conflict with the U.S. Constitution. If the Supreme Court finds that a law or action violates the Constitution, the law is struck down.

The Supreme Court's Decision Is Final. Most cases must go through other state courts or federal courts before they reach the Supreme Court. The Supreme Court is the final court for a case, and the justices decide which cases they will review. After the Supreme Court hears a case, it may agree or disagree with the decision by a lower court. When the Supreme Court makes a ruling, its decision is final. In December 2000, the Supreme Court made a decision that meant George W. Bush was the winner of the November election for president.

Who Is on the Supreme Court? Below are the nine justices who were on the Supreme Court at the beginning of its 2001-2002 session.

Back row *(from left to right): Ruth Bader Ginsburg, David H. Souter, Clarence Thomas, Stephen Breyer.*
Front row *(from left to right): Antonin Scalia, John Paul Stevens, Chief Justice William H. Rehnquist, Sandra Day O'Connor, Anthony M. Kennedy.*

SUPREME COURT HANDSHAKE *Every day before they go into court and at the start of their private conferences where they discuss cases together, each justice shakes hands with the other 8. Justice Melville W. Fuller started this practice in the late 1800s. He wanted the justices to remember that, despite differences of opinion, they all share the same purpose.*

HOW A BILL BECOMES A LAW

STEP 1 Senators and Representatives Propose Bill.

A proposed law is called a **bill**. Any member of Congress may propose (introduce) a bill. A bill is introduced in each house of Congress. The House of Representatives and the Senate consider a bill separately. A member of Congress who introduces a bill is known as the bill's **sponsor**. Bills to raise money always begin in the House of Representatives.

STEP 2 House and Senate Committees Consider the Bill.

The bill is then sent to appropriate committees for consideration. A bill relating to agriculture, for example, would be sent to the agriculture committees in the House and in the Senate. A committee is made up of a small number of members of the House or Senate. Whichever party has a majority in the House or Senate has a majority on each committee. When committees are considering a bill, they hold **hearings** at which people can speak for or against it.

STEP 3 Committees Vote on the Bill.

The committees can change the bill as they see fit. Then they vote on it.

STEP 4 The Bill is Debated in the House and Senate.

If the committees vote in favor of the bill, it goes to the full House and Senate, where it is debated and may be changed further. The House and Senate can then vote on it.

STEP 5 From the House and Senate to Conference Committee.

If the House and the Senate pass different versions of the same bill, the bill must go to a **conference committee,** where differences between the two versions must be worked out. A conference committee is a special committee made up of both Senate and House members.

STEP 6 Final Vote in the House and Senate.

The House and the Senate then vote on the conference committee version. In order for this version to become a law, it must be approved by a majority of members of both houses of Congress and signed by the president.

STEP 7 The President Signs the Bill into Law.

If the bill passes both houses of Congress, it goes to the president for his signature. Once the president signs a bill, it becomes law.

STEP 8 What if the President Doesn't Sign the Bill?

Sometimes the president does not approve of a bill and decides not to sign it. This is called **vetoing** it. A bill that has been vetoed goes back to Congress, where the members can vote again. If the House and the Senate pass the bill with a two-thirds majority vote, it becomes law. This is called **overriding** the veto.

◄ President Franklin D. Roosevelt, signing a bill

255

SCRAMBLED STATES

This map is a little mixed up. Can you put these eight sections of the United States in their proper place on the numbered grid below? You can only see some of each section. But if you look carefully, there should be enough clues to help see where the pieces should go. You can use the map at the top of the page for reference.

1	2	3	4
5	6	7	8

ANSWERS ON PAGES 314-317. FOR MORE PUZZLES GO TO
WWW.WORLDALMANACFORKIDS.COM

United States History TIME LINE

THE FIRST PEOPLE IN NORTH AMERICA: BEFORE 1492

14,000 B.C.– 11,000 B.C.

Paleo-Indians use stone points attached to spears to hunt big mammoths in northern parts of North America.

11,000 B.C.

Big mammoths disappear and Paleo-Indians begin to gather plants for food.

AFTER A.D. 500

Anasazi peoples in the Southwestern United States live in homes on cliffs, called cliff dwellings. Anasazi pottery and dishes are well known for their beautiful patterns.

AFTER A.D. 700

Mississippian Indian people in Southeastern United States develop farms and build burial mounds.

40,000 B.C.

40,000 B.C.– 11,000 B.C.

First people (called Paleo-Indians) cross from Siberia to Alaska and begin to move into North America.

9500 B.C.– 1000 B.C.

North American Indians begin using stone to grind food and to hunt bison and smaller animals.

1000 B.C.–A.D. 500

Woodland Indians, who lived east of the Mississippi River, bury their dead under large mounds of earth (which can still be seen today).

700–1492

Many different Indian cultures develop throughout North America.

COLONIAL AMERICA AND THE AMERICAN REVOLUTION: 1492–1783

1492

1492
Christopher Columbus sails across the Atlantic Ocean and reaches an island in the Bahamas in the Caribbean Sea.

1513
Juan Ponce de León explores the Florida coast.

1524
Giovanni da Verrazano explores the coast from Carolina north to Nova Scotia, enters New York harbor.

1540
Francisco Vásquez de Coronado explores the Southwest.

1565
St. Augustine, Florida, the first town established by Europeans in the United States, is founded by the Spanish. Later burned by the English in 1586.

BENJAMIN FRANKLIN (1706-1790)

was a great American leader, printer, scientist, and writer. In 1732, he began publishing a magazine called *Poor Richard's Almanack*. Poor Richard was a make-believe person who gave advice about common sense and honesty. Many of Poor Richard's sayings are still known today. Among the most famous are "God helps them that help themselves" and "Early to bed, early to rise, makes a man healthy, wealthy, and wise."

1634

1634
Maryland is founded as a Catholic colony, with religious freedom for all granted in 1649.

1664
The English seize New Amsterdam from the Dutch. The city is renamed New York.

1699
French settlers move into Mississippi and Louisiana.

1732
Benjamin Franklin begins publishing *Poor Richard's Almanack*.

1754-1763
French and Indian War between England and France. The French are defeated and lose their lands in Canada and the American Midwest.

1764-1766
England places taxes on sugar that comes from their North American colonies. England also requires colonists to buy stamps to help pay for royal troops. Colonists protest, and the Stamp Act is repealed in 1766.

1607
Jamestown, Virginia, the first English settlement in North America, is founded by Captain John Smith.

1609
Henry Hudson sails into New York Harbor, explores Hudson River. Spaniards settle Santa Fe, New Mexico.

1619
The first African slaves are brought to Jamestown. (Slavery is made legal in 1650.)

1620
Pilgrims from England arrive at Plymouth, Massachusetts on the *Mayflower*.

1626
Peter Minuit buys Manhattan island for the Dutch from Man-a-hat-a Indians for goods worth $24. The island is renamed New Amsterdam.

1630
Boston is founded by Massachusetts colonists led by John Winthrop.

FAMOUS WORDS FROM THE DECLARATION OF INDEPENDENCE, JULY 4, 1776

"We hold these truths to be self-evident, that all men are created equal, that they are endowed by their Creator with certain unalienable rights, that among these are life, liberty, and the pursuit of happiness."

1770
Boston Massacre: English troops fire on a group of people protesting English taxes.

1773
Boston Tea Party: English tea is thrown into the harbor to protest a tax on tea.

1775
Fighting at Lexington and Concord, Massachusetts, marks the beginning of the American Revolution.

1776
The Declaration of Independence is approved July 4 by the Continental Congress (made up of representatives from the American colonies).

1781
British General Cornwallis surrenders to the Americans at Yorktown, Virginia, ending the fighting in the Revolutionary War.

THE NEW NATION: 1783-1900

WHO ATTENDED THE CONVENTION?

The Constitutional Convention met in Philadelphia in the hot summer of 1787. Most of the great founders of America attended. Among those present were George Washington, James Madison, and John Adams. They met to form a new government that would be strong and, at the same time, protect the liberties that were fought for in the American Revolution. The Constitution they created is still the law of the United States.

THE LOUISIANA PURCHASE (1803)

1784

1784
The first successful daily newspaper, the *Pennsylvania Packet & General Advertiser*, is published.

1787
The Constitutional Convention meets to write a Constitution for the U.S.

1789
The new Constitution is approved by the states. George Washington is chosen as the first president.

1800
The federal government moves to a new capital, Washington, D.C.

1803
The U.S. makes the Louisiana Purchase from France. The Purchase doubles the area of the U.S.

The Trail of Tears

"THE TRAIL OF TEARS"

The Cherokee Indians living in Georgia were forced, by the state government of Georgia, to leave in 1838. They were sent to Oklahoma. On the long march, thousands died because of disease and the cold weather.

UNCLE TOM'S CABIN

Harriet Beecher Stowe's novel about the suffering of slaves was an instant bestseller in the North and banned in most of the South. When President Abraham Lincoln met Stowe, he called her "the little lady who started this war" (the Civil War).

1836

1836
Texans fighting for independence from Mexico are defeated at the Alamo.

1838
Cherokee Indians are forced to move to Oklahoma, along "The Trail of Tears."

1844
The first telegraph line connects Washington and Baltimore.

1846–1848
U.S. war with Mexico: Mexico is defeated, and the United States takes control of the Republic of Texas and of Mexican territories in the West.

1848
The discovery of gold in California leads to a "rush" of 80,000 people to the West in search of gold.

1852
Uncle Tom's Cabin is published.

1804

Lewis and Clark, with their guide Sacagawea, explore what is now the northwestern United States.

1812–1814

War of 1812 with Great Britain: British forces burn the Capitol and White House. Francis Scott Key writes the words to "The Star-Spangled Banner."

1820

The Missouri Compromise bans slavery west of the Mississippi River and north of 36°30' latitude, except in Missouri.

1823

The Monroe Doctrine warns European countries not to interfere in the Americas.

1825

The Erie Canal opens linking New York City with the Great Lakes.

1831

The Liberator, a newspaper opposing slavery, is published in Boston.

CIVIL WAR DEAD AND WOUNDED

The U.S. Civil War between the North and South lasted four years (1861-1865) and resulted in the death or wounding of more than 600,000 people. Little was known at the time about the spread of diseases. As a result, many casualties were also the result of illnesses such as influenza, measles, and infections from battle wounds.

1898

Spanish-American War: The U.S. defeats Spain, gains control of the Philippines, Puerto Rico, and Guam.

1858

Abraham Lincoln and Stephen Douglas debate about slavery during their Senate campaign in Illinois.

1860

Abraham Lincoln is elected president.

1861

The Civil War begins.

1863

President Lincoln issues the Emancipation Proclamation, freeing most slaves.

1865

The Civil War ends as the South surrenders. President Lincoln is assassinated.

1869

The first railroad connecting the East and West coasts is completed.

1890

Battle of Wounded Knee is fought in South Dakota—the last major battle between Indians and U.S. troops.

261

UNITED STATES SINCE 1900

WORLD WAR I

In World War I the United States fought with Great Britain, France, and Russia (the Allies) against Germany and Austria-Hungary. The Allies won the war in 1918.

1900

1903
The United States begins digging the Panama Canal. The canal opens in 1914, connecting the Atlantic and Pacific oceans.

1908
Henry Ford introduces the Model T car, priced at $850.

1916
Jeannette Rankin of Montana becomes the first woman elected to Congress.

1917-1918
The United States joins World War I on the side of the Allies against Germany.

1927
Charles A. Lindbergh becomes the first person to fly alone nonstop across the Atlantic Ocean.

SCHOOL SEGREGATION

The U.S. Supreme Court ruled that separate schools for black students and white students were not equal. The Court said such schools were against the U.S. Constitution. The ruling also applied to other forms of segregation— separation of the races supported by some states.

1954

1954
The U.S. Supreme Court forbids racial segregation in public schools.

1963
President John Kennedy is assassinated.

1964
Congress passes the Civil Rights Act, which outlaws discrimination in voting and jobs.

1965
The United States sends large numbers of soldiers to fight in the Vietnam War.

1968
Civil rights leader Martin Luther King Jr. is assassinated in Memphis. Senator Robert F. Kennedy is assassinated in Los Angeles.

1969
U.S. Astronaut Neil Armstrong becomes the first person to walk on the moon.

1973
U.S. participation in the Vietnam War ends.

THE GREAT DEPRESSION

The stock market crash of October 1929 led to a period of severe hardship for the American people—the Great Depression. As many as 25 percent of all workers could not find jobs. The Depression lasted until the early 1940s. The Depression also led to a great change in politics. In 1932, Franklin D. Roosevelt, a Democrat, was elected president. He served as president for 12 years, longer than any other president.

1929
A stock market crash marks the beginning of the Great Depression.

1933
President Franklin D. Roosevelt's New Deal increases government help to people hurt by the Depression.

1941
Japan attacks Pearl Harbor, Hawaii. The United States enters World War II.

1945
Germany and Japan surrender, ending World War II. Japan surrenders after the U.S. drops atomic bombs on Hiroshima and Nagasaki.

1947
Jackie Robinson becomes the first black baseball player in the major leagues when he joins the Brooklyn Dodgers.

1950-1953
U.S. armed forces fight in the Korean War.

WATERGATE

In June 1972, five men were arrested in the Watergate building in Washington, D.C., for trying to bug telephones in the offices of the Democratic National Committee. Some of those arrested worked for the committee to reelect President Richard Nixon. Later it was discovered that Nixon was helping to hide information about the break-in.

1985
U.S. President Ronald Reagan and Soviet leader Mikhail Gorbachev begin working together to improve relations between their countries.

1991
The Persian Gulf War: The United States and its allies defeat Iraq.

1999
After an impeachment trial, the Senate finds President Clinton not guilty.

2000
George W. Bush narrowly defeats Al Gore in a hotly fought battle for the presidency. The race is finally settled by the U.S. Supreme Court in December.

1974
President Richard Nixon resigns because of the Watergate scandal.

1979
U.S. hostages are taken in Iran, beginning a 444-day crisis that ends with their release in 1981.

1981
Sandra Day O'Connor becomes the first woman on the U.S. Supreme Court.

1992
Democrat Bill Clinton is elected president, defeating George Bush.

1994
The Republican Party wins majorities in both houses of Congress for the first time in 40 years.

2001
Hijacked jets crashed into the World Trade Center and the Pentagon, September 11, killing about 3,000 people.

AFRICAN AMERICANS WORK FOR CHANGE

Would you like to learn more about the history of African Americans from the era of slavery to the present? These events and personalities can be a starting point. Can you add some more?

Thurgood Marshall, the first black on the Supreme Court ▶

1619 — First Africans are brought to Virginia as slaves.

1831 — Nat Turner starts a slave revolt in Virginia that is promptly put down.

1856-57 — Dred Scott, a slave, sues to be freed because he had left slave territory, but the Supreme Court denies his claim.

1861-65 — The North defeats the South in the brutal Civil War; the 13th Amendment ends nearly 250 years of slavery. The Ku Klux Klan is founded.

1865-77 — Southern blacks play leadership roles in government under Reconstruction; 15th Amendment (1870) gives black men the right to vote.

1896 — Supreme Court rules in a case called *Plessy versus Ferguson* that segregation is legal when facilities are "separate but equal." Discrimination and violence against blacks are increasing.

1910 — W. E. B. Du Bois (1868–1963) founds National Association for the Advancement of Colored People, fighting for equality for blacks.

1920s — African American culture (jazz music, dance, literature) flourishes during the "Harlem Renaissance."

1954 — Supreme Court rules in a case called *Brown versus Board of Education of Topeka* that school segregation is unconstitutional.

1957 — Black students, backed by federal troops, enter segregated Little Rock Central High School.

1955-65 — Malcolm X (1925–65) emerges as key spokesman for black nationalism.

1963 — Rev. Dr. Martin Luther King Jr. (1929–68) gives his "I Have a Dream" speech at a peaceful March on Washington.

1964 — Sweeping civil rights bill banning racial discrimination is signed by President Lyndon Johnson.

1965 — King leads protest march in Selma, Alabama; blacks riot in Watts section of Los Angeles.

1967 — Gary, Indiana, and Cleveland, Ohio, are first major U.S. cities to elect black mayors; Thurgood Marshall (1908–93) becomes first black on the Supreme Court.

1995 — Hundreds of thousands of black men in take part in "Million Man March" rally in Washington, D.C., urging responsibility for families and communities.

2001 — Retired Gen. Colin Powell becomes first African American secretary of state, filling the top foreign policy position in the president's cabinet.

THEY MADE HISTORY

The people below fought racial barriers in order to achieve their goals.

LOUIS ARMSTRONG (1901–1971), jazz trumpet player and singer from New Orleans, Louisiana. His free-flowing style brought him fame beginning in the late 1920s. His music continues to influence musicians.

ARTHUR ASHE (1943–1993) won the U.S. Open in tennis (1968), and became the first black member of the U.S. Davis Cup team. In 1975 he won Wimbledon and was ranked #1 in the world. Off the court, he was a critic of racial injustice and helped promote awareness of AIDS, a disease he got himself from a blood transfusion following heart surgery.

REVEREND MARTIN LUTHER KING JR. (1929–1968) used his forceful speaking style, forceful personality, and belief in nonviolence to help change U.S. history. From the mid-1950s to his assassination in 1968, he was the most influential leader of the U.S. civil rights movement.

MALCOLM X (1925–1965) was a forceful Black Muslim leader who spoke against injustices toward blacks and called for blacks to keep separate from whites. He was assassinated by rivals in 1965, but his life story, *The Autobiography of Malcolm X*, became a best-seller and helped make him a hero to many in the black community.

THURGOOD MARSHALL (1908–1993) became the first African-American justice on the U.S. Supreme Court in 1967. In 1954, he won a historic case, *Brown v. Board of Education of Topeka*, before the Supreme Court. The Court ruled that separate schools for black and white students were not equal or legal.

COLIN POWELL (born 1937) became the first African-American U.S. secretary of state in 2001. In 1991, while serving as the first black chairman of the Joint Chiefs of Staff, he oversaw Operation Desert Storm in the Persian Gulf War.

A. PHILIP RANDOLPH (1889–1979) was a labor leader and civil rights activist. In 1925 he organized the Brotherhood of Sleeping Car Porters, the first union of mainly black workers to be recognized by the American Federation of Labor. He helped persuade President Franklin D. Roosevelt to create the Fair Employment Practices Committee in 1941. He was elected vice-president of the AFL-CIO in 1957.

CONDOLEEZZA RICE (born 1954) is the first African-American, and the first woman, to be National Security Advisor, giving the U.S. president advice on foreign and defense policy. She is an expert on Eastern Europe and was a professor and top official at Stanford University in California.

Condoleezza Rice

JACKIE ROBINSON (1919–1972) was the first black player in the history of Major League Baseball. He joined the Dodgers, then in Brooklyn, in 1947. In 1949, he won the National League's MVP award and in 1962 was elected to the Baseball Hall of Fame.

HARRIET TUBMAN (1821–1913) escaped slavery when she was in her twenties. Before the Civil War, she repeatedly risked her life to lead hundreds of slaves to freedom by way of a network of homes and churches called the "Underground Railroad."

NEIL DE GRASSE TYSON (born 1959) is an astrophysicist, a scientist who studies the sky, and is director of the Hayden Planetarium in New York City. An author and teacher, he makes complicated ideas understandable and fun for people who are not scientists.

OPRAH WINFREY (born 1954) has won many awards as a talk show host, actress, writer, publisher, and film producer. Through Oprah's Angel Network, she has collected millions of dollars to help people in need.

Jackie Robinson ▶

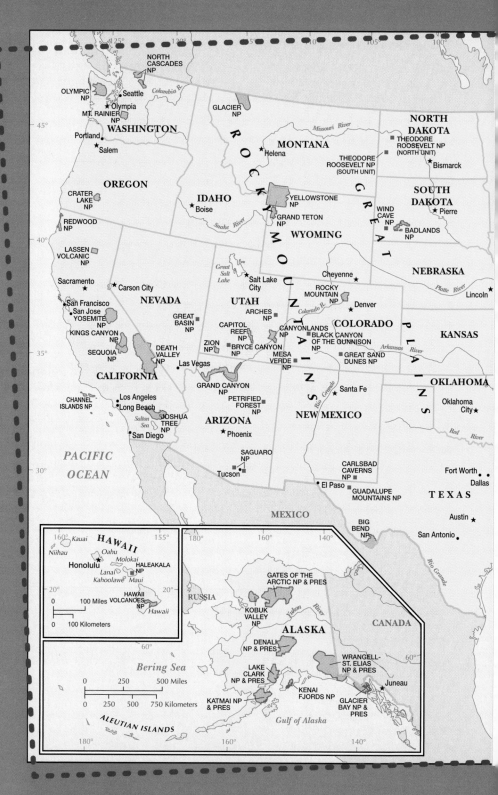

NORTH
CASCADES
NP

OLYMPIC
NP
★ Seattle
★ Olympia
MT. RAINIER
NP

WASHINGTON

Portland ●
★ Salem

Columbia R.

GLACIER
NP

Missouri River

MONTANA

Helena ●

NORTH
DAKOTA
■ THEODORE
ROOSEVELT NP
(NORTH UNIT)
■
★ Bismarck

OREGON

CRATER
LAKE
NP

IDAHO
★ Boise

Snake River

THEODORE
ROOSEVELT NP
(SOUTH UNIT)

YELLOWSTONE
NP
GRAND TETON
NP

WYOMING

SOUTH
DAKOTA
★ Pierre

WIND
CAVE
NP
■ BADLANDS
NP

REDWOOD
NP

LASSEN
VOLCANIC
NP

Sacramento ●

NEVADA

NEBRASKA

Lincoln ●

Platte River

★ Carson City

Great
Salt
Lake

★ Salt Lake
City

UTAH

Cheyenne ●

★

ROCKY
MOUNTAIN
NP

Denver ●

COLORADO

San Francisco ●
San Jose ●
YOSEMITE
NP
KINGS CANYON
NP

ARCHES
NP

GREAT
BASIN
NP

CAPITOL
REEF
NP

Colorado R.

CANYONLANDS
NP
BLACK CANYON
OF THE GUNNISON
NP

Arkansas   River

KANSAS

SEQUOIA
NP

DEATH
VALLEY
NP

ZION
NP
BRYCE CANYON
NP

MESA
VERDE
NP

GREAT SAND
DUNES NP

OKLAHOMA

CALIFORNIA

● Las Vegas

GRAND CANYON
NP

Santa Fe ●

Oklahoma
City ★

CHANNEL
ISLANDS NP

Los Angeles ●
● Long Beach

Salton
Sea

JOSHUA
TREE
NP

● San Diego

ARIZONA

★ Phoenix

PETRIFIED
FOREST
NP

Rio Grande

NEW MEXICO

Red   River

PACIFIC
OCEAN

SAGUARO
NP

Tucson ●

CARLSBAD
CAVERNS
NP

● El Paso

GUADALUPE
MOUNTAINS NP

Fort Worth ●
Dallas ●

TEXAS

Austin ★

MEXICO

BIG
BEND
NP

San Antonio ●

Rio Grande

HAWAII

160°   Kauai
Niihau
155°
Oahu
Honolulu
Molokai
Lanai   HALEAKALA
NP
Kahoolawe   Maui

20°
HAWAII
VOLCANOES
NP   Hawaii

0   100 Miles
0   100 Kilometers

180°   160°   140°

RUSSIA

GATES OF THE
ARCTIC NP & PRES

KOBUK
VALLEY
NP

Yukon   River

ALASKA

CANADA

DENALI
NP & PRES

WRANGELL-
ST. ELIAS
NP & PRES

60°

LAKE
CLARK
NP & PRES

Bering Sea

0   250   500 Miles

0   250   500   750 Kilometers

KATMAI NP
& PRES

KENAI
FJORDS NP

GLACIER
BAY NP &
PRES

Juneau ●

Gulf of Alaska

ALEUTIAN ISLANDS

180°   160°   140°

266

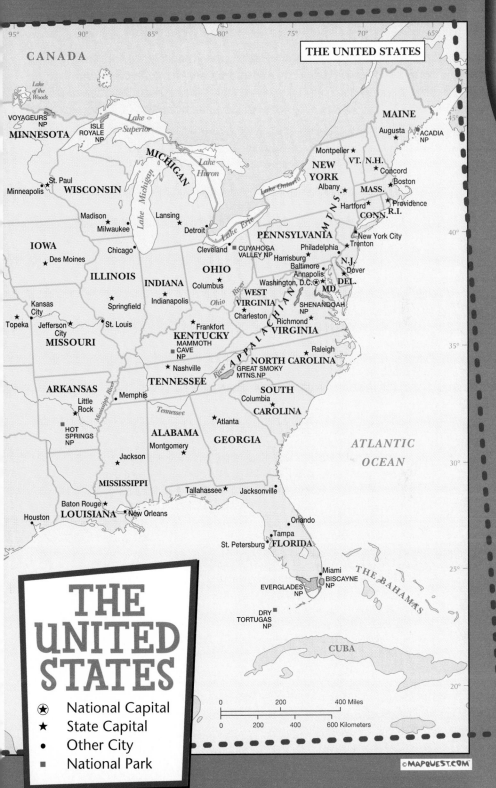

THE UNITED STATES

CANADA

Lake of the Woods

VOYAGEURS NP

MINNESOTA
ISLE ROYALE NP
Lake Superior

MICHIGAN
Lake Huron

St. Paul ★
Minneapolis
WISCONSIN
Madison
Milwaukee
Lansing
Detroit
Lake Michigan

IOWA
Des Moines ★
Chicago
Cleveland
CUYAHOGA VALLEY NP

ILLINOIS
INDIANA
OHIO
Columbus ★
Ohio River

Kansas City
Springfield ★
Indianapolis
WEST VIRGINIA

Topeka ★
Jefferson City ★
St. Louis
Frankfort ★
Charleston ★
Richmond ★

MISSOURI
KENTUCKY
MAMMOTH CAVE NP
Nashville ★
VIRGINIA
SHENANDOAH NP

ARKANSAS
TENNESSEE
GREAT SMOKY MTNS. NP
NORTH CAROLINA
Raleigh ★

Little Rock ★
Memphis
Columbia ★
SOUTH CAROLINA

HOT SPRINGS NP
Mississippi River
Tennessee River
Atlanta ★

ALABAMA
GEORGIA
ATLANTIC OCEAN

Jackson ★
Montgomery ★

MISSISSIPPI
Tallahassee ★
Jacksonville

Baton Rouge ★
LOUISIANA
New Orleans
Houston

Orlando
Tampa
St. Petersburg
FLORIDA

Miami
BISCAYNE NP
EVERGLADES NP
THE BAHAMAS

DRY TORTUGAS NP

CUBA

MAINE
Augusta ★
ACADIA NP

Montpelier ★
VT. N.H.
Concord ★
NEW YORK
Albany ★
Boston ★
MASS.
Hartford ★
Providence ★
CONN. R.I.

Lake Ontario
Lake Erie
APPALACHIAN MTNS

PENNSYLVANIA
New York City
Trenton ★
Philadelphia
N.J.
Harrisburg ★
Dover ★
Baltimore
Annapolis ★
DEL.
Washington, D.C. ⊛
MD

© MAPQUEST.COM

THE UNITED STATES

⊛ National Capital
★ State Capital
• Other City
▪ National Park

0   200   400 Miles
0 200 400 600 Kilometers

95° 90° 85° 80° 75° 70° 65°
45°
40°
35°
30°
25°
20°

FACTS ABOUT THE STATES

After every state name is the postal abbreviation. The Area includes both land and water; it is given in square miles (sq. mi.) and square kilometers (sq. km.). Numbers in parentheses after Population, Area, and Entered Union show the state's rank compared with other states. City populations come from the 2000 census.

ALABAMA (AL) *Heart of Dixie, Camellia State*

POPULATION (2001): 4,464,356 (23rd) **AREA:** 52,237 sq. mi. (30th) (135,294 sq. km.) **ENTERED UNION:** December 14, 1819 (22nd) **FLOWER:** Camellia **BIRD:** Yellowhammer **TREE:** Southern longleaf pine **SONG:** "Alabama" **CAPITAL:** Montgomery **LARGEST CITIES (WITH POP.):** Birmingham, 242,820; Montgomery, 201,568; Mobile, 198,915; Huntsville, 158,216 **IMPORTANT PRODUCTS:** clothing and textiles, metal products, transportation equipment, paper, industrial machinery, food products, lumber, coal, oil, natural gas, livestock, peanuts, cotton **PLACES TO VISIT:** Alabama Space and Rocket Center, Huntsville; Carver Museum, Tuskegee

WEB SITE *http://alaweb.asc.edu • http://www.touralabama.org*

DID YOU KNOW? *Montgomery, Alabama, was the first capital of the Confederate States of America (1861). Alabama is a major center for rocket and space research.*

ALASKA (AK) *The Last Frontier*

POPULATION (2001): 634,892 (47th) **AREA:** 615,230 sq. mi. (1st) (1,593,444 sq. km.) **ENTERED UNION:** January 3, 1959 (49th) **FLOWER:** Forget-me-not **BIRD:** Willow ptarmigan **TREE:** Sitka spruce **SONG:** "Alaska's Flag" **CAPITAL:** Juneau (population, 30,711) **LARGEST CITIES (WITH POP.):** Anchorage, 260,283; Fairbanks, 30,224 **IMPORTANT PRODUCTS:** oil, natural gas, fish, food products, lumber and wood products, fur **PLACES TO VISIT:** Glacier Bay and Denali national parks, Mendenhall Glacier, Mount McKinley

WEB SITE *http://www.state.ak.us • http://www.dced.state.ak.us/tourism/*

DID YOU KNOW? *Mount McKinley is the highest mountain in the United States. Alaska is the biggest and coldest state in the United States.*

ARIZONA (AZ) *Grand Canyon State*

POPULATION (2001): 5,307,331 (20th) **AREA:** 114,006 sq. mi. (6th) (295,276 sq. km.) **ENTERED UNION:** February 14, 1912 (48th) **FLOWER:** Blossom of the Saguaro cactus **BIRD:** Cactus wren **TREE:** Paloverde **SONG:** "Arizona" **CAPITAL AND LARGEST CITY:** Phoenix (population, 1,321,045) **OTHER LARGE CITIES (WITH POP.):** Tucson, 486,699; Mesa, 396,375; Glendale, 218,812; Scottsdale, 202,705; Chandler, 176,581 **IMPORTANT PRODUCTS:** electronic equipment, transportation and industrial equipment, instruments, printing and publishing, copper and other metals **PLACES TO VISIT:** Grand Canyon, Painted Desert, Petrified Forest, Navajo National Monument

WEB SITE *http://www.state.az.gov • http://www.arizonaguide.com*

DID YOU KNOW? *The Grand Canyon is the largest land gorge in the world and one of the world's natural wonders. It is 217 miles long and 4 to 18 miles wide at the rim.*

ARKANSAS (AR) *Natural State, Razorback State*

POPULATION (2001): 2,692,090 (33rd)
AREA: 53,182 sq. mi. (28th) (137,741 sq. km.)
FLOWER: Apple blossom **BIRD:** Mockingbird **TREE:** Pine
SONG: "Arkansas" **ENTERED UNION:** June 15, 1836 (25th)
CAPITAL AND LARGEST CITY: Little Rock (population, 183,133)
OTHER LARGE CITIES (WITH POP.): Fort Smith, 80,268, North Little
Rock, 60,433; **IMPORTANT PRODUCTS:** food products, paper,
electronic equipment, industrial machinery, metal products,
lumber and wood products, livestock, soybeans, rice, cotton, natural gas
PLACES TO VISIT: Hot Springs National Park; Arkansas House of Reptiles;
Band Museum in Pine Bluff; Ozark Folk Center, near Mountain View.

WEB SITE *http://www.state.ar.us • http://www.arkansas.com*

DID YOU KNOW? *Arkansas has the only working diamond mine in North America. Former President Bill Clinton was born in Arkansas and served as its governor.*

CALIFORNIA (CA) *Golden State*

POPULATION (2001): 34,501,130 (1st) **AREA:** 158,869
sq. mi. (3rd) (411,471 sq. km.) **FLOWER:** Golden poppy
BIRD: California valley quail **TREE:** California redwood **SONG:** "I Love You,
California" **ENTERED UNION:** September 9, 1850 (31st)
CAPITAL: Sacramento (population, 407,018)
LARGEST CITIES (WITH POP.): Los Angeles, 3,694,820; San Diego, 1,223,400;
San Jose, 894,943; San Francisco, 776,733
IMPORTANT PRODUCTS: transportation and industrial equipment,
electronic equipment, oil, natural gas, motion pictures, milk, cattle,
fruit, vegetables **PLACES TO VISIT:** Yosemite Valley, Lake Tahoe, Palomar
Observatory, Disneyland, San Diego Zoo, Hollywood, Sequoia National Park

WEB SITE *http://www.state.ca.us • http://www.gocalif.ca.gov*

DID YOU KNOW? *California has more people, cars, schools, and businesses than any other state. The world's tallest tree is a redwood tree in Humboldt County.*

COLORADO (CO) *Centennial State*

POPULATION (2001): 4,417,714 (24th) **AREA:** 104,100 sq. mi.
(8th) (269,619 sq. km.) **FLOWER:** Rocky Mountain
columbine **BIRD:** Lark bunting **TREE:** Colorado blue spruce
SONG: "Where the Columbines Grow" **ENTERED UNION:** August 1, 1876
(38th) **CAPITAL AND LARGEST CITY:** Denver (population, 554,636)
OTHER LARGE CITIES (WITH POP.): Colorado Springs, 360,890; Aurora,
276,393; Lakewood, 144,126 **IMPORTANT PRODUCTS:** instruments and
industrial machinery, food products, printing and publishing, metal
products, electronic equipment, oil, coal, cattle **PLACES TO VISIT:** Rocky Mountain
National Park, Mesa Verde National Park, Dinosaur National Monument, old mining towns

WEB SITE *http://www.state.co.us • http://www.colorado.com*

DID YOU KNOW? *The Grand Mesa in Colorado is the world's largest flat-top mountain. The highest bridge in the world (1,053 feet) is in Colorado—over the Royal Gorge of the Arkansas River. Colorado has more elk than any other state.*

CONNECTICUT (CT) *Constitution State, Nutmeg State*

POPULATION (2001): 3,425,074 (29th) **AREA:** 5,544 sq. mi. (48th) (14,359 sq. km.) **FLOWER:** Mountain laurel **BIRD:** American robin **TREE:** White oak **SONG:** "Yankee Doodle" **ENTERED UNION:** January 9, 1788 (5th) **CAPITAL:** Hartford **LARGEST CITIES (WITH POP.):** Bridgeport, 139,529; New Haven, 123,626; Hartford, 121,578; Stamford, 117,083; Waterbury, 107,271 **IMPORTANT PRODUCTS:** aircraft parts, helicopters, industrial machinery, metals and metal products, electronic equipment, printing and publishing, medical instruments, chemicals, dairy products, stone

PLACES TO VISIT: Mystic Seaport and Marine Life Aquarium, in Mystic; P. T. Barnum Circus Museum, Bridgeport; Peabody Museum, New Haven

WEB SITE http://www.state.ct.us • http://www.tourism.state.ct.us

DID YOU KNOW? *The first library for children opened in Salisbury, in 1803, and the first permanent school for the deaf opened in Hartford in 1817.*

DELAWARE (DE) *First State, Diamond State*

POPULATION (2001): 796,165 (45th) **AREA:** 2,396 sq. mi. (49th) (6,206 sq. km.) **FLOWER:** Peach blossom **BIRD:** Blue hen chicken **TREE:** American holly **SONG:** "Our Delaware" **ENTERED UNION:** December 7, 1787 (1st) **CAPITAL:** Dover **LARGEST CITIES (WITH POP.):** Wilmington, 72,664; Dover, 32,135; Newark, 28,547 **IMPORTANT PRODUCTS:** chemicals, transportation equipment, food products, chickens

PLACES TO VISIT: Rehoboth Beach, Henry Francis du Pont Winterthur Museum near Wilmington

WEB SITE http://www.delaware.gov • http://www.visitdelaware.net

DID YOU KNOW? *Delaware was the first state to agree to the Constitution and thus became the first state. Delaware had the first log cabins in America in the mid 1600s.*

FLORIDA (FL) *Sunshine State*

POPULATION (2001): 16,396,515 (4th) **AREA:** 59,928 sq. mi. (23rd) (155,213 sq. km.) **FLOWER:** Orange blossom **BIRD:** Mockingbird **TREE:** Sabal palmetto palm **SONG:** "Old Folks at Home" **ENTERED UNION:** March 3, 1845 (27th) **CAPITAL:** Tallahassee (population, 150,624) **LARGEST CITIES (WITH POP.):** Jacksonville, 735,617; Miami, 362,470; Tampa, 303,447; St. Petersburg, 248,232 **IMPORTANT PRODUCTS:** electronic and transportation equipment, industrial machinery, printing and publishing, food products, citrus fruits, vegetables, livestock, phosphates, fish

PLACES TO VISIT: Walt Disney World and Universal Studios, near Orlando; Sea World, Orlando; Busch Gardens, Tampa; Spaceport USA, at Kennedy Space Center, Cape Canaveral; Everglades National Park

WEB SITE http://www.state.fl.us • http://www.flausa.com

DID YOU KNOW? *St. Augustine, Florida, is the oldest permanent European settlement in the United States. Florida grows more citrus fruit than any other state. One out of every five people in Florida is over 65.*

GEORGIA (GA) *Empire State of the South, Peach State*

POPULATION (2001): 8,383,915 (10th) **AREA:** 58,977 sq. mi. (24th) (152,750 sq. km.) **FLOWER:** Cherokee rose **BIRD:** Brown thrasher **TREE:** Live oak
SONG: "Georgia on My Mind" **ENTERED UNION:** January 2, 1788 (4th)
CAPITAL AND LARGEST CITY: Atlanta (population, 416,474)
OTHER LARGE CITIES (WITH POP.): Augusta, 199,775, Columbus, 186,291; Savannah, 131,510 **IMPORTANT PRODUCTS:** clothing and textiles, transportation equipment, food products, paper, chickens, peanuts, peaches, clay **PLACES TO VISIT:** Stone Mountain Park; Six Flags Over Georgia; Martin Luther King Jr., National Historic Site, Atlanta

WEB SITE *http://www.state.ga.us • http://www.georgia.org*

DID YOU KNOW? *Juliette Gordon Low founded the Girl Scouts in 1912 in Savannah, Georgia. The first American Indian newspaper was published in Georgia by a Cherokee in 1828. Civil rights leader Martin Luther King Jr. (1929-1968) and baseball player Jackie Robinson (1919-1972) were born in Georgia.*

HAWAII (HI) *Aloha State*

POPULATION (2001): 1,224,398 (42nd) **AREA:** 6,459 sq. mi. (47th) (16,728 sq. km.) **FLOWER:** Yellow hibiscus **BIRD:** Hawaiian goose **TREE:** Kukui **SONG:** "Hawaii Ponoi" **ENTERED UNION:** August 21, 1959 (50th) **CAPITAL AND LARGEST CITY:** Honolulu (population, 371,657) **OTHER LARGE CITIES (WITH POP.):** Hilo, 40,759; Kailua, 36,513; Kaneohe, 34,970 **IMPORTANT PRODUCTS:** food products, pineapples, sugar, printing and publishing, fish, flowers **PLACES TO VISIT:** Hawaii Volcanoes National Park; Haleakala National Park, Maui; U.S.S. Arizona Memorial, Pearl Harbor; Polynesian Cultural Center, Laie

WEB SITE *http://www.state.hi.us • http://www.gohawaii.com*

DID YOU KNOW? *Hawaii is the only state made up entirely of islands, 122 of them. (People live on 7 of them.) Hawaii's Mauna Loa is the biggest active volcano in the U.S.*

IDAHO (ID) *Gem State*

POPULATION (2001): 1,321,006 (39th) **AREA:** 83,574 sq. mi. (14th) (216,456 sq. km.) **FLOWER:** Syringa
BIRD: Mountain bluebird **TREE:** White pine **SONG:** "Here We Have Idaho"
ENTERED UNION: July 3, 1890 (43rd) **CAPITAL AND LARGEST CITY:** Boise (population, 185,787) **OTHER LARGE CITIES (WITH POP.):** Nampa, 51,867; Pocatello, 51,466 **IMPORTANT PRODUCTS:** potatoes, hay, wheat, cattle, milk, lumber and wood products, food products
PLACES TO VISIT: Sun Valley; Hells Canyon; Craters of the Moon, near Arco; World Center for Birds of Prey, Boise; ghost towns

WEB SITE *http://www.visitid.com • http://www.state.id.us*

DID YOU KNOW? *The first hydroelectric power plant built by the federal government was the Minidoka Dam on the Snake River in Idaho; the first unit started in 1909. Two-thirds of all potatoes in the U.S. are grown in Idaho.*

ILLINOIS (IL) *Prairie State*

POPULATION (2001): 12,482,301 (5th) **AREA:** 57,918 sq. mi. (25th) (150,007 sq. km.) **FLOWER:** Native violet
BIRD: Cardinal **TREE:** White oak **SONG:** "Illinois"
ENTERED UNION: December 3, 1818 (21st) **CAPITAL:** Springfield (population, 111,454) **LARGEST CITIES (WITH POP.):** Chicago, 2,896,016; Rockford, 150,115; Aurora, 142,990; Naperville, 128,358; Peoria, 112,936;
IMPORTANT PRODUCTS: industrial machinery, metals and metal products, printing and publishing, electronic equipment, food products, corn, soybeans, hogs **PLACES TO VISIT:** Lincoln Park Zoo, Adler Planetarium, Field Museum of Natural History, and Museum of Science and Industry, all in Chicago; Abraham Lincoln's home and burial site, Springfield; New Salem Village

WEB SITE *http://www.state.il.us • http://www.enjoyillinois.com*

DID YOU KNOW? *Illinois has one of the world's busiest airports (O'Hare) and the tallest building in the U.S. (the Sears Tower in Chicago). The world's first skyscraper was built in Chicago, in 1885. Ronald Reagan and Hillary Rodham Clinton were both born in Illinois.*

INDIANA (IN) *Hoosier State*

POPULATION (2001): 6,114,745 (14th) **AREA:** 36,420 sq. mi. (38th) (94,328 sq. km.) **FLOWER:** Peony **BIRD:** Cardinal
TREE: Tulip poplar **SONG:** "On the Banks of the Wabash, Far Away"
ENTERED UNION: December 11, 1816 (19th)
CAPITAL AND LARGEST CITY: Indianapolis (population, 791,926)
OTHER LARGE CITIES (WITH POP.): Fort Wayne, 205,727; Evansville, 121,582; South Bend, 107,789; Gary, 102,746; **IMPORTANT PRODUCTS:** transportation equipment, electronic equipment, industrial machinery, iron and steel, metal products, corn, soybeans, livestock, coal **PLACES TO VISIT:** Children's Museum, Indianapolis; Conner Prairie Pioneer Settlement, Noblesville; Lincoln Boyhood Memorial, Lincoln City; Wyandotte Cave

WEB SITE *http://www.state.in.us • http://www.enjoyindiana.com*

DID YOU KNOW? *The first city to be lit with electricity was Wabash. Indiana's Lost River travels 22 miles underground. Indiana is the home of the Indianapolis 500 auto race.*

IOWA (IA) *Hawkeye State*

POPULATION (2001): 2,923,179 (30th) **AREA:** 56,276 sq. mi. (26th) (145,754 sq. km.) **FLOWER:** Wild rose
BIRD: Eastern goldfinch **TREE:** Oak **SONG:** "The Song of Iowa"
ENTERED UNION: December 28, 1846 (29th)
CAPITAL AND LARGEST CITY: Des Moines (population, 198,682)
OTHER LARGE CITIES (WITH POP.): Cedar Rapids, 120,758; Davenport, 98,359; Sioux City, 85,013 **IMPORTANT PRODUCTS:** corn, soybeans, hogs, cattle, industrial machinery, food products **PLACES TO VISIT:** Effigy Mounds National Monument, Marquette; Herbert Hoover Birthplace, West Branch; Living History Farms, Des Moines; Adventureland; the Amana Colonies; Fort Dodge Historical Museum

WEB SITE *http://www.state.ia.us • http://www.traveliowa.com*

DID YOU KNOW? *The bridge built in 1856 between Davenport and Rock Island was the first bridge to span the Mississippi River. Buffalo Bill Cody (1846-1917), near Le Claire, Iowa.*

KANSAS (KS) *Sunflower State*

POPULATION (2001): 2,694,641 (32nd) **AREA:** 82,282 sq. mi. (15th) (213,110 sq. km.) **FLOWER:** Native sunflower **BIRD:** Western meadowlark **TREE:** Cottonwood **SONG:** "Home on the Range" **ENTERED UNION:** January 29, 1861 (34th) **CAPITAL:** Topeka **LARGEST CITIES (WITH POP.):** Wichita, 344,284; Overland Park, 149,080; Kansas City, 146,866; Topeka, 122,377 **IMPORTANT PRODUCTS:** cattle, aircraft and other transportation equipment, industrial machinery, food products, wheat, corn, hay, oil, natural gas **PLACES TO VISIT:** Dodge City; Fort Scott and Fort Larned national historical sites; Eisenhower Center, Abilene; Kansas Cosmosphere and Space Discovery Center, Hutchinson

WEB SITE *http:// www.accesskansas.org • http://www.travelks.com*

DID YOU KNOW? *Kansas is located at the geographical center of the United States (excluding Alaska and Hawaii). It is one of the two biggest U.S. wheat-growing states (the other is North Dakota). The carousel with jumping horses was invented in Kansas in 1898.*

KENTUCKY (KY) *Bluegrass State*

POPULATION (2001): 4,065,556 (25th) **AREA:** 40,411 sq. mi. (37th) (104,665 sq. km.) **FLOWER:** Goldenrod **BIRD:** Cardinal **TREE:** Tulip poplar **SONG:** "My Old Kentucky Home" **ENTERED UNION:** June 1, 1792 (15th) **CAPITAL:** Frankfort (population, 27,741) **LARGEST CITIES (WITH POP.):** Lexington 260,512; Louisville, 256,231 **IMPORTANT PRODUCTS:** coal, industrial machinery, electronic equipment, transportation equipment, metals, tobacco, cattle **PLACES TO VISIT:** Mammoth Cave National Park; Lincoln's Birthplace, Hodgenville; Cumberland Gap National Historical Park, Middlesboro

WEB SITE *http:// www.kydirect.net • http://www.kentuckytourism.com*

DID YOU KNOW? *Kentucky has the longest group of caves in the world (Mammoth Caves). Abraham Lincoln was born in Kentucky. Louisville is the home of the Kentucky Derby, the most famous horse race in America.*

LOUISIANA (LA) *Pelican State*

POPULATION (2001): 4,465,430 (22nd) **AREA:** 49,651 sq. mi. (31st) (128,596 sq. km.) **FLOWER:** Magnolia **BIRD:** Eastern brown pelican **TREE:** Cypress **SONG:** "Give Me Louisiana" **ENTERED UNION:** April 30, 1812 (18th) **CAPITAL:** Baton Rouge **LARGEST CITIES (WITH POP.):** New Orleans, 484,674; Baton Rouge, 227,818; Shreveport, 200,145 **IMPORTANT PRODUCTS:** natural gas, oil, chemicals, transportation equipment, paper, food products, cotton, fish **PLACES TO VISIT:** Aquarium of the Americas, Audubon Zoo and Gardens, both New Orleans

WEB SITE *http://www.state.la.us • http://www.louisianatravel.com*

DID YOU KNOW? *The busiest port in the United States is located in Louisiana. New Orleans is known for its jazz and the colorful Mardi Gras festival.*

MAINE (ME) *Pine Tree State*

POPULATION (2001): 1,286,670 (40th) **AREA:** 33,741 sq. mi. (39th) (87,389 sq. km.) **FLOWER:** White pine cone and tassel **BIRD:** Chickadee **TREE:** Eastern white pine **SONG:** "State of Maine Song" **ENTERED UNION:** March 15, 1820 (23rd) **CAPITAL:** Augusta (population, 18,560) **LARGEST CITIES (WITH POP.):** Portland, 64,249; Lewiston, 35,690; Bangor, 31,473 **IMPORTANT PRODUCTS:** paper, transportation equipment, wood and wood products, electronic equipment, footwear, clothing, potatoes, milk, eggs, fish, and seafood **PLACES TO VISIT:** Acadia National Park, Bar Harbor; Booth Bay Railway Museum; Portland Headlight Lighthouse, near Portland

WEB SITE http://www.state.me.us • http://www.visitmaine.com

DID YOU KNOW? *Mount Katahdin, the highest spot in Maine (5,267 feet), is the first place in the United States where the sun hits in the morning.*

MARYLAND (MD) *Old Line State, Free State*

POPULATION (2001): 5,375,156 (19th) **AREA:** 12,297 sq. mi. (42nd) (31,849 sq. km.) **FLOWER:** Black-eyed susan **BIRD:** Baltimore oriole **TREE:** White oak **SONG:** "Maryland, My Maryland" **ENTERED UNION:** April 28, 1788 (7th) **CAPITAL:** Annapolis (population, 35,838) **LARGEST CITIES (WITH POP.):** Baltimore, 651,154; Frederick, 52,767; Gaithersburg, 52,613; Bowie, 50,269 **IMPORTANT PRODUCTS:** printing and publishing, food products, transportation equipment, electronic equipment, chickens, soybeans, corn, stone **PLACES TO VISIT:** Antietam National Battlefield; Fort McHenry National Monument, in Baltimore Harbor; U.S. Naval Academy in Annapolis

WEB SITE http://www.state.md.us • http://www.mdisfun.org

DID YOU KNOW? *Maryland is the narrowest state—near the town of Hancock, Maryland is only about one mile wide. The American flag on Fort McHenry during the War of 1812 inspired Francis Scott Key to write "The Star-Spangled Banner," the national anthem.*

MASSACHUSETTS (MA) *Bay State, Old Colony*

POPULATION (2001): 6,379,304 (13th) **AREA:** 9,241 sq. mi. (45th) (23,934 sq. km.) **FLOWER:** Mayflower **BIRD:** Chickadee **TREE:** American elm **SONG:** "All Hail to Massachusetts" **ENTERED UNION:** February 6, 1788 (6th) **CAPITAL AND LARGEST CITY:** Boston (population: 589,141) **OTHER LARGE CITIES (WITH POP.):** Worcester, 172,648; Springfield, 152,082; Lowell, 105,167 **IMPORTANT PRODUCTS:** industrial machinery, electronic equipment, instruments, printing and publishing, metal products, fish, flowers and shrubs, cranberries **PLACES TO VISIT:** Plymouth Rock; Minute Man National Historical Park; Children's Museum, Boston; Basketball Hall of Fame, Springfield; Old Sturbridge Village; Salem Witch Museum; Paul Revere's House, other sites on Boston's Freedom Trail

WEB SITE http://www.mass.gov • http://www.massvacation.com

DID YOU KNOW? *The Pilgrims settled in Massachusetts in 1620 and celebrated the first Thanksgiving the next year. Massachusetts had the first printing press (1639), first public school paid for by taxes (1639), and first college (Harvard, 1636).*

MICHIGAN (MI) *Great Lakes State, Wolverine State*

POPULATION (2001): 9,990,817 (8th) **FLOWER:** Apple blossom **BIRD:** Robin **TREE:** White pine **SONG:** "Michigan, My Michigan" **ENTERED UNION:** January 26, 1837 (26th) **CAPITAL:** Lansing (population, 127,825) **LARGEST CITIES (WITH POP.):** Detroit, 951,270; Grand Rapids, 197,800; Warren, 138,247; Flint, 124,943 **IMPORTANT PRODUCTS:** automobiles, industrial machinery, metal products, office furniture, plastic products, chemicals, food products, milk, corn, natural gas, iron ore, blueberries **PLACES TO VISIT:** Greenfield Village and Henry Ford Museum, Dearborn; Mackinac Island; Kalamazoo Aviation History Museum; Motown Historical Museum, Detroit

WEB SITE *http://www.michigan.gov • http://www.travelmichigan.com*

DID YOU KNOW? *Michigan is known for manufacturing automobiles. Lake Michigan is the largest lake entirely in the United States.*

MINNESOTA (MN) *North Star State, Gopher State*

POPULATION (2001): 4,972,294 (21st) **AREA:** 86,943 sq. mi. (12th) (225,182 sq. km.) **FLOWER:** Pink and white lady's-slipper **BIRD:** Common loon **TREE:** Red pine **SONG:** "Hail! Minnesota" **ENTERED UNION:** May 11, 1858 (32nd) **CAPITAL:** St. Paul **LARGEST CITIES (WITH POP.):** Minneapolis, 382,618; St. Paul, 287,151 **IMPORTANT PRODUCTS:** industrial machinery, printing and publishing, computers, food products, scientific and medical instruments, milk, hogs, cattle, corn, soybeans, iron ore **PLACES TO VISIT:** Voyageurs National Park; Minnesota State Fair, Fort Snelling; U.S. Hockey Hall of Fame, Eveleth; Walker Art Center, Minneapolis

WEB SITE *http://www.state.mn.us • http://www.exploreminnesota.com*

DID YOU KNOW? *Minnesota is the second coldest state (Alaska is the coldest). The Mall of America, in Bloomington, is the largest shopping mall in the U.S.; it has space for 12,750 cars.*

MISSISSIPPI (MS) *Magnolia State*

POPULATION (2001): 2,858,029 (31st) **AREA:** 48,286 sq. mi. (32nd) (125,061 sq. km.) **FLOWER:** Magnolia **BIRD:** Mockingbird **TREE:** Magnolia **SONG:** "Go, Mississippi!" **ENTERED UNION:** December 10, 1817 (20th) **CAPITAL AND LARGEST CITY:** Jackson (population, 184,256) **OTHER LARGE CITIES (WITH POP.):** Gulfport, 71,127; Biloxi, 50,644; **IMPORTANT PRODUCTS:** transportation equipment, furniture, electrical machinery, lumber and wood products, cotton, rice, chickens, cattle **PLACES TO VISIT:** Vicksburg National Military Park; Natchez Trace Parkway; Old Capitol, Jackson; Old Spanish Fort and Museum, Pascagoula

WEB SITE *http://www.mississippi.org • http://www.ms.gov*

DID YOU KNOW? *Mississippi was the first state to celebrate Memorial Day (originally called Decoration Day) as a holiday, in 1866. In 1884, in Columbus, Mississippi opened Mississippi University for Women, the first state-run college for women in the U.S. Jefferson Davis, president of the Confederate States of America, was born in Mississippi.*

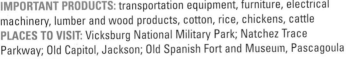

MISSOURI (MO) Show Me State

POPULATION (2001): 5,629,707 (17th) **AREA:** 69,709 sq. mi. (21st) (180,546 sq. km.) **FLOWER:** Hawthorn **BIRD:** Bluebird **TREE:** Dogwood **SONG:** "Missouri Waltz" **ENTERED UNION:** August 10, 1821 (24th) **CAPITAL:** Jefferson City (population, 39,636) **LARGEST CITIES (WITH POP.):** Kansas City, 441,545; St. Louis, 348,189; Springfield, 151,580; Independence, 113,288 **IMPORTANT PRODUCTS:** transportation equipment, electrical and electronic equipment, printing and publishing, food products, cattle, hogs, milk, soybeans, corn, hay, lead **PLACES TO VISIT:** Gateway Arch, St. Louis; Mark Twain Area, Hannibal; Harry S. Truman Museum, Independence; George Washington Carver Birthplace, Diamond; Pony Express Museum, St. Joseph

WEB SITE http://statemo.org • http://www.missouritourism.org

DID YOU KNOW? President Harry Truman, agricultural scientist George Washington Carver, and poet Langston Hughes were born in Missouri. It is said that the ice cream cone was first sold at a World's Fair in St. Louis, in 1904. Gateway Arch, in St. Louis, is the tallest monument (630 feet high) in the U.S.

MONTANA (MT) Treasure State

POPULATION (2001): 904,433 (44th) **AREA:** 147,046 sq. mi. (4th) (380,850 sq. km.) **FLOWER:** Bitterroot **BIRD:** Western meadowlark **TREE:** Ponderosa pine **SONG:** "Montana" **ENTERED UNION:** November 8, 1889 (41st) **CAPITAL:** Helena (population, 25,780) **LARGEST CITIES (WITH POP.):** Billings, 89,847; Missoula, 57,053; Great Falls, 56,690; Butte, 34,606 **IMPORTANT PRODUCTS:** cattle, copper, gold, wheat, barley, wood and paper products **PLACES TO VISIT:** Yellowstone and Glacier national parks; Little Bighorn Battlefield National Monument; Museum of the Rockies (in Bozeman); Museum of the Plains Indian, Blackfeet Reservation (near Browning)

WEB SITE http://www.visitmt.com • http://www.state.mt.us

DID YOU KNOW? Montana is the fourth-biggest state, after Alaska, Texas, and California. The most famous Indian battle in history took place in Montana, at Little Bighorn in 1876.

NEBRASKA (NE) Cornhusker State

POPULATION (2001): 1,713,235 (38th) **AREA:** 77,358 sq. mi. (16th) (200,358 sq. km.) **FLOWER:** Goldenrod **BIRD:** Western meadowlark **TREE:** Cottonwood **SONG:** "Beautiful Nebraska" **ENTERED UNION:** March 1, 1867 (37th) **CAPITAL:** Lincoln **LARGEST CITIES (WITH POP.):** Omaha, 390,007; Lincoln, 225,581 **IMPORTANT PRODUCTS:** cattle, hogs, milk, corn, soybeans, hay, wheat, sorghum, food products, industrial machinery **PLACES TO VISIT:** Oregon Trail landmarks; Stuhr Museum of the Prairie Pioneer, Grand Island; Agate Fossil Beds National Monument; Boys Town, near Omaha

WEB SITE http://www.state.ne.us • http://www.visitnebraska.org

DID YOU KNOW? Nebraska is not only a cattle state; it is the biggest meat-packing center in the world. It is also a major farm state.

NEVADA (NV) *Sagebrush State, Battle Born State, Silver State*

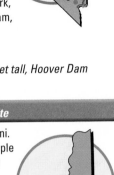

POPULATION (2001): 2,106,074 (35th) **AREA:** 110,567 sq. mi. (7th) (286,368 sq. km.) **FLOWER:** Sagebrush
BIRD: Mountain bluebird **TREES:** Single-leaf piñon, bristlecone pine
SONG: "Home Means Nevada" **ENTERED UNION:** October 31, 1864 (36th)
CAPITAL: Carson City (population, 52,457)
LARGEST CITIES (WITH POP.): Las Vegas, 478,434; Reno, 180,480;
Henderson, 175,381 **IMPORTANT PRODUCTS:** gold, silver, cattle, hay, food products, plastics, chemicals **PLACES TO VISIT:** Great Basin National Park, including Lehman Caves; Nevada State Museum, Carson City; Hoover Dam, Lake Tahoe, Pony Express Territory.

WEB SITE *http://www.state.nv.us • http://www.travelnevada.com*

DID YOU KNOW? *It rains less in Nevada than in any other state. At 725 feet tall, Hoover Dam (finished 1936) is the second highest dam in the U.S.*

NEW HAMPSHIRE (NH) *Granite State*

POPULATION (2001): 1,259,181 (41st) **AREA:** 9,283 sq. mi. (44th) (24,043 sq. km.) **FLOWER:** Purple lilac **BIRD:** Purple finch **TREE:** White birch **SONG:** "Old New Hampshire" **ENTERED UNION:** June 21, 1788 (9th) **CAPITAL:** Concord **LARGEST CITIES (WITH POP.):** Manchester, 107,006; Nashua, 86,605; Concord, 40,687
IMPORTANT PRODUCTS: industrial machinery, electric and electronic equipment, metal products, plastic products, dairy products, maple syrup and maple sugar **PLACES TO VISIT:** White Mountain National Forest; Mount Washington; Old Man in the Mountain, Franconia Notch; Canterbury Shaker Village; Flume gorge and aerial tramway

WEB SITE *http://www.state.nh.us • http://www.visitnh.gov*

DID YOU KNOW? *Mount Washington is the highest mountain in the northeast. Its peak is said to be the windiest spot on Earth. The first town-supported, free public library in the United States, opened in New Hampshire in 1833.*

NEW JERSEY (NJ) *Garden State*

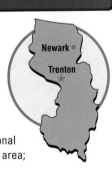

POPULATION (2001): 8,484,431 (9th) **AREA:** 8,215 sq. mi. (46th) (21,277 sq. km.) **FLOWER:** Purple violet
BIRD: Eastern goldfinch **TREE:** Red oak **SONG:** none
ENTERED UNION: December 18, 1787 (3rd) **CAPITAL:** Trenton (population, 85,403) **LARGEST CITIES (WITH POP.):** Newark, 273,546; Jersey City, 240,055; Paterson, 149,222; Elizabeth, 120,568
IMPORTANT PRODUCTS: chemicals, pharmaceuticals/drugs, electronic equipment, nursery and greenhouse products, food products, tomatoes, blueberries, and peaches **PLACES TO VISIT:** ocean beaches; Edison National Historical Site, West Orange; Liberty State Park; Pine Barrens wilderness area; Revolutionary War sites

WEB SITE *http://www.visitnj.org • http://www.state.nj.us*

DID YOU KNOW? *The electric light bulb was invented in New Jersey by Thomas Edison in 1879. The first ferryboat just for cars was built in New Jersey and placed in service in 1926. New Jersey manufactures more flags than any other state.*

NEW MEXICO (NM) *Land of Enchantment*

POPULATION (2001): 1,829,146 (36th) **AREA:** 121,598 sq. mi. (5th) (314,939 sq. km.) **FLOWER:** Yucca **BIRD:** Roadrunner **TREE:** Piñon **SONG:** "O, Fair New Mexico" **ENTERED UNION:** January 6, 1912 (47th) **CAPITAL:** Santa Fe **LARGEST CITIES (WITH POP.):** Albuquerque, 448,607; Las Cruces, 74,267; Santa Fe, 62,203

IMPORTANT PRODUCTS: electronic equipment, foods, machinery, clothing, lumber, transportation equipment, hay, onions, chiles

PLACES TO VISIT: Carlsbad Caverns National Park; Palace of the Governors and Mission of San Miguel, Santa Fe; Chaco Culture Natl. Historical Park; cliff dwellings

WEB SITE http://www.state.nm.us • http://www.newmexico.org

DID YOU KNOW? *The oldest capital city in the U.S. is Santa Fe, New Mexico. Pueblo Indians had an advanced civilization in New Mexico a thousand years ago. The deepest cave in the U.S., over 1,570 feet deep, is in New Mexico's Carlsbad Caverns*

NEW YORK (NY) *Empire State*

POPULATION (2001): 19,011,378 (3rd) **AREA:** 53,989 sq. mi. (27th) (139,831 sq. km.) **FLOWER:** Rose **BIRD:** Bluebird **TREE:** Sugar maple **SONG:** "I Love New York" **ENTERED UNION:** July 26, 1788 (11th) **CAPITAL:** Albany (population, 95,658)

LARGEST CITIES (WITH POP.): New York, 8,008,278; Buffalo, 292,648; Rochester, 219,773; Yonkers, 196,086 **IMPORTANT PRODUCTS:** books and magazines, automobile and aircraft parts, toys and sporting goods, electronic equipment, machinery, clothing and textiles, metal products, milk, cattle, hay, apples **PLACES TO VISIT:** In New York City: Museum of Natural History, Central Park, Empire State Building, United Nations, Bronx Zoo, Statue of Liberty, and Ellis Island. Niagara Falls; National Baseball Hall of Fame, Cooperstown; Fort Ticonderoga; Franklin D. Roosevelt National Historical Site, Hyde Park

WEB SITE http://www.state.ny.us • http://www.iloveny.state.ny.us

DID YOU KNOW? *New York City is the largest city in the United States and was the nation's first capital. The first pizza restaurant in the U.S. opened in New York City in 1895.*

NORTH CAROLINA (NC) *Tar Heel State, Old North State*

POPULATION (2001): 8,186,268 (11th) **AREA:** 52,672 sq. mi. (29th) (136,420 sq. km.) **FLOWER:** Dogwood **BIRD:** Cardinal **TREE:** Pine **SONG:** "The Old North State" **ENTERED UNION:** November 21, 1789 (12th) **CAPITAL:** Raleigh **LARGEST CITIES (WITH POP.):** Charlotte, 540,828; Raleigh, 276,093; Greensboro, 223,891; Durham, 187,035; Winston-Salem, 185,776; **IMPORTANT PRODUCTS:** clothing and textiles, tobacco and tobacco products, industrial machinery, electronic equipment, furniture, cotton, soybeans, peanuts

PLACES TO VISIT: Great Smoky Mountains National Park; Cape Hatteras National Seashore; Wright Brothers National Memorial, Kitty Hawk

WEB SITE http://www.state.nc.us • http://www.visitnc.com

DID YOU KNOW? *The Wright Brothers took the first airplane ride in history, in North Carolina. The first U.S. school of forestry was opened in North Carolina.*

NORTH DAKOTA (ND) *Peace Garden State*

POPULATION (2001): 634,448 (48th) **AREA:** 70,704 sq. mi. (18th) (183,123 sq. km.) **FLOWER:** Wild prairie rose **BIRD:** Western meadowlark **TREE:** American elm **SONG:** "North Dakota Hymn" **ENTERED UNION:** November 2, 1889 (39th) **CAPITAL:** Bismarck **LARGEST CITIES (WITH POP.):** Fargo, 90,599; Bismarck, 55,532; Grand Forks, 49,321; Minot, 36,567 **IMPORTANT PRODUCTS:** wheat, barley, hay, sunflowers, sugar beets, cattle, sand and gravel, food products, farm equipment, high-tech electronics **PLACES TO VISIT:** Theodore Roosevelt National Park; Bonanzaville, near Fargo; Dakota Dinosaur Museum, Dickinson; International Peace Garden

WEB SITE *http://www.ndtourism.com • http://www.discovernd.com*

DID YOU KNOW? *North Dakota is one of the two biggest wheat-growing states (the other is Kansas). Theodore Roosevelt was a rancher here before he became president.*

OHIO (OH) *Buckeye State*

POPULATION (2001): 11,373,541 (7th) **AREA:** 44,828 sq. mi. (34th) (116,103 sq. km.) **FLOWER:** Scarlet carnation **BIRD:** Cardinal **TREE:** Buckeye **SONG:** "Beautiful Ohio" **ENTERED UNION:** March 1, 1803 (17th) **CAPITAL AND LARGEST CITY:** Columbus (population, 711,470) **OTHER LARGE CITIES (WITH POP.):** Cleveland, 478,403; Cincinnati, 331,285; Toledo, 313,619; Akron, 217,074; Dayton, 166,179 **IMPORTANT PRODUCTS:** metal and metal products, transportation equipment, industrial machinery, rubber and plastic products, electronic equipment, printing and publishing, chemicals, food products, corn, soybeans, livestock, milk **PLACES TO VISIT:** Mound City Group, Indian burial mounds; Neil Armstrong Air and Space Museum; homes of and memorials to 8 U.S. presidents who lived here

WEB SITE *http://www.state.oh.us • http://www.ohiotourism.com*

DID YOU KNOW? *Seven American presidents were born in Ohio (James Garfield, Ulysses S. Grant, Warren G. Harding, Benjamin Harrison, Rutherford B. Hayes, William McKinley, William H. Taft). Ohio was the home of the first professional baseball team, the Cincinnati Red Stockings.*

OKLAHOMA (OK) *Sooner State*

POPULATION (2001): 3,460,097 (28th) **AREA:** 69,903 sq. mi. (20th) (181,049 sq. km.) **FLOWER:** Mistletoe **BIRD:** Scissor-tailed flycatcher **TREE:** Redbud **SONG:** "Oklahoma!" **ENTERED UNION:** November 16, 1907 (46th) **CAPITAL AND LARGEST CITY:** Oklahoma City (population, 506,132) **OTHER LARGE CITIES (WITH POP.):** Tulsa, 393,049; Norman, 95,694; Lawton, 92,757 **IMPORTANT PRODUCTS:** natural gas, oil, cattle, nonelectrical machinery, transportation equipment, metal products, wheat, hay **PLACES TO VISIT:** Indian City U.S.A., near Anadarko; Fort Gibson Stockade; National Cowboy Hall of Fame; White Water Bay and Frontier City theme parks; Cherokee Heritage Center

WEB SITE *http://www.travelok.com • http://www.state.ok.us*

DID YOU KNOW? *The American Indian nations called The Five Civilized Tribes (Cherokee, Chickasaw, Choctaw, Creek, and Seminole) were resettled in eastern Oklahoma by the federal government. Today, more Native Americans live in Oklahoma than in any other state.*

OREGON (OR) *Beaver State*

POPULATION (2001): 3,472,867 (27th) **AREA:** 97,132 sq. mi. (10th) (251,572 sq. km.) **FLOWER:** Oregon grape **BIRD:** Western meadowlark **TREE:** Douglas fir **SONG:** "Oregon, My Oregon" **ENTERED UNION:** February 14, 1859 (33rd) **CAPITAL:** Salem **LARGEST CITIES (WITH POP.):** Portland, 529,121; Eugene, 137,893; Salem, 136,924 **IMPORTANT PRODUCTS:** lumber and wood products, electronics and semiconductors, food products, paper, cattle, hay, vegetables, Christmas trees **PLACES TO VISIT:** Crater Lake National Park; Oregon Caves National Monument; Fort Clatsop National Memorial; Oregon Museum of Science and Industry, Portland

WEB SITE http://www.oregon.gov • http://www.traveloregon.com

DID YOU KNOW? *Hells Canyon, 7,900 feet deep at its maximum, is one of the deepest canyons in the world. Crater Lake, which gets as deep as 1,932 feet, is the deepest lake in the U. S.*

PENNSYLVANIA (PA) *Keystone State*

POPULATION (2001):12,287,150 (6th) **AREA:** 46,058 sq. mi. (33rd) (119,290 sq. km.) **FLOWER:** Mountain laurel **BIRD:** Ruffed grouse **TREE:** Hemlock **SONG:** "Pennsylvania" **ENTERED UNION:** December 12, 1787 (2nd) **CAPITAL:** Harrisburg (population, 48,950) **LARGEST CITIES (WITH POP.):** Philadelphia, 1,517,550; Pittsburgh, 334,563; Allentown, 106,632; Erie, 103,717; **IMPORTANT PRODUCTS:** iron and steel, coal, industrial machinery, printing and publishing, food products, electronic equipment, transportation equipment, stone, clay and glass products

PLACES TO VISIT: Independence Hall and other historic sites in Philadelphia; Franklin Institute Science Museum, Philadelphia; Valley Forge; Gettysburg; Hershey; Pennsylvania Dutch country, Lancaster County

WEB SITE http://www.experiencepa.com • http://www.state.pa.us.gov

DID YOU KNOW? *Pennsylvania is known for the Liberty Bell in Philadelphia, which first rang after the signing of the Declaration of Independence. Philadelphia was also the capital of the United States for most of the time between 1776 to 1800. The first hospital in the United States was built there in 1751.*

RHODE ISLAND (RI) *Little Rhody, Ocean State*

POPULATION (2001): 1,058,920 (43rd) **AREA:** 1,231 sq. mi. (50th) (3,188 sq. km.) **FLOWER:** Violet **BIRD:** Rhode Island red **TREE:** Red maple **SONG:** "Rhode Island" **ENTERED UNION:** May 29, 1790 (13th) **CAPITAL AND LARGEST CITY:** Providence (population, 173,618) **OTHER LARGE CITIES (WITH POP.):** Warwick, 85,808; Cranston, 79,269; Pawtucket, 72,958 **IMPORTANT PRODUCTS:** costume jewelry, toys, textiles, machinery, electronic equipment, fish **PLACES TO VISIT:** Block Island; International Tennis Hall of Fame, Newport; Newport Harbor; Green Animals Topiary Garden, Portsmouth

WEB SITE http://www.state.ri.us • http://www.visitrhodeisland.com

DID YOU KNOW? *Rhode Island is the smallest state. The oldest synagogue in the U.S. (Touro Synagogue, 1763) is in Newport.*

SOUTH CAROLINA (SC) *Palmetto State*

POPULATION (2001): 4,063,011 (26th) **AREA:** 31,189 sq. mi. (40th) (80,779 sq. km.) **FLOWER:** Yellow jessamine
BIRD: Carolina wren **TREE:** Palmetto **SONG:** "Carolina"
ENTERED UNION: May 23, 1788 (8th)
CAPITAL AND LARGEST CITY: Columbia (population, 116,278)
OTHER LARGE CITIES (WITH POP.): Charleston, 96,650; North Charleston, 79,641; Greenville, 56,002 **IMPORTANT PRODUCTS:** clothing and textiles, chemicals, industrial machinery, metal products, livestock, tobacco, Portland cement **PLACES TO VISIT:** Grand Strand and Hilton Head Island beaches; Revolutionary War battlefields; historic sites in Charleston; Fort Sumter; Charleston Museum

WEB SITE http://www.myscgov.com • http://www.myscgov.com/SCSGportal/static/tourism_tem1.html

DID YOU KNOW? *More battles of the American Revolution took place in South Carolina than in any other state. The first shots of the Civil War were fired at Fort Sumter in South Carolina.*

SOUTH DAKOTA (SD) *Mt. Rushmore State, Coyote State*

POPULATION (2001): 756,600 (46th) **AREA:** 77,121 sq. mi. (17th) (199,743 sq. km.) **FLOWER:** Pasqueflower **BIRD:** Chinese ring-necked pheasant **TREE:** Black Hills spruce **SONG:** "Hail, South Dakota" **ENTERED UNION:** November 2, 1889 (40th) **CAPITAL:** Pierre (population, 13,876) **LARGEST CITIES (WITH POP.):** Sioux Falls, 123,975; Rapid City, 59,607 **IMPORTANT PRODUCTS:** food and food products, machinery, electric and electronic equipment, corn, soybeans
PLACES TO VISIT: Mount Rushmore National Memorial; Crazy Horse Memorial; Jewel Cave; Badlands and Wind Caves national parks; Wounded Knee battlefield; Homestake Gold Mine

WEB SITE http://www.state.sd.us • http://www.travelsd.com

DID YOU KNOW? *South Dakota is best known for the faces of presidents carved on Mount Rushmore (Presidents George Washington, Thomas Jefferson, Abraham Lincoln, and Theodore Roosevelt).*

TENNESSEE (TN) *Volunteer State*

POPULATION (2001): 5,740,021 (16th) **AREA:** 42,146 sq. mi. (36th) (109,158 sq. km.) **FLOWER:** Iris
BIRD: Mockingbird **TREE:** Tulip poplar **SONG:** "The Tennessee Waltz"
ENTERED UNION: June 1, 1796 (16th) **CAPITAL:** Nashville
LARGEST CITIES (WITH POP.): Memphis, 650,100; Nashville, 569,891; Knoxville, 173,890; Chattanooga, 155,554 **IMPORTANT PRODUCTS:** chemicals, machinery, vehicles, food products, metal products, publishing, electronic equipment, paper products, rubber and plastic products, tobacco
PLACES TO VISIT: Great Smoky Mountains National Park; the Hermitage, home of President Andrew Jackson, near Nashville; Civil War battle sites; Grand Old Opry, Nashville; Graceland, home of Elvis Presley, in Memphis

WEB SITE http://www.state.tn.us • http://www.state.tn.us/tourdev

DID YOU KNOW? *Tennessee can claim Nashville as country music capital of the world. Frontiersman Davy Crockett was born in Tennessee. Elvis Presley and President Andrew Jackson lived in Tennessee.*

TEXAS (TX) *Lone Star State*

POPULATION (2001): 21,325,018 (2nd) **AREA:** 267,277 sq. mi. (2nd) (692,247 sq. km.) **FLOWER:** Bluebonnet **BIRD:** Mockingbird **TREE:** Pecan **SONG:** "Texas, Our Texas" **ENTERED UNION:** December 29, 1845 (28th) **CAPITAL:** Austin **LARGEST CITIES (WITH POP.):** Houston, 1,953,631; Dallas, 1,188,580; San Antonio, 1,144,646; Austin, 656,562; El Paso, 563,662; Fort Worth, 534,694 **IMPORTANT PRODUCTS:** oil, natural gas, cattle, milk, eggs, transportation equipment, chemicals, clothing, industrial machinery, electrical and electronic equipment, cotton, grains
PLACES TO VISIT: Guadalupe Mountains and Big Bend national parks; the Alamo, in San Antonio; Lyndon Johnson National Historic Site, near Johnson City; George Bush Presidential Library, College Station

WEB SITE *http://www.state.tx.us • http://texasalmanac.com*

DID YOU KNOW? *Texas is the second-largest of the states (after Alaska). Texas has more oil and natural gas than any other state and the most farmland.*

UTAH (UT) *Beehive State*

POPULATION (2001): 2,269,789 (34th) **AREA:** 84,904 sq. mi. (13th) (219,902 sq. km.) **FLOWER:** Sego lily **BIRD:** Seagull **Tree:** Blue spruce **SONG:** "Utah, We Love Thee" **ENTERED UNION:** January 4, 1896 (45th) **CAPITAL AND LARGEST CITY:** Salt Lake City (population, 181,743) **OTHER LARGE CITIES (WITH POP.):** West Valley City, 108,896; Provo, 105,166 **IMPORTANT PRODUCTS:** transportation equipment, medical instruments, electronic parts, food products, steel, copper, cattle, corn, hay, wheat, barley
PLACES TO VISIT: Arches, Canyonlands, Bryce Canyon, Zion, and Capitol Reef national parks; Great Salt Lake; Temple Square (Mormon Church headquarters) in Salt Lake City; Indian cliff dwellings

WEB SITE *http://www.utah.gov • http://www.utah.com*

DID YOU KNOW? *Utah's Great Salt Lake, which contains 6 billion tons of salt, is the largest lake in the U.S. outside of the Great Lakes. Rainbow Bridge in Utah is the largest natural arch or rock bridge in the world; it is 200 feet high and 270 feet wide.*

VERMONT (VT) *Green Mountain State*

POPULATION (2001): 613,090 (49th) **AREA:** 9,615 sq. mi. (43rd) (24,903 sq. km.) **FLOWER:** Red clover **BIRD:** Hermit thrush **TREE:** Sugar maple **SONG:** "These Green Mountains" **ENTERED UNION:** March 4, 1791 (14th) **CAPITAL:** Montpelier (population, 8,035) **LARGEST CITIES (WITH POP.):** Burlington, 38,889; Essex, 18,626 **IMPORTANT PRODUCTS:** machine tools, furniture, scales, books, computer parts, foods, dairy products, apples, maple syrup
PLACES TO VISIT: Green Mountain National Forest; Teddy Bear Factory, Shelburne; Ben and Jerry's Ice Cream Factory, Waterbury

WEB SITE *http://www.state.vt.us • http://www.1-800-vermont.com*

DID YOU KNOW? *Vermont is famous for its granite, marble, Fall leaves, maple syrup, and great skiing. Vermont passed the first state constitution (1777) to prohibit slavery and to allow all men to vote.*

VIRGINIA (VA) *Old Dominion*

POPULATION (2001): 7,187,734 (12th) **AREA:** 42,326 sq. mi. (35th) (109,391 sq. km.) **FLOWER:** Dogwood
BIRD: Cardinal **TREE:** Dogwood **SONG:** "Carry Me Back to Old Virginia"
ENTERED UNION: June 25, 1788 (10th) **CAPITAL:** Richmond
LARGEST CITIES (WITH POP.): Virginia Beach, 425,257; Norfolk, 234,403; Chesapeake, 199,184; Richmond, 197,790; Newport News, 180,150 **IMPORTANT PRODUCTS:** transportation equipment, textiles, chemicals, printing, machinery, electronic equipment, food products, coal, livestock, tobacco, wood products, furniture **PLACES TO VISIT:** Colonial Williamsburg; Arlington National Cemetery; Mount Vernon (George Washington's home); Monticello (Thomas Jefferson's home); Shenandoah National Park

WEB SITE *http://www.state.va.us • http://www.virginia.org*

DID YOU KNOW? *Virginia was the birthplace of eight presidents (Presidents William H. Harrison, Thomas Jefferson, James Madison, James Monroe, Zachary Taylor, John Tyler, George Washington, Woodrow Wilson), more than any other state.*

WASHINGTON (WA) *Evergreen State*

POPULATION (2001): 5,987,973 (15th) **AREA:** 70,637 sq. mi. (19th) (182,950 sq. km.) **FLOWER:** Western rhododendron
BIRD: Willow goldfinch **TREE:** Western hemlock **SONG:** "Washington, My Home" **ENTERED UNION:** November 11, 1889 (42nd) **CAPITAL:** Olympia (population, 42,514) **LARGEST CITIES (WITH POP.):** Seattle, 563,374; Spokane, 195,629; Tacoma, 193,556 **IMPORTANT PRODUCTS:** aircraft, lumber and plywood, pulp and paper, machinery, electronics, computer software, aluminum, processed fruits and vegetables **PLACES TO VISIT:** Mount Rainier, Olympic, and North Cascades national parks; Mount St. Helens; Seattle Center, with Space Needle and monorail

WEB SITE *http://www.access.wa.gov • http://www.tourism.wa.gov*

DID YOU KNOW? *Washington's Grand Coulee Dam, on the Columbia River, is the world's largest concrete dam. Mount Rainier is the tallest volcano in the lower 48 states. Washington is known for its apples, timber, and fishing fleets.*

WEST VIRGINIA (WV) *Mountain State*

POPULATION (2001): 1,801,916 (37th) **AREA:** 24,231 sq. mi. (41st) (62,759 sq. km.) **FLOWER:** Big rhododendron
BIRD: Cardinal **TREE:** Sugar maple **SONGS:** "The West Virginia Hills"; "This Is My West Virginia"; "West Virginia, My Home Sweet Home"
ENTERED UNION: June 20, 1863 (35th)
CAPITAL AND LARGEST CITY: Charleston (population, 53,421)
OTHER LARGE CITIES (WITH POP.): Huntington, 51,475; Wheeling, 33,099
IMPORTANT PRODUCTS: coal, natural gas, fabricated metal products, chemicals, automobile parts, aluminum, steel, machinery, cattle, hay, apples, peaches, tobacco **PLACES TO VISIT:** Harpers Ferry National Historic Park; Exhibition Coal Mine, Beckley; Monongahela National Forest

WEB SITE *http://www.state.wv.us • http://www.callwva.com*

DID YOU KNOW? *West Virginia is one of the biggest coal states. It was part of Virginia until West Virginians decided to break away, in 1861.*

WISCONSIN (WI) *Badger State*

POPULATION (2001): 5,401,906 (18th) **AREA:** 65,499 sq. mi. (22nd) (169,642 sq. km.) **FLOWER:** Wood violet **BIRD:** Robin **TREE:** Sugar maple **SONG:** "On, Wisconsin!" **ENTERED UNION:** May 29, 1848 (30th) **CAPITAL:** Madison **LARGEST CITIES (WITH POP.):** Milwaukee, 596,974; Madison, 208,054; Green Bay, 102,313; Kenosha, 90,352; Racine, 81,855 **IMPORTANT PRODUCTS:** paper products, printing, milk, butter, cheese, foods, food products, motor vehicles and equipment, medical instruments and supplies, plastics, corn, hay, vegetables **PLACES TO VISIT:** Wisconsin Dells; Cave of the Mounds, near Blue Mounds; Milwaukee Public Museum; Circus World Museum, Baraboo; National Railroad Museum, Green Bay

WEB SITE http://www.wisconsin.gov • http://www.travelwisconsin.com

DID YOU KNOW? *Wisconsin is known as America's Dairyland; it has also become a big manufacturing state. The first kindergarten in America was opened in Wisconsin in 1865.*

WYOMING (WY) *Cowboy State*

POPULATION (2001): 494,423 (50th) **AREA:** 97,818 sq. mi. (9th) (253,349 sq. km.) **FLOWER:** Indian paintbrush **BIRD:** Western meadowlark **TREE:** Plains cottonwood **SONG:** "Wyoming" **ENTERED UNION:** July 10, 1890 (44th) **CAPITAL AND LARGEST CITY:** Cheyenne (population, 53,011) **OTHER LARGE CITIES (WITH POP.):** Casper, 49,644; Laramie, 27,204 **IMPORTANT PRODUCTS:** oil, natural gas, petroleum (oil) products, cattle, wheat, beans **PLACES TO VISIT:** Yellowstone and Grand Teton national parks; Fort Laramie; Buffalo Bill Historical Center, Cody; pioneer trails

WEB SITE http://www.state.wy.us • http://www.wyomingtourism.org

DID YOU KNOW? *Wyoming is the home of the first U.S. national park (Yellowstone). Established in 1872, Yellowstone has 10,000 geysers, including the world's tallest active geyser (Steamboat Geyser).*

COMMONWEALTH OF PUERTO RICO (PR)

HISTORY: Christopher Columbus landed in Puerto Rico in 1493. Puerto Rico was a Spanish colony for centuries, then was ceded (given) to the United States in 1898 after the Spanish-American War. In 1952, still associated with the United States, Puerto Rico became a commonwealth with its own constitution. **POPULATION (2000):** 3,808,610 **AREA:** 3,508 sq. mi. (9,086 sq. km.) **FLOWER:** Maga **BIRD:** Reinita **TREE:** Ceiba **NATIONAL ANTHEM:** "La Borinqueña" **CAPITAL AND LARGEST CITY:** San Juan (population, 421,958) **OTHER LARGE CITIES (WITH POP.):** Bayamón, 203,499; Carolina, 168,164; Ponce, 155,038 **IMPORTANT PRODUCTS:** chemicals, food products, electronic equipment, clothing and textiles, industrial machinery, coffee, sugarcane, fruit, hogs **PLACES TO VISIT:** San Juan National Historic Site; beaches and resorts

WEB SITE http://www.eia.doe.gov/emeu/cabs/prico.html • http://www.gotopuertorico.com

DID YOU KNOW? *Puerto Ricans have most of the rights of American citizens, but they cannot vote in U.S. presidential elections—and do not pay federal income tax.*

WASHINGTON, D.C.
The Capital of the United States

Land Area: 61 square miles
Population (2001): 571,822
Flower: American beauty rose
Bird: Wood thrush

WEB SITE *http://www.washington.org*

HiSTORY Washington, D.C., became the capital of the United States in 1800, when the federal government moved there from Philadelphia. The city of Washington was designed and built to be the capital. It was named after George Washington. Many of its major sights are on the Mall, an open grassy area that runs from the Capitol to the Potomac River.

Capitol, which houses the U.S. Congress, is at the east end of the Mall, on Capitol Hill. Its dome can be seen from far away.

Franklin Delano Roosevelt Memorial, honoring the 32nd president of the United States, and his wife, Eleanor, was dedicated in 1997. In a parklike setting, it has sculptures showing events during the president's years of service.

Jefferson Memorial, a circular marble building located near the Potomac River. Its design is partly based on one by Thomas Jefferson for the University of Virginia.

Korean War Veterans Memorial, dedicated in 1995, is at the west end of the Mall. It shows troops ready for combat.

Lincoln Memorial, at the west end of the Mall, is built of white marble and styled like a Greek temple. Inside is a large, seated statue of Abraham Lincoln. His Gettysburg Address is carved on a nearby wall.

National Archives, on Constitution Avenue, holds the Declaration of Independence, Constitution, and Bill of Rights.

National Gallery of Art, on the Mall, is one of the world's great art museums.

National World War II Memorial, to be located between the Lincoln Memorial and the Washington Monument at the Mall, will honor all 16 million Americans who served during the war. Ground was broken in November 2000.

Smithsonian Institution has 14 museums, including the National Air and Space Museum and the Museum of Natural History. The National Zoo is part of the Smithsonian.

U.S. Holocaust Memorial Museum presents the history of the Nazis' murder of more than six million Jews and millions of other people from 1933 to 1945. The exhibit *Daniel's Story* tells the story of the Holocaust from a child's point of view.

Vietnam Veterans Memorial has a black-granite wall shaped like a V. Names of the Americans killed or missing in the Vietnam War are inscribed on the wall.

Washington Monument, a white marble pillar, or obelisk, standing on the Mall and rising to over 555 feet. From the top, there are wonderful views of the city.

White House, at 1600 Pennsylvania Avenue, has been the home of every U.S. president except George Washington.

Women in Military Service for America Memorial, near the entrance to Arlington National Cemetery. It honors the 1.8 million women who have served in the U.S. armed forces.

285

HOW THE STATES

ALABAMA comes from an Indian word for "tribal town."

ALASKA comes from *alakshak,* the Aleutian (Eskimo) word meaning "peninsula" or "land that is not an island."

ARIZONA comes from a Pima Indian word meaning "little spring place," or the Aztec word *arizuma,* meaning "silver-bearing."

Arizona

ARKANSAS is a variation of *Quapaw,* the name of an Indian tribe. *Quapaw* means "south wind."

CALIFORNIA is the name of an imaginary island in a Spanish story. It was named by Spanish explorers of Baja California, a part of Mexico.

COLORADO comes from a Spanish word meaning "red." It was first given to the Colorado River because of its reddish color.

CONNECTICUT comes from an Algonquin Indian word meaning "long river place."

DELAWARE is named after Lord De La Warr, the English governor of Virginia in colonial times.

FLORIDA, which means "flowery" in Spanish, was named by the explorer Ponce de Leon, who landed there during Easter.

GEORGIA was named after King George II of England, who granted the right to create a colony there in 1732.

HAWAII probably comes from *Hawaiki,* or *Owhyhee,* the native Polynesian word for "homeland."

IDAHO's name is of uncertain origin, but it may come from a Kiowa Apache name for the Comanche Indians.

ILLINOIS is the French version of *Illini,* an Algonquin Indian word meaning "men" or "warriors."

INDIANA means "land of the Indians."

IOWA comes from the name of an American Indian tribe that lived on the land that is now the state.

KANSAS comes from a Sioux Indian word that possibly meant "people of the south wind."

KENTUCKY comes from an Iroquois Indian word, possibly meaning "meadowland."

LOUISIANA, which was first settled by French explorers, was named after King Louis XIV of France.

MAINE means "the mainland." English explorers called it that to distinguish it from islands nearby.

MARYLAND was named after Queen Henrietta Maria, wife of King Charles I of England, who granted the right to establish an English colony there.

MASSACHUSETTS comes from an Indian word meaning "large hill place."

MICHIGAN comes from the Chippewa Indian words *mici gama,* meaning "great water" (referring to Lake Michigan).

Michigan

MINNESOTA got its name from a Dakota Sioux Indian word meaning "cloudy water" or "sky-tinted water."

MISSISSIPPI is probably from Chippewa Indian words meaning "great river" or "gathering of all the waters," or from an Algonquin word, *messipi.*

MISSOURI comes from an Algonquin Indian term meaning "river of the big canoes."

Montana

MONTANA comes from a Latin or Spanish word meaning "mountainous."

GOT THEIR NAMES

NEBRASKA comes from "flat river" or "broad water," an Omaha or Otos Indian name for the Platte River.

NEVADA means "snow-clad" in Spanish. Spanish explorers gave the name to the Sierra Nevada Mountains.

Nevada

NEW HAMPSHIRE was named by an early settler after his home county of Hampshire, in England.

NEW JERSEY was named for the English Channel island of Jersey.

NEW MEXICO was given its name by 16th-century Spaniards in Mexico.

NEW YORK, first called New Netherland, was renamed for the Duke of York and Albany after the English took it from Dutch settlers.

NORTH CAROLINA, the northern part of the English colony of Carolana, was named for King Charles I.

NORTH DAKOTA comes from a Sioux Indian word meaning "friend" or "ally."

OHIO is the Iroquois Indian word for "fine or good river."

OKLAHOMA comes from a Choctaw Indian word meaning "red man."

Oregon

OREGON may have come from *Ouaricon-sint,* a name on an old French map that was once given to what is now called the Columbia River. That river runs between Oregon and Washington.

PENNSYLVANIA meaning "Penn's woods," was the name given to the colony founded by William Penn.

RHODE ISLAND may have come from the Dutch "Roode Eylandt" (red island) or may have been named after the Greek island of Rhodes.

SOUTH CAROLINA, the southern part of the English colony of Carolana, was named for King Charles I.

SOUTH DAKOTA comes from a Sioux Indian word meaning "friend" or "ally."

TENNESSEE comes from "Tanasi," the name of Cherokee Indian villages on what is now the Little Tennessee River.

TEXAS comes from a word meaning "friends" or "allies," used by the Spanish to describe some of the American Indians living there.

UTAH comes from a Navajo word meaning "upper" or "higher up."

VERMONT comes from two French words, *vert* meaning "green" and *mont* "mountain."

VIRGINIA was named in honor of Queen Elizabeth I of England, who was known as the Virgin Queen because she was never married.

WASHINGTON was named after George Washington, the first president of the United States. It is the only state named after a president.

WEST VIRGINIA got its name from the people of western Virginia, who formed their own government during the Civil War.

WISCONSIN comes from a Chippewa name that is believed to mean "grassy place." It was once spelled *Ouisconsin* and *Mesconsing.*

WYOMING comes from Algonquin Indian words that are said to mean "at the big plains," "large prairie place," or "on the great plain."

Wyoming

NATIONAL PARKS

The world's first national park was Yellowstone, established in 1872. Since then, the U.S. government has set aside 54 other national parks. Fifty-three parks are located in the U.S.; there is also one in the Virgin Islands and one in American Samoa. You can find out more about national parks by writing to the National Park Service, Department of the Interior, 1849 C Street NW, Washington, D.C. 20240.

For information on-line, go to **WEB SITE** *http://www.nps.gov/parks.html*

BADLANDS NATIONAL PARK

covers 242,756 acres in a rugged part of South Dakota where humans, and many kinds of animals, have lived for more than 11,000 years. Both the Lakota Indians and early French trappers called the area "bad lands" in their native languages. Much of the land is bare, and there are colorful, oddly shaped rocks, ridges, and canyons. The Badlands is home to bighorn sheep, bison, antelopes, eagles, vultures, turtles, rattlesnakes, butterflies, and bluebirds. The most endangered land mammal in North America, the black-footed ferret, was reintroduced there in 1995, and is still doing well. Fossils of early ancestors of rhinoceroses, horses, pigs, and cats have been found in the park. Dinosaur fossils have been discovered nearby. Surrounded by prairie, the Badlands also has 56 species of grass and hundreds of kinds of wildflowers.

BRYCE CANYON NATIONAL PARK

in southern Utah, is famous for its "hoodoos"—colorful spires and pillars of rock shaped by erosion over millions of years. Founded in 1928 and spanning 37,277 acres, the park is named for Ebenezer Bryce, a Mormon who settled near the canyon in 1875. Paiute Indians, who were living there when Bryce arrived, believed the hoodoos were "Legend People," who had been turned to stone by Coyote, a Native American god who liked to play tricks on humans. Names for features like "Fairyland Canyon," "Inspiration Point," and the "Silent City," were inspired by the magical appearance of the rock formations.

EVERGLADES NATIONAL PARK

EVERGLADES NATIONAL PARK is a swampy, subtropical wilderness at the southwestern tip of Florida. It was created in 1934 especially to preserve the varied plant and animal life there. Most of the 1,399,078 acres are covered by shallow water during the wet season—one reason why the Everglades are called the "river of grass." There are 300 species of birds, 120 kinds of trees, 25 varieties of orchids, and 1,000 kinds of other plants. Thirty-six endangered animal species live there, including alligators, crocodiles, Florida panthers, and manatees, also known as sea cows. The manatees are sea creatures with thick gray skin. They are big (they can be 15 feet long and can weigh up to 1,200 pounds), but they are very gentle.

SEQUOIA AND KINGS CANYON NATIONAL PARK

SEQUOIA AND KINGS CANYON NATIONAL PARK, founded in 1890, is the second oldest national park (after Yellowstone). Located in central California, it is home to the world's largest living thing, the General Sherman Tree. At 275 feet tall this giant sequoia is not the tallest of all trees, but it is the most massive. It measures 102 feet round at the base of the trunk and weighs some 1,385 tons! The park is also the location of Mount Whitney, the highest peak in the United States outside Alaska, at 14,494 feet. Visitors to the park can take a guided tour of the Crystal Cave, a marble cavern with many rock formations.

YOSEMITE NATIONAL PARK

YOSEMITE NATIONAL PARK, established in 1890, covers 761,266 acres in east-central California. It has the world's largest concentration of granite domes—mountain-like rocks that were created by glaciers millions of years ago. You can see many of them rising thousands of feet above the valley floor. Two of the most famous are Half-Dome, which looks smooth and rounded, and El Capitan, which is the biggest single granite rock on earth. Skilled climbers come from all over the world to scale this 4,000-foot-high wall of rock. Yosemite Falls, which drops 2,425 feet, is the highest waterfall in North America, and the fifth highest in the world. It is actually two waterfalls, called the upper and lower falls, connected by a series of smaller waterfalls. Yosemite also features lakes, meadows, and giant sequoia trees, and is home to bighorn sheep and bears.

WEATHER

What 5 letters aren't used to start hurricane names? ➤page 291

WEATHER WORDS

BAROMETER An instrument that measures atmospheric pressure. Falling pressure means stormy weather, while rising pressure means calm weather

BLIZZARD A heavy snowstorm with strong winds.

FREEZING RAIN Water that freezes as it hits the ground.

FRONT Boundary between two air masses.

HAIL Water droplets that get coated with ice as they are blown upward into colder temperatures, often again and again. As they get heavy they fall to the ground as hailstones.

HUMIDITY Amount of water vapor (water in the form of a gas) in the air.

PRECIPITATION Water that falls from clouds as rain, snow, hail, or sleet.

RAIN Water falling in drops.

SLEET Water that reaches the ground as ice pellets or a mixture of snow and rain.

SNOW Small white ice crystals that form in clouds and fall.

TORNADO A violently rotating column of air (wind) that forms a funnel. A tornado can suck up and destroy what is in its path, and also cause severe damage from flying debris.

WIND CHILL A measure of how cold it feels when there is a wind. When it is 35°F and the wind is 15 miles an hour, it will feel like 25°F.

CLOUDS

Clouds come from moisture in the atmosphere that cools and forms into tiny water droplets or ice crystals. The science of clouds is called **nephology**. The names we still use for clouds come from a lecture given in December 1802 by the English meteorologist Luke Howard. Here are some of the cloud types that he named:

altostratus clouds form a smooth gray or bluish sheet high over the sky. The sun or moon can usually be seen faintly.

cirrocumulus clouds are high ice clouds with a wavelike or patchy appearance. The sunlight can make them look like fish scales, which makes for a "mackerel sky." ❶

cirrus clouds are thin, wispy, high-altitude clouds made of ice crystals. They often appear in nice weather. ❷

cumulonimbus clouds, also known as storm clouds, are darkish and ominous-looking. They can bring heavy storms, often with thunder and lightning. ❸

cumulus clouds are puffy white vertical clouds that get biggest during mid-afternoon. They form many different shapes. ❹

nimbostratus clouds form a shapeless dark layer across the sky blocking out the sun and moon. They often bring a long period of rain or snow.

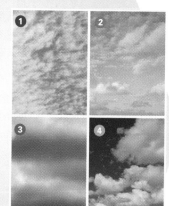

WHAT IS A HURRICANE?

Hurricanes are the largest storms. They form over warm, usually tropical, oceans. As the warm seawater evaporates into the air, the pressure drops and winds begin to circulate, creating a huge wall of clouds and rain, wrapped around a calm center. As warm, moist air continues to feed the storm, it gets stronger and can spread out to an area 300 miles wide. Winds up to 250 miles an hour can rip trees out by their roots and tear roofs off buildings. Torrential rains and giant waves caused by the fierce wind can cause flooding and massive damage before the storm finally moves out over land and dies down.

HURRICANE NAMES IN THE NORTH ATLANTIC

Until the 20th century, people named storms after saints. In 1953, the U.S. government began to use women's names for hurricanes. Men's names were added in 1978.

2002: Arthur, Bertha, Cristobal, Dolly, Edouard, Fay, Gustav, Hanna, Isidore, Jospehine, Kyle, Lili, Marco, Nana, Omar, Paloma, Rene, Sally, Teddy, Vicky, Wilfred

2003: Ana, Bill, Claudette, Danny, Erika, Fabian, Grace, Henri, Isabel, Juan, Kate, Larry, Mindy, Nicholas, Odette, Peter, Rose, Sam, Teresa, Victor, Wanda

DID YOU KNOW? **HURRICANE NAMES CAN BE RETIRED** *Hurricane names come from a set of six lists that are used in turn, one list per year. But if a hurricane is particularly destructive, its name will be retired—much as the jersey number of a great athlete is retired when the athlete steps down. After deadly Hurricane Hugo (1989), for instance, "Hugo" was replaced on the lists by "Humberto." After 1998, "Mitch" was replaced by "Matthew," and after 1999 "Floyd" was replaced by "Franklin."*

All About... LIGHTNING

Cumulonimbus (thunder) clouds may stretch upward for miles, to where freezing temperatures turn the moisture in the cloud into ice particles. Those particles sink by gravity, then they rise with the cloud's air movement, and along the way they bump into each other and separate each other's electrical charges. The negatively charged ice particles drop lower down in the cloud and attract positive particles from the ground below: in lightning rods, trees, and anything else nearby. When the negative charges connect with the positive ones—zap!—there is a huge transfer of electricity, which we see as lightning. Lightning generates between 100 million and 1 billion volts of electricity and can heat the air around it to over 50,000°F. The rapid movement of air as it heats and cools makes the shockwaves you hear as thunder. Because light travels faster than sound, the thunder takes longer to reach your ears than the lightning does to reach your eyes. The sooner you hear thunder after lightning the closer the lightning is.

Being struck by lightning is unusual—but it happens! In the United States, lightning hits the earth an estimated 25 million times a year. On average, about 70 people in the U.S. are killed by lightning each year, and hundreds suffer injury. For safety, follow the "30-30 Rule": Go indoors if you hear thunder 30 seconds or less after you see lightning, and don't go back out until 30 minutes after the last thunderclap. For more information, visit

WEB SITE http://www.lightningsafety.noaa.gov/factsheet.htm

TAKING TEMPERATURES

HOW TO MEASURE TEMPERATURE Two systems for measuring temperature are used in weather forecasting. One is Fahrenheit (abbreviated F). The other is Celsius (abbreviated C). Another word for Celsius is Centigrade. Zero degrees (0°) Celsius is equal to 32 degrees (32°) Fahrenheit.

TO CONVERT FAHRENHEIT TEMPERATURES TO CELSIUS:

1. Subtract 32 from the Fahrenheit temperature value.
2. Then multiply by 5.
3. Then divide the result by 9. Example:
   To convert 68 degrees Fahrenheit to Celsius,
   68 – 32 = 36; 36 x 5 = 180; 180 ÷ 9 = 20

TO CONVERT CELSIUS TEMPERATURES TO FAHRENHEIT:

1. Multiply the Celsius temperature by 9.
2. Then divide by 5.
3. Then add 32 to the result.
   Example: To convert
   20 degrees Celsius to Fahrenheit,
   20 x 9 = 180; 180 ÷ 5 = 36; 36 + 32 = 68

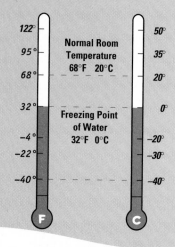

Normal Room Temperature
68°F 20°C

Freezing Point of Water
32°F 0°C

THE HOTTEST AND COLDEST PLACES IN THE WORLD

CONTINENT	HIGHEST TEMPERATURE	LOWEST TEMPERATURE
Africa	El Azizia, Libya, 136°F (58°C)	Ifrane, Morocco, –11°F (–24°C)
Antarctica	Vanda Station, 59°F (15°C)	Vostok, –129°F (–89°C)
Asia	Tirat Tsvi, Israel, 129°F (54°C)	Verkhoyansk, Russia, and Oimekon, Russia, –90°F (–68°C)
Australia	Cloncurry, Queensland, 128°F (53°C)	Charlotte Pass, New South Wales, –9°F (–23°C)
Europe	Seville, Spain, 122°F (50°C)	Ust'Shchugor, Russia, –67°F (–55°C)
North America	Death Valley, California, 134°F (57°C)	Snag, Yukon Territory, –81°F (–63°C)
South America	Rivadavia, Argentina, 120°F (49°C)	Sarmiento, Argentina, –27°F (–33°C)

HOTTEST PLACES IN THE U.S.

State	Temperature	Year
California	134°F	1913
Arizona	128°F	1994*
Nevada	125°F	1994*

* Tied with a record set earlier

COLDEST PLACES IN THE U.S.

State	Temperature	Year
Alaska	–80°F	1971
Montana	–70°F	1954
Utah	–69°F	1985

WEATHER OR NOT

CAN YOU TELL WHICH OF THESE ARE TRUE?

1. Clouds come from moisture in the atmosphere.
2. The science of clouds is called nephrology.
3. Altostratus clouds are white and puffy.
4. Storm clouds are dark and ominous looking.
5. A rising barometer usually means stormy weather.
6. The sooner you hear thunder after lightning, the closer the lightning is.
7. Lightning actually cools off the air around it.
8. Zeke and Zelda are both hurricane names.
9. If you want to be comfortable at night, you should try to keep the temperature around 68 degrees Celsius.
10. Temperatures up to 134 degrees Fahrenheit have been recorded in the United States.

ANSWERS ON PAGES 314-317. FOR MORE PUZZLES GO TO
WWW.WORLDALMANACFORKIDS.COM

WHO AM I?

By attaching a key to a kite string, I proved to the world that lightning is electricity and not some supernatural force. From there I went on to invent the lightning rod, just as I invented bifocals and a new type of iron stove. I was a pioneer in fire prevention and public libraries; I was a witty and popular writer whose autobiography is still widely read; and I helped draft the Declaration of Independence. ⤳ Answer: Benjamin Franklin

To read more about the weather try the Weather Channel at *http://www.weather.com* or try the government's National Oceanic and Atmospheric Administration at *http://www.noaa.gov*

WEIGHTS & MEASURES

Where did the metric system get its start? ➤ page 297

THE EARLIEST MEASUREMENTS

We use weights and measures all the time—you can measure how tall you are, or how much gasoline a car needs. People who lived in ancient times—more than 1,000 years ago—developed measurements to describe the amounts or sizes of things. The first measurements were based on the human body and on everyday activities.

Ancient measure			
	1 foot = length of a person's foot	**1 yard =** from nose to fingertip	**1 acre =** land an ox could plow in a day
Modern measure	12 inches	3 feet or 36 inches	43,560 square feet or 4,840 square yards

MEASUREMENTS WE USE TODAY

The system of measurement used in the United States is called the U.S. customary system. Most other countries use the metric system. A few metric measurements are also used in the United States, such as for soda, which comes in 1-liter and 2-liter bottles. In the tables below, abbreviations are given in parentheses the first time they are used.

LENGTH, HEIGHT, and DISTANCE

The basic unit of length in the U.S. system is the inch. Length, width, depth, thickness, and the distance between two points all use the inch or larger related units.

1 foot (ft.) = 12 inches (in.)
1 yard (yd.) = 3 feet or 36 inches
1 rod (rd.) = 5½ yards
1 furlong (fur.) = 40 rods or 220 yards or 660 feet
1 mile (mi.) (also called statute mile) = 8 furlongs or 1,760 yards or 5,280 feet
1 league = 3 miles

AREA

Area is used to measure a section of a flat surface like the floor or the ground. Most area measurements are given in square units. Land is measured in acres.

1 square foot (sq. ft.) = 144 square inches (sq. in.)
1 square yard (sq. yd.) = 9 square feet or 1,296 square inches
1 square rod (sq. rd.) = 30¼ square yards
1 acre = 160 square rods or 4,840 square yards or 43,560 square feet
1 square mile (sq. mi.) = 640 acres

CAPACITY

Units of **capacity** are used to measure how much of something will fit into a container. **Liquid measure** is used to measure liquids, such as water or gasoline. **Dry measure** is used with large amounts of solid materials, like grain or fruit.

Dry Measure Although both liquid and dry measures use the terms "pint" and "quart," they mean different amounts and should not be confused. Look at the lists below for examples.

1 quart (qt.) = 2 pints (pt.)

1 peck (pk.) = 8 quarts

1 bushel (bu.) = 4 pecks

Liquid Measure Although the basic unit in liquid measure is the **gill** (4 fluid ounces), you are more likely to find liquids measured in pints or larger units.

1 gill = 4 fluid ounces

1 pint (pt.) = 4 gills or 16 ounces

1 quart (qt.) = 2 pints or 32 ounces

1 gallon (gal.) = 4 quarts = 128 ounces

For measuring most U.S. liquids,
  1 barrel (bbl.) = 31½ gallons

For measuring oil,
  1 barrel (bbl.) = 42 gallons

Cooking Measurements Cooking measure is used to measure amounts of solid and liquid foods used in cooking. The measurements used in cooking are based on the **fluid ounce**.

1 teaspoon (tsp.) = ⅙ fluid ounce (fl. oz.)

1 tablespoon (tbsp.) = 3 teaspoons or
               ½ fluid ounce

1 cup = 16 tablespoons or 8 fluid ounces

1 pint = 2 cups

1 quart = 2 pints

1 gallon = 4 quarts

VOLUME

The amount of space taken up by an object (or the amount of space available within an object) is measured in **volume**. Volume is usually expressed in **cubic units**. If you wanted to buy a room air conditioner and needed to know how much space there was to be cooled, you could measure the room in cubic feet.

1 cubic foot (cu. ft.) = 1,728 cubic inches
                    (cu. in.)

1 cubic yard (cu. yd.) = 27 cubic feet

DEPTH

Some measurements of length are used to measure ocean depth and distance.

1 fathom = 6 feet

1 cable = 120 fathoms or 720 feet

1 nautical mile = 6,076.1 feet or
                1.15 statute miles

WEIGHT

Although 1 cubic foot of popcorn and 1 cubic foot of rock take up the same amount of space, they wouldn't feel the same if you tried to lift them. We measure heaviness as **weight.** Most objects are measured in **avoirdupois weight** (pronounced a-ver-de-POIZ), although precious metals and medicines use different systems.

1 dram (dr.) = 27.344 grains (gr.)

1 ounce (oz.) = 16 drams or 437.5 grains

1 pound (lb.) = 16 ounces

1 hundredweight (cwt.) = 100 pounds

1 ton = 2,000 pounds (also called short ton)

THE METRIC SYSTEM

Do you ever wonder how much soda you are getting when you buy a bottle that holds 1 liter? Or do you wonder how long a 50-meter swimming pool is? Or how far away from Montreal, Canada, you would be when a map says "8 kilometers"?

Every system of measurement uses a basic unit for measuring. In the U.S. customary system, the basic unit for length is the inch. In the metric system, the basic unit for length is the **meter**. The metric system also uses **liter** as a basic unit of volume or capacity and the **gram** as a basic unit of mass. The related units are made by adding a prefix to the basic unit. The prefixes and their meanings are:

MILLI- = 1/1,000	**DECI- = 1/10**	**HECTO- = 100**
CENTI- = 1/100	**DEKA- = 10**	**KILO- = 1,000**

FOR EXAMPLE:

millimeter (mm)	=	1/1,000 of a meter	milligram (mg)	=	1/1,000 of a gram
centimeter (cm)	=	1/100 of a meter	centigram (cg)	=	1/100 of a gram
decimeter (dm)	=	1/10 of a meter	decigram (dg)	=	1/10 of a gram
dekameter (dm)	=	10 meters	dekagram (dg)	=	10 grams
hectometer (hm)	=	100 meters	hectogram (hg)	=	100 grams
kilometer (km)	=	1,000 meters	kilogram (kg)	=	1,000 grams

To get a rough idea of what measurements equal in the metric system, it helps to know that a liter is a little more than a quart. A meter is a little over a yard. And a kilometer is less than a mile.

► If you were 2 meters tall, you would be a little over 6 feet, 6 inches in height.

► A five-kilometer race is about 3 miles.

► A 100-kilogram man weighs more than 220 pounds.

METRIC BRAIN TEASER!

Lori lives 12 kilometers from the toy store. The deli is 8 kilometers north of her house. The mall is 3 times as far from her home as the bookstore. The distance from her home to the toy store is 2 times the distance from her home to the mall. The distance from her home to the deli is 4 times the distance from her home to the pet store. The bookstore is south of Lori's house.

How far (in *miles*) does Lori have to travel?
❶ To get her hair cut at the mall.
❷ To go to the pet store to buy hamster food.
❸ To go to the bookstore and back.
❹ To go to the deli, then the bookstore, then home.

ANSWERS ON PAGES 314-317. FOR MORE PUZZLES GO TO WWW.WORLDALMANACFORKIDS.COM

HOW TO CONVERT MEASUREMENTS

Do you want to convert feet to meters or miles to kilometers? You first need to know how many meters are in one foot or how many kilometers are in one mile. The tables below show how to convert units in the U.S. customary system to units in the metric system and how to convert metric units to U.S. customary units.

If you want to convert numbers from one system to the other, a calculator would be helpful for doing the multiplication.

Converting U.S. Customary Units to Metric Units

If you know the number of	Multiply by	To get the number of
inches	2.5400	centimeters
inches	.0254	meters
feet	30.4800	centimeters
feet	.3048	meters
yards	.9144	meters
miles	1.6093	kilometers
square inches	6.4516	square centimeters
square feet	.0929	square meters
square yards	.8361	square meters
acres	.4047	hectares
cubic inches	16.3871	cubic centimeters
cubic feet	.0283	cubic meters
cubic yards	.7646	cubic meters
quarts (liquid)	.9464	liters
ounces	28.3495	grams
pounds	.4536	kilograms

Converting Metric Units to U.S. Customary Units

If you know the number of	Multiply by	To get the number of
centimeters	.3937	inches
centimeters	.0328	feet
meters	39.3701	inches
meters	3.2808	feet
meters	1.0936	yards
kilometers	.621	miles
square centimeters	.1550	square inches
square meters	10.7639	square feet
square meters	1.1960	square yards
hectares	2.4710	acres
cubic centimeters	.0610	cubic inches
cubic meters	35.3147	cubic feet
cubic meters	1.3080	cubic yards
liters	1.0567	quarts (liquid)
grams	.0353	ounces
kilograms	2.2046	pounds

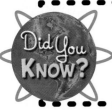

Did You KNOW?

THE METRIC SYSTEM started in France. In 1795 the French Academy of Science announced that the length of a meter was exactly 39.370008 inches. They calculated the length of an imaginary line from the North Pole—passing through Paris—to the equator. Then they divided that distance into 10,000,000 equal parts. One of those parts was a meter.

WORLD HISTORY

What famous king died at the age of 16? ➤ page 299

HIGHLIGHTS OF WORLD HISTORY

Each of the five sections within this chapter covers a major region of the world: the Middle East, Africa, Asia, Europe, and the Americas. Major events from ancient times to the present are described under the headings for each region.

THE ANCIENT MIDDLE EAST 4000 B.C.–1 B.C.

4000–3000 B.C.

► The world's first cities are built by the Sumerian peoples in Mesopotamia, now southern Iraq.
► Sumerians develop a kind of writing called cuneiform.
► Egyptians develop a kind of writing called hieroglyphics.

2700 B.C.
Egyptians begin building the great pyramids in the desert. The pharaohs' (kings') bodies are buried in them.

1792 B.C.
Some of the first written laws are created in Babylonia. They are called the Code of Hammurabi.

ACHIEVEMENTS OF THE ANCIENT MIDDLE EAST

Early peoples of the Middle East:
❶ Studied the stars (astronomy).
❷ Invented the wheel.
❸ Created written language from picture drawings (hieroglyphics and cuneiform). ▼
  ❹ Established the 24-hour day.
  ❺ Studied medicine and mathematics.

1200 B.C.
Hebrew people settle in Canaan in Palestine after escaping from slavery in Egypt. They are led by the prophet Moses.

THE TEN COMMANDMENTS

Unlike most early peoples in the Middle East, the Hebrews believed in only one God (monotheism). They believed that God gave Moses the Ten Commandments on Mount Sinai when they fled Egypt.

1000 B.C.
King David unites the Hebrews in one strong kingdom.

ANCIENT PALESTINE
Palestine was invaded by many different peoples after 1000 B.C., including the Babylonians, the Egyptians, the Persians, and the Romans. It came under Arab Muslim control in the 600s and remained mainly under Muslim control until the 1900s.

336 B.C.
Alexander the Great, King of Macedonia, builds an empire from Egypt to India.

63 B.C.
Romans conquer Palestine and make it part of their empire.

AROUND 4 B.C.
Jesus Christ, the founder of the Christian religion, is born in Bethlehem. He is crucified about A.D. 29.

▼ The pyramids and sphinx at Giza

All About... MUMMIES OF EGYPT

The pyramids of Egypt, built beginning around 2700 B.C., were tombs of the pharaohs who ruled ancient Egypt. The remains of about 70 pyramids still exist.

Egyptians believed that the pharaohs would need their bodies in the next life. They developed advanced techniques for embalming and drying out bodies so that they could last for thousands of years. The Egyptian art of embalming peaked around 1600 to 1100 B.C. and came to an end around the A.D. 300s. At that time, many Egyptians were becoming Christians, and preserving bodies after death became less important. (A form of embalming is widely practiced today, but it is not long-lasting.)

Mask of King Tutankhamen

Perhaps the most famous mummy belongs to an Egyptian boy pharaoh named Tutankhamen. King Tut, as he's often called, ruled for less than 10 years, in the late 1300s B.C. He died of unknown causes when he was 16 years old. His tomb, discovered in 1922, was filled with rich treasures.

GODS AND GODDESSES

The ancient Greeks worshipped gods who they believed lived on Mount Olympus. The Romans had similar gods, with different names. For more information on ancient Greece and Rome, see pages 306-307.

GREEK NAME	ROMAN NAME	KNOWN AS
Zeus	Jupiter	All-powerful king of the gods. Used a lightning bolt to strike down wrongdoers.
Hera	Juno	Zeus's wife and sister. Angered Zeus by playing favorites with mortals.
Poseidon	Neptune	Zeus's brother and god of the sea. He could unleash storms. Sailors prayed to him for a safe voyage.
Hades	Pluto	Zeus's brother, god of the underworld, where the dead lived as ghostly shadows.
Athena	Minerva	Zeus's daughter, goddess of wisdom. Scholars, soldiers, and craftsmen prayed to her for sharp wits.
Aphrodite	Venus	Goddess of love. She could make people fall in love. Using this skill against other gods made her powerful.
Hephaestus	Vulcan	Son of Zeus and Hera, god of craftsmen and blacksmiths. Ugly and lame, he could work magic with a hammer and anvil.
Apollo	none	Zeus's son and god of the sun, medicine, poetry, and music. Every day, Apollo drove his golden chariot (the Sun) across the sky. He was handsome, coolheaded, and fierce in battle.
Artemis	Diana	Apollo's twin sister, goddess of the moon and the hunt. She punished those who killed animals unnecessarily.

ISLAM: A RELIGION GROWS IN THE MIDDLE EAST 570–632

Muhammad is born in Mecca in Arabia. Around 610, as a prophet, he starts to proclaim and teach Islam, a religion which spreads from Arabia to all the neighboring regions in the Middle East and North Africa. His followers are called Muslims.

THE KORAN

The holy book of Islam is the Koran. It was related by Muhammad beginning in 611. The Koran gives Muslims a program they must follow. For example, it gives rules about how one should treat one's parents and neighbors.

632 Muhammad dies. By now, Islam is accepted in Arabia as a religion.

641 Arab Muslims conquer the Persians.

LATE 600s Islam begins to spread to the west into Africa and Spain.

711–732 Umayyads invade Europe but are defeated by Frankish leader Charles Martel in France. This defeat halts the spread of Islam into Western Europe.

1071 Muslim Turks conquer Jerusalem.

1095–1291 Europeans try to take back Jerusalem and other parts of the Middle East for Christians during the Crusades.

THE SPREAD OF ISLAM

The Arab armies that went across North Africa brought great change:

1. The people who lived there were converted to Islam.
2. The Arabic language replaced many local languages as an official language. North Africa is still an Arabic-speaking region today, and Islam is the major faith.

Dome of the Rock and the Western Wall, Jerusalem ▼

ACHIEVEMENTS OF THE UMAYYAD AND ABBASID DYNASTIES

The Umayyads (661–750) and the Abbasids (750–1256) were the first two Muslim-led dynasties. Both empires stretched across northern Africa across the Middle East and into Asia. Both were known for great achievements. They:

1. Studied math and medicine.
2. Translated the works of other peoples, including Greeks and Persians.
3. Spread news of Chinese inventions like paper and gunpowder.
4. Wrote great works on religion and philosophy.

1300–1900s The Ottoman Turks, who are Muslims, create a huge empire, covering the Middle East, North Africa, and part of Eastern Europe. The Ottoman Empire falls apart gradually, and European countries take over portions of it beginning in the 1800s.

1914–1918 World War I begins in 1914. The Ottoman Empire has now broken apart. Most of the Middle East falls under British or French control.

1921 Two new Arab kingdoms are created: Transjordan and Iraq. The French take control of Syria and Lebanon.

1922 Egypt becomes independent from Britain.

JEWS MIGRATE TO PALESTINE

Jewish settlers from Europe began migrating to Palestine in the 1880s. They wanted to return to the historic homeland of the Hebrew people. In 1945, after World War II, many Jews who survived the Holocaust migrated to Palestine. Arabs living in the region opposed the Jewish immigration. In 1948, after the British left, war broke out between the Jews and the Arabs.

THE MIDDLE EAST 1940s–2000s

1948 The state of Israel is created.

THE ARAB-ISRAELI WARS Arab countries near Israel (Egypt, Iraq, Jordan, Lebanon, and Syria) attack the new country in 1948 but fail to destroy it. Israel and its neighbors fight wars again in 1956, 1967, and 1973. Israel wins each war. In the 1967 war, Israel captures the Sinai Desert from Egypt, the Golan Heights from Syria, and the area known as the West Bank from Jordan.

1979 Egypt and Israel sign a peace treaty, providing for Israel to return the Sinai to Egypt.

THE MIDDLE EAST AND OIL
Much of the oil we use to drive our cars, heat our homes, and run our machines comes from the Arabian peninsula in the Middle East. For a brief time in 1973-1974, Arab nations would not let their oil be sold to the United States because of its support of Israel. The United States still relies less heavily on oil imports from the region today.

THE 1990s AND 2000s

▶ In 1991, the United States and its allies go to war with Iraq after Iraq invades neighboring Kuwait. Iraq is defeated and signs a peace agreement but is accused of violating the peace terms, especially by making weapons of mass destruction.

▶ Israel and the Palestine Liberation Organization (PLO) agree to work toward peace (1993). However, tensions increase, fueled by the assassination of Israeli Prime Minister Yitzhak Rabin, suicide bombings by Palestinians, and Israeli military actions in the occupied territories.

Oil fire in Kuwait during the Persian Gulf War ▶

ANCIENT AFRICA 3500 B.C.–A.D. 900

ANCIENT AFRICA In ancient times, northern Africa was dominated, for the most part, by the Egyptians, Greeks, and Romans. However, we know very little about the lives of ancient people in Africa south of the Sahara Desert (sub-Saharan Africa). The people of Africa south of the Sahara did not have written languages in ancient times. What we learn about them comes from such things as weapons, tools, and other items from their civilization that have been found in the earth.

2000 B.C. The Kingdom of Kush arises just south of Egypt. It becomes a major center of art, learning, and trade. Kush dies out around A.D. 350.

500 B.C. The Nok culture becomes strong in Nigeria, in West Africa. The Nok use iron for tools and weapons. They are also known for their fine terra-cotta sculptures of heads. ▶

AROUND A.D. 1 Bantu-speaking peoples in West Africa begin to move into eastern and southern Africa.

50 The Kingdom of Axum in northern Ethiopia, founded by traders from Arabia, becomes a wealthy trading center for ivory.

300s Ghana, the first known African state south of the Sahara Desert, takes power in the upper Senegal and Niger river region. It controls the trade in gold that is being sent from the southern parts of Africa north to the Mediterranean Sea.

660s–900 The Islamic religion spreads across North Africa and into Spain.

Niger River, Mali ▶

301

900 Arab Muslims begin to settle along the coast of East Africa. Their contact with Bantu people produces the Swahili language, which is still spoken today.

1050 The Almoravid Kingdom in Morocco, North Africa, is powerful from Ghana to as far north as Spain.

1230 The Mali Kingdom begins in North Africa. Timbuktu, a center for trade and learning, is its main city.

1464 The Songhay Empire becomes strong in West Africa. By around 1500, it has destroyed Mali. The Songhay are remembered for their bronze sculptures.

1505-1575 Portuguese settlement begins in Africa. Portuguese people settle in Angola, Mozambique, and other areas.

THE AFRICAN SLAVE TRADE

Once Europeans began settling in the New World, they needed people to harvest their sugar. The first African slaves were taken to the Caribbean. Later, slaves were taken to South America and the United States. The slaves were crowded onto ships and many died during the long journey. Shipping of African slaves to the United States lasted until the early 1800s.

1652-1835

❶ Dutch settlers arrive in southern Africa. They are known as the Boers.

❷ Shaka the Great forms a Zulu Empire in eastern Africa. The Zulus are warriors.

❸ The "Great Trek" (march) of the Boers north takes place. They defeat the Zulus at the Battle of Bloody River.

1899: BOER WAR The South African War between Great Britain and the Boers begins. It is also called the Boer War. The Boers accept British rule but are allowed a role in government.

1948 The white South African government creates the policy of apartheid, the total separation of blacks and whites. Blacks are banned from restaurants, theaters, schools, and jobs considered "white." Apartheid sparked protests, many of which ended in bloodshed.

1983 Droughts (water shortages) lead to starvation over much of Africa.

THE 1990s AND 2000s

Apartheid ends in South Africa. Nelson Mandela becomes South Africa's first black president in 1994. Also in 1994, civil war in Rwanda leads to the massacre of 500,000 civilians. Meanwhile, the disease AIDS kills thousands each year. Africa accounts for 70 percent of AIDS cases worldwide. In Zimbabwe, for example, one out of every four adults has HIV/AIDS.

▲ Nelson Mandela

COLONIES WIN THEIR FREEDOM

Most of the countries on the African continent and nearby islands were once colonies of a European nation such as Britain, France, or Portugal, but later became independent. Here are some major African countries that achieved independence in the 1900s.

Country	Became Independent	From
Egypt	1952	Britain
Morocco	1956	France
Sudan	1956	Britain
Ghana	1957	Britain
Burkina Faso	1960	France
Cameroon	1960	France
Congo, Dem. Rep. of	1960	Belgium
Côte d'Ivoire	1960	France
Mali	1960	France
Niger	1960	France
Nigeria	1960	Britain
Zimbabwe	1960	Britain
South Africa	1961	Britain
Tanzania	1961	Britain
Algeria	1962	France
Uganda	1962	Britain
Kenya	1963	Britain
Malawi	1964	Britain
Angola	1975	Portugal
Mozambique	1975	Portugal

ANCIENT ASIA 3500 B.C.–1 B.C.

3500 B.C. Communities of people settle in the Indus River Valley of India and Pakistan and the Yellow River Valley of China.

2500 B.C. Cities of Mohenjo-Daro and Harappa in Pakistan become centers of trade and farming.

AROUND 1523 B.C. Shang peoples in China build walled towns and use a kind of writing based on pictures. This writing develops into the writing Chinese people use today.

1500 B.C. The Hindu religion (Hinduism) begins to spread throughout India.

AROUND 1050 B.C. Chou peoples in China overthrow the Shang and control large territories.

700 B.C. In China, a 500-year period begins in which many warring states fight one another.

563 B.C. Siddhartha Gautama is born in India. He becomes known as the Buddha—which means the "Enlightened One"—and is the founder of the Buddhist religion (Buddhism).

551 B.C. The Chinese philosopher Confucius is born. His teachings—especially the rules about how people should treat each other—spread throughout China and are still followed today. ▶

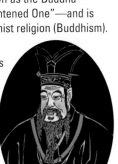

TWO IMPORTANT ASIAN RELIGIONS

Many of the world's religions began in Asia. Two of the most important were:

❶ **Hinduism.** Hinduism began in India and has spread to other parts of southern Asia and to parts of the Pacific region.

❷ **Buddhism.** Buddhism also began in India and spread to China, Japan, and Southeast Asia. Today, both religions have millions of followers all over the world.

320–232 B.C.: INDIA

❶ Northern India is united under the emperor Chandragupta Maurya.

❷ Asoka, emperor of India, sends Buddhist missionaries throughout southern Asia to spread the Buddhist religion.

221 B.C. The Chinese ruler Shih Huang Ti makes the Chinese language the same throughout the country. Around the same time, the Chinese begin building the Great Wall of China. Its main section is more than 2,000 miles long and is meant to keep invading peoples from the north out of China.

202 B.C. The Han people of China win control of all of China.

ACHIEVEMENTS OF THE ANCIENT CHINESE

❶ Invented paper.
❷ Invented gunpowder.
❸ Studied astronomy.
❹ Studied engineering.
❺ Invented acupuncture to treat illnesses.

The Great Wall of China

320 The Gupta Empire controls northern India. The Guptas are Hindus. They drive the Buddhist religion out of India. The Guptas are well known for their many advances in the study of mathematics and medicine.

618 The Tang dynasty begins in China. The Tang dynasty is well known for music, poetry, and painting. They export silk and porcelains as far away as Africa.

THE SILK ROAD ▶

Around 100 B.C., only the Chinese knew how to make silk. Europeans were willing to pay high prices for the light, comfortable material. To get it, they sent fortunes in glass, gold, jade, and other items to China. The exchanges between Europeans and Chinese created one of the greatest trading routes in history—the Silk Road. Chinese inventions such as paper and gunpowder were also spread over the Silk Road. Europeans found out how to make silk around A.D. 500, but trade continued until about 1400.

960 The Northern Sung dynasty in China makes advances in banking and paper money. China's population of 50 million doubles over 200 years, thanks to improved ways of farming that lead to greater food production.

▼ *Statues from Angkor Wat temple, Cambodia*

1000 The Samurai, a warrior people, become powerful in Japan. They live by a code of honor known as Bushido. ▶

1180 The Khmer Empire based in Angkor is powerful in Cambodia. The empire became widely known for its beautiful temples.

1206 The Mongol people of Asia are united under the ruler Genghis Khan. He builds a huge army and creates an empire that stretches all the way from China to India, Russia, and Eastern Europe.

1264 Kublai Khan, the grandson of Genghis Khan, rules China as emperor from his new capital at Beijing.

1368 The Ming dynasty comes to power in China. The Ming drive the Mongols out of the country.

1467–1603 WAR AND PEACE IN JAPAN

❶ Civil war breaks out in Japan. The conflicts last more than 100 years.
❷ Peace comes to Japan under the military leader Hideyoshi.
❸ The Shogun period reaches its peak in Japan (it lasts until 1868). Europeans are driven out of the country and Christians are persecuted.

1526 THE MUGHALS IN INDIA

❶ The Mughal Empire in India begins under Babur. The Mughals are Muslims who invade and conquer India.
❷ Akbar, the grandson of Babur, becomes Mughal emperor of India. He attempts to unite Hindus and Muslims but does not succeed.

1644 The Ming dynasty in China is overthrown by the Manchu peoples. They allow more Europeans to trade in China.

1739 Nadir Shah, a Persian warrior, conquers parts of western India and captures the city of Delhi.

EUROPE 300 B.C.–A.D. 800s

264 B.C.–A.D. 476
ROMAN EMPIRE The city of Rome in Italy begins to expand and captures surrounding lands. The Romans gradually build a great empire and control all of the Mediterranean region. At its height, the Roman Empire includes Western Europe, Greece, Egypt, and much of the Middle East. The Roman Empire lasts until A.D. 476.

ROMAN ACHIEVEMENTS
1. Roman law. Many of our laws are based on Roman law.
2. Great roads to connect their huge empire. The Appian Way, south of Rome, is a Roman road that is still in use today.
3. Aqueducts to bring water to the people in large cities.
4. Great sculpture. Roman statues can still be seen in Europe.
5. Great architecture. The Colosseum, which still stands in Rome today, is an example of great Roman architecture.
6. Great writers, such as the poet Vergil, who wrote the Aeneid.

49 B.C. A civil war breaks out that destroys Rome's republican form of government.

45 B.C. Julius Caesar becomes the sole ruler of Rome but is murdered one year later by rivals in the Roman army. ▶

27 B.C. Octavian becomes the first emperor of Rome. He takes the name Augustus. A peaceful period of almost 200 years begins.

THE CHRISTIAN FAITH
Christians believe that Jesus Christ is the Son of God. The history and beliefs of Christianity are found in the New Testament of the Bible. Christianity spread slowly throughout the Roman Empire. The Romans tried to stop the new religion and persecuted the Christians. They were forced to hold their services in hiding, and some were crucified. Eventually, more and more Romans became Christian.

337 The Roman Emperor Constantine becomes a Christian. He is the first Roman emperor to be a Christian.

410 The Visigoths and other barbarian tribes from northern Europe invade the Roman Empire and begin to take over its lands.

476 The last Roman emperor is overthrown.

THE BYZANTINE EMPIRE, centered in modern-day Turkey, was made up of the eastern half of the old Roman Empire. Byzantine rulers extended their power into western Europe. The great Byzantine Emperor Justinian ruled parts of Spain, North Africa, and Italy. The city of Constantinople (now Istanbul, Turkey) became the capital of the Byzantine Empire in 330.

768 Charlemagne becomes king of the Franks in northern Europe. He rules a kingdom that includes parts of France, Germany and northern Italy.

800 Feudalism becomes important in Europe. Feudalism means that poor farmers are allowed to farm a lord's land in return for certain services to the lord.

▼ *The Colosseum, Rome*

The Temple of Saturn, Rome

EUROPE 800s–1500s

896 Magyar peoples from lands east of Russia found Hungary.

800s–900s Viking warriors and traders from Scandinavia begin to move into the British Isles, France, and parts of the Mediterranean.

Viking helmet ▼

989 The Russian state of Kiev becomes Christian.

1066 William of Normandy, a Frenchman, successfully invades England and makes himself king. He is known as William the Conqueror.

1096–1291 THE CRUSADES In 1096, Christian European kings and nobles sent a series of armies to the Middle East to try to capture the city of Jerusalem from the Muslims. Between 1096 and 1291 there were about ten Crusades. During the Crusades the Europeans briefly captured Jerusalem. But in the end, the Crusades did not succeed in their aim.

One of the most important results of the Crusades had nothing to do with religion: trade increased greatly between the Middle East and Europe.

1215 THE MAGNA CARTA The Magna Carta was a document agreed to by King John of England and the English nobility. The English king agreed that he did not have absolute power and had to obey the laws of the land. The Magna Carta was an important step toward democracy.

1290 The Ottoman Empire begins. It is controlled by Turkish Muslims who conquer lands in the eastern Mediterranean and the Middle East.

Ottoman Palace of Ciragan, Istanbul ▶

1337–1453 WAR AND PLAGUE IN EUROPE

❶ The Hundred Years' War (1337) begins in Europe between France and England. The war lasts until 1453 when France wins.

❷ The bubonic plague begins in Europe (1348). The plague, also called the Black Death, is a deadly disease caused by the bite of infected fleas. Perhaps as much as one third of the whole population of Europe dies from the plague.

1453 The Ottoman Turks capture the city of Constantinople and rename it Istanbul.

1517 THE REFORMATION The Reformation led to the breakup of the Christian church into Protestant and Roman Catholic branches in Europe. It started when the German priest Martin Luther opposed some teachings of the Church. He broke away from the pope (the leader of the Catholic church) and had many followers.

1534 King Henry VIII of England breaks away from the Roman Catholic church. He names himself head of the English (Anglican) church.

▲ *Queen Elizabeth I*

1558 The reign of King Henry's daughter Elizabeth I begins in England. During her long rule, England's power grows.

1588 The Spanish Armada (fleet of warships) is defeated by the English navy as Spain tries to invade England.

MODERN EUROPE 1600s-2000s

1600s The Ottoman Turks expand their empire through most of eastern and central Europe.

1618 The Thirty Years' War begins in Europe. The war is fought over religious issues. Much of Europe is destroyed in the conflict, which ends in 1648.

1642 The English civil war begins. King Charles I fights against the forces of the Parliament (legislature). The king's forces are defeated, and he is executed in 1649. But his son, Charles II, eventually returns as king in 1660.

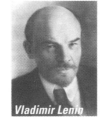

Vladimir Lenin

1762 Catherine the Great becomes the Empress of Russia. She allows some religious freedom and extends the Russian Empire.

1789 THE FRENCH REVOLUTION

The French Revolution ended the rule of kings in France and led to democracy there. At first, however, there were wars, much bloodshed, and times when dictators took control. Many people were executed. King Louis XVI and Queen Marie Antoinette were overthrown in the Revolution, and both were executed in 1793.

1799 Napoleon Bonaparte, an army officer, becomes dictator of France. Under his rule, France conquers most of Europe by 1812.

1815 Napoleon's forces are defeated by the British and German armies at Waterloo (in Belgium). Napoleon is exiled to a remote island and dies there in 1821.

1848 Revolutions break out in countries of Europe. People force their rulers to make more democratic changes.

Napoleon Bonaparte ▶

1914-1918 WORLD WAR I IN EUROPE At the start of World War I in Europe, Germany, Austria-Hungary and the Ottoman Empire opposed England, France, and Russia (the Allies). The United States joined the war in 1917 on the side of the Allies. The Allies won in 1918.

1917 The czar (emperor) is overthrown in the Russian Revolution. The Bolsheviks (Communists) under Vladimir Lenin take control. Huge numbers of people are jailed or killed under dictator Joseph Stalin (1929-1953).

THE RISE OF HITLER Adolf Hitler became dictator of Germany in 1933. He joined forces with rulers in Italy and Japan to form the Axis powers. By 1939, the Axis had started World War II. They fought against the Allies— Great Britain, the Soviet Union, and the U.S. By 1945, Hitler and the Axis powers were defeated. During his 12-year reign, Hitler killed millions of Jews (the Holocaust) and others.

1945 The Cold War begins. It is a long period of tension between the United States and the Soviet Union. Both countries build up their armies and make nuclear weapons but do not go to war against each other.

THE 1990s Communist governments in Eastern Europe are replaced by democratic ones. Divided Germany becomes one nation. The Soviet Union breaks up. The European Union (EU) takes steps toward European unity. The North Atlantic Treaty Organization (NATO) bombs Yugoslavia in an effort to protect Albanians driven out of the Kosovo region.

2002 The euro becomes the single currency in 12 European Union nations.

THE AMERICAS 10,000 B.C.–A.D. 1600s

10,000–8000 B.C.
People in North and South America gather plants for food and hunt animals using stone-pointed spears.

AROUND 3000 B.C.
People in Central America begin farming, growing corn and beans for food.

▲ *The landing of Columbus*

1500 B.C.
Mayan people in Central America begin to live in small villages.

500 B.C.
People in North America begin to hunt buffalo to use for meat and for clothing.

100 B.C.
The city of Teotihuacán is founded in Mexico. It becomes the center of a huge empire extending from central Mexico to Guatemala. Teotihuacán contains many large pyramids and temples.

A.D. 150
Mayan people in Guatemala build many centers for religious ceremonies. They create a calendar and learn mathematics and astronomy.

900
Toltec warriors in Mexico begin to invade lands of Mayan people. Mayans leave their old cities and move to the Yucatan Peninsula of Mexico.

1000
Native Americans in the southwestern United States begin to live in settlements called pueblos. They learn to farm.

1325
Mexican Indians known as Aztecs create huge city of Tenochtitlán and rule a large empire in Mexico. They are warriors who practice human sacrifice.

Mayan pyramid, Yucatan Peninsula, Mexico ▶

1492
Christopher Columbus sails from Europe across the Atlantic Ocean and lands in the Bahamas, in the Caribbean Sea. This marked the first step toward the founding of European settlements in the Americas.

1500
Portuguese explorers reach Brazil and claim it for Portugal.

1519
Spanish conqueror Hernán Cortés travels into the Aztec Empire in search of gold. The Aztecs are defeated in 1521 by Cortés. The Spanish take control of Mexico.

WHY DID THE SPANISH WIN?
How did the Spanish defeat the powerful Aztec Empire in such a short time? One reason is that the Spanish had better weapons. Another is that the Aztecs became sick and died from diseases brought to the New World by the Spanish. The Aztecs had never had these illnesses before and, as a result, did not have immunity to them. Also, many neighboring Indians hated the Aztecs as conquerors. Those Indians helped the Spanish to defeat them.

1534
Jacques Cartier of France explores Canada.

1583
The first English colony in Canada is set up in Newfoundland.

1607
English colonists led by Captain John Smith settle in Jamestown, Virginia. Virginia was the oldest of the Thirteen Colonies that turned into the United States.

1619
First African slaves arrive in English-controlled America.

1682
The French explorer Robert Cavelier, sieur de la Salle, sails down the Mississippi River. The area is named Louisiana after the French King Louis XIV.

EUROPEAN COLONIES By 1700,
most of the Americas are under the control of Europeans:

Spain: Florida, southwestern United States, Mexico, Central America, western South America.

Portugal: eastern South America.

France: central United States, parts of Canada.

England: eastern U.S., parts of Canada.

Holland: eastern U.S., West Indies, eastern South America.

1700 European colonies in North and South America begin to grow in population and wealth.

1775–1783 AMERICAN REVOLUTION

The American Revolution begins in 1775 when the first shot is fired in Lexington, Massachusetts. The thirteen original British colonies in North America become independent under the Treaty of Paris, signed in 1783.

SIMÓN BOLÍVAR: LIBERATOR OF SOUTH AMERICA In 1810, Simón Bolívar
began a revolt against Spain. He fought for more than 10 years against the Spanish and became president of the independent country of Greater Colombia in 1824. As a result of his leadership, ten South American countries had become independent from Spain by 1830. However, Bolívar himself was criticized as being a dictator. ▶

1810–1910 MEXICO'S REVOLUTION
In 1846, Mexico and the United States go to war. Mexico loses parts of the Southwest and California to the U.S. A revolution in 1910 overthrows Porfirio Díaz.

BECOMING INDEPENDENT

Most countries of Latin America became independent of Spain in the early 1800s. Some took longer.

COUNTRY	YEAR OF INDEPENDENCE
Argentina	1816
Bolivia	1825
Brazil	1822[1]
Chile	1818
Colombia	1819
Ecuador	1822
Guyana	1966[2]
Mexico	1821
Paraguay	1811
Peru	1824
Suriname	1975[3]
Uruguay	1825
Venezuela	1821

[1]From Portugal.
[2]From Britain.
[3]From the Netherlands.

1867 The Canadian provinces are united as the Dominion of Canada.

1898 THE SPANISH-AMERICAN WAR
Spain and the U.S. fight a brief war in 1898. Spain loses its colonies Cuba, Puerto Rico, and the Philippines.

U.S. POWER IN THE 1900s During
the 1900s the U.S. strongly influenced affairs in the Americas. The U.S. sent troops to various countries, including Mexico (1914; 1916–1917), Nicaragua (1912–1933), Haiti (1915–1934; 1994–1995), and Panama (1989). In 1962, the U.S. went on alert when the Soviet Union put missiles on Cuba.

1994 The North American Free Trade Agreement (NAFTA) is signed to increase trade between the U.S., Canada, and Mexico.

2001 Terrorists crash planes into U.S. targets, killing about 3,000 people; the U.S. launches a "war on terrorism."

ANNIVERSARIES

IN 2003

50 YEARS AGO—1953

- Edmund Hillary and Tenzing Norgay became the first humans to climb to the top of Mount Everest, the world's highest mountain.
- Francis Crick and James Watson figured out the structure of DNA, opening up a new era in biology. ▶
- The New York Yankees won the World Series for a record-breaking fifth straight time. They beat the Brooklyn Dodgers, four games to two.
- Subway fares in New York City jumped from 10 cents to 15 cents, making many people mad.
- Reaching a speed of more than 760 mph as she flew her Sabre jet, Jacqueline Cochran became the first woman to fly a plane faster than the speed of sound.
- A cease-fire agreement ended the Korean War.

100 YEARS AGO—1903

- Bicycle riders raced 1,500 miles across France's countryside, as the now-famous Tour de France was held for the first time.
- In the first World Series, the Boston Pilgrims upset the Pittsburgh Pirates, five games to three.
- Orville Wright took off on a 12-second, 120-foot flight at Kitty Hawk, North Carolina, the first successful airplane flight in history. ▶
- The silent film *The Great Train Robbery* became the first major American movie. It was also the first movie with a realistic plot.
- Mary Harris Jones led hundreds of workers, including children, in a 100-mile march from Philadelphia to New York to protest their long hours of work in mills and factories.
- Pierre and Marie Curie shared the Nobel Prize in Physics for their work with radioactive elements, including two that they had discovered (radium and polonium).

IN 2004

50 YEARS AGO—1954

- In a landmark decision, the U.S. Supreme Court ruled that segregating white and black students into different schools violated the U.S. Constitution.
- The first nuclear-powered submarine, the USS *Nautilus*, was launched in Groton, Connecticut.
- A vaccine against polio, developed by Dr. Jonas Salk, came into use and nearly wiped out this crippling disease in most of the world.
- Baseball legend Hank Aaron joined the Milwaukee Braves, and his dazzling major league career took off.
- The first automated toll machine was placed in service, on the Garden State Parkway in New Jersey.
- Charles Lindbergh won the Pulitzer Prize for *The Spirit of St. Louis*, the story of his historic solo flight across the Atlantic in 1927.

100 YEARS AGO—1904

- The New York City subway system opened. This system grew to become the biggest in the U.S., and one of the largest in the world.
- Denton True "Cy" Young became the first player in major league history to pitch a perfect game, allowing no batter to reach first base. ▶
- The first comic books were published; they were collections of popular cartoons and comic strips that had already appeared in newspapers.
- The first Olympic Games in the United States were held in the summer in St. Louis, Missouri. They were part of the World Exposition celebrating the 100th anniversary of the Louisiana Purchase.
- Helen Keller, who was both blind and deaf, graduated from Radcliffe College; she had already written a famous book, *The Story of My Life* (1902).

HISTORY SEARCH

Find all the words in the Word Box. They go across, up, down, backward, and diagonally. Some letters are used for more than one word, and a few are not used at all.

```
A  D  A  M  R  A  Z  I  G
X  C  O  A  E  A  B  U  C
A  Z  N  Y  V  T  U  T  E
N  A  U  A  O  I  L  K  L
A  R  J  L  L  T  S  U  T
H  A  M  M  U  R  A  B  I
G  J  T  R  T  E  M  M  C
R  A  K  R  I  A  U  I  G
U  H  E  L  O  T  R  T  N
C  O  L  O  N  Y  A  X  A
B  A  R  A  C  N  I  P  T
```

WORD BOX

Arab	Ghana	Oil	Troy
Armada	Giza	Rajah	Turk
Boer	Hammurabi	Revolution	Tut
Celtic	Helot	Samurai	Zulu
Colony	Inca	Tang	
Cuba	Juno	Timbuktu	
Czar	Maya	Treaty	

PUZZLE ANSWERS

ANIMALS, Page 31: WORM WORD SEARCH

```
S   C   O   C   O   O   N   C   M
C   U   R   R   F   A   R   U   S
S   A   N   A   H   O   L   C   E
E   W   S   A   P   L   Z   P   G
T   K   G   T   E   V   F   J   M
A   Y   U   T   I   L   K   K   E
E   Y   I   P   D   N   C   Y   N
K   L   R   Y   K   D   G   W   T
C   M   U   C   U   S   Q   S   S
```

BOOKS, Page 47: FIND THAT NAME

AUTHORS
JACK PRELUTSKY
KATHRYN LASKY

NORTON JUSTER
MILDRED TAYLOR

BOOK TITLES
The Gargoyle on the Roof
Visions of Beauty: The Story of Sarah Breedlove Walker
The Phantom Tollbooth
The Land

COMPUTERS, Page 58: COMPUTER CROSSWORDS

¹P	A	²S	S	W	O	R	³D	
		M					A	
⁴C	H	I	P		⁵B	Y	T	E
		L			U		A	
		E			G		B	
⁶A		Y		⁷V			A	⁸M
S			⁹G	I	G		S	O
¹⁰C	P	U		R			E	D
I				U				E
¹¹I	C	O	N	S			¹²R	O	M

ENVIRONMENT, Page 73: RAIN FOREST MAZE

FOR MORE PUZZLES GO TO
WWW.WORLDALMANACFORKIDS.COM

HEALTH, Page 93: WHICH DOESN'T BELONG?

The nose is the item that doesn't belong. Humans only have one nose. All of the other parts shown (ears, eyes, feet, hands) come in pairs.

LANGUAGE, Page 106: LANGUAGE MAZE

The letters spell out **COMMUNICATE**. (they also spell "I can commute")

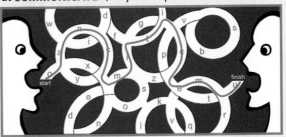

MONEY, Page 115: COIN TRIANGLE CHALLENGE

NUMBERS,

Page 166: ROMAN NUMERALS   **CDLXXVI**

Page 171: PUZZLE 1

three parts   **six parts**

PUZZLE 2: 15 days. PUZZLE 3: 36 children. PUZZLE 4: 4.

PUZZLE 5: The numbers of the squares needed to get to the end of the NUMBER MAZE are (in order) 2,3,2,1,2.

SIGNS & SYMBOLS, Page 199:

1. World Almanac for Kids
2. I Have News for You

FOR MORE PUZZLES GO TO
WWW.WORLDALMANACFORKIDS.COM

POPULATION, Page 177: A CITIZENSHIP TEST

1. 13.
2. They represented the 13 original colonies.
3. George W. Bush.
4. The Electoral College.
5. Yes.
6. The legislature of the United States; it is composed of two separate bodies, the Senate and the House of Representatives.
7. The people (registered voters).
8. To interpret laws.
9. See pages 268-285.
10. November.

UNITED STATES, Page 256: SCRAMBLED STATES

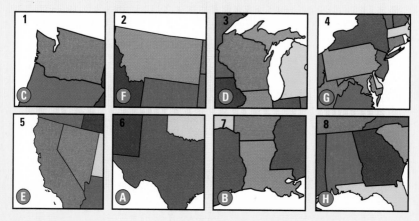

WEATHER, Page 293: WEATHER OR NOT

1. True.
2. Not! Nephrology is the science of kidneys. The science of clouds is *nephology*.
3. Not! They are gray or bluish sheets in the sky.
4. True.
5. Not! It usually means good weather.
6. True.
7. Not! It heats the air around it, possibly to as high as 50,000 degrees Fahrenheit.
8. Not! The letters Q, U, X, Y, and Z are not used to start hurricane names.
9. Not! Room temperature is 68 degrees Fahrenheit. 68 degrees would be 154 degrees Fahrenheit, a little too hot!!
10. True. That temperature was recorded in California in 1913.

FOR MORE PUZZLES GO TO
WWW.WORLDALMANACFORKIDS.COM

WEIGHTS & MEASURES, Page 296:

1. 6 kilometers/3.726 miles
2. 2 kilometers/1.242 miles
3. 4 kilometers/2.484 miles
4. 20 kilometers/12.42 miles

WORLD HISTORY, Page 296: HISTORY SEARCH

```
A D A M R A Z I G
X C O A E A B U C
A Z N Y V T U T E
N A U A O I L K L
H R J L L T S U T
H A M M U R A M I
G J T R T E A M C
R A K R I A U I G
U H E L O T T T N
C O L O N Y A X A
B A R A C N I P T
```

WORMS, Page 333:

```
                            ¹C
                             H
             ²H              A
              E      ³P      R
              R   ⁴C L I T E L L U M
              M    A        E
             ⁵C A S T I N G ⁶S S
              P    A        E D
              H    R        G A
              R    I        M R
             ⁷C O C O O N   E W
              D    A        N I
              I    N        T N
              T             S
              E
```

FOR MORE PUZZLES GO TO
WWW.WORLDALMANACFORKIDS.COM

317

INDEX

T

WORMS

Kids in the Pomfret, Vermont, 4th grade class have been studying worms. By doing tons of experiments on them, we learned that they are invertebrates. They are also hermaphrodites which means they are both boy and girl.

CHARLES DARWIN

Did you know that Charles Darwin was one of the best and earliest wormology scientists? One time he tried playing very low notes on the piano and the worms reacted by digging under the soil in their flower pot which was on the piano. The reason the worms reacted to this effect was because worms are sensitive to vibration. Darwin once even calculated that there were 50,000 worms on a piece of farm land and every one of those worms brought up 18 tons of soil—36,000 pounds! Darwin studied worms for over 40 years. The more Charles Darwin studied worms, the more he wanted to learn.

Amazing Facts About Worms!

► Did you know that worms aren't really bothered by red light? They are bothered by regular light.

► Did you know that worms don't really have one heart? They have five pairs of tubes that act like a heart by pumping blood.

► Did you know that worms are translucent? For example, if you take a piece of wax paper you can kind of see through it, the sun can shine through it too, but it's not clear like plastic wrap which is transparent.

► Did you know worms breathe through their skin? All worms breathe oxygen through their skin and breathe out carbon dioxide.

DIGESTION

The worm eats the dirt and then grinds the soil to get its food. It eats a lot of dirt to get enough food. What the worm doesn't use, it poops out through a part of the body called the **anus**. The piles of poop are called worm **castings**. When the worms are in the dirt, they loosen it up. It improves the dirt.

TYPES of WORMS

The Planarian is a flatworm.

The Leech is a segmented worm.

The Bootlace is a ribbon worm.

The Hookworm is a roundworm

HERMAPHRODITES

The ancient Greeks believed that there was a god called Hermaphrodites. Hermaphrodites had boy body parts and girl body parts. When scientists found an animal that had boy and girl body parts, they called that animal a hermaphrodite. One end of each worm is a girl and one end is a boy. So when worms mate they have to face in opposite directions.

WORM FACTS

MOUTH The mouth is a bump on the head where the worm eats.

PHARYNX When a worm eats, the food goes to the pharynx.

ESOPHAGUS After the food has gone to the pharynx it passes to the esophagus.

CROP The crop is a temporary storage compartment for grains of sand, which help break up the worm's food.

GIZZARD After the crop, the food goes into the gizzard where the food gets mushed up.

INTESTINE The mushed up food gets forced down the intestine and out the anus.

ANUS The anus is the opening at the end of the worm where the castings come out.

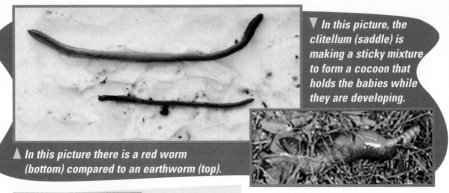

▼ In this picture, the clitellum (saddle) is making a sticky mixture to form a cocoon that holds the babies while they are developing.

▲ In this picture there is a red worm (bottom) compared to an earthworm (top).

◄ This is a worm bin. We keep earthworms and red worms in it. We hope to keep it all year!

HOW TO MAKE A WORM BIN

1 You need to shred newspaper for bedding.

2 You need a bin that has holes.

3 You need water to make it moist, but not too wet.

4 Put in red worms which are called Eisenia fetida.

5 Put in leftover food like apple cores or bread crust.

The worms turn the food into soil. They also make cocoons in the bin.

The length of our bin was 19 inches. The width was 15 inches. The height was 13 inches. We needed 15 pounds of water and 5 pounds of newspaper.

REPRODUCTION

The reproduction system is very interesting. Some worms can lay over 100 eggs a year. Now isn't that amazing!

When a worm lays eggs, the temperature around the eggs has to be just right or they will not hatch properly.

When worms mate, they exchange sperm with each other. The sperm is used to fertilize its own eggs. After 3-4 weeks the worms hatch.

PARTS OF A WORM

setae
anus
segments
mouth

CROSSWORD

ACROSS

4 The mucus that holds the worm babies while they are developing is made by the ...

5 Another word for worm poop is ...

7 A baby hatches out of a ...

DOWN

1 A famous wormologist was ...

2 What do you call a worm that is half boy and half girl?

3 A flatworm is called a ...

6 Worm bodies are divided into ...

ANSWERS ON PAGES 314-317.
FOR MORE PUZZLES GO TO
WWW.WORLDALMANACFORKIDS.COM

333

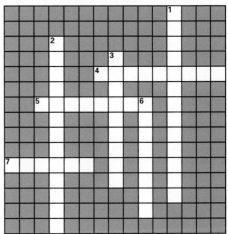

The World Almanac for Kids
"YOU BE THE EDITORS"
Classroom Contest

Your class can win the chance to be in the next edition of THE WORLD ALMANAC FOR KIDS!

The "You Be The Editors Contest" — sponsored by Weekly Reader, World Almanac Education Library Services, and The World Almanac for Kids — gives classes in grades 3 to 8 the chance to design the artwork and provide the content for a two-page spread in the next edition of *The World Almanac for Kids*.

Get together with your teacher and your class, pick a topic that you think could be included in *The World Almanac for Kids*, and design your two-page spread (see pages 332–333 for this year's winning entry).

▲ *Contest Winners for 2002: Fourth grade class at the Pomfret School, Pomfret Vermont, with teachers and staff, and Almanac editor Bill McGeveran*

The Grand Prize–winning entry — along with a picture of the winning class — will be printed in *The World Almanac for Kids 2004* (available in July 2003) and will receive the prizes listed below. Ten runner-up classes will be awarded the runner-up prizes below.

Winners will be judged for creativity, originality, content, design, and humor/fun, as well as appropriateness for inclusion in the book. Grade level will be taken into consideration. All entries should include the teacher's name and the school name, address, and phone number. Entries should be sent to the address below.

The contest begins on August 15, 2002, and all entries must be received by January 15, 2003.

GRAND PRIZE

Winning Class:
- ▶ A *World Almanac for Kids* Deluxe 25-book classroom kit
- ▶ A year's subscription to *Weekly Reader*
- ▶ Your class will be interviewed for *Weekly Reader*

Each Member of the Winning Class:
- ▶ A copy of *The World Almanac for Kids 2003*
- ▶ A limited edition World Almanac for Kids T-shirt
- ▶ A gift certificate for a CD or cassette of their choice

RUNNER-UP PRIZES

10 Runner-Up Classes:
- ▶ Their class name and school listed in *The World Almanac for Kids 2004*

Each Member of the 10 Runner-Up Classes:
- ▶ A limited edition World Almanac for Kids T-shirt

For More Information, including suggestions about the best way to submit the layout, visit The World Almanac for Kids Online (*www.worldalmanacforkids.com/class-contest*) or contact:

S. De Vos, World Almanac for Kids, 512 Seventh Avenue, New York, NY, 10018, (800) 777-3865 (phone), sdevos@waegroup.com (e-mail).

ILLUSTRATION AND PHOTO CREDITS

ILLUSTRATION: Teresa Anderko: 53, 60; Dolores Bego: 66, 79, 83, 84, 86, 200; Olivia McElroy: 91; Joe Tucciarone: 34–35; Kerria Seabrooke: 73, 106.

PHOTOGRAPHY: 9: Vincent Laforet/The NY Times. **10:** World Trade Center, AP/U.S. Navy by Jim Watson; Pentagon, AP/Wide World Photos. **11:** Bush, AP/Wide World Photos; Giuliani, AP/Wide World Photos; Memorial, by Edward A. Thomas; U.S. soldiers, U.S. Army Photo. **12:** All, NASA. **13-14:** All, AP/Wide World Photos. **15:** Baha Men, Fashion Wire Daily/AP; Mandy Moore, AP/Wide World Photos. **16:** Spider-Man, motion picture, © Columbia Pictures Industries, Inc., Spider-Man character ® & © 2002 Marvel Characters, Inc. All Rights Reserved. **17:** AFP. **18:** Animal Planet. **19-23:** All, AP/Wide World Photos. **31:** Licker the Dachshund, © Jeff Rutzky. **36:** Pigs, AP/Wide World Photos. **39:** Aldrin, NASA; Parks, Library of Congress, Prints & Photographs Div. (LC-USZ62-109426); Witherspoon, AP/Wide World Photos. **40:** Powell, U.S. Dept. of State; Kennedy, Library of Congress, Print & Photograph Div. (USZ62-117124 DLC); Portman, Fashion Wire Daily/AP. **41:** Berry, AFP; James, Library of Congress, Print & Photograph Div. (LC-USZ62-3854); Piazza, AP/Wide World Photos. **42:** Clinton, U.S. Senate; Boone, Library of Congress, Prints & Photographs Div. (LC-USZ62-16240); Beethoven, Library of Congress, Prints & Photographs Div. (LC-USZ62-29499). **43:** *Harry Potter and the Goblet of Fire* by J. K. Rowling, HARRY POTTER, characters, names, and all related indicia are trademarks of Warner Bros. © 2002. **44:** *Any Small Goodness: A Novel of the Barrio* by Tony Johnston, Courtesy of Scholastic; Tolkien, AP/Wide World Photos. **46:** *A Single Shard* by Linda Sue Park, Clarion Books/Jacket art: Jean & Mou-sien Tseng. **49:** Pentagon, U.S. Dept. of Defense. **57:** iPod, Courtesy of Apple. **58:** U.S. Army Photo. **60:** Solar car, Schenck & Schenck 2001. **74:** PARCHEESI ™ & © 2002 Hasbro, Inc. Used with permission. **76:** Wagner card, AP/Wide World Photos; Atomic Wedgie, Courtesy of BattleBots Inc. **77:** Lionel image courtesy of Lionel LLC. **95:** Red Nose Day, by Timothy Bryk. **96:** Segway Human Transport, Courtesy of Segway LLC. **97:** Titanium Power Book, © Jeff Rutzky. **99:** MARV Jr., Sandia National Laboratories. **108:** Black Hawks, U.S. Dept. of Defense. **109:** Stealth, U.S. Air Force; Predator, U.S. Dept. of Defense; Tamerlane, by Daniel C. Waugh. **110:** U.S. Dept. of Defense. **112:** Quarters, U.S. Mint; gold coin, Smithsonian Institution, NNC, Douglas Mudd. **116:** "ICE AGE" © 2002 Twentieth Century Fox. All rights reserved. **117:** *The Lord of the Rings*, AP Photo/New Line Cinema. **118:** "SpongeBob SquarePants" created by Stephen Hillenburg, © 2002 Viacom International Inc. All rights reserved. Nickelodeon, SpongeBob SquarePants and all related titles, logos and characters are trademarks of Viacom International Inc. **119:** Hathaway, AP/Dimitrios Kambouris-Fashion Wire Daily; Christensen, AP/Fashion Wire Daily. **120:** The Children's Museum of Utah. **121:** Jamestown-Yorktown Foundation. **122:** Wright Flyer, Smithsonian National Air & Space Museum. **124:** The Beatles, AP/Wide World Photos. **126:** Lil' Romeo, AP/Wide World Photos. **128:** Afghanistan, AP/Wide World Photos. **176:** Library of Congress, Prints & Photographs Div. (LC-B201-5202-13). **178:** Annan, UN/DPI PHOTO; Kim Dae Jung, Embassy of the Republic of Korea in U.S. **179:** Powell, U.S. Dept. of State; Lee, Courtesy of the Mobile Register 2001 © All rights reserved. Reprinted with permission, by Mike Kittrell. **180:** AFP. **190:** Cat, TAMU College of Veterinary Medicine. **191:** Edison, Library of Congress, Prints & Photographs Div. (LC-USZ62-98067). **192:** Kid at museum, Dirk Fletcher, Museum of Science and Industry, Chicago. **193:** Lisa Lazzara. **197:** Code talkers, Official U.S. Marine Corps Photo. **202:** Uranus, Neptune, Pluto, Courtesy of NASA/JPL/Caltech. **203:** Mars Odyssey, Courtesy of NASA/JPL/Caltech. **208:** Courtesy of NASA/JPL/Caltech. **209:** Space Station, Courtesy of NASA/HSF. **211:** Sosa, Jonathan Daniel/AllSport. **211:** Bonds, AP/Wide World Photos; Mays & Campanella, Courtesy of Library of Congress, NY World-Telegram & the Sun Newspaper Photograph Collection (LC-USZ62-112029); Aaron plaque, © Jay Jaffe. **212-220:** Jordan, Leslie, Bird, Warner, Crouch, Woods, Iginla, figure skaters, AP/Wide World Photos. **220:** Olympic snowboarder, © Jay Jaffe; **222:** Hughes, AP/Wide World Photos. **223:** Donavan, © JBW/ISI. **224:** Special Olympics, AP/Wide World Photos. **226:** Hawk, Allsport USA. **235:** Roller coaster, Six Flags Magic Mountain. **245-250:** Presidents 1-36, © 1967 by Dover Publications. **250:** Nixon, Courtesy of Richard Nixon Library; Ford, Courtesy of Gerald R. Ford Museum; Carter, Courtesy of Jimmy Carter Library; Reagan, Courtesy of Ronald Reagan Library; G. H. W. Bush, Courtesy of Bush Presidential Material Project; Clinton, Courtesy of the White House; G. W. Bush, Eric Draper—The White House. **251:** Lincoln, Kennedy, Madison, Roosevelt, Washington, Library of Congress, Prints & Photographs Division; Laura Bush, Eric Draper—The White House. **253:** Johnson, © 1967 by Dover Publications; Clinton, Courtesy of the White House. **254:** Courtesy of the Supreme Court Historical Society. **262:** Model T, Courtesy of The Center for American History, Univ. of Texas at Austin. **263:** Robinson, Courtesy of Library of Congress-Serial & Government Publications Div. (LC-USZC4-6147). **264:** Courtesy of Library of Congress, NY World-Telegram & the Sun Newspaper Photograph Collection (LC-USZ62-111236). **265:** Rice, The White House; Robinson, Courtesy of Library of Congress, Look Magazine Photograph Collection (LC-L9-54-3566-O,#7). **298:** Hieroglyphs, © Edward A. Thomas. **334:** Nancy McGeveran.

FRONT COVER: Sosa, Jonathan Daniel/AllSport; Wright Brothers plane, Library of Congress Prints & Photographs Div. (LC-W86-20); ASIMO humanoid robot, Courtesy of American Honda Motor Co., Inc; Space Station, Courtesy of NASA/HSF.

BACK COVER: iPod: Courtesy of Apple.

INSIDE COVER: Wagner card, AP/Wide World Photos.

THE WORLD ALMANAC FOR KIDS 2003
"KIDS SPEAK OUT!" Contest

Win An All-Expense-Paid Trip For Four To Washington, D.C.!

The *World Almanac for Kids 2003* is proud to present its annual "Kids Speak Out!" Contest. One Grand Prize Winner and 1,000 Runners-Up will be chosen from among the entries received.

▶ The Grand Prize Winner will receive an all-expense-paid trip for four to Washington, D.C.

▶ 1,000 Runners-Up will receive a limited edition *World Almanac for Kids* T-shirt

The Grand Prize includes transportation to Washington, D.C., lodging for four nights, and three meals per day for four days. The winner will receive the opportunity to meet with a member of Congress, plus the chance to visit such noted national landmarks as the White House, the Capitol, the Washington Monument, the Lincoln Memorial, the Air & Space Museum, Arlington National Cemetery, and much more.

To enter, kids must write and explain:

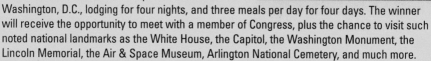

> If you became President of the U.S. tomorrow, what are the first three things you would try to do to help make America and the world a better place?

Entry is limited to kids aged 6-14 and all entries must be received by February 28, 2003. All entries must include the respondent's name, complete address, age, and daytime phone number. Entries should be sent via our Web site www.worldalmanacforkids.com or via mail, fax, or e-mail to:

World Almanac Books
World Almanac for Kids
"Kids Speak Out!" Contest
512 Seventh Avenue, 22nd Floor
New York, NY 10018
Fax: (646) 312-6839
E-mail: sdevos@waegroup.com

Scott Skophammer from Iowa, winner of The World Almanac for Kids 2002 *"Kids Speak Out!" Contest* ▶